PLAN YOUR FINANCIAL FUTURE

A COMPREHENSIVE GUIDEBOOK TO GROWING YOUR NET WORTH

SECOND EDITION

Keith R. Fevurly

Apress®

Plan Your Financial Future: A Comprehensive Guidebook to Growing Your Net Worth

Keith R. Fevurly
METROPOLITAN STATE UNIV OF DENVER, DENVER, Colorado, USA

ISBN-13 (pbk): 978-1-4842-3636-9	ISBN-13 (electronic): 978-1-4842-3637-6
https://doi.org/10.1007/978-1-4842-3637-6

Library of Congress Control Number: 2018945472

Copyright © 2018 by Keith R. Fevurly

This work is subject to copyright. All rights are reserved by the Publisher, whether the whole or part of the material is concerned, specifically the rights of translation, reprinting, reuse of illustrations, recitation, broadcasting, reproduction on microfilms or in any other physical way, and transmission or information storage and retrieval, electronic adaptation, computer software, or by similar or dissimilar methodology now known or hereafter developed.

Trademarked names, logos, and images may appear in this book. Rather than use a trademark symbol with every occurrence of a trademarked name, logo, or image, we use the names, logos, and images only in an editorial fashion and to the benefit of the trademark owner, with no intention of infringement of the trademark.

The use in this publication of trade names, trademarks, service marks, and similar terms, even if they are not identified as such, is not to be taken as an expression of opinion as to whether or not they are subject to proprietary rights.

While the advice and information in this book are believed to be true and accurate at the date of publication, neither the authors nor the editors nor the publisher can accept any legal responsibility for any errors or omissions that may be made. The publisher makes no warranty, express or implied, with respect to the material contained herein.

Managing Director, Apress Media LLC: Welmoed Spahr
Acquisitions Editor: Shiva Ramachandran
Development Editor: Laura Berendson
Coordinating Editor: Rita Fernando

Cover designed by eStudioCalamar

Distributed to the book trade worldwide by Springer Science+Business Media New York, 233 Spring Street, 6th Floor, New York, NY 10013. Phone 1-800-SPRINGER, fax (201) 348-4505, e-mail orders-ny@springer-sbm.com, or visit www.springeronline.com. Apress Media, LLC is a California LLC and the sole member (owner) is Springer Science + Business Media Finance Inc (SSBM Finance Inc). SSBM Finance Inc is a **Delaware** corporation.

For information on translations, please e-mail rights@apress.com, or visit www.apress.com/rights-permissions.

Apress titles may be purchased in bulk for academic, corporate, or promotional use. eBook versions and licenses are also available for most titles. For more information, reference our Print and eBook Bulk Sales web page at www.apress.com/bulk-sales.

Any source code or other supplementary material referenced by the author in this book is available to readers on GitHub via the book's product page, located at www.apress.com/9781484236369. For more detailed information, please visit www.apress.com/source-code.

Printed on acid-free paper

*This book is dedicated to Vivian Louise,
my own personal reason for wealth management
and accumulation.*

Contents

About the Author vii
Foreword to the First Edition ix
Acknowledgments xi
Preface. xiii

Part I:	The Financial-Planning Process 1
Chapter 1:	Understanding the Challenge: The Need to Begin 3
Chapter 2:	Do You Need a Financial Planner? 19
Chapter 3:	Elements of Personal Financial Planning and the Wealth-Management Process. 31
Part II:	Protecting Yourself, Your Family, and Your Property 47
Chapter 4:	Insuring Yourself and Your Family. 49
Chapter 5:	Insuring Your Health and Long-Term Care 59
Chapter 6:	Insuring Your Earning Power. 79
Chapter 7:	Insuring Your Property 87
Chapter 8:	Optimizing Your Employment Benefits 101
Part III:	Accumulating Wealth 117
Chapter 9:	Investing in Financial Assets 119
Chapter 10:	Investing in Real Assets. 137
Chapter 11:	Investing in Use Assets 147
Part IV:	Defending Wealth 159
Chapter 12:	Income-Tax Planning and Management. 161
Chapter 13:	Transfer-Tax Planning and Management 175
Chapter 14:	Life Events that Endanger Wealth 189

Contents

Part V: **Distributing Wealth During Your Lifetime.... 207**

Chapter 15: Planning for Your Child's Higher Education 209
Chapter 16: Planning for the Financial Aspects of Retirement 229
Chapter 17: Planning for the Lifestyle Needs of Retirement.......... 255
Chapter 18: Planning for Other Lifetime Financial Goals 273

Part VI: **Distributing Wealth at Death 285**

Chapter 19: Estate Planning 287
Chapter 20: Philanthropy 303

Part VII: **Summarizing the Personal Financial-Planning Process 317**

Chapter 21: Reaping the Rewards 319
Appendix A: Sample Data-Gathering Form 321
Appendix B: Sample Budget 333
Appendix C: Power of Attorney................................. 335
Appendix D: Declaration as to Medical or Surgical Treatment and Medical Durable Power of Attorney 341
Appendix E: Sample Personal Letter of Instruction................. 349
Glossary 351
Index 365

About the Author

Keith R. Fevurly is an investment advisor with Integra Financial and a senior lecturer in finance at Metropolitan State University of Denver. He also conducts a private practice in estate planning in Centennial, Colorado. Previously he served as the vice president of education at the College for Financial Planning in Denver, Colorado and served as the executive director of Kaplan Financial's financial-planning program. Dr. Fevurly has assisted in the financial education of approximately 50,000 financial planners and authored more than 20 refereed articles on financial planning. For more than 20 years, he was a member of the Editorial Review Board of the *Journal of Financial Planning*, the major academic and professional journal for personal financial planners; and he has written proprietary textbooks on investment planning, income-tax planning, and estate planning for Kaplan University. He is a licensed attorney in Colorado and Kansas and has been a CFP certificant since 1986.

Foreword to the First Edition

It is my pleasure to write this foreword to *Plan Your Financial Future* by my friend and associate Keith Fevurly, MBA, JD, Esq., LLM (Taxation), CFP. I have my own successful financial-planning firm, Integra Financial, in Greenwood Village, Colorado, and have $40 million of assets under management [editor note: now over $50 million as of March 2018]. Every day, Integra Financial addresses and solves the financial-planning issues discussed by Keith in this book for a roster of upper-middle-class and upper-class families. From his ability to teach financial planning in CFP classes to his prowess at analyzing complex investment, retirement, and estate-tax issues, Keith's expertise is unsurpassed. He boils down complex issues and explains them in terms that both our clients and you can understand.

In this book, Keith describes a novel way of analyzing and putting into place the personal financial-planning process, which he entitles the PADD process. The first step in this process is protecting yourself, your family, and your property. Next comes accumulating wealth, a section that will likely be of the most interest to a broad range of consumers and those who are engaged in financial planning in order to achieve financial independence. Third, Keith looks at the defense of accumulated wealth, notably discussing income-tax planning, with taxes being one of the two great "usurpers" of wealth (the other being the impact of inflation). Finally, Keith takes up the "fun" part of the financial-planning process: the distribution of accumulated wealth during an individual's lifetime, notably retirement, as well as at death, which is the date of focus for most estate-planning techniques. Keith also provides a glossary of financial-planning terms at the conclusion of the book and cross-references these terms in each chapter by boldfacing them. Although there are no guarantees in life, particularly in today's volatile economic marketplace, if you follow the process outlined in this book, you will have a more-likely-than-not chance of accumulating and preserving wealth during your lifetime.

It is our hope that this book will give you a level of comfort about your financial future. I like to say that my retired and debt-free clients live not only in different neighborhoods than those who are struggling financially but on different planets. Using the strategies presented in this book, with or without a good financial advisor, can help you to live on a different planet with the few others who actually achieve financial success. That is a rare feat in today's marketplace!

Willis G. Ashby, CFP
Integra Financial, Inc.
Greenwood Village, Colorado

Acknowledgments

I would like to thank Willis G. Ashby, CFP, for writing the foreword to the original edition of this book. I also would like to thank all the financial planners and wealth managers I have taught over the years. To be an effective teacher, the instructor should learn at least as much from his students as he teaches them. I can honestly say that has been my experience!

Thank you also to the Apress Business team, particularly Morgan Ertel and Rita Fernando. You folks are the best!

Preface

A number of events have occurred since the publishing of the first edition of *Plan Your Financial Future: a Comprehensive Guidebook to Growing Your Net Worth* in 2013, most notably the election of a new President of the United States, Donald J. Trump, in 2016. In that vein, major new tax legislation was passed and signed into law by President Trump on December 22, 2017: the Tax Cuts and Jobs Act of 2017, identified in this edition by the abbreviation *TCJA of 2017* or *2017 TCJA*. The second edition fully updates the content to reflect relevant changes made by the TCJA of 2017 as well as experience to date with the implementation of another piece of major legislation, the Patient Protection and Affordable Care Act of 2010 (PPA), commonly known as *Obamacare*.

As before, this book is intended for the educated consumer as well as the financial-planning or services professional. If you are engaged in your own personal financial planning (the "educated consumer"), you will find the contents of the book invaluable as you seek to establish and grow your wealth. Alternatively, if you are a financial planner or advisor (the "financial-planning or services professional"), you will find the content to be helpful in assisting clients whom you are advising. You may even see the need to have your client purchase the book in the planning and advising process! If so, the book can be purchased online at the Apress web site, www.apress.com, or at the Amazon web site.

Also, as in the original edition, I provide a glossary of financial-planning terms at the conclusion of the book and cross-reference these terms in each chapter by boldfacing the applicable term.

Finally, I have attempted diligently to catch and remove any technical and grammatical errors in this (and the original) edition. However, I bear sole responsibility for any errors that may still be present in this edition. To that end, I beg your indulgence!

Keith Fevurly, Esq., CFP
Centennial, Colorado
March 2018

PART I

The Financial-Planning Process

CHAPTER 1

Understanding the Challenge: The Need to Begin

The process of personal financial planning is both a challenge and an opportunity. A *challenge* because of the need to sometimes perform rigorous financial calculations, and an *opportunity* because of the ability to grow, often significantly, your wealth (or, in financial-planning language, your *net worth*). This chapter introduces a new way to engage in personal financial planning: the Protect Accumulate Defend Distribute (PADD) process. More broadly, the book describes, in depth, the challenge of the process and the opportunity that comes from effectively engaging in it.

© Keith R. Fevurly 2018
K. R. Fevurly, *Plan Your Financial Future*, https://doi.org/10.1007/978-1-4842-3637-6_1

Wealth and the PADD Approach

You need to understand one thing up front: this is *not* a book about how to get rich quickly (although if you follow the advice given in these pages, you may very well become rich). Rather, this is a book about slowly and consistently becoming wealthy.

Wealthy, as defined by *Merriam-Webster's Collegiate Dictionary*, is the state of "having wealth" or becoming "extremely affluent." There is no mention of actual money in this definition, but most people can't become wealthy without also being rich. In other words, the number of dollars you have (either in your pocket or invested in financial or real assets) is equivalent to wealth. This book attempts to go *beyond* the standard definition of monetary accumulation (or what most people think of when they hear the word *rich*) to characterize wealth as a process of achievement involving not only financial independence, but also an emotional and psychological state of looking forward to and being comfortable with the future. Indeed, when we substitute the word *successful* for *wealthy*, we see that what most individuals want is a successful and fulfilling future that involves much more than purely monetary riches!

So how do you achieve wealth? This question has both a hard (monetary) and a soft (psychological) answer, but certainly having financial affairs that are not in order complicates the summative belief that you've achieved a wealthy life. Thus, implementing a financial plan to manage the future is important. If you have not assembled such a plan, or even if you have not thought about how best to manage the future, don't worry—*you're not alone!* Americans are notoriously *bad* planners (and notoriously *good* procrastinators), but the important point to understand is that financial planning and wealth accumulation are a journey and not a destination!

You need to begin the financial-planning process and then (hopefully) continue it as best as possible, with or without professional assistance. This book is designed to help you do both—that is, as a do-it-yourself planner (as many individuals are inclined to be, either by conscious decision or by default of circumstances) or by becoming an educated consumer when seeking the help of a financial planner. In addition, the book introduces you to a simple way of thinking about the financial-planning process: the PADD approach to achieving lifetime wealth. The steps in this approach are as follows:

- *Protect* your assets.
- *Accumulate* monetary wealth.
- *Defend* your wealth.
- *Distribute* this wealth during your lifetime for the benefit of yourself and your family (and for the benefit of your heirs after your death).

Let's begin!

Steps in the Financial-Planning Process

As put forward in the Certified Financial Planner Board of Standards *Financial Planning Practice Standards*, there are six steps in the personal financial-planning process:

1. Establishing and defining the relationship with the financial-planning client
2. Gathering client data and determining goals and expectations
3. Determining the client's financial status by analyzing and evaluating client information
4. Developing and presenting the financial plan
5. Implementing the financial plan
6. Monitoring the financial plan

Although these steps are intended for the professional Certified Financial Planner (CFP) certificant, there are several tasks that you, as an individual intent on beginning the financial-planning process, should also undertake.

The first task is to gather your financial and personal records. Appendix A includes a formal, detailed data-gathering form and personal financial-planning questionnaire to help you with this undertaking. Keeping good personal records has one obvious advantage: it lets you know where and how you are currently spending your money. In turn, these records will assist you in constructing a budget for your monthly income and expenses—a critical money-management tool for most individuals. (We talk about budgets shortly.) Record keeping also assists you in determining where you are financially today. You can't begin the journey of personal financial planning without knowing your starting point.

What type of financial and personal records should you keep, and for how long should you keep them? In most instances, there is no single answer to these questions, because the type and number of records you need depends on personal preference. Some of us keep everything (for as far back as we can imagine), whereas others try to rid ourselves of paper almost as soon as we receive it. However, documents such as copies of insurance policies, brokerage account statements, mortgage statements, deeds and leases, notes receivable, and current statements of vested amounts in 401(k) plans or other company-sponsored retirement plans should be kept indefinitely. Moreover, it is important to keep personal income-tax returns for at least three years.

No single document can tell you more about your financial life than your annual income-tax return. Think about it: this return forces you to not only disclose the *amount* of your income, but also identify the *source* of that income—an extremely important part of the budgeting and financial-planning process. Under law, you are required to keep (unless you're committing fraud) your income-tax return and supporting details for only three years from April 15th of any given year. However, because of the wealth of information provided by the return and its importance as a guide to your financial past, you may wish to consider retaining it for much longer.

Once you have determined what type of financial and personal records you should keep, the next step is to determine where to keep them. Again, there is no single answer to this question, but I tell my estate-planning clients (for more on wills and estate-planning documents, see Chapter 19) to keep these documents somewhere in their home where they can easily be obtained in the event of an emergency. The reason that I advise them in this way is to encourage them to consider the disadvantages of a safe-deposit box. In addition to the often high fees charged for safe-deposit box rentals, many individuals make the mistake of listing only their name as a signatory for access to the box. In the event of an unanticipated injury or death, no other individual can access the important documents stored in it. You should consider instead a locked desk or fireproof case kept in your house or apartment for storing all your important records.

Another critically important task to launch you on the path toward financial independence is to specify in writing your long-term (more than ten years), medium-term (five to ten years), and short-term (one to five years) financial goals. Be as specific as you can with respect to these goals. For example, "to become wealthy" not only is hard to quantify for most people but, as mentioned previously, may not even mean the accumulation of actual dollars. If monetary wealth is important to you (as it is for many people), determine how many dollars you need to accumulate in order to satisfy your written financial goals.

Here are some of the most common financial goals mentioned to financial planners:

- To retire early or at normal retirement age with an adequate level of income
- To fund a child's (or children's) college education
- To buy a house or vacation home
- To make home improvements
- To take a dream vacation

- To reduce debt service (for example, to pay off credit cards with an outstanding balance)
- To buy a luxury car
- To minimize income or transfer (estate) taxes
- To start my own business

You may add other objectives to this list, depending on your own personal and financial situation, but it is important to recognize that these goals should be quantified and monitored. In other words, you should establish a plan to meet these goals and then track how you are doing. As with determining an investor's *time horizon*, it is important to match your goals to a specified time frame and categorize them according to a long-term, medium-term, or short-term planning period.

What about the possibility that your goals cannot be achieved with your current financial resources? In that event, you have one of three (or a combination of three) choices:

- You can prioritize away the meeting of some financial goals (in other words, recognize that only some, but not all, of your specified financial goals are achievable in the specified time frame).
- You can attempt to increase cash inflows (your income potential).
- You can reduce your cash outflows (adjust your standard of living).

Until you have determined your financial goals and specified a time frame for their achievement, you likely won't know how to begin planning, which may keep you from planning at all!

Determine Where You Are Now

One of the primary assumptions of the financial-planning and wealth-building process is that your net worth (assets minus liabilities) should experience a steady increase as you continue to invest. There is no benchmark percentage increase (or dollar amount) by which your net worth should grow annually, only the suggestion that you should strive for as great a percentage increase as possible given your current financial resources. For example, if you are in your peak wage-earning years (typically age 45 to 55), you should establish a goal of at least a 10 percent increase in your net worth annually. When we apply the **Rule of 72** to this increase (72 divided by 10), your net worth will double in a period of only 7.2 years.

Creating a Personal Balance Sheet

You should monitor and track the increase (or decrease) in your net worth at least once a year. (Many individuals calculate this number at year-end). How do you go about tracking and determining this important number? By preparing the first of two personal financial statements that you should keep among your important financial records: the *statement of personal financial position*, commonly referred to as the *personal balance sheet*. Generally, you should prepare a statement of personal financial position at least annually to keep track of how you are doing in increasing your wealth.

An example of a statement of personal financial position is produced in Table 1-1. Before you examine it closely, you should keep a few considerations in mind when preparing and interpreting such a statement:

1. Be sure to list all assets at their current fair market value without reducing them to reflect any outstanding indebtedness; for example, list your personal residence at the value you believe it will sell for in the local market without taking into account the mortgage balance you may currently owe.

2. Break down your assets into cash equivalents, investments, and use assets. Cash equivalents are those assets that you can access quickly to pay ongoing expenses (bills) or, in the event of a financial emergency, without fear that they may be worth less than when you purchased them. Alternatively, investments are longer-term assets (greater than one year in maturity or holding period) that may experience a fluctuation in daily value.

3. List liabilities at their current balance or what you owe to the creditor as of that given point in time.

There is no right or wrong answer when preparing your statement of financial position. Certainly, as you proceed along the path of wealth building, the objective is that the value of your assets will exceed the balance of your liabilities (thereby increasing your net worth), but do not become too judgmental of yourself as you construct your first statement. The danger is that you will become discouraged (or even give up), which runs counter to the reasons for preparing the statement in the first place—as a tool to help you assess your current financial situation and what you want to see happen in the future.

Table 1-1. Statement of Personal Financial Position (as of 12/31/2017)

ASSETS		LIABILITIES AND NET WORTH	
Cash Equivalents		*Liabilities*	
Cash on Hand	$_____	Primary Residence Mortgage	$_____
Checking Account	$_____	Vacation Home Mortgage	$_____
Savings Account	$_____	Real Estate Investment Mortgage	$_____
Money Market Accounts or Funds	$_____	Auto Loans Balance	$_____
Certificates of Deposit (less than one year maturity)	$_____	Personal Loans	$_____
		Student Loans	$_____
		401(k) Loans	$_____
Cash Value of Life Insurance	$_____	Credit Card Balances	$_____
Total Cash Equivalents	$_____	Rent	$_____
		Other (for example, alimony or child support)	$_____
Investments		Total Liabilities	$_____
Stocks	$_____		
Bonds	$_____		
Mutual Funds Balance	$_____		
Certificates of Deposit (one year or more maturity)	$_____		
Real Estate Investments	$_____		
Vested Employer Pension Benefits	$_____		
Participant IRAs	$_____		

(continued)

Table 1-1. (continued)

ASSETS		LIABILITIES AND NET WORTH	
Rollover IRAs	$_____		
401(k) Account	$_____		
Other	$_____		
Total Investments	$_____	Net Worth (Assets – Liabilities)	$_____
(Assets – Liabilities)	$_____		
Use Assets			
Primary Residence	$_____		
Vacation Home	$_____		
Automobiles	$_____		
Home Furnishings	$_____		
Jewelry	$_____		
Artwork	$_____		
Total Use Assets	$_____		
Total Assets	$_____	Total Liabilities and Net Worth	$_____

When planning your estate, it is helpful to identify on the statement of personal financial position how each asset is titled. For example, if your primary residence is held in joint tenancy with right of survivorship between you and your spouse, place a *JT* for *joint tenancy* next to Primary Residence. Note, however, that retirement accounts, such as individual retirement accounts (IRAs), may be owned only individually, even in community-property states such as California or Texas.

Creating a Cash-Flow Statement

In addition to preparing a statement of personal financial position, you need to track your ongoing expenses and sources of income. A second reference document, the *personal cash-flow statement* or *worksheet*, should be completed at least quarterly (better done monthly, if possible). Here are the reasons:

- The cash-flow statement lets you see where you are spending your money. (It will tell you whether you are living within or beyond your means.)
- It gives you an idea of your ability to save.
- It pinpoints your financial strengths and weakness with respect to your current standard of living.
- It can serve as a practice document before preparing a budget for future cash-flow management. (The cash-flow statement reviews past financial performance, or *looks backward*, whereas the budget *looks forward*.)

Just as the statement of personal financial position has three general categories (assets, liabilities, and net worth), so does the personal cash-flow statement. On the cash-flow statement, you should separately identify cash inflows (sources of income), cash outflows (ongoing expenses), and any resulting cash surplus or cash deficit. A cash surplus or deficit is merely the difference between your cash inflows and cash outflows. Of course, what you want at the end of the quarter (or month) is a cash surplus, sometimes known as *discretionary income*, because that amount is available for saving. A little mental trick to help you save: include a fixed savings amount or percentage of income on the first line of the Cash Outflows column. In other words, *pay yourself first*, and treat the savings amount the same as you would any other fixed expense. You should strive to save at least 10 percent of your gross income monthly.

An ongoing issue with respect to the preparation of the cash-flow statement is whether to show income and Social Security taxes as a separate expense or cash outflow (alternatively, you would show the after-tax amount among your cash inflows because your paychecks reflect this). The better practice is to list these taxes as a cash outflow, because (again) one of the purposes of the cash-flow statement is to show how you are spending your money. Including a separate line item for income and Social Security taxes among the cash outflows forces you to account for what may be an otherwise invisible expense.

Table 1-2 is an example of a properly prepared personal cash-flow statement.

Table 1-2. Personal Cash-Flow Statement (for 2017)

CASH INFLOWS	
Salaries	$_____
Bonuses	$_____
Self-Employment Income	$_____
Interest Received	$_____
Dividends Received	$_____
Capital Gains (from sale of assets)	$_____
Rents and Royalties	$_____
Pension and Annuities	$_____
Social Security	$_____
Other Income	$_____
Total Cash Inflows	$_____
CASH OUTFLOWS	
Savings	$_____
Rent/Mortgage Payments	$_____
Repairs, Maintenance, Improvements	$_____
Utilities	$_____
Auto Loan Payments	$_____
Credit Card Payments	$_____
Food	$_____
Clothing	$_____
Insurance Premiums:	
Life	$_____
Health	$_____
Long-Term Care	$_____
Disability	$_____
Auto	$_____
Homeowner (if not included in mortgage payment)	$_____
Umbrella Liability	$_____

(continued)

Table 1-2. (continued)

CASH INFLOWS	
Total Insurance Premiums	$_____
Medical Expenses	$_____
Property Taxes (if not included in mortgage payment)	$_____
Income Taxes	$_____
Social Security and Medicare Taxes	$_____
Child-Care Expenses	$_____
Recreation and Entertainment	$_____
Other Expenses	$_____
Total Cash Outflows	$_____
CASH SURPLUS (OR DEFICIT)	$_____

You may be wondering how both statements (the statement of personal financial position and the personal cash-flow statement) tie together. A cash surplus from the cash-flow statement at the end of the year (or for whatever period you choose to list your income and expenses) *increases* your net worth, as reflected on the statement of personal financial position. Conversely, a cash deficit *decreases* your net worth. Increasing net worth is a financial strength, whereas decreasing net worth (particularly if the decrease continues over a long period of time) is a financial weakness. In other words, if a cash deficit continues (you are spending more than you are earning), you need to do something to reverse the situation. If you don't, your financial goal of future wealth accumulation is impossible.

Budgeting

For many people, putting together and sticking to a budget is one of life's little burdens. Sometimes the thought of limiting their spending (and therefore their lifestyle) is so threatening that people refuse to even think about preparing a budget. I have heard it said, "What budget? I spend what I make, so that's my budget!" However, living without a budget damages your long-term financial health. Look at a budget as an opportunity to prove your own financial self-discipline. You could even pay yourself (and add to your savings) if you come in under budget each month and show that you can live within your means. Over time, that practice will significantly increase your net worth.

As mentioned, a budget looks forward and is a benchmark for what you plan to spend. It may take you a few months to get it right, but get it right you must if you want to accumulate wealth! If you are just starting to prepare (and comply with) a budget, be conservative in the assumptions you make. For example, an underlying assumption of any budget is that your current employment is secure; if it is not (if you anticipate a job change or layoff), you probably need to set aside even more savings and spend even less. This will help you build up an emergency or contingency fund—another financial-planning practice that is critical to your long-term financial well-being.

Normally, a budget is developed in several steps. First, it is helpful to have determined your financial goals and the amount of savings necessary to accomplish them. Next, be as realistic as you can when estimating your future income and forecasting your anticipated expenses for the budget period. Finally, a well-developed budget should be flexible enough to accommodate financial emergencies or one-time major expenses (hence the need for the emergency fund).

A sample of a detailed budget is included in Appendix B, but take this to heart: *a budget has value only if you intend to use it.* If you do not use it, you are likely better off attempting to meet your short- and long-term financial goals by focusing on some other planning technique (say, by hoping to win the lottery)!

Cash Flow and Debt Management

As a matter of financial prudence, you should maintain an emergency or contingency fund for unanticipated expenses. This fund should be kept in *liquid assets* (those that may be converted quickly to cash without a significant loss in value) and equal in amount to three to six months of expenses. (For example, if your monthly expenses average $5,000, you should have a contingency fund of at least $15,000—$5,000 times 3—in a checking, savings, or money market account or mutual fund.) The size of this fund will vary depending on the nature of your employment and the constancy (or variability) of your income. A self-employed individual who has no employer to provide benefits (such as sick or personal days) to serve as a safety net should consider an even larger fund to compensate for lost income.

An investment trade-off exists, however, when establishing a contingency fund. This trade-off is a lower investment rate of return from money kept in more conservative cash equivalents. For this reason, you may wish to consider establishing an unsecured line of credit with a bank or a home-equity line of credit to substitute as emergency fund assets. Be careful: if you do this, you must arrange for the credit line *before* the financial emergency occurs. For example, if you lose your job (for whatever reason), the bank is unlikely to extend you any credit. Plus, if you are using a credit line as your emergency fund and you need to access the line after you have lost your job, you will incur even more debt—probably the last thing you need when you are no longer employed.

Let's move on to a great tragedy or success story (depending on how you look at it)—the amount of debt carried by the average consumer.

We read a great deal in the media about the negative savings rate of many Americans. Is that bad? It depends. There is both good and bad debt. *Good* debt is generally any debt incurred for the purchase of an asset that is likely to appreciate—for example, your home or real estate in some parts of this country. More specifically, good debt is any interest rate assumed on an obligation where you are paying less than what you can make, in terms of investment return, on the asset for which you have borrowed the money. Another example (in a rising stock market) is the margin interest incurred on the purchase of an individual stock or mutual fund from which you can potentially earn a far greater return than what you must pay the broker to make the purchase.

Bad debt is any debt incurred on an asset that is likely to *depreciate* in value, such as a new car or automobile. Another type of bad debt is credit card debt, which not only carries extremely high rates of interest (18 to 21 percent annually, on average), but also "revolves" from month to month so that it is difficult to completely satisfy the obligation. Both automobile and credit card debt share the income-tax disadvantage: because they are considered personal or consumer debt, the interest paid generally is not deductible and therefore won't reduce your annual income-tax liability.

So how do you go about reducing bad debt? The obvious answer is not to incur it in the first place (by paying cash for a new car, for example), but often this is impractical. Here are some tried-and-true debt-reduction techniques:

- Focus on one type of bad debt to the exclusion of others. For instance, adopt a payment schedule and amount to pay off on your credit card debt—and stick to it! Consider it another form of paying yourself: if the interest rate on the card is 18 percent annually, it is similar to earning 18 percent on an investment. (That does not mean, however, that credit cards are a good investment.)

- Consolidate or restructure your debt. The most common example of this is a college or graduate student who consolidates several smaller loans into one larger loan. Although this does not eliminate the debt, it often reduces the total amount of debt service (interest).

- Borrow from your cash-value life insurance or 401(k) plan. The advantage of these alternatives is that you are, in essence, borrowing from yourself. But be careful: you need to repay this money in a timely manner, or you will reduce the amount of your life insurance coverage and retirement plan benefits payable in the future. If you die and still owe a balance on the life insurance policy loan, the insurance company will pay only the policy proceeds *less* the outstanding loan balance to your named beneficiary or beneficiaries. Similarly, if you leave your employer with an outstanding 401(k) loan balance, the company will likely pay only a net amount in your final paycheck or severance payment. Alternatively, the company will require payment of the outstanding loan balance before it remits your final paycheck.

- Switch to debit cards. Debit cards work much like ATM machines, because the money comes out of your checking account immediately. Although a debit card does not stop you from excessive spending, it does make you account for the cash-flow consequences much more quickly than would a traditional credit card.

Finally, it cannot be stressed enough that poor cash-flow and debt management can put you on the path to financial ruin. Fortunately, credit counselors and some financial planners can assist you in reducing your debt load. If you think you have a problem with debt, you probably do! If you can't solve the problem, the wealth-building techniques discussed in this book will take much longer to work for you—if they work at all.

Monitor Your Progress and Life-Cycle Planning

How often you review your financial progress depends on your age and the time frame you have specified to meet your financial goals. In most cases, an annual review is sufficient. This may be done with or without the assistance of a professional financial planner. (The question of whether you need a financial planner is addressed in the next chapter.) If you go it alone, ask yourself the following questions:

- What life cycle or life stage are you in? Are your short- and long-term goals representative of peers in the same financial-planning cycle or stage? In other words, are your financial goals realistic?

- Have these goals remained the same throughout the review period?

- Are you living at or below your means?
- How much money did you save during the review period?
- With respect to your savings, are you earning the investment rates of return you need to meet your goals?
- Has anything changed in your personal and financial situation that may cause you to reconsider either the priority of the financial goals you established or the time frame in which you anticipate meeting them?

It is generally agreed that there are four financial-planning life cycles. Although there are no hard-and-fast ages at which an individual transitions from one life cycle to the next, certain financial goals are typically more important than others during each stage.

The first of these stages is the *accumulation stage* (between ages 25 and 45 for most consumers). In this stage, individuals are usually in the early-to-middle years of their employment career and often raising young children. Typically, their net worth is relatively small, and their debt load may be excessive, normally due to student or personal loan obligations. Their major financial goals are likely to be reducing their debt, buying a house, and beginning the financing of their children's higher education.

The next of the financial-planning life cycles is the *consolidation stage* (ages 45 to 62 or other normal retirement age). In this stage, individuals are typically past the midpoint of their careers and are likely approaching their peak wage-earning years. Most, if not all, of their debts have been paid off and their net worth is growing rapidly. Their children are in college or graduate school, and those expenses have also been satisfied or are in the course of payment. Financial goals for individuals in the consolidation stage of life are likely to include making home improvements, taking a dream vacation, buying a luxury car or vacation home, and minimizing income taxes.

The third life-cycle stage, the *spending phase* (ages 62 to 90), is sometimes combined with the fourth phase, the gifting phase. The spending phase is characterized by the individual's approaching retirement or the early years of retirement. In this phase, their peak earning years have likely concluded and, from an investment perspective, the focus turns from growth to income. The individual's children have likely begun their own careers and have moved from the family home. Financial goals for individuals in the spending stage shift to early retirement, retirement with adequate income, and, perhaps, the starting of their own business.

Finally, the fourth and final life-cycle phase, the *gifting phase*, is synonymous with an individual's retirement years. Excess assets, if any, may be used to benefit family members during life or in the event of the individual's death. Estate planning becomes important in this phase, and as such a primary financial goal is the minimization of transfer (estate and gift) taxes. Also characteristic of this phase is a conservative investment approach and withdrawal rate, due to the fear of outliving the amount of retirement monies the individual has saved.

Now, let's proceed to an often-asked question: Do I need a professional financial planner to help me get control of my financial life, or can I do it myself? The answer to this question is the focus of the next chapter.

CHAPTER 2

Do You Need a Financial Planner?

Often, the first question in the personal financial-planning process is, "Do I need help (that is, should I engage the services of a personal financial planner)?" or, alternatively, "Can I complete the process myself?" The answer to this latter question is sometimes "Yes," simply because of the desire to avoid the anticipated expense involved in securing the help of a professional planner. But is this the best decision? This chapter describes the types of financial planners, and questions to ask them when deciding to seek assistance, as well as factors to be considered should you choose the do-it-yourself option.

A Word About Self-Help

Now that you know about the basics of the financial-planning process, do you think you can do it yourself? Only you can answer that question, but here are several important factors to consider as you attempt to do so:

- Financial planning is a lot like preparing your own income-tax return. As a matter of fact, income-tax planning is one of the subjects covered by the Certified Financial Planner (CFP) certification examination, so CFP certificants must demonstrate competence in that area. Like income-tax planning, financial planning is a *dynamic* process that requires the planner to stay abreast of many laws and regulations that may impact the planning result.

- Retirement income (and other) computations require knowledge and application of **time value of money** (present and future value) principles. Although you can learn how to apply these principles with the use of a financial function calculator or computer software program, a learning curve is still involved for the average consumer.

- Certain financial planners, like CFPs, must comply with a professional code of ethics that requires them to act at all times in your exclusive best interest. Of course, you will not hesitate to act at all times in your own best interest, but without extensive knowledge of the economic, legal, and regulatory environment in which we all live and work, you may not be aware of what your best interest is.

- Finally, as with a New Year's resolution, many individuals vow to get their financial life in order, but because of common, everyday pressures, fail to do it. Will you be the exception to the rule?

Assuming you have made the decision to seek the assistance of a professional financial planner, the question becomes a matter of *when* you should seek assistance. That question, like so many others in financial planning, has no definitive answer, but one determining factor is the complexity of your financial life. Generally, the *more money* people make, the *more complicated* their financial life is. This is certainly true of corporate executives and self-employed individuals. In addition, higher-net-worth individuals (such as business owners) are more likely to recognize the need to have a financial planner as part of their advisory team.

Beyond all that, middle-income America is quickly appreciating the need for more detailed guidance with respect to their financial lives. As you will learn, the two biggest obstacles to a lifetime of wealth accumulation and distribution are inflation and taxes. Although the former is a fact of economic life that the average Joe (or Jane) can do little to prevent, a professional financial planner can help minimize the deteriorating effect of inflation on your overall portfolio return. The latter (income taxes) can also be managed with the assistance of a skilled professional, such as a Certified Public Accountant (CPA).

One significant warning: *seeking professional assistance does not absolve you of responsibility for your own financial future.* It is *your* financial life, and the goals you establish are *your* financial goals. A financial planner can ideally direct you on a path to wealth in the fullest sense of the term, but you must still make the necessary decisions with respect to your financial well-being.

Types of Financial Planners

You should seek a financial planner you trust and with whom you can establish a rapport. From a compensation standpoint, there are three types of planners in today's marketplace.

The first type of planner is paid solely by commission from the sale of financial products. These products include insurance (usually life insurance), mutual funds, stocks and bonds, and fixed and variable annuities. Typically, the commission received by the planner is taken off the top of these products and, at least to you, is invisible. However, it does add to the cost of the product you are buying. *Commission-only planners* are prevalent at banks, broker/dealers (securities firms), and insurance agencies.

A great deal of controversy exists within the financial-planning profession with respect to whether a commission-only planner can be objective. In other words, "Does the planner have an inherent conflict of interest?" After all, the more the planner sells of a particular product, regardless of whether it is actually suitable for your needs, the more money they make. This question has no definitive answer (inherently, just because a planner is paid by commission only, that does not *automatically* mean the planner is not acting in your best interest), but it is something to consider as you decide which type of planner to work with.

The second type of planner is a *fee-and-commission planner*, sometimes referred to as a *fee-based planner*. These planners are paid in two ways. First, for their planning activities (an example would be the preparation of a statement of personal financial position), the planner charges an hourly or fixed fee. In addition, they receive a commission for any products you buy from them, such as mutual funds with a service charge or *load*. Some fee-and-commission planners offer investment advisory services based on a percentage of the amount of money they manage for you. This fee, known as a *wrap fee* or *advisory fee* in the trade, typically ranges from 1 percent to 2.5 percent of the money managed annually. Although arguably the fee is not a commission, because it is paid by you to the planner and does not come off the top like a product sale, you will likely think of it as constituting a commission all the same.

The third (and rapidly growing) type of planner is a *fee-only planner*. These planners typically do business independently and accept no commissions. Rather, they charge an hourly fee for financial-planning advice and, usually, a fixed fee for developing a comprehensive financial plan. Like fee-based planners, they also charge an annual percentage fee for assets under management (again, 1 to 2.5 percent annually), but they do not sell securities and are not normally employed by or associated with a broker/dealer. As such, the fee-only planner works only for the client. Often, fee-only planners are (or work for) a Registered Investment Advisor (RIA). Historically, this type of planner has tended to work primarily with high-net-worth or higher-income clients, but recently these planners are reaching out to more middle-income clients.

As you will see in the list of questions to ask a financial planner provided later in this chapter, one of the things you want to know before engaging the services of a planner is how they are paid. However, more important than this is your level of comfort with the planner and defining the scope or range of services they will provide. Many a professional engagement or relationship has been made more difficult by not reaching a clear initial understanding of the respective responsibilities of the client and the planner. Remember, this is *your* financial life and future, so use the planner as an advisor and not as a substitute decision-maker.

The Certified Financial Planner Professional and Other Financial-Planning Designations

Although other financial planners have distinguished themselves in today's marketplace with one or more professional designations, probably the best-known financial-planning credential is the CFP certificant. Individuals who have achieved this credential are subject to a mandatory Code of Ethics and Standards of Conduct that is enforced by the Board of Professional Review, a subsidiary of the CFP Board of Standards responsible for awarding the CFP license. As a part of this code, the planner must agree to assume a fiduciary duty under law, meaning they must act at all times in the exclusive and best interest of the client. In addition, a planner who achieves this credential must participate in mandatory continuing education in the specified subject areas of financial planning, as well as complete a separate refresher course in the principles and rules of the ethics code. CFP planners must also have graduated from college, have at least three years of financial-planning experience, complete a formal education program covering specified financial-planning topics (including, beginning in 2012, comprehensive case studies), and successfully pass a rigorous, comprehensive, six-hour examination in these topics.

Another meaningful credential for a financial planner is the Chartered Financial Consultant (ChFC). This designation is awarded by the American College of Financial Services in Bryn Mawr, Pennsylvania, to individuals who have completed an eight-course curriculum, some of which can substitute for the CFP educational program requirement. The American College was originated and first funded by the life insurance industry, so its education probably tends to emphasize insurance matters more than broad-based financial planning. However, the designation is well respected among financial planners generally.

A third highly recognized financial-planning professional designation is one available only to Certified Public Accountants (CPAs) and is offered by the American Institute of Certified Public Accountants (AICPA). A CPA who also holds the designation of Personal Financial Specialist (PFS) has passed a written examination covering the personal financial-planning subject matter and has practical experience in the area. Currently, only approximately 11,000 CPAs have this designation, although personal financial planning is a much-sought-after service requested by clients of CPAs.

In addition to these three broad-based financial-planning credentials, several other specialized credentials exist in today's marketplace. These other credentials indicate that the financial planner has completed a particular course of instruction and commands specialized experience, such as in retirement or estate planning.

You may wish to consider including a CFP certificant or other financial-planning professional among a team of financial advisors. (High-net-worth individuals and small business owners have been doing this for years.) Specifically, financial advising teams have traditionally consisted of a financial planner, a life insurance or property and casualty insurance agent, an accountant (usually a CPA), an estate-planning attorney, and, sometimes, a bank trust officer. Each fulfills the following roles:

- *Financial planner:* Typically, this individual has the broadest knowledge of your financial life and, as such, is often considered the quarterback of the financial advising team. They often prepare paperwork and financial documents used by other members of the team in properly advising you, the client. The financial planner also normally handles money management and investments for the client.
- *Life insurance, or property and casualty, agent:* Because separate state licenses are required to sell life insurance and homeowner/automobile insurance policies, you often need to contact two different professionals to buy each

respective policy. The life insurance agent or broker can obtain needed life insurance protection, and the property/casualty agent can do the same with respect to protecting your important property. Sometimes insurance agents have both state licenses, but not often.

- *Accountant:* Normally, the accountant performs income tax–related tasks, including the preparation of your annual income-tax return. However, this professional can also work closely with your financial planner in advising how best to organize and operate a small business and when it may be most appropriate to sell assets in a tax-efficient manner (such as appreciated **stock** and **mutual funds**).

- *Estate-planning attorney:* The role this professional fulfills as a member of the financial advising team is indicated in their title. The estate-planning attorney is responsible for the proper drafting of wills, trusts, and power-of-attorney documents with respect to your financial life, as well as certain business-planning documents if you are also a small business owner.

- *Bank trust officer:* This member of the financial advising team is generally involved only in the event that you (a) have drafted a **trust** with the assistance of the estate-planning attorney/team member and (b) have elected to use a professional **trustee** to manage and distribute the trust assets. However, you may also be the **beneficiary** of a trust established by someone else and might interact with the bank trust officer in this manner.

It is possible that any of these professionals may perform several roles. For example, many accountants not only advise clients with respect to taxes, but also have broadened their services to include traditional financial-planning advice. To provide both services, they may hold and maintain not only the CPA state license, but also the CFP professional credential.

Questions to Ask a Financial Planner

As you can likely appreciate by now, if you choose to work with a financial planner, selecting the planner is not an easy task. This is complicated by the fact that, unlike that for doctors and lawyers, there is no formal licensing, and accompanying regulation, of financial planners. Right now, anyone can call themselves a financial planner—even a taxicab driver in New York City. If you work with an unqualified advisor, your financial future may be at risk, so be careful!

Plan Your Financial Future

How do you protect yourself against this possibility? One answer is to work only with someone who demonstrates considerable financial services experience and expertise, such as an individual with an advanced business degree or a well-respected financial-planning designation. However, in addition to this preliminary screen, you should also ask the planner or advisor certain basic questions, such as those listed next from the Financial Planning Association (FPA), the major professional association of personal financial planners. The FPA's web site is www.fpanet.org.

The FPA suggests that you ask the following ten questions of any prospective financial planner with whom you are considering working. I have added commentary to each to assist you even further in deciding which planner might be best for you:

1. *What experience do you have?* Experience in any industry or profession is important, but in the rapidly changing world of financial services, such experience is invaluable. If the planner has not spent at least five years advising and working with clients, you may wish to keep searching until you find a planner who has.

2. *What are your qualifications?* Qualifications mean educational and professional designations that you can trust with respect to expertise in the financial-planning process.

3. *What services do you offer?* In most instances, a financial planner offers *investment advisory services* when implementing the financial plan for a client. Therefore, they must either have a Series 65 or Series 66 Financial Industry Regulatory Association (FINRA) securities license or have been waived from this requirement by virtue of earning an approved designation, such as the CFP certification. In addition, most planners offer other services that may require separate state or federal licensing.

4. *Can I have your engagement agreement in writing?* The first step in the personal financial-planning process for the professional planner is to establish and define the client-planner relationship. As a part of this step, the planner should offer to define for you in writing the scope of the engagement, which is the totality of services that the planner and client agree is necessary and appropriate, and that the planner is qualified and willing to provide. A CFP certificant *must* define the scope of the engagement in writing. In mutually defining this scope, the client and planner may agree to only parts of the financial-planning process (segmented financial planning or goal-specific planning) or the completion of a comprehensive financial plan.

5. *What is your approach to financial planning?* This question usually involves a discussion of the planner's investment approach (for example, does the planner adopt a more conservative or aggressive approach when investing a client's money?), but some planners adopt more of a financial life planning approach than others. Financial life planning is difficult to define but generally tries to anticipate life events and prepare for them at a point much earlier in time than does traditional financial planning. Financial life planning also explores more fully the psychology of money and attempts to complement more completely the merging of an individual's financial goals and lifestyle needs.

6. *Will you be the only person working with me?* Like any professional, the practicing financial planner usually has staff who work in the same office. These individuals may or may not have the same expertise as the planner, not to mention the same rapport with you. If this is a concern to you, you should ask the planner how much time they will personally spend on your particular case file. In addition, if the planner works as a member of a financial-planning advisory team, you may wish to ask for the names of the other team members and investigate their qualifications and background.

7. *How much do you typically charge?* The total amount that the financial planner will charge for their services depends on the nature and extent of those services. Nevertheless, the planner should be able to provide you with an hourly fee (if they charge in that manner) or flat fee or the percentage of commissions or investment assets under management that is standard for their practice.

8. *How are you paid?* As discussed, financial planners are paid on a commission-only, fee-and-commission, or fee-only basis. As a part of the written engagement letter that the planner should provide at the beginning of the relationship, the planner should explain how they are paid. Some planners also provide an estimate of the total amount of fees or commissions that will be due.

9. *Have you ever been publicly disciplined for any unlawful or unethical actions in your professional career?* This is an important question to ask. Although public *discipline* of a planner is a matter of record, you probably do not know where to find such information. If you know (or ask) what

licenses are maintained by the planner, you can check the records of those particular regulatory bodies or agencies, but it is better to have a simple conversation with the planner about any past disciplinary problems. If the planner objects to this conversation, it may be because he or she has, indeed, incurred regulatory sanctions.

If the planner provides investment advice and is registered as an investment advisor with the U.S. Securities and Exchange Commission (SEC) or the state securities commission, under securities law they must provide you with a disclosure form entitled *SEC Form ADV Part II* or the state equivalent. If the planner is employed by a securities firm that is registered as an investment advisor, the firm's disclosure form must be given to you.

10. *Can anyone other than me benefit from your recommendations?* (Stated another way: *Do you have any potential or current conflicts of interest?*) Another big question! This is perhaps even more important than the public discipline inquiry.

    If a planner has a current conflict of interest (for example, if they are on the board of directors of a company whose stock you are considering purchasing), it should be disclosed to you initially—preferably, in writing. In addition, if during the course of the engagement a potential conflict of interest arises for the planner, it should be disclosed to you as well. An advantage of working with a CFP certificant is that, under their applicable code of ethics, both current and potential conflicts of interest *must* be disclosed to you in writing. It is then your decision whether you wish to begin working with (or continue working with) the CFP certificant.

    In addition to these questions, I would ask two more:

11. *What is the typical net worth and annual income level of your clients?* Unfortunately, many financial planners and investment advisors prefer to work with individuals who have already made considerable money or accumulated a sizable amount of assets and want to increase their annual income or net worth even further. If this is not you, do not despair! More and more planners are focusing on middle-income Americans and their need for financial security.

When searching for a financial planner, ask the candidates you are considering to draw you a mental picture of their clients with respect to their average income level and net worth. You may want to ask about the financial goals and life-cycle status of a typical client and compare their situation to yours. If there is a great disparity, or you feel inferior in some manner, you may wish to consider another planner.

12. *Do you construct an investment risk profile for your clients? And, if so, can you explain to me in simple terms how you evaluate and use this profile?* It is likely that among the first issues you will address with the planner is how to build your wealth through investment in real or financial assets or both. To properly analyze this issue, it is necessary to determine your tolerance for assuming investment risk (your *risk tolerance*). This is a complicated determination for many individuals. Many people consider themselves conservative investors and expect their investment advisor to know what this means. Skilled financial planners and investment advisors know how to probe for the real meaning of the term *conservative* (and its polar opposite, *aggressive*) by providing real examples of investment situations and asking how you would react if these situations happened to you.

For example, consider this question: "If you had $50,000 invested in the stock market, how much of this amount could you tolerate losing—and over what time period—and still sleep at night?" If the answer is none or a very small amount, you are likely a conservative investor. However, be aware that this answer means your investment return (reward for risk) is also likely to be greatly reduced. Generally, as we age, we become *more conservative* in our investment outlook, although as you will learn later, this does not mean you should avoid investment risk altogether. Indeed, there are many forms of investment risk, and just because you may avoid the risk of loss to the principal of an investment, you may instead assume the loss of future purchasing power due to inflation. A skilled financial planner can assist you in determining what level of investment risk you are comfortable with and, accordingly, how well you are able to sleep at night.

Since the severe decline in the stock market and Great Recession of 2007—2009, many investors have come to more properly appreciate their assumed level of risk. Until December 2007, many younger investors had never experienced a market in which a consistent decline in the market value of securities was the norm. As a result, some investors are reevaluating the allocation of their portfolio and moving into financial assets that are deemed to be "safer" (commonly defined in the investor's mind as shorter-term US government securities).

The next chapter addresses personal financial planning and the wealth-management process. Wealth management is an extension of personal financial planning and focuses on high-income and high-net-worth clients. Wealth management also emphasizes the investment process within financial planning, because high-income clients typically have a larger amount of discretionary income than middle-income investors. This book is designed to show you how to reach the status of a higher-net-worth individual by increasing your current wealth.

CHAPTER 3

Elements of Personal Financial Planning and the Wealth-Management Process

Chapter 3 | Elements of Personal Financial Planning and the Wealth-Management Process

Academic studies have shown that following a financial plan will help you build wealth more rapidly than is possible without one. This is because a financial plan enforces self-discipline, the key to any future accumulation of wealth. People earning between $50,000 and $100,000 per year who follow a financial plan typically have up to twice as much savings as those in the same income bracket who have no financial plan. For those earning more than $100,000 per year and following a financial plan, the savings rate is some 60 percent greater than that of their peers. Clearly, people who adhere to some form of a financial plan—either in writing or informally by matching their savings practice to a predetermined set of financial goals—have a significant advantage. Bottom line: *you have to convince yourself of reasons to save, or you will probably not do it.* One of the purposes of this book is to provide you with those reasons.

Personal Financial Planning and Wealth Management

The profession of personal financial planning has had an interesting and somewhat complicated past. Although financial planning has always been about the process of determining whether and how individuals can meet their financial goals through the proper management of financial resources, planners have occasionally been sidetracked and focus too much on the *resources* component of the definition instead of the *process* component. In other words, financial *products*—such as an attractive stock or the newest insurance product—that are necessary to implement the planning process become predominant.

Alternatively, some financial planners prefer to think of themselves as *wealth builders* or *wealth managers* to differentiate themselves from the product side of the business and, hopefully, attract the client with a higher net income or net worth. No academic subject in the personal financial-planning process is likely more important than the others, but planners who think of themselves as primarily wealth builders tend to emphasize investment selection and investment management. As a result, those planners prefer to work only with high-net-worth clients and specify a minimum amount of investable assets (usually in the high six figures or even in the low seven figures) that can immediately be put to work in the capital markets. But wealth managers and financial planners are really beginning at the same place: the client's financial goals. It is only the amount of financial resources a client can bring to bear in accomplishing their goals that distinguishes a financial planner from a wealth builder or wealth manager.

Regardless of whether these financial professionals think of themselves more as wealth managers or planners, they typically provide six main services for their clients:

- Insurance and risk management
- Employment benefits (often simply referred to as *fringe benefits*)
- Investments
- Income-tax planning and management
- Planning for retirement
- Estate planning

I suggest that you use these general categories to examine and review your own financial life. Keep in mind that numerous issues need to be addressed within each of these areas. Determining your own status in each category may help you begin the process of record keeping. Additionally, a professional financial planner will orient their work around each of these areas, and some will demonstrate a specialty in one or more of the subjects.

Is there any importance to the order in which I have listed the general areas of financial planning? In terms of thinking about your financial life, yes, there is! Your employment status determines whether you have any employment benefits to consider, but think of these benefits as nothing more than a temporary safety net that you can use to protect your financial well-being. When you change jobs, these benefits may or may not be portable (they probably will not be). This is why it is much better to build a *permanent* safety net constructed from individual life insurance and other benefits that you purchase on your own and are intended to remain with you throughout your lifetime, regardless of your employment status. Because both temporary and permanent benefits are primarily obtained so as to provide protection against possible future financial loss, they should be thought of sequentially as *first* in the financial-planning process.

The PADD approach to building and managing wealth places the general categories of personal financial planning in a real-life context that can be used as a blueprint to financial independence:

- *Protect* yourself against the risk of catastrophic financial loss.
- *Accumulate* wealth through investments.
- *Defend* that wealth through prudent income-tax planning and management.
- *Distribute* that wealth for your retirement and as part of your estate at death.

First, however, because of their importance in the overall financial-planning process as the "engine" in generating substantial wealth, we need to spend some time discussing investments and investment strategies. This begins with the need for a well-thought-out investment policy statement.

The Need for an Investment Policy Statement

Many planners refer to the *investment policy statement* (IPS) as the third mandatory personal financial statement (in addition to the statement of personal financial position and the cash-flow statement discussed in Chapter 1). The IPS helps the investor specify realistic investment goals while also forcing them to consider the risks and costs of investing. For example, specifying that you wish to obtain an average 15 percent annual rate of return on an investment in an individual stock begs the question of whether you also expect the stock to increase in price by this same amount consistently every year. If so, you need to engage in a reality check! Such thinking ignores the risk of stock investing, because the market price of stocks can fluctuate dramatically from year to year. This is known as **volatility**, which you need to understand and accept as a risk prior to investing in the stock market.

Any well-developed investment policy statement has four basic sections. With allowances for the specific wording of any customized statement, these sections are as follows:

- Statement of the investor's objectives
- Statement of investor constraints or limitations
- Meeting the investor's objectives and allocation of investment resources
- Monitoring the performance of the investment plan

Statement of the Investor's Objectives

The formulation and statement of the investor's objectives are your primary input to the statement and should explain your investment goals in terms of investment risk and return. A careful analysis of your risk tolerance should precede any discussion of return objectives. As we have discussed, you typically will not know how to adequately define your risk tolerance; accordingly, this is one of the benefits of using a financial planner, who will help assess and clearly specify the amount of risk you are willing to assume.

A person's return objectives may be stated in terms of a percentage, but they also may be stated in words. For example, *capital preservation* means investors seek to maintain the purchasing power of their investment—therefore, the necessary return must be no less than the rate of annual inflation. Alternatively, *capital appreciation* is an appropriate objective when the investor wants to achieve growth of their investment through real capital gains (a return considerably more than annual inflation). A *current income* objective means the investor wants the manager to invest in dividend-paying stocks or interest-earning bonds to generate income. Finally, a *total return* strategy implies that the investor seeks to increase the value of investments by taking advantage of both capital gains and reinvesting any current income back into the investment for future growth of principal.

Statement of Investment Constraints or Limitations

In this section of the statement, you need to specify your *investment time horizon*, or the time period in which you intend to invest. Concomitant to this time period is your need to access the money without a significant loss to principal (also known as *liquidity*). Investors with longer investment horizons, such as an investor who is saving for retirement, generally require less liquidity and can thus tolerate more investment risk. Investors with shorter time horizons, such as an investor already in retirement, generally seek greater liquidity and less-risky investments because losses cannot be overcome nearly as quickly.

Additional factors or limitations that you will typically wish to consider when developing a policy statement are the current and expected state of the overall economy and sectors of the economy in which you may be considering investing (for example, technology). The current tax status of any previous investments should also be taken into account. For example, an individual who is saving for retirement and is taking advantage of the tax-deferred nature of an individual retirement account (IRA) may engage in more-frequent investment transactions than someone who holds these investments in a taxable portfolio where capital gains must be recognized at the date of sale.

A final, often-included limitation covers the unique circumstances or preferences of the investor. Here is where you should state any preference to invest only in socially responsible companies. Similarly, you should give some thought to your current or anticipated cash flow. For example, if one of your goals is to purchase a vacation home during a shorter, specified time period, you will need to invest in relatively liquid assets. Alternatively, if you expect to receive a large inheritance during the time period (thus providing additional money for investment), you should discuss what you want to do with this money.

Meeting the Investor's Objectives and Allocation of Investment Resources

Although the typical investment policy statement does not indicate specific stocks or bonds the investor should purchase or sell, it should provide guidelines with respect to which asset classes to include and the relative percentages of each. In other words, the investment policy statement should provide an **asset allocation** strategy.

The assets in which you may wish to invest may not be the same as those of the typical investor, based on your risk-tolerance level, desired rate of return, and investment time horizon. However, most investment policy statements use only three categories or classes of investment assets:

- Stocks
- Bonds
- Cash or cash equivalents (savings accounts, short-term certificates of deposit, money-market funds, and any asset that is relatively liquid)

Investment percentages are assigned to each class.

Note Sometimes a fourth category, referred to as *alternative investments*, is also used as an asset class. These are any assets other than stocks, bonds, and cash (such as gold or silver).

Many methods are used to allocate the investment percentages, including some involving computer software. There are also a few rules of thumb. For example, one commonly cited rule is that you should subtract your age from 100 to determine the percentage amount that should be devoted to stock or stock mutual fund investments. The rest should be split between bonds and cash or cash equivalents, with only a relatively small percentage allocated to cash, given its lack of relative return. Here are four sample asset-allocation scenarios for a young, mid-life, pre-retiree, and retired investor of moderate risk tolerance:

- *Young investor (age 25 to 44)*: 75 percent stocks, 20 percent bonds, 5 percent cash or cash equivalents
- *Mid-life investor (age 45 to 55)*: 60 percent stocks, 30 percent bonds, 10 percent cash or cash equivalents
- *Pre-retiree investor (age 55 to 64)*: 50 percent stocks, 35 percent bonds, 15 percent cash or cash equivalents
- *Retired investor (age 65 plus)*: 40 percent stocks, 40 percent bonds, 20 percent cash or cash equivalents

Once the asset-allocation process has been determined, you should consider a mix of assets that have the highest probability of meeting your financial goals at a level of risk with which you are comfortable. As you get closer to meeting your financial goals, you should adjust this asset mix. For example, if you are several years away from meeting your goals, *safety* of principal should become more important to you than *growth* of that principal; accordingly, you should adjust the percentage of asset mix *toward* short-term bonds and cash equivalents and *away from* stocks.

Asset allocation generates **portfolio diversification**, which is the key to reducing your investment risk. We will talk more about diversification later in this chapter, but for now you should understand that a well-thought-out asset-allocation strategy is the foundation of any effective investment policy statement.

Monitoring the Performance of the Investment Plan

The drafting of a policy statement will assist you in judging the performance of your investment manager. Typically, the statement should include a model or benchmark portfolio against which the performance of the manager may be judged. For example, if you choose to invest in large-capitalization stocks (companies that have a large amount of outstanding public stock), you will likely want to compare the performance of the manager against the benchmark annual return of Standard & Poor's index of 500 stocks. Alternatively, if you choose to invest in smaller-capitalization stocks, a benchmark portfolio of similar stocks, such as the Russell 2000 Index, should be used. Because benchmark portfolios set an objective performance standard, the investment policy statement acts as a starting point for periodic portfolio review and assessment of investment manager performance.

The Basics of a Diversified Portfolio

A diversified portfolio should be diversified in two respects: *between* asset classes and *within* asset classes. Therefore, in addition to allocating your assets among stocks, bonds, and cash equivalents, you need to mix your investments within each of these three asset classes. The key to doing this successfully is to identify investments that may perform differently under different market conditions. For example, you should locate a stock that does not go down (or does not go down much) in a declining, or *bear*, market. The search for a stock that behaves in this manner, also known as *correlation*, is not easy; in essence, finding such a stock is how portfolio managers earn their money. Investment textbooks available at public libraries can tell you outline broadly how this can be done. A word of advice, however: leave this to the pros! If you choose to go about trying to select lower positively correlated or negatively correlated stocks on your own, you will quickly expend a lot of research time and possibly money and probably still not pick the stocks correctly.

Because achieving effective diversification is not easy, you may prefer to purchase numerous mutual funds. *Mutual funds* are a type of professionally managed asset, selected by an investment company, that pools money from many investors and invests in stocks, bonds, and financial assets. Such a fund makes it easy for the individual investor to own a small portion of a great number of investments. However, be careful: a mutual fund investment does *not* necessarily guarantee instant diversification. For example, the mutual fund may be investing only in stocks issued by companies involved in the same industry (called a *sector fund*). Thus, if you purchase a sector mutual fund, you have diversified *between* asset classes but not *within* asset classes. A mutual fund investing only in the stocks of technology companies is not participating in the broader market, which includes the stocks of many more types of companies and industries.

There are also ways to purchase mutual funds that are automatically diversified based on your age and life stage. A *life-cycle fund* is a diversified mutual fund that automatically shifts toward a more conservative mix of investments (more bonds, fewer stocks) as it approaches a particular year in the future, known as its *target date*. Given a considerable boost by pension plan legislation passed in 2006, life-cycle funds are frequently used by investors who prefer to hold a prepackaged number of investments to meet their financial goal—usually, saving for retirement. The managers of life-cycle funds make all decisions with respect to the asset allocation, diversification, and rebalancing of the fund. Such funds are easy to recognize, because they usually have a target retirement date (the year 2030, 2035, 2040, and so on) included in their name.

The Basics of Rebalancing

Rebalancing is a fundamental aspect of the initial asset-allocation decision and is necessary to bring your portfolio back to its original asset mix or percentages. Why is this required? Over time, some of your investments and asset classes will grow more quickly (or decline more) than other classes, thus deviating from the original percentages you specified as a part of your investment policy statement.

Let's say the stock market had a "good year" (a year in which the asset values of the majority of stocks increased in price). As a result, your initial stock allocation of 60 percent has now increased to 75 percent of your total portfolio. This also means your percentage allocations to bonds and cash equivalents have decreased. You are faced with either selling off some of your stock investments or purchasing more investments from the bonds and cash or cash equivalent asset classes, assuming that you wish to remain true to the asset allocation you established when the investment policy statement was prepared. This is not a bad thing. One of the steps in the financial-planning process that often is not done well is step 6: the monitoring part of the plan. Portfolio rebalancing is an automatic trigger that will assist you in the practical accomplishment of this step.

How often should you rebalance your portfolio? Like many other questions in financial planning and wealth building, this one has no definitive answer. If you have engaged the services of an investment advisor or professional financial planner, and a separate account has been established to hold your assets, the advisor should notify you when it is time to rebalance. Alternatively, if you are proceeding on your own, this decision is yours to make, although an annual rebalancing is likely prudent. Whatever the time frame, before you rebalance your portfolio, consider any transaction fees or income-tax consequences that may result from the rebalancing.

If you have invested in a taxable account and experienced a loss on the value of your stocks or bonds, consider selling those assets now and using the loss against your income taxes. By doing so, you also avoid one of the biggest mistakes of the average investor: refusing to let go! Some securities will *never* return to their original value. Even if they do, think of what you could have made with your money in the meantime. The opportunity cost of what you could have done with your money—but did not—is rarely considered by the average investor.

Investment Strategies

The number of investment strategies that may be pursued to build your wealth is probably limited only by the constraints of your own imagination and securities law, but let's talk about a few of the most common strategies.

Dollar-Cost Averaging and Share Averaging

Dollar-cost averaging is sometimes euphemistically referred to as "the poor man's method of saving." Using dollar-cost averaging, an investor purchases additional shares of stock in a mutual fund at regular intervals, usually in equal amounts, regardless of market conditions. Often, this is done through the use of an automatic withdrawal plan offered by the stock issuer or mutual fund company. When withdrawals are made from your paycheck in order to make **401(k) plan** contributions, you are essentially pursuing a dollar-cost averaging strategy.

The practical result of dollar-cost averaging is to gradually increase the number of mutual fund shares you own over a long period of time. In the event that the current price of the fund is below its previous price, you have succeeded in purchasing more shares of the investment. Because more shares are acquired when the price of the fund declines, this has the effect of reducing the average cost per share. Subsequently, if the price of the fund rises, you earn more profits on lower-priced shares, thereby increasing your overall rate of percentage return.

For example, assume that you purchased a $5,000 portion of ABC mutual fund in January 2018, when its share price was $20. You purchased a total of 250 shares ($5,000 divided by $20). Now, instead, assume that you made five separate purchases of ABC mutual fund during 2018 using this same $5,000, but you did so in $1,000 increments, when the price of the fund fluctuated as follows:

Month	Share Price	# of Shares Purchased
March 2018	$22.00	45.45
May 2018	$19.50	51.28
July 2018	$18.00	55.55
September 2018	$17.50	57.14
December 2018	$20.25	49.38
		Total: 258.80

Further assume that you plan to sell all the separately purchased ABC shares in January 2020, when ABC's per share price is estimated to be $24. Your total sale price will be $6,211.20 ($24 times 258.80 shares), and you will have **recognized** a gain of $1,211.20 ($6,211.20 less $5,000). What if you had sold your original January 2018 shares? Your gain would have been only $1,000 ($6,000 less $5,000). Using dollar-cost averaging, you increased your annual compounded rate of return by almost 2 percent (from 9.54 percent to 11.46 percent).

As the previous example illustrates, dollar-cost averaging works best when markets are declining or fluctuating. It does not work well when the market is steadily increasing; in that event, you are better off buying as many shares as possible, as soon as possible, when the price per share is lower. If an experienced investor learns one lesson throughout their years of investing, it is that markets rarely go straight up or straight down. Rather, fluctuation in share values is the rule and not the exception. Therefore, dollar-cost averaging should be a valuable wealth-building strategy for you, as it has been for millions of other investors.

A variation of the dollar-cost averaging technique is share averaging. When an investor *dollar-cost averages*, the number of dollars spent on stock or mutual fund purchases at regular intervals is held constant, but the number of shares purchased with these dollars varies. Conversely, when an investor *share averages*, the number of shares purchased remains constant, but the number of dollars spent to make those purchases varies. With share averaging, the investor purchases a *fixed* number of shares, regardless of how low the price falls. Thus, they do not obtain the reduction in the average cost of the shares to the same extent as is possible with dollar-cost averaging. This is why, as a wealth-building technique, more investors implement dollar-cost averaging than share averaging.

Averaging Down

As you can see from our example involving dollar-cost averaging, an investor can leverage their gain by buying more shares when the price of a certain asset declines (as long as the price eventually goes back up before the investor sells). Is there a strategy that results in buying additional shares only when the price goes down? Yes. It is referred to as *averaging down*. In our example, you would have bought ABC shares only in May 2018, July 2018, and September 2018, when the share price fell below the original $20 purchase price, and not in March 2018 and December 2018, when the price was more than $20.

Is pursuing this strategy a good idea? The answer depends on whether you are more interested in purchasing the stock or the company issuing the stock. If you are interested only in the *stock,* averaging down may not be a good strategy, because (as with dollar-cost averaging) the ability to make a profit ultimately depends on the share price increasing. If the share price does not increase, you will have purchased more shares of a stock that you likely should have considered selling in the first place. In other words, you will now have more shares of a losing stock. Alternatively, if you are purchasing the *company* issuing the stock, presumably you have researched the prospects of that company and the industry in which it does business. Accordingly, you should have greater confidence in the possibility for an increase in the price of that company's stock, as well as reasonable assurance that a decline in price is only temporary. Therefore, if you are using the strategy in this manner, averaging down may make more sense as a long-term investment technique.

In any event, proceed carefully! Unless you are an experienced investor, averaging down is an investment strategy you should not try without the help of a professional.

Dividend Reinvestment Programs

Unlike averaging down, which is for only experienced investors, stocks that offer a dividend reinvestment program (DRIP) should be considered by any investor. With a DRIP, dividends declared are automatically reinvested in the stock, adding to the investor's overall ownership share. If you want to build an ownership percentage in a company, this is the way to do it!

DRIPs offer other advantages. If the dividends are reinvested automatically—instead of paid directly to the shareholder—the investor purchases the additional shares of company stock without having to incur a broker's commission. Also, because the company tracks your purchases and keeps records of the purchase price, it can easily provide you with **cost basis** information in the event that you want to sell.

Many mutual funds have similar programs. If you are working with an investment advisor or financial planner who has positioned your holdings in some form of advisory account, ask them whether you can opt to reinvest any capital gain or dividend distributions (or both) into the purchase of additional shares of the fund. If this option is available, consider taking advantage of a DRIP as an easy way to save and build wealth.

Laddering

You can go about laddering, or staggering, the maturity of fixed income investments, such as **bonds** or certificates of deposit, in a number of ways. The most popular is to figure out the longest- and shortest-term maturities you want to assume and then sequence your purchases between those maturity dates.

For example, if you have $50,000 to invest, and you want to invest in bonds with a maturity of no longer than ten years and no shorter than one year, consider ten purchases of bonds in $5,000 increments with a maturity date each year from the end of year one to the end of year ten. This has the effect of minimizing the impact of the price changes in the bonds due to interest-rate fluctuations, also known as *interest-rate risk*. In addition, as the short-term bonds mature, their principal may subsequently be invested at potentially higher market interest rates.

You can adopt the same approach with respect to bank certificates of deposit and obtain the advantage of Federal Deposit Insurance Corporation (FDIC) insurance on each certificate, as long as the total ownership in each bank and certificate does not exceed $250,000 per depositor.

Buy and Hold

Another phrase that describes the buy-and-hold investment strategy is **passive portfolio management**. In other words, the investor does not intend to actively trade the stocks, bonds, or other assets in their portfolio and instead chooses to own those investments for a relatively long time. Buy and hold, coupled with dollar-cost averaging, is a common strategy for building wealth to meet the average investor's saving-for-retirement financial-planning goal.

The buy-and-hold strategy has several advantages:

- You can minimize your acquisition and trading costs in the trading of securities, leading to considerable savings over time.

- It will assist you in managing your income-tax obligations. For example, if you do not sell a security in a given year, you do not need to recognize a capital gain or loss on your income-tax return.

- Academic studies have shown that the most significant gains in the securities markets are made during several trading days throughout the year; a buy-and-hold strategy ensures that you will not be out of the market during those days.

A warning: many individuals say they are buy-and-hold investors when, in fact, they are not. Most of us allow changing market conditions to influence our buy-and-sell trading decisions. In other words, we let short-term emotions get in the way of our long-term investment decisions. Mega-investor Warren Buffett has made his investors rich in part by not permitting emotions to dictate his investment philosophy. If you are a pure buy-and-hold investor, you will remain in the market for a long time with little concern for market volatility.

Market Timing

Market timing is the behavioral opposite of the buy-and-hold strategy. It is an attempt to predict the overall direction of the securities market and to take advantage of the market's volatility, whether that general direction is up (a bull market) or down (a bear market).

Market timing should not be confused with the rebalancing strategy discussed earlier in this chapter. You should rebalance your portfolio to maintain consistent asset-allocation percentages over time. However, when you rebalance, you are responding to rules and conditions that *you* have established—through an asset-allocation strategy, included in an investment policy statement, that is intended to culminate in the meeting of your financial goals. Market timing responds to *external* market circumstances—rules and conditions that have been established by the market—over which you have no control. In practice, portfolio rebalancing is proactive, whereas market timing is reactive.

Does market timing work? Probably not, largely for the reason mentioned earlier: an investor needs to stay invested in the market all year long to experience the greatest gains. Nevertheless, if done properly, market timing can have value. For example, as an investor, you should pay attention to reports that indicate whether a large number of market timers are either buying or selling over a period of several weeks. This may give you some perspective with respect to overall market sentiment (and, accordingly, whether the market in the future is likely to go up or down).

Value vs. Growth Investing

Value and growth investing are just different sides of the same investment coin. In this case, the investment coin is the **price-to-earnings (P/E) ratio** of stocks.

Value investing is an investment strategy that is concerned with the market price of stocks: specifically, finding stocks that are currently undervalued by the market. Thus, investors who practice value investing attempt to find stocks with high dividend yields and low P/E ratios. This strategy assumes that the current P/E ratio of the stock is below its proper level (or what the ratio should be, given current market conditions) and that an efficient market will soon accommodate for this discrepancy and drive up the price of the stock.

Growth investing, on the other hand, focuses on the potential earnings of the company issuing the stock. As a result, growth investors look for growth stocks—stocks of a company that has shown a proven ability to develop products quickly and efficiently with a minimum of marketplace competition. Such stocks usually have a superior rate of earnings growth (typically 10 percent a year or more), low dividend yields, and an above-average P/E ratio.

There is some practical evidence that, in a bull market, a growth investing strategy tends to outperform a value investing approach. Conversely, in a declining or fluctuating market, value investing may be more appropriate. As an investor, you should likely consider both strategies as appropriate methods of building wealth.

Investing in Real Estate

Most Americans have made an investment in real estate—whether they realize it or not—in the form of their own home. Is your home a good investment? Although the answer to this question depends on many factors, not the least of which is the geographical location of your home, studies have shown that the average annual real (after inflation) return on residential real estate historically lags that of stocks and bonds. According to a Fidelity Research Institute report, which used data obtained from Global Financial Data and Winans International that predated the Great Recession of 2007–2009, the average annual ten-year real (after inflation) rate of return on residential real estate is only 1.62 percent. This compares to an average annual real rate of return of 5.85 percent for stocks and 3.18 percent for bonds over the same period. Indeed, experts say to expect only a future, annual real return on homes of one-quarter to one-half percentage point greater than the annual inflation rate.

Despite this low rate of real return, home ownership is important in our society because it allows the investor-homeowner to build equity, which is the difference between the fair market value of their home and the amount the investor-homeowner owes on it. In addition, the financial obligation of making mortgage payments may make the investor or homeowner a better saver than an individual who rents. The ability to save (or, more accurately, the exercise of financial self-discipline) is an important trait for any effective wealth builder. As a result, studies show that the net worth of homeowners is some eight times greater on average than that of renters, regardless of age or income level.

In Chapter 9 and Chapter 10 of this book, when discussing the accumulation step in the PADD approach to wealth, we will cover in more detail investing in financial vs. real assets. However, as noted in the Fidelity Research report, the average investor should be wary of over-investing in real estate. This is especially true when certain financial assets, such as stocks and bonds, have proven their superiority as wealth-building vehicles over time.

We have now covered the basics of the financial-planning process. Next we will go into detail about the specified subject-matter areas of the process, beginning with the protection of your lifetime earning capacity, your family, and your property.

PART II

Protecting Yourself, Your Family, and Your Property

CHAPTER 4

Insuring Yourself and Your Family

This section of this book introduces the first step in the PADD approach to accumulating and managing wealth: *protecting yourself* against the risk of catastrophic financial loss. In this chapter, we discuss the most important form of risk management: insuring your life (and protecting your loved ones from the resulting loss of income at death) by purchasing life insurance.

Before we begin, you should keep in mind the following guiding principles with respect to purchasing any type of insurance:

- Never risk more than you can afford to lose. Buy only the amount of insurance required to ensure that you and your family will be restored to the before-loss status quo.

- Do not buy insurance you don't need. This is particularly important when considering the purchase of an annuity, an insurance product providing for lifetime income, but also including a death benefit. If you do not need the death benefit, think twice before purchasing the annuity, because there are less expensive ways to provide for a lifetime income stream.

© Keith R. Fevurly 2018
K. R. Fevurly, *Plan Your Financial Future*, https://doi.org/10.1007/978-1-4842-3637-6_4

Do I Need Life Insurance? How Much?

Few financial questions are likely to be more troublesome than, "Do I need life insurance?" This is in part because it prompts the asker to confront his or her own mortality. In addition, the need for life insurance is a philosophical issue for some individuals. For example, historically, farmers and people who make their living off the land and intend to pass this land down to their families do not believe that a financial product such as life insurance can substitute for something God did not create.

Let's accept for a moment that we are all going to die someday. Once you have accepted your mortality, figure out what you want to have happen in the event of your death. Most people with spouses and children want to protect the financial lifestyle of their heirs. In other words, they do not want their families to have to suffer financially because they have lost a source of income. It makes sense, then, that the amount of life insurance you need is primarily determined by how much income needs to be replaced after your death.

As a rule of thumb, many life insurance agents say that you should purchase a life insurance death benefit to replace between five and seven times your annual gross income. For instance, if your annual gross income is $100,000, you should purchase between $500,000 and $700,000 of life insurance coverage. But, like most rules of thumb (and contrary to the financial-planning process that should guide your decision), nowhere in this rule is any consideration given to financial goals or particular individual needs and family circumstances. As such, two primary methods are used by most financial planners to determine the amount of life insurance that an individual should purchase.

The first of these two methods is the *human life value approach*. This approach estimates the amount of income your family would need, based on the financial loss they would incur, if you were to die today, anticipating the number of possible working years that remained. This amount is then adjusted downward for what you would have personally consumed or paid in taxes (referred to as the *family's share of earnings*). Utilizing a rate of return known as a *discount rate*, the present value of your life to your family is estimated. For example, let's say you currently make $70,000 per year in salary and have approximately 20 years left in your working career. Your amount of personal consumption and taxes due on this income is $20,000, resulting in a family's share of earnings of $50,000 ($70,000 less $20,000). By applying a rate of return to these earnings of 5 percent annually and using a financial function calculator or software program, we can determine a life insurance need of approximately $625,000.

The human life value approach focuses *only* on your income-earning potential and the income loss to your survivors resulting from your death. As such, it is a relative method that assumes that your life has value only as it impacts the financial life of your survivors. It does not consider the recurring nature of your dependents' expenses or any unusual expenses that may result from your death, such as the future need for college education for minor children. Rather, these expenses are part of the alternative computation known as the *needs approach* to life insurance planning.

The *needs approach* to determining the optimal amount of life insurance an individual should purchase is sophisticated and usually computed via a computer software program. Briefly, the approach considers your marital status, whether your spouse is employed outside the home, the size of your family, and any separate income earned by your dependents (children or elderly parents). For example, an individual who is single and has no dependents has little need for life insurance coverage. As a result, life insurance for this person may be necessary only to repay debts and expenses related to their death. A married person or single working parent who supports dependents has a need for life insurance to continue the flow of income to these dependents in the event of the person's death. The needs approach is suitable to determine the amount of this need.

Here are some of the typical needs of an insured person and their family in the event of death:

- Burial or cremation expenses, including funeral costs
- An adjustment fund, which is a short-term fund intended to cover one-time expenses incurred by the family as it adjusts to the loss of the primary (or other) wage-earner
- An income continuation fund, including an amount for mortgage payoff (if the insured's house is not paid off by the time of death)
- An educational fund for the college education of minor children
- An amount to provide a lifetime income for the surviving spouse, the need for which arises if the spouse is unemployed and does not have the necessary skills to enter the workforce or cannot otherwise earn sufficient income to replace the insured's income

As the potential insured of a single-income family, you should consider that even if your surviving spouse could generate sufficient income to cover the loss of your earnings, your spouse's entry into the workforce might not be preferable to purchasing additional life insurance for this need. In other words, do you intend to *require* your spouse to work? The answer depends on your agreements with your spouse, but if you do not wish to have this discussion, you should purchase the necessary additional life insurance.

Term vs. Cash Value Insurance

Many life insurance companies offer various life insurance policies. All these policies generally consist of only two basic methods of providing life insurance: term (also known as *temporary* life insurance) and cash value (also known as *permanent* life insurance). **Term insurance** protects you only for a specific period; if you die during this period and are current in your premium payments, the company will pay your family the contractual death benefit that is due. **Cash value insurance** protects you for life and offers a savings component in the form of a cash value buildup. Types of term life insurance policies include annual renewable term, level premium term, and decreasing term insurance. Types of permanent life insurance policies featuring a cash value buildup include traditional whole life, universal life, variable life, and variable universal life (VUL) coverage.

Both term and cash value life insurance can be valuable in protecting yourself and your family. You should not think of either term or cash value insurance as an all-or-nothing proposition; many thoughtful individuals purchase both forms of coverage. But generally, as you age, term insurance coverage will become *more expensive*, whereas the cost of cash value coverage will remain *fixed*. The reason is that cash value expenses are front-loaded as part of the policy structure, because some of the premium expenses (beyond the pure mortality cost associated with any life insurance policy) go to build a cash reserve or cash fund that you can potentially access for emergency needs.

Just as in determining the amount of life insurance that may be needed, rules of thumb pertain to whether it is best to purchase term or cash value insurance. One of the most common is to "buy term insurance and invest the difference." In other words, given the fact that term is at least initially less expensive than cash value (the *younger* you are, the *longer* your life expectancy and the *less* the mortality costs associated with term insurance), take the savings and invest it in higher-yielding financial investments, such as mutual funds. Although the appeal of this strategy is obvious, permanent insurance advocates counter that the buy-term-and-invest-the-difference concept depends on several flawed assumptions:

- The difference will always be diligently invested every year the insured owns term insurance, regardless of the insured's personal financial circumstances or ongoing standard of living.
- The alternative investment will always be financially superior to the incremental cash value buildup.
- Somehow the need for insurance will magically disappear as the insured ages.

Ultimately, the final decision of how to best meet your life insurance needs is yours. In providing for these needs, you should remember that life insurance should be purchased to *protect yourself and your family*; investments, on the other hand, should be purchased to *accumulate wealth*. Although cash value policies have some investment characteristics (particularly the newer forms of universal and variable universal life), life insurance is first and foremost a risk-management product and, generally, *not* a product designed to generate significant investment growth.

Types of Term Insurance

Today, most buyers of term insurance purchase either annual renewable term or level premium term. Historically, decreasing term insurance has been a popular form of temporary protection and has been used as a mortgage-payoff vehicle at the insured's death. However, decreasing term has fallen out of favor in recent years, primarily because it does not reduce protection at the same rate as the typical mortgage balance, thus resulting in an unnecessary premium cost to the insured. With annual renewable term, you pay the premium each year, and the policy remains in force. As you age, the cost to the insurance company increases, and the premium goes up each year. But the level of protection—the death benefit—afforded your family remains constant.

Level premium term insurance, on the other hand, initially costs more per year than annual renewable term, but the premium remains level for a fixed period of time (generally anywhere from 5 to 30 years). Thus, as you age, presuming you still want a relatively inexpensive temporary life insurance policy, you should probably consider replacing annual renewable term with level premium term. But beware: as you approach the expiration date of your level term policy, you should begin to set aside additional funds for premium payments after the policy expires. Typically, depending on your age, health, and the length of your original level term policy, you will experience a significant increase in premiums when you purchase a new term policy.

An attractive feature of some term policies is the ability to convert from term, or temporary, coverage to cash value, or permanent, life insurance protection *without* evidence of insurability. This means you can obtain permanent protection without having to pass a medical examination. Accordingly, the opportunity to convert is particularly valuable for insureds whose health may have declined during the term. As such, if your health has changed for the worse and you currently own a term policy, you should probably consider converting to a cash value policy as soon as possible, because it is unlikely that you will be able to qualify for permanent coverage at a later date.

Types of Cash Value Insurance

There are three basic types of cash value policies: traditional whole life, universal life, and variable life. A fourth type, variable universal life (VUL), combines the features of universal and variable policies.

Traditional whole life is the standard form of cash value insurance that has been offered by life insurance companies for many years. It features a fixed premium for the life of the policy as well as a savings component that grows on a tax-deferred basis. The policy is initially relatively expensive and, unless you continue to make premium payments, will lapse, potentially causing you to lose coverage. In addition, at your death, your beneficiaries will receive only the death benefit payable from the policy and not the accumulated cash value. If you choose to access the cash value or savings portion during your lifetime, you must do so through a policy loan or withdrawal, which in turn reduces the amount of the death benefit paid.

Next, *universal life* takes the concept of "buy term and invest the difference" in a new direction. Yes, you are able to invest the premium amounts charged in excess of pure term coverage and generate additional return, but you must do so by investing in what the insurance company chooses for you—which are usually conservative, fixed-income vehicles, such as investment-grade bonds. Thus, the return generated by a universal life policy, although higher than that of a traditional whole life policy, still lags that of a variable life policy, in which equities (common stocks) are the primary form of investment. The primary advantage of a universal life policy is its flexibility with respect to premium payments. The policy premium is not fixed or tied to the amount of death benefit protection purchased, except in the first year of the policy. The premiums are then deposited into an accumulation fund from which the insurance company withdraws monthly mortality charges. A minimum payment is required to keep the policy in force only when the accumulation fund is close to zero. The policyholder, subject to their continued insurability, may increase the death benefit of a universal life policy.

The third kind of cash value insurance, *variable life insurance*, differs from traditional whole life and universal life in one primary respect: you (and not the insurance company) are in charge of your investment choices. Variable life policies allow you to invest in various combinations of stocks, bonds, and mutual funds and feature subaccounts in which you can allocate your assets (similar to the variable annuity form of insurance product). Although the premium payments due on a variable life policy are fixed (as in traditional whole life), the death benefit may increase, as can the underlying cash value accumulated within the policy subaccounts. The VUL policy, finally, takes this concept one step further by combining a choice of investments and increasing death benefit protection with the ability to make flexible premium payments.

Which of these cash value life insurance forms is best? It almost invariably depends on your comfort level with assuming investment risk. If you consider yourself to be a moderately aggressive or aggressive investor (remember, a primary advantage of working with a financial planner is that the planner helps you determine your risk-tolerance level), a variable life or VUL policy may be preferable. If you are relatively uncomfortable with assuming investment risk or you do not like making investment decisions, a traditional whole life or universal life policy may be more to your liking.

Table 4-1 summarizes the types of term and cash value policies available, to help you weigh your options.

Table 4-1. Types of Life Insurance

Type of Policy	Description	Insurance Need	Death Benefit	Premium Structure	Who Should Buy It?
Annual Renewable Term	Pure life insurance with no cash value	Temporary	Fixed	Increases each year	Insured with limited funds
Level Premium Term	Pure life insurance with no cash value	Temporary	Fixed	Level for period of years and then increases	Insured with limited funds
Traditional Whole Life	Cash value accumulation; predictable maximum cost	Permanent	Fixed	Level for insured's lifetime	Insured with need for predictable savings
Universal Life	Cash value accumulation; flexible cost	Permanent	Adjustable (may increase)	Flexible with minimum payment	Conservative investor
Variable Life	Cash value accumulation based on investment performance	Permanent	Guaranteed minimum (fluctuates)	Level for insured's lifetime	Risk-tolerant investor
Variable Universal Life (VUL)	Features of both variable and universal life policies	Permanent	Adjustable with guaranteed minimum	Flexible with minimum payment	Risk-tolerant investor

Now that we have considered the types of life insurance policies available for purchase, let's move on to choosing an insurance company.

Insurance Company Selection and Ratings

Before purchasing any type of life insurance policy, even a term policy, find out the financial strength of the insurance company underwriting (or insuring) it. Remember, the purpose of the policy—to provide for your family members in the event of your death—will not be realized until sometime in the (hopefully) distant future. You want the company from whom you buy the policy to be in business when it comes time for the death benefit to be paid. Moreover, should you need to access a portion of the death benefit during your life through one of the popular **accelerated death benefit riders** available today, you want to ensure that the company will be there to provide it.

The primary measure that most financial planners use to assess the financial strength of an insurance company is to consult an independent rating service. There are five primary insurance company rating organizations: A.M. Best, Standard & Poor's, Moody's, Fitch Ratings, and Weiss Research. Their rating letters are different, but all use A+ or some variation thereof to rate the highest companies, and several use F as the lowest rating. Table 4-2 shows the top six ratings from each organization, as well as the lowest ratings.

Table 4-2. Insurance Company Rating Agencies and Ratings

	A.M. Best	Standard & Poor's	Moody's	Fitch Ratings	Weiss Research
Highest Rating	A ++	AAA	Aaa	AAA	A+
Second-highest rating	A+	AA+	Aa1	AA+	A
Third-highest rating	A	AA	Aa2	AA	A−
Fourth-highest rating	A−	AA−	Aa3	AA−	B+
Fifth-highest rating	B++	A+	A1	A+	B
Sixth-highest rating	B+	A	A2	A	B−
Lowest rating	F	D	C	CCC−	F

None of these ratings organizations is any more preferable than the others; they all provide valuable information and basically review the same data on each insurance company. However, it is important to understand which organization's ratings are being cited. For example, a company rated A by A.M. Best means the company is of the third-highest quality, whereas the same company rating provided by either Standard & Poor's or Fitch Ratings indicates a level of only the sixth-highest quality. Regardless, with the number of insurance companies in business today, you should likely seek out only those of the highest or second-highest rating, using any rating measure. Typically, companies that deserve those ratings are well-known and have been conducting business for many years.

One final point to consider: some financial planners and insurance advisors believe that an insurance company's financial strength is not as important a consideration for those who plan to purchase a variable life or VUL cash value policy as it is for those who plan to purchase a traditional whole life or universal life policy. This is because the insurance company uses its general assets to stand behind a claim filed with respect to a traditional whole life or universal life policy but does not with the variable forms of life insurance. In these latter types of policies, the cash value accumulates in a separate subaccount that is *not* subject to the claims of the insurance company's other general creditors. As such, the financial viability of the company to pay your claim on a variable form of life insurance policy may not be quite as critical.

Another form of insurance protection—much in need today—is that of health insurance. Whereas most health insurance is offered, if at all, on a *group* level basis, the primary emphasis of "Obamacare" is directed toward the mandatory purchase of health insurance at the *individual* level. (Note that the 2017 TCJA *repealed* the individual mandate to purchase health insurance, but not effective until the beginning of year 2019.) By providing for increased competition among insurers in the form of state health insurance exchanges, it is hoped that the number of uninsured individuals will decline, thus forcing down health insurance costs. Although the success of these state health insurance exchanges to date is arguable in actually reducing costs, the next chapter reviews the major provisions of Obamacare as well as indemnity and managed care options.

CHAPTER 5

Insuring Your Health and Long-Term Care

The issues of health insurance and health insurance coverage are controversial and politically charged, particularly given individual preferences about national health insurance vs. a private-payer system. The potential necessity for long-term care insurance, however, is not nearly as well-known or discussed. According to the US Department of Health and Human Services, individuals reaching the age of 65 have an approximately 40 percent chance of entering a nursing home and requiring chronic, custodial care. Candidates for long-term care suffer from chronic or disabling conditions that require nursing-home care or other constant supervision. The cost of this care can be expensive—even financially catastrophic—for many individuals and their families.

One way to provide for the cost of this care is to purchase long-term care insurance while you are still healthy and young enough to qualify for it. But other alternatives exist, as discussed later in this chapter. Let's look first at the factors that should be considered in selecting an individual health insurance policy and the types of policies available in today's marketplace.

© Keith R. Fevurly 2018
K. R. Fevurly, *Plan Your Financial Future*, https://doi.org/10.1007/978-1-4842-3637-6_5

Considerations in Selecting a Health Insurance Policy

This section presents five general considerations to keep in mind when selecting the right health insurance policy.

Not Having Health Insurance Is Expensive. *Health insurance costs a lot, but not having it costs a great deal more.* Quite by accident, as a result of a recruitment tool used to entice veterans returning from World War II, the United States has an employer-based health insurance system. Accordingly, a majority of Americans are covered through group health insurance policies provided by their employers. However, many self-employed individuals and their employees do not have health insurance, given the prohibitive cost of coverage. The same is true for salaried individuals who are laid off as a result of a weak economy.

When it comes to health care expenses, studies show that if one family member is not covered by health insurance and suffers an accident, the resulting medical bills will have an impact on the future economic health of the entire family. The obligation to pay high medical bills is the number-one reason for personal bankruptcy filings today. As such, the need for group or individual coverage is important. If you are not covered by an employer or individual health plan, follow these steps as recommended by health care advocates and consultants:

1. Get in touch with your state's insurance department to find a list of health care plans that provide coverage in your state. Because of the extensive cost of health care to the uninsured, and the continuing inability of some individuals to qualify for health insurance, some states have established health insurance pools that offer coverage for high-risk individuals.

2. Contact the top-ranked plans in your state for details regarding premiums and costs for major medical procedures.

3. Find out whether any preexisting conditions are excluded from coverage. If you have previously been covered by a group policy, the Health Insurance Portability and Accountability Act of 1996 (HIPAA) may assist you in obtaining individual coverage, even if you have a preexisting condition as specified by the insurance carrier. Moreover, since the implementation of the Patient Protection and Affordable Care Act of 2010 (PPA), an insurance carrier is generally prohibited from denying coverage based on a preexisting condition.

Consider Participating in Your Employer's Plan

If your employer offers a group health plan, you are likely better off participating in that plan than purchasing individual health insurance. This can be a tough lesson to learn if you are young and healthy. As a young person in good health covered by a group plan, you may be overinsured, given that you are paying for a great deal of coverage that you may never use. You can minimize this cost by selecting as high a deductible and co-payment as the plan permits. You are still probably ahead cost-wise by participating in the group plan rather than purchasing individual coverage. In addition, you need to establish coverage under a group plan so as to exercise certain continuation rights that may be necessary in the event that you change or lose your job (otherwise known as COBRA rights, after the Consolidated Omnibus Budget and Reconciliation Act of 1985 that provided for these rights).

Carefully Review Plan Details

Review the co-payment and deductible provisions under health insurance plans carefully. Under most managed care plans—including health maintenance organizations (HMOs) and preferred provider organizations (PPOs))—the insured pays a fixed charge each time they see a medical doctor or fill a covered prescription. This is known as a *co-payment* and should be distinguished from *co-insurance*, through which the plan provider and the insured share the cost of covered medical expenses after the plan deductible has been met. Generally, you want the co-payment to be as small as possible, unless you do not anticipate using the insurance policy heavily during the year (if you are young and healthy, for example). In this case, you may want to opt for as high a co-payment as possible, which in turn should reduce your premium cost.

Many health care plans, particularly in recent years as the cost of health insurance has skyrocketed, require each insured to retain a certain portion of their health care expense risk in the form of a deductible. This is an out-of-pocket amount that the insured must pay before any insurance coverage is afforded. Once the covered medical expenses equal the plan deductible (usually on an individual or family basis), further expenses then qualify for the co-insurance provision. Typically, after the co-insurance provision is triggered, the insured must then pay 20 percent of the expenses until a certain maximum amount is reached (known as a *stop-loss*), at which point the insurance company pays 100 percent of the excess.

If your employer offers a **flexible spending account (FSA)** to help you with the payment of any deductibles or co-payments associated with its health insurance plan, put as much money into this account as you can afford or as allowed under current law. An FSA is a special form of employee benefit that allows you to pay for certain medical expenses (such as deductibles and

Chapter 5 | Insuring Your Health and Long-Term Care

co-payments) with *before-tax* dollars, thus reducing your taxable income. We will talk more about FSAs later; but as a general rule of tax planning, whenever you can pay for an expense with before-tax rather than after-tax dollars, doing so will usually prove advantageous.

Flexibility Costs Money

The more flexibility you have in selecting health care providers, the more the plan will cost you. Many insureds do not need to concern themselves with this fact, because their employer has already taken this flexibility away from them. For example, employers who offer only HMO enrollment to their employees have substantially restricted the employees' right to choose their own primary care physicians and specialists. But insureds who participate in other forms of health insurance plans, such as PPO plans, may typically see either an in-network physician or one who does not participate in the network (an out-of-network provider). This same concept also applies to participating and nonparticipating hospitals. If you want to see an out-of-network doctor or hospital, you will likely pay more for the privilege, but at least your choice is preserved.

As a result, if you are participating in a PPO managed care plan, one of the questions you should research is whether your preferred doctor or hospital is a member of the plan's network of medical providers. Usually, you can check out the network physicians and hospitals participating in the plan before signing up.

Know Your Rights

Make sure you know your legal rights if you leave your job (and the employer-provided coverage). In the past, two legislative acts—the Consolidated Omnibus Reconciliation Act of 1985 (COBRA) and the Health Insurance Portability and Accountability Act of 1996 (HIPAA)—have gone a long way to ensure continuing health insurance coverage for individuals who once had health insurance protection. Unfortunately, neither of these acts do much to address the ongoing problem of the uninsured or, just as important, the rising cost of health insurance premiums.

Note See the subsequent discussion in this chapter of the 2010 Patient Protection and Affordable Care Act, sometimes referred to as *Obamacare*, which was passed in part to address the problem of the uninsured and rising health care costs.

Plan Your Financial Future

We will talk in more detail about the COBRA and HIPPA acts shortly, but you should be aware that if you once had health insurance coverage but lost or changed jobs, it is relatively easy to continue that coverage for a period of time. Although your share of the health insurance premium may increase (if you exercise your COBRA rights, you have to incur the portion of the group health insurance previously paid by your employer), it is still much better than going without coverage. As mentioned earlier, no single event can threaten your future economic security or that of your family more than incurring substantial medical bills for which you have no individual, employer-provided, or government-mandated insurance.

Patient Protection and Affordable Care Act of 2010

On March 23, 2010, US President Barack Obama signed into law the **Patient Protection and Affordable Care Act** (or PPA). It is also commonly known as *Obamacare*. The purpose of this act was to assist consumers, particularly those with preexisting conditions, in purchasing health insurance coverage through the *individual* insurance marketplace. As a result, the group insurance marketplace was left largely unchanged. Among PPAs most important provisions are the following:

- A mandate requiring all individuals and certain employers to maintain or offer a minimum essential amount of health care insurance or face a penalty. The constitutionality of this mandate (as a penalty tax) was upheld in the US Supreme Court case of *National Federation of Independent Business, et al. v. Sebelius, Secretary of Health and Human Services, et al.* (decided June 28, 2012) and was effective beginning January 1, 2014. The requirement of automatic enrollment provisions for all employees covered under group health insurance, subject to certain specified opt-out rights, was also effective beginning January 1, 2014, and impacts all employers who employ more than 50 full-time equivalent (FTE) employees. Even part-time employees who work 30 hours or more per week are counted among the 50 FTEs. As mentioned in the last chapter, the individual mandate (not the employer mandate) is repealed by the 2017 TCJA for years beginning *after* 2018.

- The prohibition of waiting periods to be covered under a health insurance policy of more than 90 days, effective January 1, 2014.

- The prohibition of preexisting condition exclusions, first made effective in 2010 for children under the age of 19, and subsequently made effective for all individuals beginning January 1, 2014.
- The requirement that all new policies issued cover preventive services, such as cancer screening, with no out-of-pocket costs to the insured, effective for policies with plan years beginning on or after September 23, 2010.
- Extended coverage for dependents up to age 26, effective for policies with plan years beginning on or after September 23, 2010.
- A cap on health care contributions to FSAs of $2,500 per year beginning January 1, 2013, which is indexed for inflation thereafter.

The PPA also includes several provisions to help finance health care reform. Among the most important of these is an increase in the threshold for medical expense deductions from 7.5 percent to 10 percent of a taxpayer's adjusted gross income (AGI) for individuals under the age of 65; a new 3.8 percent surtax on unearned income (such as dividends and interest) for taxpayers with annual modified adjusted gross income (MAGI) over $200,000 (single filer) and $250,000 (joint filers); and an increase in the Medicare payroll tax from 1.45 percent to 2.35 percent for taxpayers with an annual gross income over $200,000 (single filers) and $250,000 (joint filers). All of these provisions became effective January 1, 2013, although the 2017 TCJA reduced the threshold for medical expense deductions from 10 percent to 7.5 percent of AGI for *all* taxpayers temporarily for the 2018 tax year.

Types of Health Insurance Policies

Historically, there have been only two basic types of health insurance policies: indemnity (or fee-for-service) policies and managed care policies. In recent years, however, a third type of health insurance coverage—the health savings account (HSA)—has come onto the scene, spurred by Congressional legislation. The first two types of policies dominate the employer-provided range of coverage, whereas the HSA represents a new way of looking at the individual health insurance problem. The HSA is designed to make the *individual*—rather than their employer—the party responsible for making financial decisions related to health. For this reason, the HSA and its predecessor, the medical savings account (MSA), are part of what is now referred to as *consumer-driven health care*.

Indemnity (Fee-for-Service) Policies

True *indemnity policies* do *not* include a deductible or co-payment and as such are sometimes referred to as *first-dollar coverage* (because they pay from the first dollar of medical expenses incurred). Over time, indemnity policies, which historically have included separate first-dollar coverage for hospital, surgical, and physician's expenses (often known as *basic medical insurance*), have evolved into the *comprehensive major medical policy*. The *major med policy*, as it has come to be called, includes both a deductible and a co-insurance provision, as well as a maximum dollar limitation of coverage, which usually amounts to at least $1 million in lifetime medical expenses.

As a rule, indemnity policies, including major med, cover only accidents and illnesses and do *not* cover preventative care. In addition, they pay a benefit based only on the usual, customary, and reasonable (UCR) rates in your area, *not* on the actual bill or expenses incurred. Individuals insured under indemnity policies are often billed by their medical providers, submit claims to the insurance company, and are subsequently reimbursed for expenses. Insureds usually have complete freedom with respect to which medical providers they use, thereby driving up costs for both the insured and the employer-sponsor. Primarily because of the cost implications, indemnity policies have largely been replaced by managed care policies in recent years.

Managed Care Policies

In the mid to late 1990s, *managed care* became the most popular form of health care, and some of its benefits were integrated into major comprehensive medical policies. Notably, managed care introduced the concepts of co-payments (rather than annual deductibles) and the *primary care physician*, also known as the gatekeeper physician, or *PCP*. Another innovation of managed care was the coverage of routine physical exams and other forms of preventative care, in furtherance of the belief that it is less expensive to treat disease in its early stages of development rather than waiting until more extensive treatment is warranted. Managed care has three primary approaches: health maintenance organizations (HMOs), preferred provider organizations (PPOs), and point-of-service (POS) plans.

An *HMO* offers medical services to its subscribers for a monthly fee (commonly referred to as a *capitation fee*). The members of the organization must use the HMO's on-site doctors unless they are referred to a specialist by their assigned primary care physician. The organization provides all medical services and administrates all medical claims filed by the insured. As such, an HMO is not technically an insurance company, because there is no third party to whom the insurance risk is transferred. Rather, the organization provides only prepaid medical services.

A *PPO*, on the other hand, is most often administered by an insurance company that is acting as an intermediary between medical care providers and the health care consumer. Generally, the various providers affiliated with the PPO, referred to as *in-network providers*, accept reduced fees in exchange for the insurance company paying their fee more rapidly and for guaranteeing payment. Many PPOs allow consumers to receive care outside the network of preferred providers; however, if an out-of-network provider is used, the insured pays a higher co-payment or deductible.

Finally, a *POS* plan combines attributes of the HMO and PPO. If contracted providers in a POS plan are used, their services are available for a low co-payment or are covered completely (as with an HMO). However, if an out-of-network provider is used, the insured pays a higher co-payment, and some preventative care may not be covered (as with a PPO). Newly enrolled policyholders are required to choose a primary care physician to direct their medical treatment. This physician becomes the insured's point of service and is chosen from a list of preapproved physicians in the plan's medical care network.

Health Savings Accounts

The *HSA*, a policy that any individual who does not participate in an employer-sponsored plan may establish separately, is the latest entry in the health insurance marketplace. An employer may also contribute to an HSA that was established by an employee if it so chooses. Today, many HSAs offer investment options, ranging from money market accounts to mutual funds to individual stocks. Most of these investment options are currently underutilized because participants have historically favored only cash to fund HSAs.

An HSA is set up more or less like an individual retirement account (IRA), except that the tax-deductible contributions made to an HSA may be used only to reimburse the account owner for qualifying medical expenses. If they are not used for this purpose prior to the owner reaching the age of 65, a 20 percent penalty is imposed. As in an IRA, earnings generated by HSA investments accumulate income-tax-free. Therefore, if the distributions from the HSA are used to pay for qualified medical expenses (including long-term care insurance premiums), the account is *never taxed*—not when contributions are made, not while these contributions are generating earnings, and not when the contributions and earnings are withdrawn.

Generally, any individual below Medicare age (age 65) who is not covered by any group or individual health plan can establish an HSA. A high deductible is required on the health insurance policy, and limitations are specified on the annual amount of tax-deductible contributions that may be made to the account. However, unlike with an IRA, there are no income caps for individuals claiming the HSA deduction, nor is the claiming of the deduction dependent on whether the individual itemizes their tax deductions at year-end.

Who should implement an HSA? Certainly, any younger, healthier individual who is unlikely to have large medical bills in the near future and does not participate in an employer plan should consider the option. In addition, older, self-employed individuals who will not have the advantage of retiree health insurance should look closely at the savings opportunities presented by the HSA. Upper-income and relatively healthy persons may also find HSAs attractive if they switch to a high-deductible insurance policy and then take advantage of the deduction for contributions to offset their taxable income. An often-overlooked benefit of establishing an HSA is that you can roll over money from an IRA to an HSA without incurring income tax and avoid a tax bill altogether if you then use the money for qualifying medical expenses.

Continuation of Health Insurance Coverage After You Have Left Your Job

Many health care consumers are not aware that if they lose their job, voluntarily or involuntarily, they can continue their previous group health insurance coverage. Under the federal COBRA law, employers with 20 or more employees must let you remain enrolled in their policy at your own expense. Typically, this right must be afforded for a period of up to 18 months after you leave your job.

Although it may require some new cash-flow planning to pay not only your previous share of the employer group policy premiums but the employer's share as well, it is still probably wise to pursue your COBRA rights. Most group policies (including those of your potential new employers) have waiting periods before you are entitled to coverage. In some cases, the waiting period may be as long as six months. (Of course, with the implementation of the prohibition on waiting periods beyond 90 days under Obamacare, this has changed since 2014.) Taking this into consideration, as well as the possibility that it may take you some time to find another job, flexing your COBRA rights is prudent cash-flow management.

Other COBRA qualifying events include the death of a covered spouse, divorce or legal separation that causes an employee's spouse or dependent children to lose coverage, and attaining Medicare age. In these events, the term of coverage afforded under COBRA may be as long as 36 months after the so-called triggering event.

Portability of Health Insurance Coverage

The phrase *portability of health insurance coverage* is a bit of a misnomer. It does not mean that you can literally transfer the same group policy from your previous employer to your new employer. However, it does mean that, under HIPAA, as long as you have been covered under a group policy for a specified period of time, an insurance company cannot deny you coverage, even if you have become seriously ill in the meantime. Specifically, HIPAA states that there cannot be enforcement of a preexisting medical condition clause by the new insurance company if the following are true:

- You were covered by a prior employer's health insurance plan for at least 12 months.
- Fewer than 63 days have elapsed since you lost coverage under the prior employer's plan.

Again, however, these limitations have become less important with the general prohibition of refusing coverage to anyone because of preexisting conditions under the provisions of Obamacare.

How do you know that you have lost coverage under your prior employer's plan? Your previous employer must provide you with a certificate of coverage that states the length of your insurance coverage and the date when you lost it. Keep this certificate! Should you enroll in a new group health insurance plan that applies a preexisting condition exclusion, proof of prior coverage often guarantees that you can avoid the application of this exclusion. Unfortunately, HIPAA does not regulate premium costs, so there is no guarantee that you will be able to afford the new insurance to which you are legally entitled!

Medicare and Medigap

Medicare is a federal government health insurance plan that covers individuals when they reach the age of 65. Historically, Medicare consisted of two major parts: Part A, hospital insurance; and Part B, supplementary medical insurance. In 2003, Congress passed a third major part of Medicare: Part D, prescription drug coverage. Part D became fully effective on January 1, 2006, but unlike Parts A and B of the plan, Part D coverage is not included within the traditional Medicare program. Instead, beneficiaries must elect to enroll in one of many hundreds of Part D plans offered by private insurance companies, with the US government providing premium support to these policies.

Medicare Part A coverage is provided at no premium cost to eligible participants and covers four broad categories:

- In-patient hospital care up to 90 days. The patient pays a deductible for the first 60 days and a co-payment after 60 days, up to the 90-day maximum.
- Skilled nursing care benefits.
- Home health services.
- Care in a hospice for the terminally ill (defined as a person with a life expectancy of six months or less).

Perhaps the most misunderstood part of Medicare Part A coverage is that long-term nursing-home coverage (referred to as *custodial care* under most long-term care insurance policies) is *not* provided. Rather, a short-term limited benefit known as the *skilled nursing care benefit* is available. While custodial care may be required, Medicare will pay for only 100 days of care, and it must be following a hospital stay. Notably, the skilled nursing care benefit means the patient must enter a skilled nursing facility at the direction of a medical doctor within 30 days after leaving a hospital where the patient was treated for a serious illness for three or more consecutive days.

This leads to the question of how to financially provide for an aging parent who needs continuing care. We will address this issue when we discuss long-term care alternatives later in this chapter; but, speaking as someone who has personally wrestled with the problem, there are three basic choices:

- You can attempt to self-fund, using either your own money or that of your parent.
- You can investigate whether it is still possible for your parent to qualify for coverage under a long-term care insurance policy.
- You can attempt to take advantage of the strict requirements to qualify the parent for Medicaid assistance.

The practical problem is that most of us either do not have the money to self-fund the coverage or wait so long that our parent no longer qualifies for or can afford the purchase of a long-term care policy. Thus, the purchase of a long-term care insurance policy for yourself or for aging parents is increasingly becoming a cornerstone of proper wealth management.

In contrast to Part A, Medicare Part B coverage is not free to the participant; rather, it entails the payment of a specified monthly premium by the insured and, further, is *means tested*, meaning those with higher incomes pay a higher premium. Moreover, a deductible must be paid by the insured as well as co-insurance toward covered expenses in any calendar year. Currently, this co-insurance percentage is coordinated with the percentage share of most indemnity medical plans, or 80 percent on the part of the government and 20 percent on the part of the insured. You can opt out of Medicare Part B coverage, but at the time you qualify for Medicare Part A coverage, you must tell the Social Security Administration (which also administers Medicare) that you do not wish to participate in Part B coverage.

As you can likely appreciate, individuals who are eligible for Medicare may have substantial medical costs for which they are responsible in excess of the covered expenses. The reimbursement of these excess expenses is why you (or your parent) should purchase a Medicare supplemental health insurance policy, colloquially referred to as a *Medigap policy*.

Medigap policies consist of 14 supplemental policies that have been standardized by federal legislation and are identified by the letters A through N for the types of benefits provided. (Effective June 1, 2010, Plans E, H, I, and J are no longer sold, although if purchased before this date, they are still valid.) Generally, you must have both Part A and Part B coverage under Medicare before a Medigap policy may be purchased. Under law, seniors (defined here as individuals aged 65 or over) may be sold only one Medigap policy at a time. The policy must accept all applicants within the first six months of qualification for Medicare, *regardless* of any preexisting conditions. Medigap policies can be obtained through a variety of companies and organizations, including the most popular source, the American Association of Retired Persons (AARP), which is headquartered in Washington, DC.

Seniors may also wish to consider a second form of Medicare coverage: the Medicare Advantage plan, which is *private* insurance subsidized by the federal government that offers the same basic coverage provided by Medicare but also includes the most important features of Medigap policies. There are two types of Medicare Advantage plans: those that include the attributes of managed care plans as well as private fee-for-service plans (or PFFS plans), featuring open access to health care providers with few restrictions. PFFS plans are currently the fastest growing type of alternative Medicare coverage and are provided for under Part C of the Medicare Act of 1965.

The Importance of Long-Term Care Insurance in Protecting Your Wealth

The need for long-term care can mean different things to different people, but generally it results from any chronic or disabling condition that requires nursing-home care or constant medical supervision. Long-term care insurance policy provisions cover not only care in a nursing-home facility, but also nursing care in your own home. Payment for care received in your own home is the number one reason you may want to consider purchasing a long-term care insurance policy for yourself or your parent.

Long-term care is expensive, no matter where you or your aging parent resides, and most people cannot afford to cover the cost of this care for long. For example, the average cost of a nursing home for a private room in the United States in 2018 is approximately $96,000 per year—and it may be considerably higher, depending on the level of care received and the location of the nursing home. Fortunately, the average stay in a nursing home is less than three years (2.7 years, to be exact), but this is the *average*. You or your parent may reside in such a home for much longer than three years, sometimes even as long as 15 to 20 years. You should keep this statistic in mind when deciding how long a benefit period you wish to purchase as part of a long-term care policy. As a general rule, the *greater* the benefit period, the *higher* the long-term care insurance policy premium.

Since 1996, when the HIPAA legislation was passed, most long-term care policies have been issued as qualified policies. Although the primary advantages of a qualified long-term care policy are the accompanying income-tax benefits, another real advantage is the fact that it must be *guaranteed renewable*. This means you have the right to continue the policy for as long as the premiums are paid. Thus, the insurance company cannot cancel the policy if your health declines, nor can it increase the policy premiums, unless it does so for all members of the same class of insureds covered by the policy. In addition, long-term care policies may be issued on a *noncancellable* basis, meaning they must have a fixed, guaranteed level premium throughout your lifetime. However, given the rapidly increasing cost of providing long-term care, no insurance company is currently underwriting a policy for which the premiums cannot be increased. Indeed, in recent years, some big insurance companies, such as Met Life, have stopped underwriting long-term care insurance entirely!

If a long-term care policy is tax-qualified, premiums paid by the policyholder are deductible as itemized medical expenses up to a dollar limit that depends on the policy owner's age. Also, benefits paid from a qualified policy are income-tax-free without limit. If an employer pays for long-term care insurance coverage for its employees (a *group* long-term care policy), the premiums are tax-deductible to the employer and are not considered to be taxable income to the employee.

> **Note** A non-tax-qualified form of long-term care policy also exists that does not provide any tax advantages. However, nonqualified plans require only "medical necessity" as an acceptable condition to be eligible for benefits, whereas tax-qualified plans require "the failure to perform certain activities of daily living (ADLs)" for benefit eligibility.

From an income-tax standpoint, it has just been mentioned that qualified long-term care premiums are deductible as medical expenses within certain limits. What is this limitation? Specifically, all medical expenses are deductible only to the extent that they exceed 7.5 percent of AGI floor effective only for 2018; beginning in 2019, goes back to 10 percent of AGI floor. This means that you probably will *not* be able to deduct the premium until *after* you enter a nursing home and begin incurring substantial medical expenses. The primary advantage the policy affords you is the income-tax-free nature of the benefits paid. Remember, though, that most long-term care benefits received are likely to be paid in reimbursement of medical expenses and therefore are not subject to income tax under current law.

Eight basic types of coverage are afforded by a qualified long-term care policy, only a few of which (such as skilled nursing care) are covered under Medicare. Even so, the qualifying conditions under the policy are likely to be much more favorable than those under Medicare law. In addition, as mentioned, the major benefit of custodial care coverage in a long-term care policy is *not* included among Medicare coverage provisions. The basic types of long-term coverage (in order of level of care) are as follows:

- *Skilled nursing care:* This is the highest level of medical care available and is provided in traditional nursing homes on a daily basis, typically to those individuals recovering from a severe life-threatening illness such as a stroke. Such rehabilitative care has to be given at the direction of a physician.

- *Memory care*: Arguably, this is as high a level of care as skilled nursing care. Memory care is specialized care for those with severe dementia, Alzheimer's disease, and other forms of brain-related memory conditions. Such care is typically provided in an assisted-living environment.

- *Intermediate nursing care:* This is similar to skilled nursing care, except that the care is provided only occasionally and not on a daily basis.

- *Custodial care:* This is traditional nursing-home care and does not have to be ordered by a physician. It is provided to individuals with a chronic health condition that does not permit them to take care of themselves.

- *Assisted living:* These are facilities that provide apartment-style housing (often including meals) and support services for individuals who need only intermittent assistance with the tasks of daily living.
- *Home health care:* This is care that allows the patient to remain at home and receive part-time skilled nursing care or other rehabilitative assistance.
- *Hospice care:* This is care for terminally ill patients (generally, within six months of expected date of death) and may be administered daily or less frequently. The care usually occurs at the patient's home, but it may also be delivered at a hospice care center.
- *Adult day care:* This care is provided for persons who need assistance and supervision during the day at home and whose spouse or family members work outside the home.

Most long-term care policies have two criteria that must be met before benefits are payable. The insured must meet *either* one of these two criteria:

1. The insured must be chronically ill as defined in the policy. *Chronically ill* is defined as being unable to perform, without substantial assistance, two of the six activities of daily living (ADLs) for at least 90 days. The six ADLs are as follows:
   - Eating
   - Bathing
   - Dressing
   - Transferring from bed to chair
   - Using the toilet
   - Maintaining continence
2. Substantial services are required to protect the insured from threats to health and safety because of brain damage resulting from, for example, strokes, dementia, or Alzheimer's disease.

Usually, in proving that you meet either of these criteria, written verification by one or more physicians is required, but some policies will pay benefits upon the submission of a claim and an internal investigation (no doctor's letter is required).

Let's now address some of the more common exclusions and limitations on benefits that you should be aware of before purchasing a long-term care policy. The most important of these are the following:

- *Daily benefit amount:* Each policy typically guarantees a daily benefit amount, or dollar amount, payable per day based on the level of care being provided by the facility. A good place to begin in determining what this amount should be is to check the daily rate of nursing homes in your area. You may wish to consider an inflation rider to account for future increases in this rate.

- *The elimination, or waiting, period:* This period is the number of days you must wait before benefits are paid under the policy. During this time, you have to pay for the cost of care you receive out of your own private funds or those of your family. As may be expected, the *shorter* the elimination period, the *greater* the long-term care insurance period. The standard elimination period for most policies is 90 days.

- *The benefit period:* As mentioned earlier, the average time spent in a nursing-home facility is 2.7 years. As such, you may wish to consider a three-year benefit period or less. Because this is the *average* time spent in a nursing-home facility, you may also wish to consider a longer period. Policies are available for lifetime benefit, but the longer the benefit period, the higher the policy premium.

- *Preexisting-condition limitation:* A preexisting condition is a condition for which a physician recommended medical treatment within six months before the effective date of insurance coverage. Some long-term care policies include a preexisting condition limitation. If they do, it means benefits will not be payable for long-term care related to the medical recommendation. (It is possible to find policies without any preexisting condition limitations, but they are more expensive.)

- *Policy exclusions:* The most common exclusion is for long-term care that is necessary because of alcohol or drug addiction. Almost uniformly, policies do not cover this condition.

Alternatives to Long-Term Care Insurance

The first question that should come to mind with respect to long-term care insurance alternatives is whether you are likely to require long-term care during your lifetime. For some people, the answer is relatively simple, based on problematic family medical history or current poor health. For others, the answer is much less clear-cut. However, statistics bear out that approximately four out of ten people aged 65 or over will require long-term care assistance at some point during their lifetimes. These are relatively good odds! Thus, the question becomes not so much a matter of *if*, but rather *when* long-term care will be needed, and how it will be paid for.

Historically, three choices have been available with respect to paying for long-term care:

- Pay for such care yourself or rely on the financial resources of family members.
- Attempt to qualify for government assistance in the form of Medicaid.
- Purchase a long-term care insurance policy.

Recently, a fourth method has become available in the form of the purchase of an *accelerated death benefits* or *living benefits rider* as part of your life insurance coverage. This rider accelerates payment of the death benefit if the insured contracts a terminal disease or becomes chronically ill. In other words, the insured must be certified by a physician as unable to perform, without assistance, certain ADLs.

There is a difference in the income-tax treatment of a policy cashed in using this rider. If an insured is *terminally ill* (generally defined as being expected to die within 24 months from the date of the onset of disease), they can use the proceeds *for any purpose* during their lifetime. Thus, there is *no* taxable gain to a terminally ill insured individual. However, if the insured is only *chronically ill*, they must use the proceeds *only for long-term care* to avoid taxation on the gain (defined as the cash value of the policy less any premiums paid to date).

For example, assume you are terminally ill but previously purchased a $250,000 universal life insurance policy with an accelerated benefits rider. To date, you have paid $50,000 in premiums, and the policy has accumulated a cash value of $75,000. You have $25,000 ($75,000 less $50,000) of potentially taxable gain (**ordinary income** and *not* **capital gain**). Because you are *terminally ill*, you can use the $75,000 cash value for any purpose free of income tax. However, if you are only *chronically ill*, you must use the cash value of $75,000 only for long-term care expenses if you want to avoid paying taxes on the $25,000 gain.

Many individuals—either intentionally or by reason of financial circumstances—choose to self-fund the payment of long-term care. A savings or investment plan may help you do so. However, this option requires financial self-discipline, a trait that some of us do not possess in considerable quantity. You may also rely on the equity in your home to cover your long-term care costs. For example, you can either downsize to a less expensive home and use the savings to fund possible long-term care costs, or you can enter into a *reverse mortgage*, whereby the lender pays you a monthly income based on a percentage of the amount of equity in your home. But given the vicissitudes of residential real estate markets in many areas of the country, this option entails some risk as well.

If you are unable to self-fund the payment of your long-term care, you might consider turning to Medicaid, which is a joint federally and state-funded program for low-income and low-net-worth individuals providing for both health and long-term care. To qualify for coverage, applicants must meet income and asset tests as determined by the state where they live. Some relatively wealthy individuals have attempted to deliberately qualify for long-term Medicaid coverage by "spending down" their assets and income to the specified level. However, a series of laws dating back to the 1980s have curtailed this activity, notably through the implementation of a look-back period in which most assets that are gifted to others ("spent down") are not ignored. For example, individuals who transfer assets to family members (usually members other than their spouse) during a period of 60 months prior to applying for Medicaid may find themselves penalized and prohibited from receiving Medicaid assistance for a significant period of time. For this reason, if you can afford to self-fund your long-term care, relying on government assistance to help you with these expenses may not be the most prudent planning alternative. On the other hand, if you have otherwise been attempting to qualify for Medicaid assistance but find that you must unexpectedly enter a nursing home, consider purchasing a long-term care insurance policy to cover the requisite look-back period. This means that the applicable benefit period of the policy will likely have to be at least five years before you apply for Medicaid coverage.

As a final alternative to long-term care insurance, check to see if your state of residence has adopted a so-called *filial support* law with respect to long-term care expenses. Such a law may be used to require reimbursement by a patient's family for unpaid long-term care expenses incurred by a family member. Currently, 30 states have such a law, but the laws are becoming more prevalent, given the rapidly increasing Medicaid expenses paid out by states on behalf of insured individuals.

This leads us back to the possible purchase of a long-term care insurance policy. If you believe that family or personal circumstance might warrant the purchase of such a policy, here are some factors you should consider:

- *When (at what age) should I buy the policy?* The guideline is that you should purchase a long-term care policy while you are still relatively healthy and young, but not so young as to pay premiums for an inordinate period of time. Generally, the optimal time to purchase a long-term care insurance policy is around age 55, as you are approaching your retirement years but can still qualify for policy coverage without major health questions.

- *What type of long-term care are you likely to need?* Certainly, skilled nursing care is not desired by anyone, but payment for home health care services is likely an objective of most prospective purchasers. You may wish to purchase a long-term care insurance policy just to provide for this possibility.

- *How much can you afford to pay for long-term care?* The answer to this question usually determines what the elimination period under the policy will be and how long you can make payments before the private insurance coverage becomes effective.

- *What is your attitude with respect to leaving an estate for your spouse or children?* Nothing can decimate the size and distribution of your accumulated estate to others more quickly than a prolonged stay in a nursing-home facility. Accordingly, the purchase of a long-term care insurance policy may be thought of as a stopgap measure to preserve at least some portion of your estate.

We have now covered one of the biggest potential threats to your ability to accumulate wealth: unanticipated medical expenses for which you have no means of payment. The next chapter deals with another major threat to your ability to become wealthy: the threat of losing your earning power. This type of risk can be managed by the purchase of an individual disability policy, likely among the most needed form of insurance in today's marketplace.

CHAPTER 6

Insuring Your Earning Power

Ask any financial planner or insurance agent what the most neglected or underinsured financial risk is, and they are likely to say the risk of losing your ability to earn a living. Most individuals do *not* give sufficient attention to this possibility and, if they do, believe that they are adequately covered. They believe they will never lose their earning power! However, according to the **Commissioner's Individual Disability Table A**, one in three working Americans will suffer some form of disability that lasts at least 90 days before they reach the age of 65. In addition, one in seven employees will be disabled for five or more years prior to their retirement. You are *two to three times* more likely to become disabled during your working career than you are to die during this same period. These are impressive (and somewhat frightening) numbers.

Many individuals believe they are adequately insured against the loss of future earning power because they are covered by a group disability income policy at their place of employment. However, this belief has two major flaws:

- Most employer policies replace only 50–60 percent of your monthly income.
- The replacement income provided by this benefit is likely income-taxable, because the employer paid the cost of the insurance premium while you were working. In turn, this means you will receive less than the 50–60 percent of monthly income promised to you.

© Keith R. Fevurly 2018
K. R. Fevurly, *Plan Your Financial Future*, https://doi.org/10.1007/978-1-4842-3637-6_6

How can this often-forgotten risk be adequately covered? Most commonly through the purchase of an individual disability income policy.

Is the Loss of Your Earning Power Already Adequately Covered?

There are other forms of insurance that you may rely on to protect your earning power in the event that you are unable to work. Among these is *supplemental income insurance*, which is designed to pay your living expenses while you are disabled. The best known of these policies is issued by American Family Life Assurance Company—better known as AFLAC. Quack, quack!

In addition to supplemental policies, employee benefits from your employer are typically available, as mentioned previously. For short-term illness, your employer may provide sick leave, short-term disability income protection, or both. Furthermore, all employers are mandated by the state to provide worker's compensation benefits in the event of a serious injury while on the job. Keep in mind, however, that most employers provide only group *long-term disability* policies. Benefits from these types of policies begin when short-term benefits, if there are any, stop. Long-term benefits then generally continue until you reach age 65 (the Medicare age for receiving benefits) or until you return to work. Group policies include a cap, or limitation, on the amount they will pay—usually no more than 60 percent of your monthly income. Plus, as with most employee benefits, when you leave your current place of employment, the disability income coverage is terminated.

Social Security income protection, on the other hand, is a disability benefit provided under the Social Security system, but qualifying for it is not easy. Specifically, to qualify for a disability benefit under Social Security, you must

- Have been disabled for at least five full calendar months
- Have a disability expected to last at least 12 months or end in death
- Be unable to engage in any substantial gainful occupation, and not just your own occupation, at the time your disability begins

As with funding possible long-term care needs, many individuals (if they have given any thought to their chances of becoming disabled) attempt to self-fund for disability through investment. To determine what you would need to self-fund for this possibility, review the basics of what we have discussed so far—most notably, how to prepare and analyze a personal cash-flow statement—and see what your monthly expenses are. Then multiply this amount by 12 and determine the amount of your total annual expenses. Doing so gives you some idea of the funds needed to take you through one year of disability. Most long-term disabilities last more than a year, so you should now be able to appreciate the actual amount of savings needed to cover the risk of loss to your earning power. Most people cannot afford to self-fund for long, which brings us back to considering the purchase of an individual disability income insurance policy.

Definitions of Disability

The most important part of any disability income insurance policy (and the single most important consideration for you) is the language used by the policy to define *disability*. Fortunately, there are only three definitions:

- *Own Occupation (Own Occ):* This is the most favorable definition of *disability* from the point of view of the insured. The definition states that the insured is considered totally disabled (and therefore eligible for benefits payments) if they are unable to engage in the primary duties of their own occupation. For example, a medical surgeon would be unable to engage in their own occupation if they suffered an injury to the hands. This would be the case even if the surgeon were still able to diagnose illnesses as a general practitioner of medicine.

- *Modified Any Occupation (Modified Any Occ):* This definition is slightly less restrictive than the Any Occupation definition but not as liberal as the Own Occ definition. Modified Any Occ defines *disability* as the insured's inability to engage in any occupation for which they are reasonably suited by education or experience and for which they could easily become qualified. Applying this definition to the medical surgeon example, if the surgeon could become a general practitioner reasonably easily after the injury to their hands, the policy probably would not pay a benefit.

- *Any Occupation (Any Occ):* This is the practical opposite of the Own Occ definition and requires the insured to be unable to perform the duties relating to any gainful occupation before they are considered to be totally disabled. It is not unlike the Social Security definition of *disability*, except that there is no five-month waiting period and expected length of disability. The Any Occ definition is usually limited to blue-collar workers, although white-collar workers and professionals may also obtain a policy with this definition. The reason these individuals would want to do so is to achieve premium cost savings.

Group long-term disability policies usually use a combination of the Own Occ and Modified Any Occ definitions (called a *split-definition policy*). Such policies permit the insured to receive benefits for a period of months or years under the Own Occ criteria; then, after the insured has been retrained for another position, the policies apply the stricter Modified Any Occ definition. Why? By design, the split definition encourages the worker to return to work and remain with the company, even though it may be in a new position or occupation.

It is also possible to write an individual disability income policy with a loss-of-income definition. With this kind of policy, the type of disability is not defined; rather, if, as a result of injury or sickness, the insured suffers a loss of income, benefits based on that loss are payable *regardless* of whether the insured returns to work in the same or a related occupation. Given that it does not usually provide as great a benefit, the loss-of-income policy is not as popular among professionals or other workers as the Own Occ definition. But insurance companies like the loss-of-income standard because it establishes a simple benchmark from which to measure the amount of benefits payable.

Additional Important Provisions in an Individual Disability Policy

Many of the same provisions that are included in a long-term care insurance policy are found in an individual disability income policy. For example, like long-term care policies, disability insurance includes an elimination (or waiting) period, a benefit period, and a benefit amount.

The elimination period in disability insurance essentially works the same way as that included in a long-term care policy. In other words, an *elimination period* is the period of time *after* the insured has met the qualifying conditions to collect under the policy but *before* any benefit payments are made. In the case of disability insurance, an elimination period of 90 days is probably optimal when considering the trade-off between covering the required payments from personal funds for a number of days and the need for as low an insurance premium as possible. Longer elimination periods naturally reduce policy premiums, but the *longer* this period, the *greater* the need for personal savings or other alternatives to cover the insured's ongoing living expenses.

A somewhat novel and increasingly popular alternative that insurance agents are recommending to cover the elimination period is the separate purchase of a *critical illness* insurance policy. Critical illness insurance is an insurance policy that makes a lump sum cash payment if the insured is diagnosed with one of the critical illnesses listed in the policy and survives a minimum number of days (typically 30) from the date of diagnosis. Such a policy may be underwritten to require payment for the same illness or condition that prompts the insured to make a claim under their disability policy—and to make the payment *immediately* rather than some 90 days later.

The maximum number of months or years that a disability income policy will pay a benefit is referred to as the *benefit period*. Most disability policies written today provide benefits until the insured becomes eligible for Medicare or reaches age 65. Nonetheless, some insurance companies will write a policy that ensures disability payments are made throughout the life of the insured. Remember: the *longer* the benefit payment period, the *higher* the insurance policy premium. As such, you should think carefully about whether this trade-off is financially worth it. During retirement, if you are looking for a financial product to make lifetime payments, some form of annuity policy is likely a less expensive way to ensure an income stream, rather than an extremely long disability insurance benefit period.

Finally, what most people are interested in when purchasing a disability income policy is the *benefit amount* that is payable. The general approach in the underwriting of all disability income policies is to pay individuals slightly less than their net after-tax income if they were able to work, thus encouraging them to return to work as soon as possible. This typically works out to a benefit payable of somewhere between 50 and 60 percent of an employee's previous monthly gross pay. If you are covered at work by a group long-term disability policy at the time you apply for individual coverage, the amount of new disability insurance that you can obtain will probably be limited because of underwriting restrictions. If this is the case, ask your insurance agent if the company will sell you a *rider*—an addition to the insurance policy with specified benefits or conditions—that allows you to increase the benefit amount without having to undergo a qualifying medical exam. Or, better yet, purchase and implement an individual disability policy *before* you participate in the group policy; then you can receive *both* benefits in the event that you leave the company.

You should also consider whether and how much of your disability insurance income may be taxable. In other words, how much of this income do you get to keep? Fortunately, unless you are self-employed, the answer is relatively simple. If the employer pays the disability income insurance premiums on your behalf, the disability income payments are *taxable*. Alternatively, if you pay the disability insurance premiums yourself, the disability income payments are *income-tax-free*. Therefore, when coupling a group policy with individual disability coverage, the group payments are taxable, whereas those payments made from an individual policy are not. In summary, you are now in the same position you would be in if you had been able to continue working and were receiving a steady paycheck.

Let's now address two other questions you should be sure to ask before purchasing an individual disability insurance policy. Each of these questions has to do with continuing policy coverage in the future and the price you must pay to obtain it.

Policy Continuation Provisions

The first question you should ask with respect to policy continuation is whether the policy can ever be canceled. In contrast to group policies, individual disability income policies may be underwritten as *noncancellable*. This is a guarantee that not only can the insurance company *not* cancel the policy, but it also cannot *increase* the policy premiums unless otherwise provided for in your contract. This kind of guarantee does not come cheap, particularly in today's inflationary society, but you want the cash-flow protection if you can get it.

The second question to ask with respect to policy continuation is whether the company can raise your premiums. Certainly, if you have been fortunate enough to secure a noncancellable policy, the answer is no. However, what if you cannot or do not want to incur the additional cost of a noncancellable policy? In that case, you have another option: you can purchase a guaranteed renewable policy. A *guaranteed renewable* policy allows the insurance company to increase the premiums but *not* to change the terms of the policy once written. The company also guarantees that you can renew the policy at the date of expiration as long as you have paid the premiums on a timely basis. In addition, the company cannot single you out for any rate increase; it may increase the premiums only for an entire class of similarly rated insureds.

Guaranteed renewable policies generally have lower premiums than noncancellable policies. Insurance companies are loath to increase the premiums on guaranteed renewable policies after they're issued for fear of creating disgruntled policyholders. As such, it may be possible for you to get essentially the same level of protection with a guaranteed renewable policy as with a noncancellable policy but at a much lower cost.

Additional Policy Benefits to Consider

Many individual disability policies offer additional benefits, usually in the form of a policy rider. Here are some of the more important possible additional benefits:

- *Cost-of-living adjustment (COLA) rider*: The most common form of this rider increases the disability benefit paid after you start to collect benefits, thus protecting you against inflation. Another form increases the policy benefits by a specified percentage (usually five percent) each year before you become disabled, thus ensuring your constant purchasing power after you begin to draw benefits.

- *Return of premium*: This benefit requires the insurance company to refund a portion of your premium if no claims are made for a specified period of time.

- *Waiver of premium*: This benefit allows you to stop paying the premium on the policy if you are disabled for a period of time, usually 90 days.
- *Partial disability rider*: This benefit is triggered when you are unable to perform important duties of your own occupation but are able to perform enough other duties to allow you to return to work part-time. In this event, the policy pays a partial benefit, such as 50 percent, of the total that would otherwise be payable.
- *Residual disability rider*: This rider provides that if you are able to return to work full-time but at lesser pay than before due to a disability, the policy will pay the difference between your former pay and the current pay for the benefit period.
- *Guaranteed insurability rider* (also known as an *increase-in-benefits rider*): This rider guarantees you the opportunity to increase the benefit amount payable under the policy at specified time periods, regardless of your physical or mental health at the time. A usual requirement to obtain this rider is that you must have initially purchased a disability policy that is at least 80 percent of the maximum benefit amount that the insurance company would approve.

Policy Exclusions

Just as with other insurance contracts, it is important to know what is *not* covered under a disability income policy. These are known as *policy exclusions* and, with respect to disability income policies, refer to particular injuries or illnesses that may result in the insured not being able to work. Those that are most frequently encountered are disabilities resulting from the following:

- War or an act of war
- Pregnancy or complications from childbirth
- The insured committing or attempting to commit a crime
- A period when the insured was incarcerated
- An injury or disease that was self-inflicted, including those related to or caused by drinking alcoholic beverages or the illegal use of drugs

Remember, if your disability results from any one of these exclusions, the policy will likely *not* pay benefits.

Questions to Ask Before Purchasing an Individual Disability Income Policy

The following are questions you should ask before buying an individual disability income policy:

- What is the definition of *disability* in my policy?
- What is the amount of benefit payable from my policy?
- Do I have to pay taxes on that benefit?
- How long are my benefits payable?
- Is my benefit adjusted for inflation (and if so, in what amount)?
- Is there an elimination, or waiting, period before I can begin to receive my benefit (and if so, how long is it)?
- Is there a way I can ensure that payments are made during this waiting period?
- Can I renew my policy without undergoing a medical examination?
- Can the company increase my policy premiums?
- What are the policy exclusions, and do they affect me?

This chapter concludes our look at *personal* risk exposures. Now, let's consider a risk exposure that most of us also have: the risk of loss or damage to our *property*, such as a home or automobile. Business insurance for self-employed individuals is also addressed in the next chapter.

CHAPTER 7

Insuring Your Property

Typically, an individual's most important possessions are their home and automobile. Now that you have learned how to insure your life, health, and earning power, you want to be sure that your home(s) and automobile(s) are protected against significant financial loss as well.

As you prepare to read this chapter, keep in mind that, unlike homeowner's insurance, which generally is not mandatory unless you are required to purchase it by your mortgage lender, automobile liability insurance *is* required by many states. Specifically, states require all drivers to be financially responsible for damages or injuries caused to others as a result of automobile ownership. Liability insurance must be carried by every driver. However, insurance reimbursement for damage to your car or property (collision and comprehensive insurance) need *not* be carried. As such, you may choose to drop collision coverage and obtain only comprehensive (also known as *other-than-collision*) insurance for older automobiles. This is good cash-flow planning, because it makes little sense to insure a car that is worth only $1,500 for collision coverage when the annual premiums for such coverage may be $300 or more after a $500 or more deductible.

© Keith R. Fevurly 2018
K. R. Fevurly, *Plan Your Financial Future*, https://doi.org/10.1007/978-1-4842-3637-6_7

What to Consider When Insuring Your Home

Homeowner's insurance insures your home (commonly referred to as "the dwelling" in the insurance policy) and the personal belongings that are in the home. In almost all cases, insurance companies write a package policy, meaning the policy covers not only damages to the home but also liability for any injuries you or family members cause to others while they are on your property. Various types of homeowner policies insure property based on the kind of dwelling you own, and most include the following general forms of coverage:

- Coverage A: dwelling
- Coverage B: other structures
- Coverage C: contents (personal property)
- Coverage D: loss of use
- Coverage E: personal liability
- Coverage F: medical payments to others

You should also be aware that damage from some natural disasters is commonly excluded in the standard homeowner's policy. Notably, damages caused to your home by flooding or earthquakes are *not* covered. However, federal flood insurance, underwritten as part of the National Flood Insurance Program (NFIP), may be purchased through your property and casualty insurance agent or broker. If the federal policy is insufficient for your needs, you should consider buying excess flood coverage from a private insurance company. Similarly, you can insure against earthquake damage by purchasing an earthquake endorsement to your standard homeowner's policy. For example, in the state of California, an earthquake endorsement must at least be offered to the homeowner (although purchase of the endorsement is not required under state law).

Coverage A: Dwelling

Some homeowners make a huge mistake by covering only the fair market value of their home. Instead, your policy should cover the cost of rebuilding in the event of severe damage or destruction, which is otherwise known as insuring your home for its *replacement cost*. To receive the full benefit of such coverage, you need to cover your home for at least 80 percent of its replacement cost. Otherwise, you will likely be paid only the actual cash value (ACV) for your home, which is its replacement cost less a depreciation charge that the insurance company figures in based on the house's age and condition. In other words, if actual cash value applies, you are paid only a percentage of the damage or partial loss to your home. A total loss is paid without reference to this limitation as long as the loss is within the coverage limits of your policy.

Some insurance companies offer an extended policy rather than guaranteed replacement cost coverage. An extended policy pays a certain limit—generally, 25 to 30 percent over and above the fair market value of your home—for the purpose of rebuilding. For example, if the fair market value of your home is $500,000, an extended policy would pay to rebuild your home up to a cost of $625,000 ($500,000 times 1.25).

How do you determine the replacement cost of your home? Generally, a local developer or construction expert can provide an estimated rebuilding cost. Sometimes local property appraisals may help, but be careful: appraisals of your property for property-tax purposes may be undervalued or overvalued, depending on the need for revenue in your particular community. You can also go online to obtain an estimate of replacement cost at web sites such as www.hmfacts.com. Moreover, as part of the annual insurance checkup that you should be doing with your property and casualty agent, ask the agent what they show as the replacement cost for your home.

Coverage B: Other Structures

This second type of homeowner's coverage amounts to 10 percent of the dwelling coverage (Coverage A) and insures outbuildings on your property, such as an unattached garage or storage shed. For example, if your dwelling is insured for $500,000, you will see separate structure (sometimes referred to as *dwelling extensions*) coverage in the policy of $50,000 ($500,000 times 0.10). Typically, this amount provides adequate coverage, although if you have built a considerable structure not attached to your home but still on the property, such as a guesthouse, you may wish to consider purchasing a higher amount of coverage.

Coverage C: Contents or Personal Property

This type of coverage insures all the personal property included in your home unless the property is specifically excluded or limited in the amount of coverage. Coverage is generally 50 percent of Coverage A, and, unless you pay a higher premium and obtain replacement cost for personal property items, the policy will pay you only the actual cash value (or depreciated value) of the property.

Particularly valuable items usually are *not* adequately covered in a typical homeowner's policy. For example, jewelry and furs, if stolen, are typically limited to a value of no more than $2,500 per article lost. Any item that is worth more than the limits specified in the policy should be covered with an endorsement to the homeowner's policy or through a separate policy known as a *personal articles floater* (PAF). If you do not know the replacement cost of the personal property but suspect it is considerably more than your current policy limits, have the property appraised before purchasing coverage.

The advantage of a **floater** is that the listed property is insured at the appraised value for damage or loss, often without any deductible applied. However, once an item is insured via a floater, it is no longer covered under the basic limits of Coverage C. Therefore, if your jewelry is appraised at $10,000 (and "scheduled" for this amount), for example, you would not receive a reimbursement of $12,500 ($10,000 plus $2,500) if the jewelry was stolen; rather, coverage would be limited to only $10,000.

Would you remember all your personal property items if your home were destroyed by fire? Most people would not. For this reason, it is time and money well spent to record your belongings and separately store the video footage on a personal computer. Put this video in a fireproof safe in your home and another copy in a safe-deposit box. You will be glad you did!

Coverage D: Loss of Use

If your home is damaged by fire or one of the other listed perils in the standard homeowner's policy, Coverage D pays your living expenses during the time required to repair or rebuild your house. Usually, the amount is 30 percent of Coverage A or sometimes Coverage C, depending on the type of policy. You typically want the limitation tied to Coverage A, because it will result in a much higher reimbursement amount.

Coverage E: Personal Liability

Coverage E insures certain liability risks, including in the event of an invited guest being injured on your property, regardless of whether you are home at the time of the injury. If the injured individual was not an invited guest, under most state laws you are relieved from liability. Regardless, the amount of liability coverage you obtain is usually important. Many people maintain a maximum of only $100,000 per occurrence for personal liability. In today's litigious society, however, this amount generally is not enough, particularly if you are a professional, such as a physician or lawyer. To obtain additional supplemental liability coverage (referred to as **umbrella liability insurance**), many companies require you to maintain underlying liability coverage of at least $300,000 per occurrence in your homeowner and automobile policies. We discuss the possibility of obtaining umbrella coverage to protect you and your family later in this chapter.

Coverage F: Medical Payments to Others

This type of coverage is designed to pay the medical costs of individuals who are *not* residents of your home but are on the premises with your permission and are injured. Medical costs may also be paid for individuals who reside away from your premises but are injured by the actions of your pets (for example, a dog that has temporarily left the premises). The coverage is usually limited to $1,000 per occurrence, but with today's rising medical costs, it is not unusual to see higher limits (some as high as $5,000 per occurrence). Some states, such as Colorado, now require a minimum level of medical payments to others under law.

Types of Homeowner's Policies (and the One You Want)

Although it is important to understand the various types of homeowner's policies and what each insures you against (known as a *peril* in insurance language), it is equally important to know what is *not* covered. We have already mentioned the two most common exclusions: damages caused by *flooding* or *earthquakes*. There are six other, common exclusions (in other words, when your property is *not* covered against potential loss):

- If your dwelling is condemned or does not comply with local building codes and has to be replaced or destroyed.
- Losses resulting from power failure or interruption of power from the utility company.
- Losses resulting from neglect by the insured. (If you have not reasonably maintained your home and you incur a loss, you are not covered.)
- Losses caused by war.
- Losses resulting from a nuclear hazard.
- Any damage resulting from an intentional act of the insured. (If you burn down your house, the insurance company will not cover this loss.)

Now, let's mention the perils that *are* covered under the **standard homeowner's (HO) policy**. This is where the types of policies diverge—for example, a standard HO-1 policy covers only specified *basic* perils, whereas an HO-2 policy extends this coverage to additional and specified *broad* perils.

Basic perils are losses to your property resulting from the following:
- Fire
- Lightning
- Wind (tornado or hurricane)
- Hail
- Riot or civil commotion
- Aircraft collision
- Vehicle collision
- Smoke
- Vandalism or malicious mischief
- Explosion
- Theft
- Volcanic eruption

To these basic perils, the *broad* form of homeowner's coverage adds losses to your property resulting from the following:
- Falling objects (for example, tree limbs)
- Weight of ice, snow, or sleet
- Accidental discharge from a sprinkler, heating, or air-conditioning system
- Sudden and accidental damage to a hot-water tank or air-conditioning, heating, or sprinkler system
- Freezing of a plumbing, heating, air-conditioning, or sprinkler system
- Sudden and accidental damage from an artificially generated electrical current (for example, an electrical generator)

As a homeowner, generally, you do not want either an HO-1 or HO-2 policy that specifies named perils. Rather, you should ask for an HO-3 type of policy that provides for special, or *open peril*, coverage. Open peril coverage means you are protected against all losses (even from unknown perils) unless the cause of that loss is specifically excluded under the terms of the policy. In addition, many companies offer a rider to an HO-3 policy (known as an *HO-15 endorsement*) whereby you can also provide for open peril coverage on all the personal property included within your dwelling. Still other companies have combined the HO-3 policy and HO-15 endorsement into one standard HO-5 policy. If you can obtain an HO-5 policy in your state, do so, because it provides you with the most protection for each premium dollar you expend.

You should also be aware that many insurance companies that write property insurance policies do not call them HO-1, HO-2, and so on, as developed by the Insurance Services Office (ISO), but instead market them under their own proprietary names. Nonetheless, all homeowner's policies track the coverage and limitations that have been mentioned. If you are in doubt, ask your insurance agent to enumerate the types of perils or causes of loss against which you are protected, and then check them off from the lists in this chapter.

If you rent an apartment or home, you should ensure that you have an HO-4 (renter's insurance) policy. If you are an owner of a condominium or co-op property, an HO-6 policy is preferable.

If a centuries-old, historic home is destroyed, insurance coverage is often limited. This is because the cost to rebuild the home by using new construction materials and methods will likely exceed the home's replacement cost. As such, only a modified insurance coverage policy, known as an *HO-8 policy*, is available in today's marketplace. If you live in a much older home, you should make sure you have this type of homeowner's policy.

Table 7-1 lists the types of homeowner's policies, categorized by the kind and extent of losses covered (basic, broad, or open peril).

Table 7-1. Comparing Types of Standard Homeowner's Policies

	HO-1	HO-2	HO-3	HO-4	HO-5	HO-6	HO-8
Coverage A: Dwelling	Basic	Broad	Open peril	N/A	Open peril	Broad	Basic
Coverage B: Other Structures	Basic	Broad	Open peril	N/A	Open peril	N/A	Basic
Coverage C: Personal Property	Basic	Broad	Broad*	Broad	Open peril	Broad	Basic
Coverage D: Loss of Use	Basic	Broad	Open peril	Broad	Open peril	Broad	Basic

* Can be combined with an HO-15 endorsement to provide for open peril coverage on all personal property located within the dwelling.

What to Consider When Insuring Your Automobile

Like homeowner's insurance, many forms of automobile coverage are available in today's insurance market. However, most types of coverage derive from a standardized form of policy known as the **personal automobile policy** (**PAP**). The PAP has four general coverages for which it provides protection:

- Coverage A: personal liability
- Coverage B: medical payments
- Coverage C: uninsured motorist coverage
- Coverage D: physical damage or loss coverage

Most states have laws that require drivers to obtain a certain amount of personal liability insurance. Increasingly, however, these amounts are not generally viewed as sufficient. If you have obtained only the state-minimum amount of liability insurance, you likely are *underinsured*. One way to remedy this situation is to purchase additional liability insurance as a part of your current policy. But another, often-overlooked solution is to purchase an umbrella liability policy from the same company that insures your car, your home, or both.

Coverage A: Personal Liability

Personal liability limits are quoted on the basis of either a split-liability limit or single-limit liability. If the liability limit is specified using a split liability and you are at fault in an accident, the maximum amount that is paid by your insurance company is partitioned among several individual limits of coverage. For example, if you are quoted a policy with liability coverage limits of 50/100/25, it means you have protection of up to $50,000 for injuries to *one* individual resulting from an automobile accident, up to $100,000 for injuries to *all* individuals per accident, and up to $25,000 per accident for *property damages* to the car you hit and for which you were at fault. Alternatively, if the liability limit is a single limit, one maximum amount applies to all bodily injuries and property damages per accident, without regard to a per person maximum. In either instance, if the injured party has expenses over and above your policy's personal liability limits, generally they must sue you and hope you have sufficient assets to cover those expenses.

A common question about liability insurance concerns for whom this personal liability coverage is provided. For example, is liability coverage provided if someone borrows your car with your permission? Yes, and it applies whether the injured party is related to you or not. For instance, if you lend your car to your employer, who then is involved in an accident, your employer is covered under your policy for damages to another person or property. However, if your employer injures another person or damages property while using your car as a delivery vehicle (for a business reason), it is likely that the insurance company will deny coverage under a prevailing liability exclusion in the personal automobile policy. A commercial liability policy would be required in this instance.

Another frequently asked question about liability coverage concerns what qualifies as a covered automobile for the purposes of liability protection. The standard PAP defines a covered vehicle as follows:

- Any vehicle shown in the declaration page of the policy (that is, your car or cars)
- A newly acquired vehicle—however, normally only for a period of 30 days (in other words, you need to let the insurance company know to extend insurance coverage within 30 days of acquiring the new car)
- Any trailer owned by the insured
- Any car that is being used as a temporary substitute automobile (such as a rental car or loaner)

Be careful! Your insurance company may have a different, lesser time period under which it insures a newly acquired vehicle for collision coverage (for example, only 14 days). As a result, it is good practice to notify your insurance company agent or broker *as soon as* you purchase a new car and ask how to optimally insure the car in your state.

Coverage B: Medical Payments

This type of coverage pays your medical bills and those of your family or any other occupant of the car if you are hurt in an automobile accident. It also covers any medical expenses that you may incur as a result of being struck by an automobile while you are a pedestrian. However, any payments that are made to you as a result of the liability coverage of another driver who is at fault reduce your medical payments coverage. Furthermore, if you collect under your employer's group or individual health insurance policy, doing so may reduce pro rata the amount of benefits you can collect under Coverage B.

Coverage C: Uninsured Motorist's Coverage

Uninsured motorist's insurance is an agreement that pays the amount the insured could have collected from the insurance company of a negligent driver if the driver had maintained automobile insurance. Logically, given state laws requiring personal liability insurance on the part of all drivers, uninsured motorist's coverage makes little sense. Nevertheless, practically, such coverage is necessary for your or your family's adequate protection. The persons insured under uninsured motorist's coverage might be you, your family members, and any other occupant of your vehicle at the time of an accident.

Like Coverage A of the PAP, the *higher* the bodily injury limits under Coverage C, the *better*. As a recommended limit, if you are quoted a split-liability policy, you should obtain at least $250,000 per individual and $500,000 per accident of uninsured motorist's coverage. If you are quoted a single-liability policy, the higher limit of $500,000 is preferable. Given the fact that uninsured motorist's coverage essentially acts as a secondary liability policy, many insureds use their personal liability limits as the limit for uninsured motorist's protection (without the property damage component).

Coverage D: Physical Damage or Loss Coverage

Physical damage protection for your car is available through two separate types of coverage under the PAP:

- *Collision* coverage applies whenever your car hits another car, a fence, a telephone pole, a tree, or a building (essentially, any *inanimate* object). Collision coverage pays for damages to your car regardless of who was at fault in an accident.

- *Other-than-collision,* or comprehensive, coverage is for property damage to your car that results from something other than collision, such as a broken windshield, damage from fire or hail, theft, or damage from collision with animals (any *moving* object).

Depending on the company issuing the policy, physical damage coverage may or may not apply for rental cars. Typically, for short-term rentals (less than 30 days), coverage is afforded; however, the issue is much less clear for longer-term rentals. You should check with your insurance company before renting a car for longer than a month, because you likely are *not* covered. As a substitute (unless you are renting a car in certain foreign countries), you may be able to obtain coverage if you rent the car with a major credit card, such as MasterCard, Visa, or American Express.

You can reduce your car insurance premium substantially if you choose the highest deductible available with respect to collision and comprehensive coverage. Better yet, if you can afford the loss of a car damaged beyond repair ("totalled"), purchasing physical damage coverage of any form probably is not wise. However, if your car is financed and pledged as collateral for a loan, the lender generally requires physical damage coverage, regardless of its estimated salvage value.

No-Fault Insurance

The traditional method of settling claims resulting from an automobile accident is through the tort system of state law. A *tort* is a civil wrong wherein one driver generally is found to be at fault in an accident. (Negligence is the most common example of a tortuous act.) Under the tort system of liability, the at-fault driver's insurance carrier is required to pay for damages suffered by the other parties to the accident. This means that if you are the driver at fault in an accident, your insurance company will likely either raise your premiums or, worse, cancel any further coverage.

An alternative method of settling claims is the no-fault insurance system. In this system, the insured's insurance company pays the insured for their damages and then seeks reimbursement from the at-fault driver and their insurer. Most states that employ a no-fault system have adopted a *modified* form that permits a lawsuit by the injured party only when the insured's policy limits are exceeded. However, to combat the rising costs of premiums, many states are abandoning the no-fault system altogether and returning to the tort liability system.

Umbrella Liability Insurance

Umbrella liability policies are extended personal liability insurance—that is, they supplement, or add to, your existing, or underlying, personal liability coverage under your homeowner's or automobile policy. For example, if you are sued for negligence in an automobile accident and the plaintiff wins a verdict of $1 million in damages, an umbrella policy will cover you for this amount, even though the underlying maximum limit on your personal automobile policy for injuries to all individuals is only $300,000.

An umbrella liability policy may not only increase your liability coverage amounts, but also broaden such coverage. Most automobile and homeowner's policies exclude the risks of libel or slander from liability protection; in contrast, an umbrella policy typically includes them. Additional risks may be covered by an umbrella policy; however, because most policies are customized to the needs of the insured, the covered risks may vary. Keep in mind that the nature of an umbrella policy limits the number of claims that the insurance company experiences and potentially has to pay.

The premiums charged for umbrella coverage are relatively inexpensive. This is primarily because an umbrella policy is written on an excess basis—the policy pays only when the underlying coverage limits from your automobile or homeowner's policy or both have been used up. When the umbrella policy is the only coverage for a claim (for example, if slander is alleged and proven), the policy typically has its own deductible or self-insured retention amount, which may be as high or low as the insured chooses. Alternatively, if the liability claim is covered by one of the underlying policies (for example, automobile negligence), the deductible for the underlying policy is also effectively the deductible for the umbrella.

You should think of an umbrella policy exactly as the name implies. The excess coverage provided by the "umbrella" protects you against sizable damage amounts that may be awarded as a result of litigation. Purchasing umbrella coverage is particularly important for individuals who are often the subject of lawsuits, including professionals (lawyers, doctors, accountants, engineers, and so on) and any person of higher net worth. Be aware that any claim arising out of a business activity in which you or any other insured are engaged is *not* covered under an umbrella policy; rather, to be protected against these types of claims, a professional liability policy (typically, a malpractice or errors-and-omissions policy) is necessary.

Business Property Insurance

There are two types of business property insurance: a *commercial package policy* (CPP) and a *business owner's policy* (BOP). The type of policy you purchase depends on the size and organizational form of your business. For example, the CPP is usually required by *larger* businesses, typically corporations, whereas the BOP is designed for *small to medium* businesses, usually operating in an unincorporated form as a sole proprietorship or partnership.

The CPP combines commercial property, liability, and business automobile coverage into a single policy. As a result, each part of the CPP specifies covered business property, an applicable deductible, valuation provisions, and a requisite cause of loss. In practical effect, these types of property coverage are similar to a homeowner's policy, but they are much broader and comprehensive in scope. Hence, the advantage of listing and insuring business property in this manner is that there are fewer gaps in coverage. In addition, you may achieve administrative savings that can lead to lower premiums.

The general liability portion of the CPP protects the business against legal liability arising from business activities, excepting injuries incurred by employees while on the job, for which separate worker's compensation insurance is needed. Typically, the CPP includes additional coverage for business automobile liability, but all claims arising out of employee injury must be handled as part of the worker's compensation policy that most businesses are required to maintain by state law. It is also possible to write a separate policy for commercial general liability, although this may result in additional cost to the business.

The BOP, on the other hand, is specifically designed for the needs of small- to medium-sized businesses and covers all business-related real and personal property without a separate listing. This policy has two forms: basic and special. The *basic* form covers the possibility of loss from all listed perils, and the *special* form covers loss from all perils not excluded. All forms of the BOP cover liability for bodily injury and property damage caused by employees while engaged in an activity on behalf of the business.

If you are business owner, you should be aware that another type of policy protects business property while that property is in transit to another location. This is known as an *inland marine policy* and covers domestic goods while they are being moved from one location to another, mobile equipment and property, and certain types of property that are still in the dealer's store (such as inventory). The term *inland marine* has nothing to do with water or oceanic activities, as the name may seem to imply.

We have now concluded our look at personal and property risk exposures and how to insure them. However, if you are employed, additional forms of insurance benefits may be available to you in *group form*. Such forms, along with other benefits commonly offered by an employer, are the subject of our next chapter.

CHAPTER 8

Optimizing Your Employment Benefits

Our discussion on how to *protect* your wealth concludes with this chapter on how best to take advantage of benefits offered by your employer. Unlike the humorous television commercial, benefits offered by your employer do not come from France ("French benefits") but rather are commonly referred to as *fringe benefits*. The nature and amount of fringe benefits you receive from your workplace depends on your employer, its current and future cash flow, and its attitude toward providing (usually) tax-free benefits to its employees. Typically, employers offer fringe benefits not only for competitive reasons, but also because they receive an income-tax deduction for doing so, which thereby assists them with the management of their future cash flow.

Perhaps the most popular benefit for employees that has evolved throughout the years is employer-provided group medical and dental insurance. Other common benefits are group term life insurance coverage, accidental death insurance coverage, group long-term disability coverage, dependent care assistance (usually through some form of flexible spending account), educational assistance, and group long-term care insurance. In addition, many employers have implemented retirement savings options, such as the Section 401(k) retirement plan (so-named after the Internal Revenue Code section of the same number). Finally, executives of companies may have special or discriminatory benefits established to encourage performance goals.

This chapter considers how you, as a valued employee, can best take advantage of these benefits to help meet your financial goals.

Group Medical and Dental Insurance

In Chapter 5, we discussed what an informed purchaser of health care services should take into account before selecting a health insurance policy. However, most wage earners have only the option of selecting whatever group medical and dental plans are offered by their employer. Historically, the most popular type of group medical plan provided by employers has been comprehensive major medical coverage, sometimes known as fee-for-service programs. Recently, though, **managed care health insurance plans** such as health maintenance organizations (HMOs) and preferred provider organizations (PPOs) have come onto the scene; and more recently still, employers have begun to offer a close cousin of the health savings account (HSA): the health reimbursement arrangement (HRA).

An *HRA* is an employer-sponsored HSA that permits employees to accumulate funds for health expenses. Unlike with an HSA, however, there is no limit on the amount of money an employer may contribute to the employee's HRA. Employers offering HRAs typically pair them with a high-deductible group health insurance plan in order to cover any sizable medical expenses incurred by the employee. Once the funds set aside in the HRA by the employer are used up in a given year, the employee's health expenses are then covered by the high-deductible plan after the deductible and co-insurance requirements are met. If any funds remain in the HRA at the end of the year, these funds may be carried over to the following year, which allows employees to "save" for their future medical expenses.

A major advantage of an HRA from the point of view of the employee is that preventative care, such as routine physicals and child immunizations, is *not* charged against the fund. In addition, because of the savings element associated with the arrangement, HRA participants have an incentive to use their health care dollars wisely. Employers, for their part, like HRAs because they help minimize health-care insurance costs: the underlying policy providing coverage has a high deductible, and the policy may never be used by relatively healthy employees.

Unfortunately, most group dental insurance coverage plans have not yet adopted the HRA approach to payment of expenses. Most dental insurance uses managed care as a model, operating either as an HMO or PPO. If you have a dental HMO, the premium payments on your group coverage are sent directly to your dentist or specialist. If your plan is structured as a PPO, a network of participating dentists has agreed to provide services for a reduced fee to group insureds. You may go out of the network to an unaffiliated provider, but you pay a higher deductible and co-payment to do so.

In summary, unless you participate in an HRA at work, your group medical plan probably provides you with little incentive to save your health care dollars. Further, the high cost of paying for your own medical care will likely dissuade you from purchasing an individual policy. As a result, you have to seek ways of paying for your share of the group medical costs (deductibles and co-payments) in as tax-efficient a way as possible, such as by participating in a flexible spending account (FSA). You should also turn your attention to other employment-provided benefits that may need to be supplemented with individual coverage, such as life insurance and disability income insurance.

Group Life Insurance

The most common form of life insurance offered by employers is *group term* insurance. By its nature, this form of insurance is temporary and covers you only for a specific period, normally only as long as you work for the employer that is providing coverage. As such, you need to keep in mind that you will probably *lose* coverage when you leave your job. However, at that point in time, you typically will have the opportunity to convert your group term coverage into some form of permanent insurance (either whole life or universal life) offered by the same insurance company. Generally, this conversion privilege is available for only 30 to 60 days following the date the employee is no longer employed. But if you take advantage of it, the privilege of converting is usually a *guaranteed benefit* (you cannot be denied coverage regardless of your health status at the time).

Group term life insurance is generally offered to employees as a multiple of their salary. For example, the death benefit provided by the policy is one or two times the employee's current salary. Often, however, the employer portion of this benefit is capped at a specified amount, usually $50,000. This is because the employee is limited to a $50,000 cost-of-coverage exclusion under tax law before the employee must be attributed some cost of the protection as a taxable employee benefit. Stated another way, if the employer pays for more than $50,000 of group term life insurance on your life, then you must report the economic benefit of the extra insurance as taxable income. (The benefit amount is typically reported on the IRS Form W-2 at the end of the year.) Fortunately, this attributed amount of income is relatively small, and the cost that the employer pays for the insurance is still probably much less than you would have to pay if you tried to obtain the insurance coverage on your own. Plus, as mentioned previously, you probably have the right to convert the group term insurance after you have left that employer.

Nevertheless, even with group term insurance coverage, you should analyze whether you have *enough* life insurance protection. Don't assume you have enough coverage simply with what the insurance provides; and remember, unless you convert, you will lose the insurance when you leave the job. Rather, look at the group term coverage only as a starting point to be supplemented with individual life insurance, either an individual term or a permanent policy—or perhaps both.

Another commonly provided group insurance is **accidental death benefit (ADB)** insurance, sometimes referred to as *double indemnity insurance*. Historically, this type of insurance has been purchased as a rider to a group life policy and doubles the death benefit payable to an employee's beneficiary if death results from an accident while the employee is conducting employer business. Like group term insurance coverage, the ADB is typically limited in amount. However, this is to minimize employer cost and not to minimize the income-tax consequences for the employee. If you have ADB insurance protection, consider yourself one of the lucky few, because increasing numbers of employers are dropping such coverage. Moreover, it is difficult to envision a situation in which your need for life insurance protection is greater in the case of accidental death than it is under normal circumstances of death. Therefore, the doubling of the benefit is essentially free money that you would not have otherwise provided for your heirs.

More and more employers are offering group *permanent* types of life insurance policies to their employees—notably, group universal life insurance. A group universal life insurance policy is similar in structure and provisions to an individual universal life policy, except that the group coverage is provided (up to a policy limit) *without* any evidence of insurability. Therefore, an employee in poor health who may not be able to qualify for individual coverage may obtain insurance through group underwriting. Also, unlike group term policies, group universal life policies are *portable*, meaning you can take the coverage with you when you leave the job (although a higher premium may then be charged).

Group Disability Insurance

Individuals with disability insurance generally receive it through their employer in the form of group long-term coverage. (As has been discussed, if your employer does not offer you disability insurance, you are unemployed, or you are self-employed, the purchase of an *individual* disability income insurance policy is probably one of the best moves you can make to protect your future wealth.) A group long-term disability policy normally has an elimination period of 30 to 180 days before you can draw benefits, but this period may be even longer if the policy is coupled with short-term disability coverage. Therefore, you need to find some way to cover your expenses while you wait for the long-term benefits to take effect, ideally by maintaining an adequate emergency or contingency fund.

If you are fortunate, your employer also offers short-term disability coverage. This coverage may have an elimination period that is as short as seven days for illness and one day for injury. If written to cover illness, short-term policies generally function as a kind of sick leave from your job insofar as they pay you a specified dollar amount that is not tied to a percentage of your monthly compensation—as is the norm with long-term coverage. If written to cover injury or disability, the short-term definition of disability that is used is usually that of total disability, which precludes payment if you are only partially disabled or temporarily experience a loss of income.

Group disability coverage is often less expensive than individual coverage. However, it is important to realize that you cannot customize coverage in a group policy nearly as effectively as you can with an individual policy. For example, in an individual disability policy, you can purchase coverage that will pay when you are unable to perform your own occupation. This is generally *not* possible with a group long-term policy that uses a combination of *Any Occupation* and *Modified Any Occupation* definitions of disability. See Chapter 6 for more on disability. Additionally, the group policy may not provide you with a cost-of-living increase in benefits as is possible with the purchase of a rider to an individual policy. Finally, you pay taxes on any disability benefits received from the policy if the employer pays the cost of the policy premiums during your employment years.

Group Long-Term Care Insurance

The offering of group long-term care insurance by employers is a relatively new phenomenon. As a result of the rising cost of long-term care (and the relative paucity of government-provided benefits to assist in the payment of this cost), more employers are encouraging their employees to plan for this need and are helping them do so through group insurance plans.

There are essentially three types of group long-term care plans, and the one that is right for you depends on the status of your current health. The most liberal and favorable type of these group long-term care policies, but also the most expensive, is a *true group* policy. This type of policy is underwritten as *guaranteed issue*, meaning no employee can be denied coverage, even if they already have a debilitating health condition that would preclude them from otherwise obtaining coverage. The price for this coverage is high, in part to discourage what is known in the insurance industry as *adverse selection*—meaning the sickest and most disabled employees are most likely to want coverage.

A secondary form of true group long-term care policy is known as a *modified guaranteed issue* policy. This type of policy uses no medical underwriting but asks one or more disqualifying questions intended to eliminate the sickest and most disabled employees from the plan. The premiums are lower on modified guaranteed issue policies, and if you are relatively healthy (and could otherwise qualify for individual coverage), a policy of this nature may prove preferable to a true group policy.

The third type of group long-term care plan—the *individual long-term care plan*—is offered to employers for group coverage to their employees on a discounted basis (typically, anywhere from 5 to 15 percent below the individual plan premium). Although these types of plans are medically underwritten (in other words, they are neither guaranteed issue nor modified guaranteed issue), they allow for more benefit options for employees. Employers like to "carve out" these policies for a select group of employees (usually executives), because the benefits are significant but the policies cost much less than true group policies. If you are an executive in a company, a discounted individual long-term care plan is probably best for you.

If you currently do not have a group long-term care policy available to you as an employee, ask your human resources department to investigate the possibility of offering such a benefit. It is possible to offer a group policy on a ten-year paid-up basis—something that is generally not available with an individually obtained policy. Oh, and one last thing: the frequency of claims made on individual long-term care policies is relatively high—so high that many insurance companies are choosing *not* to enter the long-term care market or are getting out of the business of underwriting *individual* long-term care policies altogether. Accordingly, that is all the more reason you should be investigating whether your employer will offer a *group* policy for the benefit of all employees.

Dependent Care Assistance

Your employer can provide you with a substantial amount of dependent care assistance as a nontaxable fringe benefit. Currently, you can take advantage of up to $5,000 per year of such benefits per family (or the total amount of the lower-paid spouse's salary, if less than $5,000) without having to include this assistance in your taxable income. If your employer does not provide you with dependent care assistance, you may alternatively wish to reduce your salary and contribute $5,000 to an FSA on your own behalf. Two primary reasons for doing so are as follows:

- You can pay dependent care costs, such as full-time child care, after-school day care, or the cost of a nanny, out of this account and receive reimbursement on a tax-free basis.

- You never pay any income or Social Security tax on the amount you contribute to the account; as such, you are contributing to the account from your paycheck on a pretax basis.

You also need to be aware of two related income-tax consequences as you consider whether to fund an FSA in order to pay for child care expenses:

- You may not claim the child and dependent care tax credit for any child-care cost that is reimbursed out of the account (in other words, it is an either/or proposition).
- You lose any amount contributed to the account that is not spent on employment-related child-care costs during the year. Unlike an HSA, which you can use as a savings vehicle for the next and subsequent years, an FSA is contributed to on a use-it-or-lose it basis.

As a general rule, the *higher* your taxable income, the *more advantageous* it is for you to use the FSA salary reduction in the payment of child-care expenses. Conversely, the *lower* your taxable income, the *less advantageous* the salary reduction and the *more valuable* is the child and dependent care tax credit.

Do not overlook the possibility of dependent care assistance for more than your young child or children. Under current law, the tax exclusion is available not only for expenses incurred on behalf of a dependent child under the age of 13, but also for any individual who is physically or mentally incapable of caring for themselves and who resides with the taxpayer in their principal place of residence for more than six months out of the year. Therefore, the $5,000 exclusion from income is also potentially available to help pay for dependent elderly parents or a dependent spouse for whom you are the primary caregiver.

Employer Educational Assistance

Some employers, particularly those who need highly skilled employees, offer educational assistance benefits to their workers. In most instances, under employer rules to achieve reimbursement, employers offer payment assistance only for educational expenses that are job-related. However, under current tax law, an exclusion from employee income of up to $5,250 per year for educational assistance is permanently allowed, even for non-job-related educational courses. Further, the exclusion is not limited to continuing education programs; the employer payment may be in reimbursement for either undergraduate or graduate degree courses. As a result, you may be able to obtain and be reimbursed for that doctoral degree in underwater basket-weaving you have always wanted.

Previous to 2018, a second related educational benefit in tax law was available without getting your employer involved. This was an itemized tax deduction (subject to a 2 percent of AGI "floor") for unreimbursed educational expenses that you pursue in advancement of your career. Unlike the exclusion provision, this education deduction must have been related to your career. For example, if you are an accountant, pursuing a master's degree in accounting qualifies as job-related education. The major issue here for many young fast-track employees is whether educational costs expended for a master's degree in business administration qualify for the tax break. Generally, the answer is yes; however, if your current job is significantly unrelated to traditional business activities (say, you are a professional musician), you may find it difficult to make a strong argument that the deduction should be permitted. The itemized deduction for education is scheduled to come back into the law after the year 2025 with the "sunset" of the 2017 TCJA.

Saving for Retirement Through Employer-Sponsored Plans

In recent years, employer-provided plans designed to provide for retirement have undergone major changes. Historically, employers promised their employees a pension at a certain age (usually 65) as long as the employee completed a specified number of years of service. As such, the employer assumed the risk of investment performance on the retirement monies that were set aside, with the intention of making good on its pension promise.

Beginning in the 1990s, the methodology of providing for an employee's retirement began to change from a guaranteed employer-provided pension to one in which employees were made responsible for their own financial future. In other words, *defined contribution retirement plans*—in which the amount of retirement benefit is *not* guaranteed but rather depends on the employee's own investment expertise to accumulate the needed savings—became predominant. According to Boston College's Center for Retirement Research, among workers with retirement plans, 83 percent had traditional employer-provided pensions in 1980. It is estimated that, in 2017, only 11 percent of private sector workers participated in a pension plan. This percentage, however, is much greater (approximately 84 percent) among public sector workers, such as police and fire department employees. Nevertheless, a major problem occurred in the shift away from pensions and toward defined-contribution plans: most employees did not possess the investment expertise to optimally plan for their own retirement. This is still the case today. Recent legislation has been passed to make it easier for employers to assist employees with their retirement investment decisions, but employees generally are not yet well-educated enough to take on the responsibility of making retirement plan investment choices. Hopefully, after finishing this book, you will feel more comfortable about making such choices. If not, I strongly urge you to seek the assistance of a Certified Financial Planner or other retirement planning professional.

Section 401(k) Retirement Plans

Many employees today are participating in one or more types of defined-contribution retirement plans at work, but the Section 401(k) plan has become the savings plan of choice. Although many employees believe that employers match a percentage of their 401(k) plan contributions primarily for altruistic reasons, this is not usually the employers' motivation. Rather, special **nondiscrimination tests** must be met before the employer can offer and maintain a 401(k) plan on behalf of any employee, including **highly compensated employees**, whose job satisfaction and performance are usually the employer's primary concern. Because highly compensated employees are the kind of employees most likely to already contribute to a Section 401(k) plan, the employer needs to motivate non-highly compensated employees to contribute to satisfy nondiscrimination tests under law. As a result, employers typically encourage non-highly compensated employees to contribute via a matching-of-employee-contributions program.

According to Vanguard Investments in its *How America Saves* 2016 report, the average 401(k) plan contribution (or salary deferral percentage) in the year 2015 was only 6.8 percent of income. Moreover, only approximately 75 percent of employees participate in 401(k) plans, per the Center for Retirement Research at Boston College. This means the net employee-only savings rate was only 5.1 percent (6.8 percent times 75 percent). Even with a 3 percent employer match of employee contributions (the most common matching-of-employee contributions in the United States is 50 percent of the first 6 percent of salary deferrals), the aggregate, total employer-plus-employee savings rate is only 7.35 percent (6.8 percent plus 3 percent times 75 percent). This is not nearly enough for most 401(k) plan participants to live adequately during their retirement years. Instead, the rate should be between a 10 and 15 percent annual aggregate savings rate.

If you are lucky enough to work for an employer that sponsors a Section 401(k) plan, the first thing you must do is *participate*. You should then elect to defer on a pretax basis as much of your salary as possible into the 401(k) plan. Certainly, you should be deferring at least 3 percent of your salary (or whatever percentage your particular employer will match), because doing so results in a guaranteed 100 percent investment return on your money. But beyond that, a total annual contribution of at least 10 percent of your own money should be your goal. If you are closer to retirement and have wasted the prime saving years of your 30s and 40s, you will need to save an even greater percentage of your current income to fund retirement. Either that, or you will need to consider one of two unpleasant alternatives: 1) work longer and extend your planned retirement date, or 2) reduce your post-retirement standard of living.

> **Note** Although there are annual dollar limits on how much of your salary you can defer into a 401(k) plan, these limits are usually important only for highly compensated employees, such as corporate executives.

As a result of the Pension Protection Act (PPA) of 2006, many 401(k) plans are adopting automatic enrollment plans. This alternative, also known as a *negative election*, allows an employer to enroll employees in its Section 401(k) plan without the employee's consent, as long as the employee has the right to opt out of contributing. Some employers are also supplementing the automatic enrollment with a progressive savings feature, meaning they automatically increase an employee's savings deferral percentage by a set amount (for example, 1 percent, each year that the employee participates in the plan). These two features, when used together, may go a long way in helping employees—and particularly those who have opted out in the past—save for their own retirement.

As an incentive for offering automatic enrollment, the PPA of 2006 included relief from employer liability if the employer provides investment advice to 401(k) plan participants. To be eligible for this relief, however, the employer's investment advice arrangement must include an unbiased computer model certified by an independent expert that creates a recommended portfolio for a participant's consideration. As a result, life-cycle investment funds or target-date retirement funds are now being adopted as an employer's default investment option for employees who are automatically enrolled. Overall, this is not a bad thing, particularly if you are an employee who would not save otherwise. But if you are at all serious about saving for your own retirement (you're reading this book, aren't you?), you can probably invest your retirement plan contributions more wisely than the default option. At the very least, you—or your financial advisor—should try!

Section 403(b) Retirement Plans

The Section 403(b) plan, also referred to as a *tax-sheltered annuity*, is the functional equivalent of the Section 401(k) plan for employees who work for specified not-for-profit employers, such as public or private schools, churches, and some hospitals. The maximum annual salary reduction contributions for the 403(b) plan are generally the same as those allowable for the Section 401(k) plan, as are the nondiscrimination rules that must be met by the employer. Today, more and more not-for-profit employers are matching the salary reduction contributions made by their employees (historically, many 403(b) plans were funded solely by employee salary reductions with no employer matching).

However, the 403(b) and 401(k) retirement plans differ. Only certain not-for-profit employers (called *501(c)(3) organizations* after the Internal Revenue Code section of the same number) may implement a 403(b) plan. As mentioned, these employers include schools and churches, so if you are a public school elementary or secondary school teacher, you probably have a 403(b) plan and not a 401(k) plan. I use the word *probably* here because increasing numbers of not-for-profit employers have been implementing a Section 401(k) plan, or the alternative Section 401(a) plan, and adding it to or substituting it for a Section 403(b) plan.

Why are not-for-profit employers increasingly adopting Section 401(k) plans in lieu of Section 403(b) plans? For starters, a Section 401(k) plan generally has more investment choices than the Section 403(b) offering. For example, a Section 403(b) plan must be invested in either a fixed or variable **annuity** or mutual funds. It cannot be invested in individual stocks or bonds. Therefore, if you are a qualifying not-for-profit employee who likes to "play the market," a Section 403(b) plan *limits* your investment options. Another advantage of the Section 401(k) plan is that it grants participants the ability to elect a special income-tax treatment if they choose to take a lump-sum distribution. This special election, known as *ten-year averaging tax treatment*, allows 401(k) plan participants born before 1936 to pay income taxes on a lump-sum distribution in one year as if they were paying it over ten years, thereby significantly lowering their tax bill. This option is not available for Section 403(b) plan participants.

With the exception of these two advantages of the 401(k) plan, the 403(b) is probably the more favorable of the two. We will not discuss the other technical reasons why this is so, but the 403(b) plan generally beats the 401(k) for one big reason: you can contribute more money to the 403(b) plan, the closer you are to your planned retirement date. For example, if, as a not-for-profit employee, you have worked for the same or another qualifying employer for at least 15 years, you may be able to contribute as much as $15,000 per year to the plan in addition to the normal contribution limits. As such, you can attempt to make up for those years in your 30s and 40s when you did not or were not able to adequately save for your own retirement. You cannot do this with the 401(k) plan, because the special catch-up annual contribution exception does not apply.

Other Retirement Plans

Chapter 16 discusses other employer-sponsored retirement plans and IRAs, when we address distributing your wealth at the time of retirement; but some employers offer plans in addition to the Section 401(k) and Section 403(b) plans. If they do, they may permit you to make contributions to these plans on an after-tax basis. These are commonly referred to as *designated Roth accounts*. This may not seem like something you want to do, particularly if you have already maxed out your before-tax contributions to the 401(k) or 403(b) plan, but consider this: if you contribute after-tax money to any employer-sponsored plan, you do not have to pay income taxes on any distribution the plan makes of those same funds, including earnings to you. Moreover, the contribution limit to a designated Roth account is considerably greater than the limit for contribution to a **Roth IRA**. As a result, if you have the opportunity to make after-tax contributions to an employer-sponsored plan and can afford to do so, you should.

Company Stock Purchase Plans

There are two basic types of company stock purchase plans: employee stock ownership plans (ESOPs) and employee stock purchase plans (ESPPs). Both plans permit employees to purchase and own employer stock, although, as the name implies, only the ESOP permits controlling ownership to be transferred to the employees.

If you work for a corporation or incorporated business, the employer may have established an ESOP. An unincorporated business, on the other hand, such as a sole proprietorship or partnership, cannot have an ESOP, because the business has no stock.

So, what is an *ESOP*? It is a retirement plan designed to invest primarily in employer stock. Some closely held (non-publicly traded) corporations also establish ESOPs to provide a market for employer stock that would otherwise not be very marketable. Thus, when a company establishes an ESOP, its employees *become* the market and ultimately the owners of the closely held business.

Aside from the perk of becoming a partial owner of the company for which you work, there is another major advantage to contributing to an ESOP: you now have a tax-favored retirement plan in which to save for your own retirement. Moreover, once the employer stock is distributed to you at the time of retirement, you do *not* have to pay any capital gains tax on the appreciation of the stock—technically known as **net unrealized appreciation (NUA)**—until you sell the shares. Any further amount of appreciation is then taxed at favorable long-term capital gains rates if you have owned the stock for at least a year.

In contrast to an ESOP, an ESPP is simply a means for you to own stock in your employer under favorable terms. Typically not structured as a retirement plan, but rather as an employee investment option, an ESPP gives the employee the right to buy company stock on a future date for an amount that is no higher than its current, publicly traded value. If the stock price increases between the time this right is granted and the time the employee purchases the stock, the employee may choose to buy the stock at the lower or discounted price. The tax advantages for ESPPs are generally the same as those for ESOPs.

Although company stock purchase plans can offer employees plenty of perks, there is a fundamental disadvantage to owning too much employer stock, as part of either an ESOP or an ESPP. This disadvantage is the inherent lack of portfolio diversification that accompanies ESOPs and ESPPs, so that if the company's financial prospects decline (or, as was case with Enron, liquidation occurs), you are left with an asset of little value. To avoid this problem, you should return to the basic asset-allocation principles discussed in Chapter 3 and make sure you have diversified into other assets *in addition to* your employer's stock. If you suspect you are not as diversified as you should be and are holding too much of your employer's stock as a total percentage of your portfolio (say, over half of your net worth), I advise you to see your investment advisor as soon as possible.

Stock Options and Other Forms of Incentive Compensation

This last section about optimizing your employment benefits probably best pertains to corporate executives, because they are most likely to be offered employer stock options and other forms of incentive compensation. If you are such an individual, you should know that two main types of stock options are used to compensate executives:

- Incentive stock options (ISOs)
- Nonstatutory, or regular, stock options (also known as nonqualified stock options, or NQSOs)

Both are primarily used by larger, publicly traded corporations. Neither ISOs nor NQSOs are used much by closely held corporations, including family businesses operated as corporations, because the few owners of a closely held corporation typically do not want unrelated outsiders, or even executives, as additional owners.

An ISO plan is a tax-favored, written arrangement for compensating executives by awarding options to buy employer stock. Unlike regular stock options, ISOs generally do *not* result in regular taxable income to the executive either at the time of the grant or at the time the executive exercises the option (purchases the employer stock for which the option was granted). In other words, there is *no* regular taxable consequence to the executive until they *sell* the employer stock, the timing of which is completely at the executive's discretion.

The favorable income-tax consequence associated with ISOs is not available with NQSOs, which are much more prevalent than ISOs. When the executive exercises a regular stock option (purchases the employer stock), they have taxable compensation income to the extent of the difference between the fair market value of the shares at the date of purchase and the greatly discounted option price. This is known as the *bargain element*. At this time, the employer must also withhold and pay Social Security tax and Medicare tax with respect to this compensation income.

Why, if the tax consequences are much more favorable for the executive with an ISO than a regular stock option, is the regular stock option much more prevalent? There are two reasons:

- At the time of exercising the ISO, the executive incurs an individual alternative minimum tax (AMT) consequence—an exceedingly disadvantageous tax requiring the taxpayer to pay a *greater* amount than the already high regular tax liability.

- Unless extraordinary circumstances occur, the employer or company that grants the ISO to an executive does not ever receive a corporate income-tax deduction for the compensation, thereby potentially disrupting the cash flow of the company.

If you are an executive holding a regular stock option or numerous options, you can anticipate that, at the date of exercising these options, there will be income tax due. So, what do you do if you do not have the cash or other liquid assets necessary to pay this tax? A viable planning strategy is to undertake what is known as a *cashless exercise of options*, which takes place in three steps:

1. Exercise the regular option or options at the specified date, and borrow from a stockbroker the money needed to exercise the options.

2. Simultaneously sell at least the number of shares necessary to cover any costs, including taxes due on the exercise of the options and any broker's commission that is charged on the sale of the shares.

3. Ask your employer to pay you the net amount remaining after the sale of the shares in cash or stock and then retain any additional shares for a subsequent sale date of your own choosing.

Another planning alternative is to defer the taxation of these options by combining the options with a subsequent agreement entered into with your employer that restricts your access to the shares purchased until a later time, such as your planned retirement date.

Restricted Stock

Recently, more executives have been receiving incentive compensation in the form of restricted stock instead of employer stock options. This trend is taking place partially because of the corporate abuses that have occurred with options, including the backdating of the exercise date of options to a more favorable time for the recipient. There is also a more technical reason for this trend: under general accounting rules, corporations must now account for the value of these options (known as *expensing the options*) on their income statements. In turn, this reduces corporate earnings and, ultimately, perhaps the value of the company's publicly traded stock to its shareholders. As a result, if you are an executive, do not be surprised if you are now offered a restricted stock incentive-based compensation arrangement instead of employer stock options. Employers may also adopt a restricted stock plan to keep you from going to work for a competitor, specifically providing that if you leave the company for a rival business, your right to receive the stock at little or no cost is lost.

The taxation of restricted stock to an executive is essentially similar to that of the exercise of a regular stock option. When the restriction expires, the difference between the fair market value of the stock when substantially vested and what was paid for it, if anything, is taxable compensation income. However, there is something you can do immediately to limit the amount of tax you might end up owing when you exercise the restricted stock. If you make a special tax election (commonly referred to as a *Section 83(b) election* after the Internal Revenue Code section of the same number) to recognize income as of the date you receive the restricted stock rather than when the restriction expires, any subsequent appreciation in the value of the stock is treated as capital gains income and is potentially taxable at a much lower rate.

For example, assume that you received restricted stock in the year 2014, when its publicly traded value was $35 per share. You paid nothing for this stock. Further, assume that you anticipate that, with your efforts, the value of this stock will be $85 per share five years from now (in 2019), which is also the date when the restriction of the stock expires. If you make the Section 83(b) election, you will have $35 of compensation income in 2014, but $50 of capital gains income ($85 less $35) in 2019, which is taxable at a much lower rate (currently, no more than 20 percent). Compare this to $85 of compensation income in 2019, which is currently taxable at a rate as high as 37 percent, and you can see why making a Section 83(b) election may be a prudent planning technique.

But be careful! What happens if you leave the company and forfeit the stock before 2019 but previously had made the Section 83(b) election in 2014? In that case, you are *not* permitted to go back and amend your 2014 tax return to claim a $35 per share loss. That's right: you are gambling that the stock will increase in value from the date you make the election and that you will not leave the company prior to the restriction expiring!

Nonqualified Deferred Compensation

We end this chapter with an employee benefit that is available only to a select few—the very top echelon of many corporations and businesses. This benefit is a nonqualified deferred compensation agreement, commonly funded with life insurance or securities made payable only to the executive or their family.

Nonqualified deferred compensation is not that far removed from the employer-sponsored retirement plans in which many of us participate. Both arrangements are really forms of setting aside current compensation to be paid out later, typically at the employee's retirement date. However, employer-sponsored retirement plans generally have to be available to *all* employees, regardless of compensation level and employment status (an exempt or nonexempt employee for purposes of labor law). In contrast, nonqualified arrangements may *discriminate* in favor of whomever the employer chooses. Usually, these favored employees are the CEO and senior management of the company.

If you are lucky enough to be offered any of the several forms of nonqualified deferred compensation, such as a **rabbi trust**, be sure you do not sacrifice your future benefit security for a current tax advantage. For example, although a mere promise from an employer that it will pay your deferred compensation at some point in the future achieves tax deferral, you will have sacrificed payment of your current compensation needlessly if the employer goes out of business in the future. Fortunately, there are ways to accomplish both objectives.

Most deferred-compensation arrangements must be drafted by skilled legal counsel. The risk that you, as a valued executive, will not be adequately protected by your corporate legal office or an outside law firm is, therefore, relatively small. Nevertheless, it is always important to remember that the corporate legal office primarily represents the business; it represents you as an employee only secondarily. As such, you may wish to secure your own attorney and financial planner to advise you on how best to proceed.

This chapter concludes our look at the first part of the PADD process of financial planning: that of *protecting* yourself, your family, and your property. We now move on to the second part of the process, *accumulating* wealth, and begin by considering the advantages and disadvantages of investing in financial assets such as stocks, bonds, and mutual funds.

PART III

Accumulating Wealth

CHAPTER 9

Investing in Financial Assets

There are two basic categories of investment assets: financial assets and real assets. For the purposes of this chapter, however, we will be discussing what most people think of when the term *investment* is mentioned: financial assets, such as stocks and bonds denominated and traded in US dollars. To be properly diversified in financial assets, many financial planners recommend some exposure to foreign markets or assets denominated and traded in local (non-US-dollar) currencies in addition to maintaining holdings in more traditional investments. But even if investors invest in an American Depository Receipt (ADR) of foreign stock, they need to understand that there is a currency or exchange risk when converting the proceeds from a foreign stock into US dollars. This is in addition to other systematic risks that are assumed when accumulating wealth via financial assets.

Why, with all the inherent risks we discuss in this chapter, should you invest in financial assets? The reason is simple: to generate an investment *return*, you have to assume some form of investment *risk*. For example, some investors believe that if they hoard cash and stuff it in a mattress in their basement, they are immune to investment risk—but this is not true. Because of inflation (also known as *purchasing power risk*), when the investor is ready to spend the cash years later, they will not have as much money (purchasing power) as when the cash was first stuffed in the mattress.

© Keith R. Fevurly 2018
K. R. Fevurly, *Plan Your Financial Future*, https://doi.org/10.1007/978-1-4842-3637-6_9

Chapter 9 | Investing in Financial Assets

The key to investing in financial assets and to accumulating wealth generally is to assume as *little investment risk* as possible in order to generate as *great an investment return* as possible. The methods required to do this are the subject of another book—probably several books—but any serious investor should understand the risk/return relationship and structure their portfolio accordingly.

Cash Investments and When to Use Them

You may think you know what is meant by the term *cash*—namely, that, in the United States, it is green and tangible (you can see and touch it). However, in the investment and financial-planning world, cash has a specific meaning. It refers to investments that possess a high degree of liquidity with little or no risk to principal (the sum of money that you originally invest). Many planners use the term *cash equivalents* to differentiate a cash investment from the more general "green and tangible" definition.

In general, cash investments are short-term (not more than 12 months in maturity) interest-bearing securities and deposit accounts. As such, cash investments include not only bank deposits, such as savings accounts, short-term certificates of deposit (CDs), and money market deposit accounts, but also investments that are made in the money market, including money market mutual funds, corporate commercial paper, and US Treasury bills (T-bills). Sometimes, nonmarketable investments, such as the purchase of US government Series EE bonds, are also included among cash equivalents. None of these investments generate a great deal of investment return, but they are liquid, which is a fundamental attribute of cash equivalents.

Bank Deposits

Many conservative investors do not venture away from bank deposits as an investment strategy. This is likely because they prefer the assurance of knowing that these deposits (up to a certain limit) are insured by the Federal Deposit and Insurance Corporation (FDIC). As a result of relatively recent legislation, all non-IRA bank deposits are now insured up to an amount of $250,000 per account (up from $100,000 previously). IRAs are also insured up to an amount of $250,000 per depositor per bank.

Certificates of deposit (CDs) are probably the most popular form of bank deposit. Also known as *time deposits*, short-term CDs are monies deposited with a bank for a specified period of time, usually anywhere from 3 to 12 months. The bank typically pays a fixed rate of interest for the term of the certificate, with rates increasing with the length of the term. If you redeem the CD and convert it to cash prior to its stated expiration or maturity date, a penalty is imposed by the bank in the form of a one-time fee or a lower overall interest rate.

If you have a substantial amount of money to invest (for example, a lump-sum distribution from a retirement plan), you may wish to purchase multiple CDs rather than investing in only one certificate. In addition, in order to obtain as much FDIC insurance as possible, you may wish to purchase each of these multiple CDs at a different bank. A viable investment strategy is to sequence, or *ladder*, the maturity dates of the multiple certificates to take advantage of interest-rate fluctuations. For example, if interest rates increase, dividing an investment into two 6-month certificates (rather than one 12-month certificate) may be prudent. As each 6-month certificate matures, you can then reinvest it at a higher interest rate without penalty.

Many people are unaware that banks also offer money market deposit accounts (MMDAs) in addition to standard savings accounts. An MMDA generally pays a higher rate of interest than a savings account, but it also requires a minimum deposit and account balance to avoid bank fees. Typically, six pre-authorized transfers are permitted from the account each month, up to three of which may be by personal check. Unlike a money market mutual fund, an MMDA is federally insured and for that reason may offer a slightly lower interest rate accrual than the money market fund.

Although many investors purchase Series EE bonds through payroll deduction plans at their places of employment, you can also obtain these bonds at banking institutions. Also known as *savings bonds*, Series EE bonds are cash investments that must be purchased at 50 percent of their face amount and that range in denomination from $50 to $10,000. The value of the bond is guaranteed to double after 20 years, after which time it may be extended for another 10 years at a fixed rate of interest. An advantage of a savings bond is that the interest earned is not taxable until maturity or when the investor redeems the bond, unless the investor elects to accrue the interest annually. As discussed in Chapter 15, when funding your child's college education, there is a special type of EE bond for which the interest is entirely income-tax-free if the bond's proceeds are used to pay qualified educational expenses, provided the parents' income does not exceed a certain annual amount.

Money Market Deposits

The term *money market* is used in the investment world to refer to the market in which short-term securities are borrowed and reloaned by financial institutions. The money market is contrasted to the *capital market*, which generally involves the trading of securities with longer-term maturities or no maturity date at all (like a stock). Banks and bank deposits are part of the money market, but the term is used here to refer to cash investments obtained through brokerage firms and mutual fund companies.

Most investors are familiar with money market mutual funds, if for no other reason than because they use such funds as emergency assets and as a conduit to park money before it is invested somewhere else. An investor who works with an investment advisor or financial planner to establish a separate, fee-based account of securities typically uses a money market mutual fund to "sweep" money from one investment to another.

Money market mutual funds are offered by mutual fund companies that invest in high-quality, short-term investments, such as T-bills, corporate commercial paper, bank repurchase agreements, and large CDs. The typical minimum investment in the fund is $1,000, and funds may be withdrawn at any time by telephone or if the investor has check-writing privileges on the account. Most funds also offer owners the ability to wire-transfer money from the fund to a separate bank account.

Although money market mutual funds lack FDIC insurance protection, they are safe, primarily due to the quality of the assets in which they are invested. You can also put your money into a tax-exempt money market fund that invests only in short-term municipal securities that are backed by the full faith and credit and taxing power of the municipality. This backing not only increases the potential safety of the fund, but may also increase your after-tax return, because interest from municipal securities is typically exempt from federal taxes (and may be exempt from state and city taxes as well, if you are a resident of the state and city that issued the security).

Another type of money market deposit that you may wish to consider as a separate cash investment is a Treasury bill. T-bills are sold on a discount-from-face-value basis, and the interest portion (the difference between the issue value and the face value) is exempt from state and local taxes. T-bills are offered by the US Treasury in denominations of $1,000 and have maturity dates of 4, 13, 26, and 52 weeks. Most investors find it easier to purchase T-bills through a local bank, but they can also be purchased online at www.treasurydirect.gov. The primary T-Bill market is an auction by mail.

T-Bills are important as a reference for the benchmark short-term interest rate from which all other short-term rates are established, including bank CDs. Because the US government stands behind the issuing of all Treasury securities, including the short-term Treasury bill, T-bills are often said to be default-risk free. As such, the investor assumes no credit risk when purchasing the obligation. This is not the case with other debt obligations, such as corporate bonds (or even bank CDs in excess of the FDIC limit). Thus, if you want to determine what short-term interest rate you will receive on your cash investment, start with the 13-week T-bill rate and add a half-percentage point or so for a credit risk premium.

Like any serious investor, you should invest in securities beyond what is included in the money market. However, in the wealth-accumulation process, you should make sure you always maintain some money (known in the investment world as a *position*) in a money market fund. As mentioned earlier, this is primarily to protect yourself in the event of a financial emergency, but it is also because you may be waiting on the sidelines until broader capital market conditions improve. Regardless, remember that the money market is for short-term cash investments, whereas the capital market is for longer-term security investments!

Bonds and When to Use Them

Unlike stocks, in which you own an *equity* interest in the company issuing the stock, bonds are *debt* obligations. In other words, when you purchase a bond from an issuer—usually a corporation or government—you are making a *loan* to the issuer in exchange for the right to receive semiannual or annual interest payments from that issuer. Given that interest payments from bonds are paid on a predictable schedule, you should time the purchase of bonds to coincide with when you are interested in receiving regular income payments to assist with your ongoing cash flow. Of course, concomitant to this stream of income is the expectation that you do not need back your original investment (the *principal* of the bond) or loan to the issuer until some known date in the future, otherwise referred to as the *maturity date* of the bond.

Generally speaking, the *longer* the time until the maturity date of the bond, the *higher* the interest or **coupon rate** of payment. This is because you are loaning your money to the issuer for a longer period of time and thus want a higher interest rate for doing so (known as a *maturity premium*). But be careful: the amount of interest you will earn depends on the interest rate payable by the bond, which is determined by a number of market-related factors, a measure of which is represented by something known as the *yield curve*. This curve is published regularly in financial newspapers such as the *Wall Street Journal* and tells you roughly how much more interest you are likely to receive the longer you commit your money to the issuer of the debt or bond. If this curve is relatively flat, you probably will not receive any investment reward for promising the issuer the use of your money for a longer period of time. As such, if the trend is a flat yield curve, do not invest in bond obligations with a maturity date of more than several years. Instead, reinvest your money in another bond issue when longer-term interest rates have increased—in other words, when the yield curve has turned normal or positive.

Corporate Bonds

Bonds are usually issued by a corporation or government. Corporations issue bonds in the form of a secured obligation, known as a *mortgage bond*, or an unsecured promise, known as a *debenture*. As an investor who may be concerned about not getting all of your original investment back at the bond's maturity date (referred to as the bond's *default risk*), you may want to limit your purchases only to mortgage bonds, because the corporation pledges property as collateral that may be sold in the event of the issuer's default. However, commensurate with the investment risk/investment return trade-off, the *yield* on the bond (essentially, the income rate of return) is *less* on a mortgage bond than on a debenture, because you are assuming less risk of possible default.

Corporations may issue bonds that are callable and convertible into stock. If the corporation issues a *callable* bond, that means it can pay off, or *call*, the obligation before its maturity date. Thus, you will get your money back sooner rather than later. However, this result is not as attractive as it may appear. The corporation has likely called the bond because market interest rates *declined*, meaning it is less expensive for the corporation to pay off the existing bond and issue another one at a lower interest, or coupon, rate of payment. As an investor, you are now confronted with reinvesting the bond proceeds at the current, lower interest rate. To protect investors who are relying on the security of a fixed payment from the bond, corporations usually issue bonds with a provision that they may not be called until a certain number of years have passed. Nevertheless, if you have to choose between a callable bond and one that is not, choose the noncallable bond.

A *convertible* bond, on the other hand, gives an investor both the certainty of semiannual income payments and the opportunity for significant capital gains if the bond is converted into the underlying stock of the issuer. Actually, a convertible bond provides the investor with two opportunities for capital gains: not only is there the opportunity for underlying stock price appreciation, but as the stock increases in value, so does the price of the bond. For example, assume that a bond convertible into 30 shares of ABC common stock is issued at $1,000; and, at the time of issuance, ABC common stock is trading for $25 per share. If the price of ABC stock increases to $35 per share, the convertible bond now sells for at least $1,300 ($1,000 plus the $300 of appreciation in the value of the stock shares).

The primary alternative to a convertible bond is a standard, or *plain vanilla*, bond, which is not convertible into the common stock of the issuer. A standard bond also may or may not be callable. Since 1998, Treasury bonds must be issued as noncallable, but this restriction does not apply to corporate bonds. However, given the fact that we are in a period of historically low interest rates, and interest rates generally have nowhere to go but up, the risk of a corporation actually calling a previously issued bond is low. Still, a noncallable and nonconvertible corporate bond carries the possibility of default.

How do you minimize the default risk associated with noncallable and nonconvertible standard corporate bonds? The primary way is to invest only in *investment-grade* bonds, which are bonds of the highest quality or next-to-highest quality, as rated by one of several bond-rating organizations—notably, Standard & Poor's or Moody's Investors Service. These rating services are not infallible, but they can give you guidance in differentiating an investment-grade bond from a non-investment-grade, or high-yield, bond. (By the way: a high-yield, or "junk," bond is not, by definition, a bad investment, although it does involve greater default risk than an investment-grade bond.) This is because the issuer of a high-yield bond has to offer the bond at a higher interest rate than an investment-grade bond, indicating that the issuer's financial stability is *weaker* than that of a normal corporation.

You can use Table 9-1 to help determine what is and is not an investment-grade bond, according to Standard & Poor's and Moody's. Generally, you should purchase only investment-grade bonds, because they have the lowest default risk as determined by the rating agencies.

Table 9-1. Bond Ratings

	Standard & Poor's	Moody's
Investment grade		
Highest quality	AAA–AA	Aaa–Aa
Next-to-highest quality	A–BBB	A–Baa
Non-investment-grade		
Speculative	BB–B	Ba–B
Default	CCC–D	Caa–C
Overall range	AAA–D	Aaa–C

Government Bonds

US Treasury notes and bonds are debt obligations of the federal government that are primarily distinguished by their maturity dates. A *Treasury note* is a medium-term debt security issued with a maturity date of two, three, five, seven, or ten years. The minimum denomination is $1,000, but notes may be issued up to a maximum of $1 million. A *Treasury bond*, on the other hand, is a longer-term debt security with a fixed maturity date of more than ten years. The Treasury discontinued issuance of the *long bond* (30-year maturity date) in October 2001 but, effective February 2006, resumed the auctioning of this bond as an additional method to finance the ever-expanding federal deficit. Interest from US Treasury notes and bonds is paid semiannually to the owner and is exempt from state and local taxes. As with US Treasury bills, if the US government issues a note or bond, you do not need to be concerned about default risk.

Several other forms of US Treasury securities are popular with conservative investors, but we discuss two here. The first is a form of zero-coupon bond known as a Treasury Separate Trading of Registered Interest and Principal of Securities (STRIPS). A *zero-coupon bond* is a bond for which the semiannual interest coupons are not attached but instead are omitted, or "stripped off." An interest payment is still made on this type of bond, but it is accrued as part of the bond principal and payable only at the maturity date. As a potential investor, you would have an obligation to pay federal taxes on the accrued interest, but you would not have any cash from the bond with which to pay them. So, where is a Treasury STRIPS (or any other form of zero-coupon bond, because corporations can also issue them) best positioned? In one of two places, and for one of two purposes:

- If it is a *taxable* STRIPS, position the bond in a tax-deferred account, such as a retirement plan.
- If it is a *tax-exempt* STRIPS, include the bond as a part of a college education savings program for a child under the age of 19.

In both cases, you know with absolute certainty when the STRIPS will mature, which is the primary attraction of any zero-coupon bond. Further, you also know with certainty how much the principal and accrued interest will amount to at maturity. As such, you can match the bond's maturity to the date you need the funds to meet your financial goals. This is the beauty of any zero-coupon bond, but particularly of the Treasury STRIPS, because, as an obligation of the US government, it also has *no default risk*.

The second—and an increasingly popular—form of US Treasury security (actually, a series of securities) are Treasury Inflation Protected Securities (TIPS). TIPS were first issued in 1997 and are now auctioned by the Treasury four times each year. They are sold in 5-, 10-, and 30-year maturities and in minimum $1,000 denominations. As the name indicates, they are designed to offer protection against the effects of inflation. The principal is adjusted semiannually to keep pace with inflation, as measured by the Consumer Price Index (CPI) over the previous six-month period, but the interest rate remains fixed. At the maturity date, you receive the *greater* of the inflation-adjusted principal value of the security or its face value at the time of issue.

Simply stated, if you invest in TIPS, you are taxed annually on the interest payment plus the appreciation in the face value of the security after it's adjusted for inflation. However, you do not receive the inflation-adjusted principal until the security is sold or matures (more than likely the latter, because you should look at TIPS as a longer-term investment). To avoid this investment vehicle's potentially adverse tax consequences, it is best to hold TIPS in a tax-deferred account, such as a retirement plan or a Roth IRA.

Municipal Bonds

State and local governments typically issue bonds to finance long-term projects, such as road improvement or other infrastructure needs. Such bonds come in two types: general obligation bonds and revenue bonds, although a third type of hybrid bond—a private purpose bond—is increasingly being used to finance football stadiums and the like. General obligation and revenue bonds are issued by public municipalities, whereas private purpose bonds may be shared with a private developer or sports promoter. In addition, general obligation bonds are backed by the taxing authority of the municipality and as such are safer than revenue bonds, which must depend on the revenue from a specific project to pay the bondholders. As a result of their relative safety, general obligation bonds feature a lower interest rate than revenue bonds.

Historically, municipal bonds have been most attractive to high-income taxpayers because their semiannual interest payments are generally free from federal income tax and may also be free from state and local taxes in some circumstances. You can easily compute what your after-tax return from a municipal bond will be if you know your **marginal income-tax bracket** and the coupon rate or nominal yield of the municipal bond. Once you have computed your after-tax return, you should then compare this return to the return you would receive on a taxable obligation, such as a corporate bond, to determine the higher-paying investment.

For example, assume you are trying to decide whether to purchase a municipal bond (only federal-income-tax free) featuring a tax-exempt yield of 5 percent or a corporate bond yielding 7 percent. Also assume you are currently paying taxes in the highest marginal federal income-tax bracket of 37 percent. To compute your after-tax return on the municipal bond, use the following formula:

$$\text{tax-equivalent yield} = \frac{\text{Tax-exempt yield}}{(1-\text{marginal tax rate})}$$

In this example, your tax-equivalent yield on the municipal bond is 7.93 percent: 0.05 divided by (1 − 0.37). This compares to the corporate bond yield of 7 percent, so you should likely invest in the municipal bond. It also means you probably should not purchase the corporate bond until its yield-to-maturity exceeds 7.93 percent.

It is also possible to invest in a municipal bond or tax-exempt mutual fund, usually as part of a money market mutual fund. However, if you do so, you lose control over the time at which you have to recognize capital gains from the sale of bonds. This is a distinct disadvantage of investing in bonds via a bond mutual fund.

Bonds as a Part of Your Portfolio

It is a common misconception that as people age, they become more financially conservative, meaning that safety of principal and reliable income from that principal are paramount. Savvy investors—even retirees—know that protection of purchasing power and achieving an after-tax return in excess of inflation (a so-called *real return*) are just as important as safety of principal and preserving the value of the original investment. As mentioned when we discussed asset allocation in Chapter 3, an argument can be made for the inclusion of stocks and stock mutual funds in any retiree's portfolio. However, bonds also play an important diversification role.

Certainly, a primary relationship that you must understand before investing in an individual bond is that bond prices move in the opposite direction of market interest rates. Hence, if you believe that interest rates will probably decline in the future, you should have a position in bonds, because sizable capital gains are likely. This was proven in the bear market of late 2007 to mid-2009, when bond returns significantly exceeded that of stocks as interest rates declined at the same time. Moreover, if interest rates are likely to decline, you should also buy long-term bonds, because they will appreciate more in price than shorter-term issues.

Beyond that, as the stock market exhibits volatility—seemingly random price movements up and down—bonds compete with stocks for investors' money. If the stock market *declines* in price, investors seek a positive return and, more important, safety—and next to cash, there is no safer investment than a US Treasury security bill, note, or bond. Conversely, if the stock market *increases* in value consistently over time, investors prefer the higher returns of stocks, even though stocks carry more investment risk. Nevertheless, no matter your age, you should probably include some bonds or bond funds in your portfolio, because no one, including esteemed security analysts with many years of experience, can predict with absolute certainty whether the stock market is going to be up or down on any given day.

As you explore your bond investment choices, you will probably need to decide between an investment in individual bonds and bond mutual funds, but be aware that they exhibit different characteristics. With an individual bond, if you hold the bond to maturity, you almost always get back your original amount invested plus interest. However, with a bond mutual fund, your total rate of return is uncertain, because the value of that fund constantly fluctuates.

Stocks and When to Use Them

Stocks represent an ownership or *equity* interest in a corporation. As a shareholder, you realize a return from a corporation's earnings after it has paid all its creditors, including its bondholders. This return can come from a declaration of *dividends* each year by the corporation's board of directors, from *capital appreciation* of the shares once the earnings are reinvested back into the corporation, or from both. Dividends are taxable to you, the shareholder, if they are declared for any given year and you receive them. Capital appreciation, on the other hand, is not taxable until you sell shares—and even then it is likely taxable at favorable rates if you have owned the shares for more than one year from the date you bought them.

There are two forms of stock: common and preferred. The most widely held is *common stock*, which may or may not provide dividends, depending on whether a dividend is declared for that year by the corporation's board. Common stocks are highly *marketable*, because they can generally be bought and sold easily on publicly traded exchanges, such as the New York Stock Exchange. However, they are not very *liquid*, because the investor may or may not receive back their original investment. In fact, the value of common stocks may change significantly during the course of a single trading day. As a result, common stock can carry a significant amount of *market risk*—risk that can be minimized but not entirely eliminated by proper asset allocation and portfolio diversification.

A major advantage of owning common stocks rather than bonds is the right to vote with respect to significant company matters, such as the election of the company's board of directors. However, shareholders who do not own enough shares to be in a controlling position (more than 50 percent of the total outstanding shares) must join together as a block to influence the course of future action by the corporation. Even then, if the majority or the controlling shareholders think differently, it is unlikely that the minority shareholders' views will be considered.

Most individuals, particularly younger investors, do not purchase common stock for its income potential, but rather for its possibility of significant capital appreciation. In contrast, most investors purchase *preferred stock* for much the same reason that they purchase individual bonds: to generate income. The term *preferred* in *preferred stock* means that if a dividend is declared by the corporation's board of directors, shareholders of preferred stock are first in line before any payment is made to the common shareholders. The preferred shareholder also receives payment before the common shareholder in the event of the corporation's liquidation.

Publicly traded stocks may be thought of in various ways, but most frequently they are categorized in terms of their market behavior, the sector or industry in which they are situated, and the size of the issuing company. Examples of categorizing stocks on the basis of their market behavior include the following:

- *Income stocks:* These types of stocks consistently pay high dividends to the investor.
- *Growth stocks:* These stocks exhibit considerable capital appreciation.
- *Value stocks:* These stocks are perceived as currently undervalued in terms of price compared to their marketplace peers.
- *Defensive stocks:* These stocks do not decline as much in a bear market as other stocks.
- *Cyclical stocks:* These stocks are sensitive to current economic and market conditions.
- *Blue-chip stocks:* These are stocks of the largest and oldest companies, including many of those on the Dow Jones Industrial Average—the most frequently quoted index of market activity.

The Standard & Poor's rating service divides stocks into 11 market sectors and into many more industries within those sectors. In general, however, technology, health care, and financials tend to be the fastest-growing market sectors, whereas consumer staples and utilities tend to be more stable. Some other sectors, such as the consumer discretionary sector, tend to be cyclical in nature.

The *size* of the company issuing the stocks is referred to as its *market capitalization*, which is computed as the price per share of a company multiplied by the number of common shares it has outstanding. The *higher* the price per share and the *more* the number of outstanding shares, the *greater* is the market capitalization of the company issuing the stock. With reference to this measurement, stocks are generally classified as follows:

- *Large capitalization (large-cap):* The stocks of companies with market capitalizations of more than $5 billion
- *Medium capitalization (mid-cap):* The stocks of companies with market capitalizations of between $1 billion and $5 billion
- *Small capitalization (small-cap):* The stocks of companies with market capitalizations of less than $1 billion

There are many ways to value whether you should buy an individual stock, but the most common is a relative valuation technique known as a *price-to-earnings (P/E) ratio*. This estimation of value relies on the premise that the stock's value bears some relationship to the earnings per share generated by the issuing company or corporation. This premise is supported by remembering that the rate of return to the investor, whether in the form of dividends or capital appreciation, derives from the corporation's residual earnings after all other creditors have been paid.

For example, assume that ABC stock is trading on the stock exchange for $40 per share. It is perceived by many investors as a value stock. ABC's earnings over the next 12-month period are estimated to be $2.50 per share, and you have determined that the relevant P/E ratio for the stock is 20. Therefore, using the P/E ratio approach, ABC stock should be trading for $50 per share ($2.50 times 20) in 12 months. Because it is currently selling for only $40 per share, ABC is *undervalued*, and, if you are a value investor, you should *buy* the stock at your earliest opportunity.

Stocks as a Part of Your Portfolio

Since 1926, the average large stock has generated a compounded annual rate of return of slightly more than 12 percent. Inflation has averaged 3 percent, so that is a 9 percent real, before-tax rate of return, which is a pretty good track record, notwithstanding the gloomy results of the stock market in recent years! However, if you were to look at a risk pyramid, you would find individual common stocks near the top. That means a great deal of volatility or market risk is associated with the investment—certainly more so than with investment-grade bonds. If you are going to include an individual stock in your portfolio, then, you need to research the stock carefully before you purchase it (either that, or let your financial advisor do it). Fortunately, you can use various print services, such as *Value Line,* and online reference sources before making a potential purchase.

If you decide you want to include individual stocks as a part of your portfolio, the types of stocks you select depends on your style of or orientation to investing. For example, if you are primarily a *growth* investor, you will probably select stocks with above-average earnings potential. If you are primarily a *value* investor, you will prize a stock that is undervalued in relation to its industry or sector peers. To be properly diversified, your portfolio should consist of approximately 25 stocks spread across five or six market sectors. Particularly with stocks, you should be a long-term, or *buy-and-hold*, investor. Although you may be able to make a killing in a short period of time from purchasing a hot stock, usually stocks increase in price only over long periods of time. Buy-and-hold should not be a problematic investment strategy for you if you did sufficient research before you bought the stock and you believe in the financial prospects of the company issuing it.

Mutual Funds and When to Use Them

The proper name for a mutual fund is an *open-end investment company*, meaning the fund or company does not have a fixed number of shares to issue. Instead, the number of outstanding shares varies as investors purchase and redeem their shares. The value of a share in a mutual fund is determined by its net asset value (NAV), which is computed by dividing the value of the fund's total net assets by the number of shares outstanding. As a general practice, the NAV is computed at the *end* of each market trading day and is the price at which you must buy and sell shares.

A mutual fund is a type of *professionally managed asset*. Practically, this means you deposit a sum of money with the fund along with thousands (or millions) of other investors. In turn, the fund's professional money manager buys stocks, bonds, or other securities with that money. In this way, mutual funds are for the small investor, because they allow the "little guy" to purchase a percentage ownership in securities that they may not otherwise be able to afford. Mutual funds also allow investors to achieve instant portfolio diversification, because they now own a small piece of many stocks or bonds across many market sectors or industries. As a final bonus, investors do not have to keep track of all their holdings in the fund or the cost basis of purchasing the shares, because the fund company usually assumes these responsibilities.

There are thousands of mutual funds, including money market funds; but practically, they can be segregated into stock funds and bond funds or a combination of both stocks and bonds, known as a *balanced fund*. You can also purchase funds that invest only in foreign stocks or bonds, called *international funds*, or those that invest in foreign and US stocks or bonds, called *global funds*.

There are three basic types of *stock* mutual funds:

- *Growth fund:* This fund invests primarily in stocks that offer potentially significant capital appreciation. A subcategory of this type of fund is an aggressive growth fund, which invests in stocks of considerable risk and offers the possibility for maximum capital appreciation.

- *Income fund:* An income fund invests primarily in stocks that pay higher-than-average dividends, such as utility stocks. The name can also be used to describe a fund that invests a high percentage of assets in bonds.

- *Growth-and-income fund:* There are many names for this type of fund, including *equity income* and *total return fund*. Operationally, a growth-and-income fund invests in stocks that aim to achieve both long-term capital appreciation and current income. It is here that you find a concentration of value stocks that are of primary interest to the value style of investor.

There are also three basic types of *bond* mutual funds:

- *Corporate bond fund:* This fund invests in either short-term bonds (generally not more than a five-year maturity date) or longer-term bonds or both, as issued by corporations. Usually these bonds are investment-grade, but not always. A clue that the bond fund is investing in non-investment-grade bonds is if the name of the fund includes the phrase *high-yield*. Historically, that type of fund has been referred to as a *junk-bond fund*, although the term *junk* is likely a bit extreme, because you can find good investments among the fund's holdings.

- *US government bond fund:* This fund invests in US Treasury securities, typically Treasury notes or bonds. As mentioned, the securities in the fund are free of default risk, which is a major safety advantage but also an attribute that results in a lower yield than that of corporate funds.

- *Municipal bond fund:* This is also known as a *tax-exempt fund*, because it invests primarily in bonds issued by cities and states. Dividends paid by municipal funds are free from federal taxes; and if the purchaser is a resident of the state or city that issues the bond, the dividends are typically free of state and local taxes.

There are many mutual funds and many mutual fund companies. In fact, mutual funds and professionally managed assets are among the subjects of a previous book that I authored, *The Handbook of Professionally Managed Assets* (Apress, 2013). However, if you are looking for large and well-known mutual fund companies that offer a wide variety of mutual funds (or *families of mutual funds*), the two largest companies are Vanguard Investments of Valley Forge, Pennsylvania, and Fidelity Investments of Boston, Massachusetts.

Index Funds

An *index fund* is a mutual fund that attempts to replicate the performance of a particular market index, such as the Standard & Poor's index of 500 stocks. As such, the fund implements what is known as a *passive management* investment style: the fund manager has no actual intent to attempt to exceed the return of a specified market index. Additionally, index funds are fairly income-tax efficient, given that little selling of securities occurs within the fund, the tax consequences of which are passed along to the investor in the form of capital gains distributions.

In contrast to an index fund, most stock and bond mutual funds are *actively managed*. As such, there is an effort on the part of the mutual fund's money manager to outperform the market or some appropriate market index on a risk-adjusted basis. However, academic studies have shown that, on average, approximately 95 percent of all mutual fund money managers *fail* to outperform the Standard & Poor's index of 500 stocks on a long-term basis. This means that as a potential investor, you should seek out mutual funds with relatively low expenses that have achieved above-average market performance over at least ten years. Fortunately, this is not too difficult, given the thousands of mutual funds available in the marketplace.

Exchange Traded Funds

In recent years, a variation of the mutual fund investment has been introduced to the financial markets. Called *exchange-traded funds (ETFs)*, these funds occupy a relatively small part of the investment marketplace. Nevertheless, they are growing in popularity, particularly among tax-savvy investors.

What are ETFs? Essentially, they are index funds that trade like stocks. Instead of being priced at net asset value at the end of the day, like traditional mutual funds, ETFs trade throughout the day based on market supply and demand. This can be important in a volatile market. Most ETFs are designed to match the performances of various market benchmarks, such as the Standard & Poor's index of 500 stocks, and have interesting nicknames such as SPDRs, Diamonds, Qubes, and iShares. Other ETFs try to match the performance of a market sector, such as technology, energy, or finance. Still others are engaged in the trading of international securities or currencies.

You should be interested in ETFs as possible wealth-accumulation vehicles for two primary reasons:

- Because they act like index mutual funds, ETFs are passively managed, and therefore the expenses of operating the funds are low—sometimes even lower than they would be for an index mutual fund.

- ETFs trade equivalent securities, or what are known as *in-kind trades*. According to the IRS, this exchange of essentially similar securities does not constitute a taxable event, and thus no capital gains or losses are incurred. Thus, ETFs are income-tax efficient. Alternatively, a traditional mutual fund must trade its securities in the open market, with the investor paying taxes on those gains.

Mutual Funds as a Part of Your Portfolio

Many small investors begin and end their portfolio construction with mutual funds. They also work with an investment advisor or financial planner to position these funds in an advisory services account. If you are not inclined to work with an investment advisor or financial planner but wish to invest in mutual funds (or have to invest in such funds as part of a self-directed retirement account, such as a 401(k) plan), consider the following:

- Try to invest in no-load or low-load funds. These are funds that do not assess a sales charge for purchase. Note, however, that most advisory accounts waive the sales charge if the fund is held within the account.

- Try to invest in funds with low maintenance expenses in relation to their peers. There is no rule of thumb here except that the lower the annual expenses to operate the fund, the better. An alternative is to invest in all index funds, but you lose the potential for excess market performance that an excellent mutual fund money manager may generate.

- Try to invest in funds with a relatively low turnover of assets. Investing in a fund that does not constantly sell and buy securities is an effective tax-management technique, which, as you will see in Chapter 12, is a key component to defending the wealth you accumulate.

- Make sure the fund is investing in securities consistent with its investment objective. For example, if the fund states that it is a growth-stock fund, it should *not* be investing in short-term bonds.

- Understand how much investment risk you are willing to assume, and match your risk profile to the investment objective of the fund. This is critical in mutual-fund investing. If you are most covetous of income (generally, characteristic of a conservative risk profile), many stock funds are not for you. Alternatively, an aggressive growth risk profile usually means that investing in a US government bond fund is not the most appropriate use of your money.

In summary, you may wish to invest in a combination of actively managed mutual funds and passively managed index funds or ETFs. Many investors who have adopted this strategy are wealthier for it.

International Investing

It has frequently been said in recent years that we are becoming a globalized economy. What happens financially in one country—particularly in emerging growth economies, such as China and India—almost instantaneously impacts the economy of the United States as well. Fortunately, a globalized economy presents investment opportunities beyond purchasing only domestic stocks, bonds, or mutual funds. Unfortunately, however, international investing carries additional risk.

Currency or *exchange-rate risk* originates in the uncertainty associated with the value of foreign currencies in relation to the US dollar. For example, let's say you invest in a stock of a UK company, and you pay for it in the currency of the UK pound. Even if the share value of this stock appreciates, you may still lose money if the pound depreciates relative to the US dollar. Conversely, you may reap a double benefit, including the appreciation of the UK stock, if the pound appreciates with respect to the US dollar.

How is currency or exchange-rate risk effectively minimized? This question leads us to the investment strategy of purchasing foreign stocks by using a financial instrument known as an *American Depository Receipt (ADR)*. An ADR is a receipt issued by a US bank on foreign securities purchased by the bank through a foreign representative and held in trust for the benefit of the ADR owner. These receipts are listed on most US stock exchanges, including the New York Stock Exchange, and represent an alternative to direct foreign investment in a stock. The ADR is denominated in US dollars, meaning you have to worry less about the relationship of the foreign currency to its American counterpart.

Another way of investing internationally is to purchase shares of an international or global mutual fund. An *international* mutual fund invests in securities, either stocks or bonds or both, of companies that are located and do business *outside* the United States. Alternatively, a *global* mutual fund (also known as a *world fund*) invests in securities of international companies *and* those of US companies. There are also region-specific funds, notably in the Pacific Rim countries, such as Japan, South Korea, Singapore, and Indonesia.

You should consider international investing as another way to diversify your portfolio. In recent years, international and global investing have generated returns considerably in excess of those in the US market; and, depending on future political events in foreign countries, global investments are likely to continue to outperform domestic funds. This is particularly the case if the relevant country's currency strengthens in relation to the US dollar.

Now let's move on to the other major category of investments and wealth accumulation: investing your money in *real assets* or in real property, as discussed in the next chapter. After that, we contrast financial and real assets to use assets, with the major use asset being your home or personal residence. Historically, many people have considered their home as their one primary investment. In Chapter 11, we show why that is not how you should think of your personal residence in the PADD process, because a home, at least for most people, has *not* been proven to be an excellent long-term investment.

CHAPTER 10

Investing in Real Assets

Most individuals own real estate; in fact, approximately 64 percent of Americans own their own home as of the year 2017. Moreover, according to Wallet Hacks, an online-only management web site, in 2017, approximately 60 percent of the typical American's net worth consisted of the equity in their home. *Home equity* is defined here as the fair market value of a home less any associated liability. Therefore, it remains true that home ownership is an integral part of both the American Dream and the wealth-accumulation process.

For most people, owning a home is not an investment in the same sense that owning stocks and bonds or rental real estate is an investment. Rather, your home or primary residence should be thought of as a *use asset* and should be listed as such on the statement of personal financial position. This is to be contrasted with *direct investments* in real estate, such as the ownership of a rental home, a vacation home, or even raw land, and *indirect* investments in real estate, such as a share of a real estate limited partnership (RELP) or a real estate investment trust (REIT).

Direct Investments in Real Estate

Direct investments in real estate are made primarily by wealthy individuals who understand the real estate selection process and are comfortable with riskier assets. Many direct investments in real estate are also made for purposes of improving an individual's cash flow (income) and not only for purposes of enjoying the capital appreciation of an asset (growth).

© Keith R. Fevurly 2018
K. R. Fevurly, *Plan Your Financial Future*, https://doi.org/10.1007/978-1-4842-3637-6_10

Vacation Homes

According to *American Demographics* magazine, approximately 70 percent of Americans view the purchase of a vacation home as the number-one indication that an individual has accumulated wealth. Further, partly as a reflection of this fact, some 60 percent of Americans anecdotally say they would like to own a vacation home. Although this is a common financial goal, it is not of tantamount importance for many people, because buying a vacation home is beyond their financial means. However, if you are interested in purchasing a vacation home, you should take three major factors into consideration:

- The location of the home
- The financing costs associated with buying and maintaining the property
- How long you plan to own the home, including how you may wish to ultimately divest yourself of ownership

A standard rule in any purchase of real estate applies when buying a vacation home: the most important factor is location, location, location! As of 2013, according to the Market Watch web site, with the exception of Orlando, Florida (Disney World), all of the top-ten preferred locations for buying a second home were near the ocean or in the mountains. They were also close to or part of a major city. You can bet that those locations demand premium prices and are probably suffering from a paucity of attractive vacation properties.

As such, you may wish to take a different approach. Look for areas that more than one print publication or web site describe as "up-and-coming." For example, in recent years, properties along both coasts of Mexico have become more attractive to retiring and vacationing Americans. The same can be said of Costa Rica. If you concentrate on areas that are not yet well-known to the wealthy and those who are aspiring to be wealthy, you are less likely to buy at the top of the market and can thus anticipate that your second home will enjoy future appreciation that may not be possible in more established locations.

Financing a second home, particularly if you do not have much equity in your first home or primary residence, is always an issue. Most lenders expect you to put down at least 20 percent of the second home's fair market value before closing. Renting out the home is a good way to recover some of this down payment, but if you do so, charge a rent that is approximately 10 to 20 percent higher than your mortgage payment to take care of maintenance expenses. You will also likely need to hire a property manager, particularly if the second home is some distance from your primary residence or in another country. If you can avoid it, try not to tap into the equity of your first home to make the down payment on the second. If the property value of your first home declines, it will be all the more difficult to recover the lost equity. It will also present a cash-flow challenge if you used an interest-only adjustable-rate mortgage (ARM) to finance the first home.

Do not expect your vacation home to pay for itself immediately. Over the long term, a vacation home can be self-sustaining (particularly if you are renting it out when you are not there), but only if you exercise careful financial planning. As with most real assets, the longer you own the vacation home, the greater the chances of its significant capital appreciation. Ultimately, you must determine whether you wish to pass your vacation home on to family members now or at your death, or whether you wish to sell it and realize a (hopefully) sizable percentage return. As you will see in Chapter 19, the value of a highly appreciated vacation home may be a significant estate-planning issue, although a competent estate or financial planner can assist you in removing or reducing the value of the home from your taxable estate.

Rental Homes

Most individuals become landlords in one of two ways: as a result of a conscious decision to buy homes and rent them to others, or because their primary residence does not sell in the time frame they anticipate and they convert the residence to a rental property. The obvious practical disadvantage of becoming a landlord is that, unless you hire a property manager, you have to deal with tenants. However, there *are* tax advantages associated with rental homes. Notably, as a landlord, you can depreciate the home and, at least to a limited extent, take an annual operating loss if your annual adjusted gross income is not deemed to be too high.

Under current tax law, a rental activity is treated as a *passive activity*, or one that involves the conduct of any trade or business in which the taxpayer does not materially participate. But there is a lesser standard of participation—*active participation*—that many individuals can easily meet with respect to their rental real-estate activities. An individual meets the active-participation standard if they participate in making management decisions with respect to the rental property or arrange for others (for example, a property manager) to provide rental property services. If this lesser standard is met, you can deduct up to $25,000 of losses annually from your rental real-estate activities, *provided* your adjusted gross income (AGI) for that year does not exceed $100,000. If you pass this threshold, the $25,000 maximum is then reduced by 50 percent of the amount by which your AGI exceeds $100,000. Once you reach $150,000 of AGI, no loss deduction is permitted at all.

For example, assume that you own an apartment building that is managed by an on-site property manager. You meet frequently with the property manager and make all decisions with respect to improving the property. As such, you actively participate for purposes of the rental real-estate loss deduction.

Further, assume that your AGI for the year 2018 is $110,000, and the building generates $26,000 in losses during that year. You are allowed to deduct only $20,000 of these losses on your 2018 income-tax return, because the maximum deduction is $25,000, and the maximum deduction is reduced by $5,000 (the portion of $110,000 in excess of $100,000—or $10,000—times 0.50 equals $5,000).

As you will learn when we discuss the primary residence as a use asset in Chapter 11, generally you are *never* allowed to take an income-tax loss when selling that residence (your home). However, a favorable exclusion-of-gain provision in the tax code applies to the sale of a personal residence previously converted into rental property. The sale of a rental home is taxed in accordance with the normal capital-gain and -loss rules (remember, you have turned your home into an investment), but there is the additional tax benefit of the up-to-$25,000 annual loss provision, if you qualify. This may even be enough reward to compensate you for the daily hassles of putting up with tenants!

Commercial Real Estate

Typically, given the investment risk, only experienced investors purchase commercial real estate. Accordingly, you may wish to avoid this investment opportunity entirely. However, if you do wish to invest in commercial properties, you will probably do so for one of two reasons: to receive annual income or to hold such properties for capital appreciation before eventual sale.

Most investors who participate in the commercial real-estate market do so to generate income, because a primary reason to invest in raw land is capital appreciation. If you are after income from a commercial property, you first need to determine how much to pay for it. For that, fortunately, you can use a relatively easy computation known as the *net operating income* (NOI) formula. The formula for NOI is as follows (if you hire an appraiser to help you with the investment decision, the appraiser will likely compute the NOI for you):

       Gross rental receipts from the property

+   Nonrental or other additional income from the property

=   Potential gross income

−   Vacancy and collection of receipts losses

=   Effective gross income

−   Operating expenses (excluding interest and depreciation)

=   Net operating income (NOI)

Because NOI is a cash-flow computation from the commercial property, any charges you have incurred to finance the purchase of the property (such as interest on a loan) and tax-related charges (such as depreciation) do *not* enter into the computation.

Once you or your appraiser have computed the commercial property's NOI, you need to divide that by a prevailing **capitalization rate** (cap rate) to determine how much you should pay for the property. This cap rate is not easy to determine, but think of it as the rate of annual compounded return you would like to receive from the property. It is also the reciprocal of the number of years it will take for the property to pay for itself. For example, a standard cap rate is 12 percent, meaning you want your original investment back in slightly more than 8 years (100 divided by 12 = 8.33 years). Similarly, to achieve a 20 percent return from the property, you want your original purchase price back in 5 years (100 divided by 20 = 5). Of course, keep in mind that in this latter case, you are being more aggressive, so factor in a higher risk for your initial investment with a 20 percent cap rate than with a 12 percent cap rate.

Raw or Unimproved Land

Mark Twain is famous for saying, "Buy land; they're not making it anymore." This is true, but it does not provide a great deal of guidance if you are an investor trying to decide *where* to buy land. The most valuable land or unimproved real estate is probably land that is adjacent to already-developed or soon-to-be-developed residential or commercial property. It is likely that, before long, the adjacent property will also be developed, given that its "highest and best use" is no longer as farmland, grassland, or other land lying fallow. As a result, you will probably enjoy significant capital appreciation from this land when you subsequently sell it.

Keep in mind, though, that certain significant investment risks are associated with the purchase of any undeveloped land. Among these risks are the following:

- The land may be adversely rezoned. For example, property bought for residential development purposes may be rezoned by the city or county for commercial purposes.

- You may not be able to obtain permits from the county, city, or township to build on the land in the manner that you (or the developer) intend.

- Access to your land may be restricted by an adjacent landowner's property or property rights.

- The population growth that you anticipate in the area may not occur.

As a result, many investments in undeveloped land are extremely risky. If you have borrowed money to buy the land (known as *leveraging* your investment), you must find a way to service the debt from income or assets other than your original purchase. Otherwise, you will be forced into a position to sell the land well before you otherwise intended.

Indirect Investments in Real Estate

There are two basic ways to indirectly invest in real estate: as a limited partner owning an interest in a real estate limited partnership (RELP) or as a shareholder in a real estate investment trust (REIT). Let's look at the REIT first, because it is generally the more marketable of the two investments.

Real Estate Investment Trusts

A REIT is like a mutual fund, except that its shares are not always valued at net asset value (NAV). Instead, they are traded at a premium or discount to NAV on a publicly traded exchange. In most cases, the REIT invests in income-producing real-estate properties, such as apartment buildings, shopping centers, office parks, hotels, and, increasingly, retirement communities. Some REITs, known as *mortgage REITs*, also invest in the financing of real-estate properties.

The REIT entity is not subject to federal income tax as long as it distributes at least 90 percent of its annual income to shareholders each year. As a result, many REITs distribute 100 percent of their annual income to shareholders. Taxes are then paid by the shareholders on dividends received (like stocks or stock mutual funds) and any passed-through capital gains. Under previous tax law, REIT dividends were generally not treated as *qualified dividends*, meaning they were *not* eligible for preferential long-term capital gains treatment. Thus, such dividends were potentially taxable at the previous maximum marginal rate of 39.6 percent. However, under the 2017 TCJA, the effective tax rate on such dividends for an individual investor eligible for the 20 percent "pass-through deduction" is reduced to 29.6 percent (the new 37 percent maximum marginal tax rate times 80 percent). As a result, the attractiveness of receiving a REIT dividend should increase for many taxpayers.

There is a relatively low **correlation** between the price movement of REIT shares and that of a typical stock or stock mutual fund. A primary advantage to you, as a potential investor, then, is the opportunity to further diversify your portfolio with the purchase of a REIT. Other advantages of REITs include the following:

- Relatively stable dividend income
- High dividend yields
- The possibility of significant capital appreciation

Plan Your Financial Future

- Liquidity
- Access to professional management of the property

The long-term total return (defined as dividend income plus capital appreciation of the underlying real-estate investment) of a REIT is likely *less than* a high-performing, higher-risk growth stock, but *more than* the return of a lower-risk investment-grade bond.

Before you invest in a REIT vs., for example, a mutual fund, you must first decide that you want to invest in real-estate properties. Then you must decide in what manner you wish to invest in those properties—directly or indirectly. If you decide that you want to invest indirectly in the form of a REIT, you must decide whether you wish to invest in a publicly traded or non-publicly-traded REIT.

Finally, in what type of REIT should you invest? There are three types:

- *Equity REIT:* Generally acquires income-producing real properties
- *Mortgage REIT:* Makes construction loans and otherwise invests in the financing of real-estate ventures
- *Hybrid REIT:* Both owns properties and makes financing loans

As a general rule, a mortgage REIT is a bit *riskier* than an equity REIT, because the mortgage REIT does not have established properties from which to generate an income stream to the investor. However, your ultimate rate of return from a mortgage REIT may be *greater than* that from an equity REIT.

Real Estate Limited Partnerships

If you want a high-risk, income-generating, real-estate investment with the possibility of a high return, purchasing an interest in a RELP may be for you. A RELP is most commonly structured as a real-estate syndication with one or more general partners or real-estate developers and other investors as limited partners. The limited partners have no say in the management or control of the real property investments or in when the underlying properties may be sold.

Unlike a REIT, a RELP is permitted to pass on losses to its limited partner investors. However, because of a series of income-tax rules known as the *passive activity rules*, it is doubtful that you, as a limited partner investor, can claim this loss on your annual income-tax return. Typically, you cannot claim this loss until the general partner or syndicator sells the partnership property that has generated the loss—and be aware that, as a limited partner, you cannot legally force them to do so.

A RELP usually is *not* a publicly traded entity, so cashing in your interest at something close to what you paid for it is difficult, if not impossible. Some RELPs are organized and publicly traded in the form of **master limited partnerships** (MLPs), but the trading is thin, and tax rules generally restrict the claiming of any losses on your income-tax return. Thus, an interest held in a RELP is generally both illiquid and relatively unmarketable.

So why invest in a RELP? You would do so almost always because you want income and believe in the ability of the syndicator to develop and sell the underlying real properties for a significant profit. In addition, you are able to invest in commercial and residential real-estate properties for a relatively small amount and are limited in your potential liability as a creditor only to the extent of your investment.

The Use of Leverage in Real-Estate Investing

The financial concept of *leveraging* is the use of borrowed money to increase your profit on a real-estate investment. The concept may also be used with financial assets, most notably through the use of *margin* (borrowing money from your broker to purchase more stock), but one of the oft-cited advantages of real assets is the ability to employ leverage effectively.

For example, assume that you have directly invested $100,000 in a residential real-estate property. Further, assume that this real estate is in a good location and appreciates at a rate of 10 percent annually. At the end of year one, your investment has grown to $110,000, and at the end of year two, the property is worth $121,000. You have earned a $21,000 profit in the property. Now let's assume that you have put down $100,000 on a $500,000 tract of residential real property and have borrowed the remaining $400,000 from a bank at a low interest rate. Again, the property appreciates at the rate of 10 percent annually. Now, however, at the end of year one, your investment has grown to $550,000, and at the end of year two, the property is worth $605,000. Thus you have increased your dollar profit from $21,000 to $84,000 ($105,000 less $21,000). That is *four times* your original profit, or a total percentage return of *400 percent* before figuring in the dollars and percentage rate you have to pay to the bank for borrowing the money.

How do you put the concept of leveraging into practice as a real-estate investor? You do this by putting the minimum down on real property that has a strong likelihood of *appreciating* in future years. Generally, on any real-estate purchase other than primary home purchases, the bank will ask you to put down at least 20 percent on the initial investment. If you can find a bank that will let you put down less, and you are relatively sure that the property you are interested in will go up in value, you should be able to understand the benefits of using someone else's money to accumulate wealth. That is leverage!

However, be aware that leveraging also compounds your dollar *loss* if the property goes *down* in value. Using the previous two examples, if leverage is not used, you end up with a $19,000 loss after two years. Because you are dealing with residential rental property, you may or may not be able to claim all of that loss on your tax return, depending on your AGI at the end of year two. If you used leverage, on the other hand, your loss is $95,000, a difference of $76,000 ($95,000 less $19,000). Regardless of your AGI, you *definitely* cannot take all of that loss for income-tax purposes, because you are limited to no more than $25,000 in any given year. In addition, you still have to pay the bank for any interest incurred on the loan during the two years.

In summary, if you are going to employ leverage, stay away from purchasing questionable properties in less-than-desirable areas! As mentioned in Chapter 1, there is both *good* debt and *bad* debt. Bad debt is any debt incurred on property that is likely to *depreciate* in value over the anticipated time frame of the investment. The misuse of leveraging proves the truth of that statement many times over.

Correlation

In the financial world, *correlation* measures the direction and extent of a relationship between two investment assets. However, you can also use this concept to diversify your portfolio and accumulate wealth.

How does correlation work? A correlation of +1.0 means two assets move exactly *together* in one direction, whereas a correlation of –1.0 means the two assets move in the exact *opposite* direction of each other— when one goes up, the other goes down. Meanwhile, a correlation of 0.0 means there is *no* relationship whatsoever between the two assets— they move independently of each other.

The following list shows the correlations of various financial asset classes and real estate to the Standard & Poor's index of 500 stocks for the time period extending from 1965 through 2012, a duration that encompasses numerous market cycles:

- Large-cap US stocks: 0.96
- Developed international stocks: 0.90
- Emerging-market international stocks: 0.82
- Commodities: 0.50
- Gold: 0.10
- US Treasury notes: –0.30
- US Dollar: –0.60

These figures come from Jeremy Siegel, noted Wharton finance professor and investment commentator.

A diversified portfolio is one that consists of *low positively correlated* assets, or, optimistically, negatively correlated assets. As has historically been the case, gold continues to be a good diversifier. However, in recent years, international stocks, another historically good diversifier, have become more interconnected with U.S. large cap stocks. In contrast, real estate, specifically US REITs, have *declined* in correlation—to 0.40 from a previous correlation of 0.52 (source: National Association of Real Estate Investment Trusts, or Nareit (per their website)).

Financial or Real Assets: Which Are Better?

A great amount of wealth has been created (the *accumulation* part of the PADD process) by individuals investing in financial and real assets. Nevertheless, this process is *not* a zero-sum game. The wealth-accumulation techniques involved with each type of asset are not mutually exclusive.

Some investors prefer to invest in either financial assets or real assets, but not both. The general reason is that those investors are investing in assets they understand (or someone has convinced them they understand), or they are comfortable with only one of the two general categories of assets. If you understand your ability to assume differing amounts of risk, however, you may wish to invest in *both* financial and real assets. History has shown that adding real assets to a predominantly financial portfolio improves diversification and reduces overall risk. Remember: the goal of wealth accumulation is not only to achieve as great an annual percentage of return as possible, but also to do so with as little risk as possible! As such, you might consider investing in real-estate investments that look more like financial investments (for example, a REIT is a mutual fund that invests in real estate and real-estate properties). Alternatively, you can invest in securities issued by real-estate development companies and home builders.

Regardless of whether you decide to invest solely in financial assets, solely in real assets, or in both, do not forget this fundamental rule of investing: *if you do not understand a potential investment, you should not be investing your hard-earned money in it!* Prior to the most recent recession that began in December 2007, some investors *ignored* this basic rule and piled money into exotic derivative investments, such as credit-default swaps, whose underlying risk they did not appreciate and whose complexities they did not understand.

Now let's move on to a topic of great interest to investors and noninvestors alike: how to buy a home and take best advantage of *use* assets in accumulating wealth. The effective management of use assets is the focus of the next chapter and concludes our look at the second step in the PADD process: techniques to accumulate wealth. After that, we take up the defense of that hard-earned wealth by using effective tax management.

CHAPTER 11

Investing in Use Assets

If you think back in the financial-planning process to when you first prepared your personal financial statement, you will notice that your home and automobile were properly listed as *use assets* and not as investments. Although a profit motive may attach to some use assets (particularly luxury automobiles or antique collectibles), generally such assets are purchased so you can make efficient and enjoyable *use* of them.

Your Home as an Investment

Your home likely means a lot of things to you, not the least of which is adequate and enjoyable shelter. Further, owning your own home is an integral part of the American Dream. One of the things your primary residence or home should *not* be, however, is an investment—or, as many baby boomers are relying on, a retirement-planning vehicle.

As noted in Chapter 3, studies have shown that the average annual real rate of return on residential real estate is only 1.62 percent after considering the costs of maintenance and improvement. Moreover, it is generally *not* good financial planning to have too much of your net worth tied up in any one asset, such as your home. We discussed in Chapter 9 and Chapter 10 the importance of diversification when investing in financial and real assets, yet millions of individuals now, and when they retire, will hold approximately 60 percent of their net worth in just one asset: the equity in their home.

© Keith R. Fevurly 2018
K. R. Fevurly, *Plan Your Financial Future*, https://doi.org/10.1007/978-1-4842-3637-6_11

Chapter 11 | Investing in Use Assets

According to the *Wall Street Journal*, homeowners can easily spend up to *three times* the purchase price of a home in additional costs, such as mortgage interest, property taxes, and major home improvements. For example, today's buyer of a $300,000 single-family dwelling who finances with a 30-year fixed-rate mortgage will end up paying the price of the dwelling over again just in mortgage interest. Then add 30 years of property taxes, ongoing maintenance of the home, and several major home repairs or improvements, and the total cost of buying the home could approach $1 million.

Does this mean you should not buy a home and should instead rent? No, not at all! Since the nationwide collapse of the housing market that began in 2007, and the subsequent historic reduction in mortgage rates, it is now less expensive in some parts of the country to buy than to rent. However, the cost of home ownership does argue for a new method of analyzing why you bought your home in the first place.

A house is one of the few assets that does not violate the basic rule of debt management: *go into debt only for an asset that is likely to appreciate in value.* Notwithstanding the current housing crisis in many cities, over the long term, depending on their location, houses generally *do* increase in value. As mentioned, you may have already spent your initial purchase several times over; so, as the *Wall Street Journal* suggests, think of the sales proceeds from your home as a *rebate* of the money you spent on it. In other words, some of the thousands of dollars you spent on upkeep and improvements to your house are returned to you when you eventually sell it.

Let's look at the average cost of home ownership over the 30-year period ending in 2007, according to an Office of Federal Housing Enterprise Oversight (OFHEO) study. The OFHEO assumes a purchase price of $50,000 for a single-family home in 1977 (not much above the national median home price of $48,800 at that time). It then takes the total cost of owning the home by financing its purchase with a 30-year fixed-rate mortgage and compares it with the total cost of an all-cash purchase of the home. According to the OFHEO, the house would have appreciated to a value of $290,500 by the year 2007 at a nominal annual compounded rate of return of approximately 6.04 percent. (Note that, according to the Federal Home Mortgage Corporation, or "Freddie Mac," the average annual compounded rate of return for home ownership *declined* to 3.60 percent for the period from 1983–2013.) The average mortgage interest rate for a 30-year fixed-rate mortgage in 1977 was 8.72 percent, and the homeowner is assumed to be in a 33 percent marginal income-tax bracket. Table 11-1 shows the cost of owning this home.

Table 11-1. Average Cost of Home Ownership Over 30 Years (1977–2007)

	Mortgage Financing	All Cash
Down payment/cash price	$10,000 (20% down)	$50,000
Principal of loan	$40,000	-0-
Interest at 8.72%: $112,796 total less $40,000 principal = $72,976 interest	$50,000 ($72,976 times (1 − 0.33, or 0.67))(rounded up)	-0-
Taxes and insurance ($3,000 per year)	$90,000	$90,000
Ongoing maintenance ($150 per month)	$54,000	$54,000
Major repairs and home improvements	$150,000	$150,000
Total Costs	**$394,000**	**$344,000**
Sale value	$290,500	$290,500
Net Profit/(Loss)	**($103,500)**	**($53,500)**

There are several striking facts to recognize when analyzing this table. The first is that even an all-cash purchaser suffered a dollar loss over the 30-year period of home ownership (although not as much as the borrower, after itemizing their mortgage interest deduction). The second is that the net loss in both instances could have been turned into a net profit if not nearly as much money was expended on major repairs and home improvements. This speaks to the next major point we need to make with respect to home ownership: *exercise as much financial discipline as possible over the controllable aspects of the purchase and ongoing ownership of your home.*

Specifically, as a prospective home purchaser and owner, you have control over two significant home-owning costs: the amount of interest you pay and the extent of home improvements you make. Under the new tax law, beginning after December 31, 2017 and before January 1, 2026, the deduction for mortgage interest is limited to underlying "acquisition indebtedness" of up to $750,000 (down from the previous $1 million). So, that is still a good tax break for most of us! However, if you make your scheduled mortgage payments only in accordance with the **amortization schedule**, you are making little progress on paying down the loan principal on the typical 30-year loan. Thus, doubling up on payments and paying off the mortgage as quickly as you can results in considerable savings. Another option, if you can afford it, is to finance the purchase of the home with a 15-year fixed-rate mortgage rather than the standard 30-year note.

Limiting the number of home improvements you make is even more challenging, but the fact is that few improvements will pay off for you at the time of sale. Studies have shown that a new kitchen or bathroom returns the greatest rebate at the time of sale, but even those improvements do not often return all of the money expended. In addition, beware the temptation to add a backyard swimming pool or dog run to your home. The next buyer of your house may not have children or a dog, so these additions can be disadvantageous at the time of sale, not advantageous. Furthermore, a swimming pool can be an "attractive nuisance" to neighborhood kids, and if one of them falls in the pool and is injured, you will likely be sued, particularly if you did not enclose the pool.

In addition to accelerating your mortgage payments and limiting the extent of your home improvements, you can adopt several other planning strategies with respect to managing your home as a use asset:

- *Adopt a different attitude.* Treat your home like any other consumer purchase, and buy it at as low a price as possible. Monitor price trends in your local housing market closely, and when there is a dip in the market, consider houses to be on sale. Buy then if you can. When tracking home values, web sites such as www.zillow.com can be helpful.

- *Stay put as long as possible.* Be a "buy-and-hold" home purchaser as long as possible. The average homeowner lives in their home only seven years before moving on, usually to a more expensive residence. Depending on your area and market conditions, this probably is not long enough to ensure a net profit when you eventually sell.

- *Pay as much cash as possible.* If you can afford an all-cash purchase, doing so is preferable; but absent that, make as much of a down payment as you can. A large down payment limits the amount of principal you have to borrow and interest you have to pay.

- *Be careful about refinancing.* Yes, if you refinance, you will lower your monthly payment, but you also extend the time of your loan and thus add to your total interest payments. If you are going to refinance, consider going from a 30-year fixed-rate mortgage to a 15-year fixed-rate mortgage (especially as you grow closer to your planned retirement date).

- *Stay away from interest-only mortgages.* This is not so much a cash-management tool as it is straightforward, practical advice. Many individuals who finance their home purchases with interest-only mortgages buy more house than they can afford and thus probably pay too much. Interest-only mortgages contradict the first strategy of paying as little for the house as you can.

- *Diversify, diversify, diversify!* After accelerating your mortgage payments, take whatever money you have left and make sure you are contributing as much as possible to your employer's 401(k) retirement plan and any personal retirement savings vehicles, such as traditional or Roth IRAs. But don't go overboard: if you can pay off your house before you retire, you will increase your cash flow considerably and enjoy your retirement years that much more.

Buying vs. Renting a Home

It can be argued that buying a home with a mortgage is just another form of renting. Instead of paying the rent to a landlord, however, as a homeowner paying interest, you are paying the mortgage lender. Sure, you get a tax deduction for paying mortgage interest if you itemize your deductions; but until about the 20-year point in a standard 30-year mortgage, your interest payments are not doing much to reduce your principal. As such, you are only compromising your financial well-being when you move soon after purchasing your home. As just discussed, this is why it is so important to accelerate the payment of your mortgage as quickly as possible.

A sample home buy-vs.-rent analysis worksheet is provided next.

HOME BUY-OR-RENT ANALYSIS

Cost of Buying

1. Annual mortgage payments (12 times monthly mortgage payment)
2. Property taxes
3. Homeowner's insurance
4. Maintenance
5. After-tax cost of interest on down payment and closing costs ($ times % after-tax rate of return)
6. Total costs (sum of lines 1 to 5)

Less:

7. Principal reduction in mortgage loan balance (from amortization schedule)
8. Tax savings due to itemized mortgage-interest deduction (interest portion of mortgage payments times marginal income-tax rate)
9. Tax savings due to itemized property-tax deduction (line 2 times marginal income-tax rate)
10. Total reduction and deductions (sum of lines 7 to 9)

Equals:

11. Annual after-tax cost of home ownership (line 6 less line 10)

Plus:

12. Anticipated annual appreciation in fair market value of home, if any (percentage of price of home)

Equals: Total Cost of Buying (line 11 less line 12)

Cost of Renting

1. Annual rental costs (12 times monthly rental rate)
2. Renter's or tenant's insurance

Equals: Total Cost of Renting (line 1 plus line 2)

One important positive component of buying a home is not an issue for renters: the estimated annual appreciation in the value of the home. This underscores what was just discussed: it is critical that, as a prospective homeowner, you research the local market carefully and do *not* overpay for the property! If you *do* overpay, you limit the amount of potential appreciation in your home's value. If you happen to buy in the wrong area or at the wrong time, you may have been better off renting in the first place.

As for renting, an oft-overlooked protection strategy for the renter is the purchase of a tenant's property insurance policy. Almost every lease includes exculpatory language whereby the landlord bears no liability for damage to or theft of the tenant's personal property. A tenant's policy provides for this protection plus liability coverage for guests who may be injured while on the property. The policy also protects the tenant from the consequences of their own injurious acts, wherever they may occur.

In addition to securing a property insurance policy, a tenant should be sure to check on the status of any security deposit required by the landlord. Some landlords, in an attempt to attract tenants, invest this deposit for the tenant and pay them the interest at the end of a long-term lease. However, more commonly this deposit is simply maintained in escrow by the landlord and refunded to the tenant at the expiration of the lease, provided the rental unit is left in good physical condition As a prospective tenant, you want as low a security deposit as possible and a return on your money in the form of protected premises and timely landlord maintenance.

Selling Your Home

Most of the issues involving the sale of your home are income-tax related, but you should not overlook practical questions, such as whether to sell the home yourself or use a real-estate broker. With today's Internet-savvy society, increasing numbers of individuals are opting to list and sell their homes themselves. However, as attractive as it might seem to avoid the cost of using a real-estate broker, consider the following if you choose to sell your home on your own:

- *You must establish a reasonable price for your home.* Although this may appear easy given the widespread availability of comparable market data these days, you need to be as realistic as you can about what your home may be worth. As such, you must separate emotion and the natural tendency to ask for more money rather than less. Be as objective as possible.

- *You need to market your home.* This involves much more than simply sticking a For Sale by Owner sign in the front yard. You need your house listed in your area's multiple-listing service (MLS). According to the National Association of Realtors, over 60 percent of home sales occur with the assistance of a buyer's agent (in contrast, real-estate agents or brokers typically work only for the seller). Try to list your house with such an agent, who typically works as part of a network and represents any number of qualified buyers.

- *You need to separate the serious prospects from the merely curious.* Neighbors are notorious for taking sales brochures or flyers simply because they want to see what you are asking for your house. Instead, ask your neighbors to refer any friends or family who may be looking for a new home. You should then prequalify the serious buyers so as not to waste your time negotiating a price with someone the mortgage lender will not approve.

- *You have to close the deal!* This is where many for-sale-by-owner sellers stumble. Many buyers are skilled in the art of negotiating for the absolute lowest price (or sometimes even a below-market price). Hence, as a seller, you have to know what price you will accept while recognizing that it is the most the market will bear at that particular time.

Assuming that you or your real estate agent have been successful in getting a fair price for your home, you now have to report the tax on any gain from that sale. Fortunately, the gain from the sale of any primary residence is considered a gain on the sale of a capital asset. Depending on your income-tax bracket and whether you have owned the house for at least one year, the gain is generally taxed at either a 0 percent or a 15 percent marginal rate. More important, if you meet certain conditions, any gain on the sale of a home is taxable only to the extent that it exceeds $250,000 (or $500,000, if you file a joint return). This $250,000 or $500,000 exclusion may be used as often as once every two years.

To determine your taxable gain, you must subtract your *basis* in the home from its sales price minus all costs and commissions. This computation process underscores the importance of keeping good records, because your basis in a home is generally equal to what you paid for it plus any improvements made while you owned it. For example, assume that you paid $250,000 for your home ten years ago. While you owned it, you finished the basement at a cost of $30,000. Your adjusted basis in the home is now $280,000 ($250,000 plus the $30,000 in improvements). Also assume that you recently sold the home for $370,000 with the assistance of a real-estate broker. You must pay your broker a commission of 6 percent of the sales price. Therefore, your sales price for determining any capital gains tax due is $347,800 ($370,000 less the $22,200 broker's commission). Accordingly, your total, potentially taxable gain is $67,800 ($347,800 net sales price less $280,000 basis); but if you qualify for the $250,000 exclusion, you do not have any recognized gain for tax purposes. In other words, you do not owe any income tax if you take advantage of the available exclusion.

To qualify for the $250,000 or $500,000 exclusion, you must meet both an *ownership test* and a *use test*. Specifically, you must have

- *Owned* the residence for at least two out of the five years prior to when you sold it
- *Used* the home as your primary residence for this same period of time

If you are married and file jointly at the time of sale, either you or your spouse can meet the ownership requirement, but you *both* must meet the use requirement. This may be a particularly difficult requirement for divorced or divorcing couples in which one partner vacates the home before sale. If you fail to meet these tests due to a change in employment (for example, if your employer transfers you to a new location) or as a result of other unforeseen circumstances, you can exclude the fraction of the $250,000 or $500,000 exclusion that is equal to the fraction of the two-year period in which these tests were met.

For example, assume that you purchased a home on January 1, 2017, and on January 2, 2018, your employer transferred you to another city. You have owned your home for at least 12 months and, as a single taxpayer, are entitled to exclude up to $125,000 of any gain on the sale ($250,000 times 0.50, or 12 divided by 24). Finally, as with any other personal asset, *losses* on the sale of a home used as a personal residence are not allowed for income-tax purposes.

Automobiles: Do You Really Need That New Lamborghini?

Unlike houses, which have historically appreciated in value, no other use assets depreciate in value more quickly than automobiles. From a debt-management perspective, you should think twice before borrowing to purchase a new luxury automobile. Remember, *borrowing to buy a depreciating asset does not make financial sense*. Nevertheless, in most places in America, an automobile is not a discretionary purchase, but a necessity for getting around. What are some tips for taking the most advantage of this necessary tool of daily living?

- If you can suffer what is, for some, an indignity, purchase only a quality used automobile. An automobile broker or referencing an online web site can assist you in finding one. Then, as with a house, do not overpay for it.

- Do some research before you buy. For example, if you have decided on a pre-owned car, consult the Kelley Blue Book to determine what you should be paying as the retail price. If you are purchasing a new car, you can consult online services to find out the dealer's invoice cost. Start your negotiation with the dealer about 2 percent above that cost, and try to work down from there.

- Before you buy, try to determine whether the car you are interested in is likely to become a classic model. For example, individuals who were fortunate enough to buy a 1957 Chevrolet or a 1965 Ford Mustang transformed a depreciating asset (a car) into a collector's item (a classic automobile).

- Buy only one quality automobile at a time, and keep it for at least ten years or 100,000 miles. Fortunately, automobiles are improving in quality all the time, so this should not be too difficult.

- Keep your car in good repair and up-to-date on maintenance. It has been proven that well-tuned cars conserve gasoline and thus, in the longer term, save you money.

Another decision you may need to make with respect to an automobile is whether to buy or lease the car. Generally, when a high percentage of the car's use is for business purposes, it may be more advantageous to lease instead of buy. Not only can the business portion of the lease payments be deducted for income-tax purposes, but the business portion of the interest on the loan may be deducted. Further, depreciation of the leased vehicle, within certain limits, is also a tax deduction. Finally, if the vehicle you are purchasing is to be used for primarily personal purposes, buying and owning the car for a significant period of time is preferable. This is particularly the case if the lease agreement does not provide for an option to purchase the car at its depreciated value at the lease's expiration date (known as a *closed-end* automobile lease agreement).

Tangible Personal Property and Collectibles

Tangible personal property, such as art, stamps, and coins, may be transformed from a use asset to an investment based on the rarity and quality of the property. Likewise, a hobby, such as stamp collecting, may turn into a business depending on whether the collector intends to earn a profit from the activity as determined by the IRS and the courts.

Examples of popular investment-quality collectibles include artwork, gemstones, rare coins, antique dolls and furniture, and even baseball cards. All share certain attributes—notably, rarity and popularity within a sizable market. But collectibles generally do not provide any current income to the owner and are best held for capital appreciation. Once disposed of, the items are taxed at a special long-term capital gain rate of 28 percent.

Although there is a market for collectibles, in most cases it is not an *organized* market. As a result, both buyers and sellers are at a disadvantage, because unless they are very skilled, they are unlikely to know what constitutes a fair price for the item. As with so many other consumer purchases, the Internet and a multiplicity of web sites (particularly eBay) have improved access to reliable information about collectibles. Still, by and large, the market for collectibles is inefficient.

Another problem with tangible personal property that may become a collectible is that the market may be temporary. For example, several years back, Cabbage Patch Kids dolls were a heavily sought-after item that demanded high retail prices. Today, however, the craze has passed, and the price has returned to a more normal level. This is bad news if you bought at the top of the market, intended to make a subsequent profit, and now have no practical use for the dolls.

It is possible to obtain insurance coverage for valuable tangible personal property. If you own standard-use property, you need to schedule or endorse the property for an agreed-on value with the insurance company, as mentioned in Chapter 7. If, on the other hand, your property is truly a collectible with a recognized and sustainable market, you must enter into insurance negotiations with a specialized underwriter, such as those found at the **Lloyds of London** insurance market.

The next few chapters take up the defense of accumulated wealth, most notably from the harmful effect of income taxes. It is well understood by effective wealth managers that inflation and taxes are the two primary threats to wealth accumulation. However, only one of these threats—taxes—can be managed by the average individual. The purpose of the next section of the book is to show you how to manage taxes and leave more money in your pocket rather than adding to the fisc of Uncle Sam!

PART IV

Defending Wealth

CHAPTER

12

Income-Tax Planning and Management

Now that we have discussed how to use the PADD process to *protect* and *accumulate* your wealth, we move on to the *defense* or preservation of that wealth. Specifically, this chapter focuses on income-tax planning and management, with subsequent chapters addressing transfer-tax (gift- and estate-tax) planning and life events that threaten wealth, such as divorce or loss of a job.

You must effectively manage two primary threats in order to defend your wealth: *inflation* and *taxes*. Unfortunately, the rate of inflation is largely out of your individual control. However, you can be proactive when it comes to effective tax management, and the first step is to become familiar with the basic provisions of the income-tax system.

Basics of Income-Tax Rates, Withholding, and Estimated Taxes

A basic rule of wealth accumulation and management is to determine not only how much income you have to spend or save, but also how much of this income you *get to keep*. To maximize how much of your income you get to *keep*, you need to know your federal income-tax rate. Keep in mind that you should also know what your *state* income-tax rate is if you work in a state that imposes an income tax. However, because of the wide variation in state laws with respect to income taxes, only the basics of the federal system are discussed here.

There are two types of federal income-tax rates: effective and marginal. Your *effective*, or *average*, tax rate is the total tax payable divided by your taxable income as reported on your federal income-tax return. Normally, though, when someone asks what your tax rate is, they are referring to your *marginal* income-tax rate, which is the percentage of tax applying to your *next* dollar of taxable income.

As of the year 2018 and extending through the year 2025, seven federal marginal income-tax rates apply to salaries and wages (and most other income other than capital gains income): 10, 12, 22, 24, 32, 35, and 37 percent. These seven rates clearly are more than the two income-tax rates (15 percent and 28 percent) implemented by the Tax Reform Act of 1986. But historically, seven is still a relatively small number of income-tax rates. Moreover, as a result of the **Tax Cuts and Jobs Act of 2017** TCJA of 2017, the bracket of income to which the top rate applies is significantly increased, beginning at $500,000 for single individuals and $600,000 for married couples filing jointly.

Income is taxed in each of these rates according to a range of income known as an income-tax *bracket*. Your bracket depends on the amount of taxable income you make in a year and the filing status you use to report this income (for example, single or jointly filed with your spouse). As a tax-management technique, you want to do everything legally possible to not progress into the next-higher marginal tax bracket, where all remaining income is then taxed at a greater percentage.

One strategy for minimizing your marginal tax rate involves holding investment or business property for a required length of time (currently, more than one year) before selling it. This is known as *long-term capital gain property*, and the tax rate that is assessed depends on your marginal income-tax rate. For example, if you are in the 10 or 12 percent marginal tax bracket, long-term capital gains are now permanently not taxed at all (a rate of 0 percent). Meanwhile, if your annual taxable income exceeds $425,800 for single taxpayers and $479,000 for joint filers (that is, you are in the top two individual tax brackets of 35 and 37 percent), long-term capital gains are taxed at a rate of 20 percent.

In addition, a surtax of 3.8 percent (the purpose of which is to finance the future health insurance coverage provisions of the Patient Protection and Affordable Care Act of 2010) is charged on capital gain/investment income for single taxpayers with annual modified adjusted gross income (MAGI) over $200,000 for single filers and $250,000 for joint filers. All numbers are adjusted for inflation.

Losses from investment or business property in both sets of marginal tax brackets are first offset against any capital gains and, if there is any remaining loss, are taken against salary or wages (or any other noninvestment or business property income) up to a maximum of $3,000 in any given year. Any excess loss is then carried forward indefinitely until used up. For example, assume that you or your tax preparer have reported that you have a long-term capital gain of $4,000 and a long-term capital loss of $5,000 in 2018. You are in the 12 percent marginal income-tax bracket. As such, you have no long-term capital gain (it is completely offset by the long-term capital loss), but you have incurred a remaining $1,000 long-term capital loss. As a result, you can use the total of this loss ($1,000) to reduce your salary or wages (or other noninvestment or business property income), because it is less than $3,000 in the current year.

Once you know your marginal income-tax rate (you can determine this by referring to past tax returns and checking the amount of taxable income against the bracket range), the next step is to figure out how much to withhold from your paycheck for future taxes. You do this by obtaining and completing an IRS Form W-4. Your goal in completing this form is to withhold taxes equal to 90 percent of what you think you will owe the federal government at the end of the year. How do you do this? The IRS Form W-4 lets you claim withholding allowances based on your projected income for the current year. An allowance *reduces* the amount of taxes withheld and *increases* the amount of your take-home pay. Therefore, the *greater* the number of allowances claimed, the *higher* your take-home pay; and the *lower* the number of allowances, the *lower* your take-home pay.

Some individuals, notably self-employed taxpayers, are required to pay *estimated taxes* in lieu of income taxes. However, some taxpayers must pay estimated taxes *in addition to* their income taxes. For example, if, as a salaried individual, you have a great deal of additional income, such as rental real-estate income, you may have to pay these taxes. Retirees with a large lump-sum distribution from their retirement plan also may be required to pay estimated taxes. If you are a taxpayer who is subject to estimating your taxes, your first payment is to be made by filing IRS Form 1040-ES on April 15 of the current year followed by payments on June 15, September 15, and January 15 (of the next year).

Social Security and Medicare Taxes

Under the Federal Insurance Contributions Act (FICA), all salaried employees have to pay (or have withheld from their paycheck) 7.65 percent of their salary to fund the Social Security and Medicare social insurance systems. Specifically, 6.2 percent of the total portion of 7.65 percent represents the employee's contribution to fund their own Social Security retirement or disability benefit, and the remaining 1.45 percent helps to fund the Medicare hospitalization (Part A) program. Moreover, some employees—those earning in excess of an inflation-indexed amount of $200,000 annually ($250,000 married filing jointly)—pay an additional 0.9 percent as a Medicare supplemental tax used to pay for Affordable Care Act coverage. The Social Security withholding is assessed only up to a certain amount of the employee's salary (referred to as the *taxable wage base*: for example, $128,400 in 2018) in any calendar year, whereas the Medicare withholding is assessed on an unlimited amount of employee salary.

Unlike state and local income taxes, which some taxpayers can separately deduct against their federal income taxes up to an amount of $10,000 annually, Social Security and Medicare taxes are *not* deductible. Effectively, this *increases* the overall marginal income-tax rate that an individual pays. For example, if you are in the highest marginal income-tax bracket of 37 percent, you effectively pay 10.48 percent *more* in taxes (7.65 percent plus 2.83 percent (0.37 times .0765) because you cannot deduct these amounts from your federal income taxes.

Regular Income Tax vs. Individual Alternative Minimum Tax

We just discussed the most important provisions of the *regular* income-tax system—the one that most taxpayers must protect against as an ongoing threat to their accumulated wealth. However, certain high-income (and some upper-middle-income) taxpayers must plan for *another* tax system each year. This system is referred to as the individual *alternative minimum tax (AMT)*.

The AMT is a parallel tax system originally designed to prevent a small number of high-income taxpayers from avoiding paying regular tax. Under the AMT system, taxpayers pay the *greater of* the regular tax or alternative minimum tax due in any given year. Beginning in 2018, the Tax Cuts and Jobs Act of 2017 (TCJA) increased the AMT exemption amounts to $70,300 for single taxpayers and $109,900 for married couples filing jointly. It also indexed these amounts for inflation after 2018. However, phaseouts do apply, such that once a taxpayer's income exceeds a specified amount of alternative minimum taxable income (AMTI), the exemptions no longer apply. Additionally, AMT rates of either 26 percent or 28 percent apply not to your regular taxable income, but to a separate computation of AMTI or, effectively, your regular taxable income increased by certain "add back" items from the regular system. The deductions and other regular income-tax breaks not allowed to you under the AMT system are generally referred to as *tax preference items*. Among such preference items is the income portion of an incentive stock option (ISO) occurring on the date of exercise of that option, the disallowance of the regular standard income-tax deduction, and the disallowance of any interest on student loans.

So how do you avoid the application of this onerous tax? First, understand what constitutes a tax preference item (they are described in the separate instructions to the AMT tax form), and then try to limit such items. For example, if you hold ISOs as an employee benefit from your employer, postpone exercising them for as long as possible (ideally, until your total income is relatively low in a given year). Next, as curious as it seems, you may wish to consider *accelerating income* into the current year in the hopes of increasing your regular tax liability to *above* that of the AMT. Finally, *postpone deductions* that you cannot take for AMT purposes into the next taxable year. The deductions at risk here include certain itemized deductions, including the deduction for state income taxes and property taxes. If you currently live in a high income-tax state, such as New York, you should ask your accountant or financial planner to separately compute your possible AMT liability. Also note that these last two AMT planning techniques are the exact *opposite* of what you would do in regular income-tax planning. As a result, AMT planning essentially requires you to think *backward* with respect to how you would otherwise try to minimize taxes.

Basic Tax-Planning Technique #1: Tax Avoidance

The term *tax avoidance* may be used narrowly, as when a higher-bracket taxpayer gives property to a lower-bracket taxpayer, and the lower-bracket taxpayer pays the income tax on that property at a reduced rate. Alternatively, the term may be used broadly, meaning that the higher-bracket taxpayer does not incur income taxes on the income. In the context that the term is used in this book, you should think of tax avoidance as broadly as possible.

The most common example of tax avoidance is taking full advantage of all income-tax deductions to which you are entitled under the tax law. A tax *deduction* is a percentage reduction of your taxable income based on your marginal income-tax rate. For example, if you are in the 32 percent marginal bracket, you are effectively paying tax on only 68 percent (1 less 0.32) of your income. Similarly, the standard deduction available to all taxpayers operates to exclude that specified amount of income from taxation. A third example of tax avoidance involves attempting to qualify for any income-tax credits provided under law. A tax *credit* is a dollar-for-dollar reduction against an individual's income-tax liability and therefore is not affected by the taxpayer's marginal income-tax rate. For example, if you have computed your income-tax liability before credits to be $10,000 this year, and you qualify for a credit of $1,000, you owe the government only $9,000 ($10,000 less $1,000). In practical effect and as a tax-avoidance technique, a *credit* is worth more to a *lower-bracket taxpayer* (22 percent rate and below), whereas a *deduction* is worth more to a *higher-bracket taxpayer* (24 percent and above).

As a regular taxpayer, you are entitled to choose one of two general deductions: a specified *standard deduction* under law, based on your filing status, or a series of deductions known as *itemized deductions*. You want to choose the *higher* of the two deductions, because doing so will afford you the greatest tax benefit. As a practical matter, given the doubling of the standard deduction amount in TCJA of 2017, you will likely choose the standard deduction. Only high-income homeowners or philanthropists are likely to itemize deductions. You may potentially be able to take advantage of the following deductions if you elect to itemize:

- Unreimbursed (by health insurance) medical expenses
- State and local income and property taxes (limited to a maximum of $10,000 annually)
- State and local sales taxes in lieu of state and local income taxes (again, limited to $10,000 annually)
- Home mortgage loan or "acquisition indebtedness" interest payments (limited to a home purchase amount of $750,000)
- Charitable contributions

As mentioned, regardless of whether you take the standard deduction or itemize, certain tax credits are allowable for qualified taxpayers. There are two general types of credits: refundable and nonrefundable. A *refundable* credit, such as the earned income-tax credit, is one that results in money being paid to you even though you have no income-tax liability. Conversely, a *nonrefundable* credit is one that, at best, reduces your tax liability to zero (in other words, you are not separately paid if you do not owe any taxes). Of the two, you should maximize the number of refundable credits you can take. Unfortunately, however, most credits are nonrefundable.

Among the most popular nonrefundable (or only partially refundable) credits are the following:

- The child and dependent care tax credit
- The child tax credit (partially refundable)
- The adoption credit
- The credit for the elderly or disabled
- Certain higher-education expense credits, such as the Lifetime Learning Credit

As a general strategy to avoid paying as much regular income tax as possible, you should *accelerate deductions and credits* into the current tax year and *postpone income* into the next or subsequent tax years. Salaried taxpayers typically find it difficult to postpone income, because they are not in control of when they receive it. However, self-employed taxpayers have much more latitude with respect to this tax-planning technique. For example, a self-employed taxpayer can choose to bill a client early in January of the following year rather than in late December of this year, thereby deferring taxes due on the income.

Tax Avoidance vs. Tax Evasion

While we are on the topic of tax avoidance, it is important to distinguish between income-tax avoidance planning techniques and tax evasion. *Avoidance* techniques are perfectly legal and take advantage of tax benefits, such as deductions and credits, that are afforded to you under the tax law. Conversely, tax *evasion* is illegal; it means you *intended* to not comply with the tax law. The most common form of tax evasion is the failure to report all your taxable income for the calendar year.

If, in filing your tax return for any given year, you intend to break the law, the IRS must prove this fact in court. If it does, you will be found guilty of a felony offense that is punishable by severe monetary fines or imprisonment in a federal penitentiary. Fortunately, imprisonment is rarely the punishment for tax evasion. Instead, *restitution* (paying what you should have owed) and fines are the preferred recourse of the government. Nevertheless, if you are involved in a tax-evasion case, either as the subject of the investigation or as someone who knows something about it, you should immediately contact a tax attorney to represent you to the IRS Criminal Investigation Division (CID). Do not speak voluntarily to the CID, because anything you say may be used against you later.

Basic Tax-Planning Technique #2: Tax Deferral

The most common tax-deferral technique is to contribute to a retirement plan at work or to a personal retirement savings plan, such as a **traditional IRA** or **Roth IRA**. We have already talked about the importance of contributing to your employer's 401(k) or 403(b) retirement plan and taking advantage of any matching contributions your employer may offer. However, from a tax-planning perspective, you are also deferring the tax on any contributions made to the 401(k) or 403(b) plan *and* deferring the tax on any earnings generated from those contributions. Because 401(k) and 403(b) plans are tax-deferred retirement plans under law, you must pay tax on your contributions and earnings beginning in the year after you reach the age of 70 and 6 months. In the meantime, you have enjoyed the financial advantage of the tax-free compounding of your money. Let's try to understand the importance of this advantage.

If you were asked, "Would you rather have $1,000 today or $1,000 ten years from now?" you would likely intuitively answer, "$1,000 today." Why? The logic is that if you receive $1,000 today, you can invest the lump sum and make even more money with it. Assume that you invest your $1,000 in a US Treasury note that returns 5 percent annually. At the end of ten years, you will have $1,628.89. Alternatively, if you were to take the $1,000 ten years from now, the *present value* of this same amount would be only $613.91 in today's dollars.

Now let's look at this question another way. Think of the 5 percent annual rate of return as a tax percentage. If you have an income-tax liability this year of $1,000 but you can somehow defer that liability for ten years, the present value of that liability is now only $613.91 (a savings of more than $386). And, using time-value-of-money principles, the *longer* you postpone that liability, the *lower* your present value and the *greater* your savings. Moreover, you should be aware that by year 40, your $1,000 liability is worth only $142.05 in present value dollars—approximately 14 cents on the dollar. You have generated the other 86 cents on the dollar completely income-tax free, which is the beauty of income-tax deferral with respect to retirement plan accumulations of wealth.

There are also other tax-deferral techniques involving financial products. Notably, if you purchase a tax-deferred fixed or variable annuity product, the taxes on your earnings from the after-tax contributions to that product are deferred (in some cases, until age 100). You can also purchase a tax-deferred annuity with a lump-sum distribution that you make from an employer's retirement plan (such as a 401(k)). However, because those contributions are really made with before-tax money (you never paid taxes on it), distributions must be made in the year after you reach the age of 70 and 6 months if you want to avoid paying hefty taxes on them.

Another financial product that provides for tax deferral is a cash-value life insurance policy. If you do *not* access the cash surrender amount in this policy during your lifetime, the death proceeds from the policy to your named beneficiary are completely *income-tax free*. Alternatively, the earnings on the cash value accumulated within a whole life, universal, variable, or variable/universal life insurance policy are tax-deferred until you surrender the policy, assuming that the cash value you receive is in excess of the premiums paid on the policy at the time of surrender. For example, assume that you have owned a whole life insurance policy for some time and have accumulated $70,000 of cash-surrender value. During the course of the year, you surrender this policy for cash but have paid only $50,000 in premiums on the policy to date. The portion of the lump-sum payment of $70,000 in excess of the premiums paid of $50,000 ($20,000) is taxable immediately, payable at your current marginal income-tax rate.

Basic Tax-Planning Technique #3: Conversion of Income

Ultimately, every item of income is generally classifiable as either *ordinary income* (such as salary and wages) or *capital gains* (generally, income deriving from the sale or disposition of an investment product, such as a stock or business property). As previously noted, significantly different tax rates potentially apply to each of these types of income. For example, ordinary income is taxed at a maximum rate of 37 percent, whereas long-term capital gains income is taxed at a maximum rate of only 20 percent. This rate spread of almost 20 percent suggests the prudence of following a tax-planning strategy that converts as much ordinary income as possible into capital gains income. It also underscores the importance of saving and investing as much as possible, because the appreciation on investment assets is taxable at a rate of no higher than 20 percent.

Assume that you have earned $1,000 in salary and are currently (in the year 2018) in the maximum ordinary income-tax bracket of 37 percent. Your after-tax, disposable dollars are $630 ($1,000 less $370). If you take this same $1,000 and invest it in ABC stock, which you later sell for $2,000 at least one year after you bought it, your after-tax, disposable dollars are now $800 ($1,000 less $200). Note that you incur only a 20 percent capital gains tax. If you were in the 12-percent-or-lower ordinary income-tax bracket, you would not pay any capital gains tax on this sale.

Since 2003, you can take advantage of capital gain income-tax rates on most investment income (dividends) generated from stocks or stock mutual funds. However, keep in mind that dividends payable from indirect real-estate investments, such as a **real estate investment trust (REIT)**, do not typically qualify for this same advantage (although, beginning in 2018, there is a reduction in the maximum tax rate for some REIT dividends). As such, a tax-efficient conversion of income is not completely possible with REIT investments. There is also a common *reverse conversion* of income that many taxpayers unwittingly commit without realizing it. This occurs when a taxpayer invests in mutual funds (or individual stocks and bonds) in a retirement plan—either an employer-sponsored plan, such as a 401(k), or a traditional deductible IRA. In such cases, what the taxpayer has really done is invest in a capital asset, which could potentially be taxed at a lower capital gains rate on sale, and then converted it to an asset that requires the payment of ordinary income taxes on distribution. This happens because, for income-tax purposes, a distribution from a retirement plan or IRA is considered a replacement for a salary, which would otherwise be taxable as ordinary income. Nonetheless, this disadvantageous conversion of income is likely *outweighed* by the extremely favorable, long-term tax deferral of earnings and contributions associated with an employer-sponsored retirement plan or IRA.

Tax-Smart Investing

Now that we have discussed both investing and income taxes, we need to combine the two. In other words, which type of account—tax-deferred or taxable—is most efficient to position a given type of financial asset?

Tax-deferred accounts, such as retirement plans, allow taxpayers to grow their assets over many years without having to pay taxes on the earnings. Therefore, it makes sense to position those investments that are *not* income-tax efficient in retirement plans. An example of such an investment is a zero-coupon bond, which generates taxable phantom income each year but does not distribute any corresponding cash to the bond holder. Other similarly income-tax-inefficient investments you may wish to position in retirement plans are individual corporate, investment-grade bonds and bond mutual funds, as well as Treasury Separate Trading of Registered Interest and Principal of Securities (STRIPS) and Treasury Inflation Protected Securities (TIPS). Conversely, one type of financial asset you should generally *not* position in a tax-deferred account is a municipal bond or municipal bond fund. Interest from a municipal bond is tax-exempt, so if you position it in a tax-deferred account, you are converting its tax-free status to a taxable status after it is withdrawn from the retirement plan. It is important to note that in recent years, the tax-exempt yield generated from a municipal bond—as compared to a taxable corporate bond—was so advantageous that it made economic sense to modify this strategy. However, you are generally better off refraining from positioning municipal bonds and municipal bond funds in a tax-deferred account as an income-tax strategy.

What about *taxable* accounts? As a general rule, individual stocks and stock mutual funds belong in these types of accounts, because they are more tax-efficient than bonds and bond mutual funds. Index funds or exchange-traded funds (ETFs) are also good choices for taxable accounts, because they are passively managed and generally income-tax efficient. However, with respect to stocks and stock mutual funds, an argument may be made that, given their growth potential and the total compounded dollars they have earned at the time of withdrawal, they may also optimally fit into a tax-deferred portfolio. If you are working with a financial planner or investment advisor, ask them to give you perspective with regard to this argument.

What You Can Learn From Your Own Tax Return

Although most taxpayers do not prepare their own tax returns, they should understand the entries so as to plan more effectively for the coming years. The following points provide a brief explanation of some of the basics of filing a tax return:

- *What is your filing status?* If you are married and living together throughout the year, you should file your return jointly with your spouse, because generally you will be taxed more favorably. Alternatively, if you are a single parent with a dependent child or children, you should investigate filing your return by using the advantageous head-of-household status.

- *Should you itemize or take advantage of the standard deduction?* Given that the standard deduction for single or married-filing-jointly taxpayers has been effectively doubled under the 2017 TCJA, it is likely that many fewer individuals will elect to itemize. However, if you are a homeowner with a sizable mortgage, or make a great number of annual charitable contributions, it may be to your advantage to itemize deductions.

- *Should your investment interest be taxable or tax-exempt?* As discussed, the higher your marginal income-tax rate, the greater the advantage to you of investing in tax-exempt assets, such as municipal bonds or municipal bond funds.

- *Do you have any self-employment income?* If you do (to be reported on IRS Form 1040, Schedule C), you may be entitled to a number of business deductions that you would not otherwise be able to claim.

- *Do you have capital losses (losses from the sale of any investment or business property)?* As a tax-planning technique, you should recognize capital losses in years when you have capital gains. These losses can offset capital gains and further offset ordinary income to the extent of $3,000 per year.

- *Are you required to make required minimum distributions from your IRA this year?* Just as with distributions from employer-sponsored retirement plans, you have to begin taking distributions from a traditional deductible IRA (not a Roth IRA) no later than April 1 of the year after you reach the age of 70 and 6 months.

- *Can you contribute to and deduct contributions to your IRA this year?* The answer is somewhat complicated and depends on your filing status, but if your income is low enough, you can both contribute to and deduct a specified amount annually from your IRA.

- *Do you have unreimbursed employee expenses?* The 2017 TCJA disallows a deduction for unreimbursed employee expenses. Thus, if your business expenses are not being reimbursed, you should ask your employer to establish a reimbursable, or accountable, plan.

- *What is your taxable income?* Depending on your filing status, this amount determines what marginal income-tax bracket you are in and your applicable marginal income-tax rate.

- *Do you qualify for any additional tax credits this year?* All allowable credits have qualifying conditions or limitations. However, if you qualify, a credit affords you a dollar-for-dollar tax reduction.

- *Do you owe household employment taxes?* Generally, you are responsible for paying Social Security and Medicare taxes if you employ a household domestic worker, such as a nanny. This is one of the most overlooked sections of income tax law and has resulted in the imposition of tax penalties for many salaried and self-employed workers.

- *Did you pay tax or receive a tax refund?* A goal of many taxpayers is to receive as big a refund as possible when they file their tax return, but think about it: if you receive a refund, you have just given the federal government an interest-free loan for the entirety of the previous tax year. Alternatively, you do not want to withhold so little tax that penalties are imposed for the previous year. Your goal should be a small tax payment with the filing of your individual income-tax return (for example, a payment of no more than $100).

We now move on to the other major tax that can quickly reduce your accumulated wealth: the transfer tax imposed under federal tax law. The transfer tax, which includes estate and gift taxes, is most relevant in estate planning and will be referred to again in Chapter 19. Regardless, the next chapter provides important information with respect to the provisions and application of federal estate-tax and gift-tax law in planning for your financial future.

CHAPTER 13

Transfer-Tax Planning and Management

Once an individual has *accumulated* wealth, their motivations in the financial-planning process turn to not only how to protect or defend this wealth, but also how to *distribute* it. For this reason, this chapter explains gifts and the advantages of making gifts in transfer-tax planning and management. Many individuals think that transfer-tax (gift- and estate-tax) planning is relevant for only very high-net-worth taxpayers, but this is not true. For example, did you know that you can give away $15,000 per year, regardless of the amount of your net worth, to donees without having to file a federal gift-tax return, IRS Form 709? Just as important, did you know that once you exceed this $15,000 limit, you are generally *required by law* to file a federal gift-tax return? Yes, you will also have to include Christmas gifts on that tax return if you have given away the full $15,000 limit earlier in the same year.

This chapter also considers how to minimize your taxable estate at death. Although there has been a great deal of discussion in Congress about the repeal of the estate tax (sometimes referred to as the *death tax*), it is still with us—and likely will be in some form for years to come. We talk more about

© Keith R. Fevurly 2018
K. R. Fevurly, *Plan Your Financial Future*, https://doi.org/10.1007/978-1-4842-3637-6_13

the distribution of wealth in Part 5 of this book, but the beauty of lifetime gifting is that it accomplishes two steps of the PADD process at once: the *defense* of your wealth against transfer taxes and the *distribution* of that wealth for the benefit of others (typically, your spouse and children).

The Advantages of Lifetime Gifting

You may have many reasons for making gifts. Among these may be personal reasons, such as assisting a family member or close friend in immediate financial need. You may also have tax reasons for gifting. Whereas lifetime gifting (other than to charity) does *not* generate an income-tax deduction, it does shift the income generated from the gifted property onto someone else. Numerous tax rules restrict the outright assignment of income to others, but if you gift them an income-producing asset, such as a stock, a bond, or real estate, the donee—and not you—will pay the future income tax on the gains that asset generates.

Under the gift-tax rules, there are three ways to make gifts to others without worrying about paying a gift tax. The first has already been mentioned: as of 2018, you can give up to $15,000 per year to as many donees as you like. Technically, this $15,000 allowance per donee is known as the gift-tax *annual exclusion amount*. For example, if you have ten children, you can give up to $150,000 per year ($15,000 times 10) without concerning yourself with reporting these gifts to the federal government. But be careful: some taxpayers, believe it or not, are so concerned about reducing their income- and estate-tax liability that they forget to ask a basic question before making a gift—can I afford to make this gift without sacrificing my *own* future financial security?

The second method of making a lifetime gift is to transfer assets or property to your spouse or a **qualified charity**. Unlike gifts to others, you can make a gift of *unlimited value* to your spouse or a qualified charity. Particularly as the situation relates to estate-tax planning, it may be financially beneficial to make gifts to your spouse or a qualified charity, because the gifted property is now completely removed from your taxable estate at death. However, as you will see later in this chapter, if your spouse is the recipient of your gift, you may be causing a further estate-tax problem for them if they are already of high net worth in their own right (or expect to be shortly).

The third method of prudent lifetime gifting is to pay the educational or medical expenses of a loved one. However, the payment of such gifts needs to be made *directly* to the educational institution or medical provider, not indirectly through the donee, who would then pay the institution or provider. If the donee is the intermediary, the $15,000 or other indexed-for-annual-inflation limit applies, rather than the unlimited amount that is possible if the institution or provider is the payee.

If you generally give more than $15,000 annually to any donee, you are legally required to file a gift-tax return and apply the excess amount against an overall lifetime exemption limit of $11.2 million (a $10 million indexed amount) through the end of calendar year 2018. Making a gift that is larger than the annually permitted limit has two consequences:

- You begin to use up your overall lifetime limit of $11.2 million. Once you exceed $11.2 million in lifetime taxable gifts, you pay federal gift tax out of pocket.

- The gift-tax value of the gift you make (the property's fair market value at the time you gift it) is included in the estate-tax computation as an adjusted taxable gift, meaning it adds to your potential taxable estate at death.

For example, assume that you make a gift of appreciated stock to your adult son in 2018. The fair market value of this stock at the time you give it is $100,000. Thus, you have made a taxable gift of $85,000 ($100,000 less $15,000) for which you must file a federal gift-tax return. As a result, you now have only $11,115,000 ($11.2 million less $85,000) of your lifetime exemption limit left. This taxable gift of $85,000 is also added to your taxable estate at your date of death. The good news, however, is that your gift is frozen in taxable value at that amount and cannot increase to a date-of-death fair market value (because you don't own the stock anymore)! In other words, you have removed any *future appreciation* of the gifted property from your taxable estate. In this example, let's say the $100,000 in stock that you gave your son appreciates to $600,000 at your death 20 years later. The appreciation amount of $500,000 ($600,000 less $100,000) is now forever removed from possible future transfer taxation in your estate.

You should note that the 2017 TCJA *doubled* the lifetime gift exemption limit from an indexed amount of $5.6 million to $11.2 million, effective for the year 2018. The overwhelming majority of individuals likely will never have to pay federal gift tax. However, the fact remains that high-net-worth individuals, particularly small business owners, are most likely to make gifts to family members; indeed, this group of individuals is the intended Congressional target of the gift (and estate) tax initially!

Let's go back to taking maximum advantage of the $15,000 annual gift-tax exclusion. In the example given previously, wherein each of ten children is the donee of $15,000, the person who gave the gift immediately removed $150,000 from their taxable estate and did not have to file a gift-tax return or worry about reducing their overall $11.2 million exemption limit in 2018. This strategy is known in estate planning as a *systematic annual gifting program* and takes advantage of as many gift-tax annual exclusion amounts as possible, to as many donees as possible, to reduce the donor's taxable estate. Therefore, as a transfer-tax planning technique, you should look first into adopting a systematic gifting program by making as many annual exclusion gifts as you can afford at the *beginning* of each calendar year.

Gifts to Minors

If you are going to make gifts to a minor (someone who is under the state-specified age of legal majority, usually 18), you have to be concerned not only about gift-tax laws, but also about state property laws. Minors cannot take title to property in the same way individuals of legal majority—adults—can. Instead, minors must take title through custodial arrangements as specified by each state. Historically, custodial arrangements have also been a common method of saving for a child's college education, as discussed in Chapter 15.

There are two basic types of custodial arrangements: those provided by the Uniform Gifts to Minors Act (UGMA) and those provided by the Uniform Transfers to Minors Act (UTMA). In many states, UTMA has superseded the previously enacted UGMA and is now the approved form for making property transfers to minors. Under both uniform laws, the minor is given title to property, but the property is managed by a custodian, usually the parent or grandparent of the minor. This custodian then invests and manages the gifted property on behalf of the minor and does not own the property in any respect. As such, the custodial arrangement is similar to a trust on behalf of the minor, but it lacks the complexity and cost of implementing the trust document.

All states have simple forms to title property gifted to a minor in a custodial arrangement, but be aware that custodial gifts to minors are completed gifts for federal gift-tax purposes. In other words, the gift becomes the *minor's property*, and not yours, if you are the donor. As a result, at the state-specified legal age of majority, the child can do whatever they want with the gifted property. Even if the gift was intended to finance the child's future educational expenses, they are under no obligation to go to college or pursue higher education. Meanwhile, income used for your minor child's maintenance and support is taxable to *you* if you are the child's parent, even though you may *not* be the named custodian of the custodial arrangement. This is because, under all state property laws, as the child's parent you have the legal obligation to support and raise that child until they attain the legal age of majority.

Fortunately, as discussed in Chapter 15, Congress has legislated a much better technique for saving for college than custodial arrangements. Called a *private savings plan*, this approach for funding a child's future educational expenses is made possible under Section 529 of the Internal Revenue Code.

A Basic Primer on the Use of Trusts

A *trust* is an arrangement to which there are three parties:

- The individual who establishes the trust (known as the *creator* or *grantor*)

- The trustee of the trust
- The individual or individuals for whose benefit the trust is established (known as the trust *beneficiary* or *beneficiaries*)

In any trust arrangement, the trustee must act solely and exclusively on behalf of the trust beneficiaries. The trustee has the legal title to the trust assets, but the beneficiaries have what is known in the law as *equitable title* to the assets.

Trusts carry many advantages when they are used in transfer-tax planning and management, as well as in estate planning generally. Among these are the following:

- The ability to benefit one or more specified beneficiaries
- The ability to afford the expertise of a professional or other skilled individual in the management of the investment of trust assets
- The ability to provide asset protection
- The ability to avoid probate
- The ability to achieve income- and transfer-tax savings

There are many types of trusts, including those established on behalf of minors, but all may be categorized from a transfer-tax perspective as either revocable or irrevocable trusts.

Revocable Trusts

A *revocable trust* is created during your lifetime, and you retain the power to revoke, or take back, the trust assets. Accordingly, you do not make a completed gift, nor do you lose the right to the income from the trust assets. However, if you appoint someone else the beneficiary of the trust, a gift does occur at that time. When you die, if you have not revoked the trust, the trust becomes irrevocable and can operate in lieu of a will to distribute your assets.

A revocable trust offers two major advantages, neither of which involves transfer-tax savings:

- If you transfer assets to the trust during your lifetime and retitle them in the name of the trustee (which is typically you), the trust assets avoid the probate process in the state where you die.
- If you become mentally incompetent (for example, if you contract Alzheimer's disease), the successor trustee of the trust can assume the management of your financial and personal affairs.

Additionally, you can reduce the beneficiary's estate tax by using a revocable trust—when it becomes irrevocable at your death—if the trust is drafted properly.

Keep in mind that because you keep complete control over the trust and its assets, the assets are included in your gross estate. However, if you are below the estate-tax allowable exemption amount ($11.2 million in 2018), you should not be concerned about this disadvantage. Furthermore, generally the advantages that trusts provide far outweigh the lack of transfer-tax savings your estate will suffer from the revocable trust at the time of your death.

Revocable trusts, which are also known as *living trusts* when property is retitled in the name of the trustee, are heavily promoted by trust sponsors and marketing firms as the panacea to all estate-tax problems. Although this is decidedly *not* the case, living trusts can be an effective estate-planning tool, particularly for individuals who own a vacation home or other real estate in a state other than their primary residence. For owners of out-of-state vacation homes, a second, or *ancillary*, probate proceeding is required in the state where the vacation home is located. By transferring the title of the vacation home to the trustee of the revocable trust, your estate can avoid multiple probate proceedings.

Irrevocable Trusts

An *irrevocable trust*, which may be created during your lifetime or at the time of your death, can result in estate-tax savings when you—the creator of the trust—die. The term *irrevocable* means just what it implies: *you cannot change, revoke, or amend the trust in any way after you create it.* This disadvantage alone is incentive enough for many trust creators to shy away from even considering the implementation of an irrevocable trust—with one or two notable exceptions.

The first reason you may wish to create an irrevocable trust has to do with the usual motivations of individuals who purchase life insurance policies. Most individuals purchase a life insurance policy for death-motivated reasons: that is, to protect their survivors from the loss of income resulting from their death. Given the at-death motivation and the fact that a low gift-tax value is associated with most policies, the life insurance policy is usually an excellent asset to transfer to an irrevocable trust. As such, funding a trust with only a life insurance policy, otherwise known as creating an **irrevocable life insurance trust (ILIT)**, is a commonly used estate-planning technique.

The second reason you may wish to create an irrevocable trust is for asset protection from creditors. This type of trust, which is particularly popular among doctors and lawyers and other professionals who are frequently the target of lawsuits, is known as a *foreign situs* or *offshore* trust. Be careful, though: the offshore trust is controversial, and the IRS monitors its operation carefully.

In part, this is because the income generated from property transferred to the trust is still taxable to its creator, or **grantor**. As a result, unless the trust is drafted skillfully and for appropriate estate-planning reasons, the trust may be rendered void on its face in violation of the state fraudulent conveyance laws of its creator.

Components and Valuation of the Gross Estate

Thus far in this chapter, I have mentioned the estate tax on a few occasions, but what, exactly, is the *estate tax?* This tax is ultimately assessed on an amount known as the *tentative tax base*, which is your taxable estate plus any adjusted taxable gifts made during your lifetime; but the computation begins with assets that make up the taxpayer's *gross estate*. The gross estate is similar to gross income under income-tax law, but with one major difference: in income-tax law, tax is assessed on your *annual income*, whereas in estate-tax law, tax is assessed on the fair market value of your *lifetime assets* as of the date of your death. Operationally, the income tax is a government levy on the inflow items you show on your *personal cash-flow statement*; conversely, the estate tax is a government levy on the asset items you show on your *statement of personal financial position*.

The gross estate consists of not only assets you die owning, but also certain lifetime transfers (gifts) over which you retain control or from which you enjoy benefits at the time of your death. For example, if you make a gift to an irrevocable lifetime trust but at your death are an income beneficiary of that trust, the *total* fair market value of the trust assets at your date of death is taxed. Similarly, if you have previously gifted an out-of-state vacation home to your favorite child, but you retain by agreement with that child the right to use the home whenever you want, the fair market value of that home at your date of death is taxed. For example, assume that you live in North Dakota but own a winter home in Florida. In 2018, you transfer the title to the Florida home to your oldest son but, per an oral agreement with him, are permitted to use the home whenever you want. If you die still holding this power, the fair market value of the Florida home is included in your gross estate, as if you had never transferred the title to your son in the first place.

Property is included in your estate at its fair market value as of the date of your *death*. You should contrast this with gifted property, which is valued at its fair market value as of the date of the *gift*. Most of the time, the date-of-death fair market value of property can be easily established. For example, publicly traded stock is valued based on the average of the highest and lowest trading price on the decedent's date of death. Real estate can also be relatively easily valued by referencing comparable sales in the neighborhood or area. However, if a decedent is the owner of a small, family, or closely held business, the value of their business interest may not be so easily determined. Many factors must be considered when establishing this value, not the least of which is whether the owner owns a controlling or minority interest in the business at the time of their death. If you are an owner of a closely held business, it is best to contact a qualified appraiser to help you value it properly for estate- or gift-tax purposes.

One final comment with respect to the assets included in the gross estate and their respective value: if you die owning or having incidents of ownership with respect to a life insurance policy, you have to include the *death proceeds* or *face value* of that policy in your gross estate. This is a much *greater* amount than the fair market value of the policy, which, depending on its type, is usually relatively small. For example, if you own a cash-value type of life insurance policy, its fair market value is close to its accumulated cash value. Meanwhile, if you own a term policy that has no cash value, its fair market value is close to zero. This is all the more reason to consider making a lifetime gift of a life insurance policy to a beneficiary: if you gift it, the policy has a *small* value, whereas if you die owning it, the policy has a *large* value. Assume, for example, that you die owning a whole life insurance policy with a face value of $500,000 and that the accumulated cash value in this policy at your date of death is $80,000. For estate-tax purposes, the policy is included in your gross estate at a value of $500,000. If you had previously gifted it, the policy value for gift-tax purposes would be no more than $80,000 (and probably less, because the policy would not have accumulated the same amount of cash value at your death years later).

Deductions and Credits Available to the Estate

As with the income-tax system, deductions and credits are available to the estate for transfer-tax purposes. However, unlike those that you can claim under the income-tax system, these deductions and credits are not usually limited in amount.

The two most useful—and probably the most frequently claimed—estate-tax deductions are those for property transfers at death to either your spouse or a qualified charity. Respectively, these are known as the estate-tax *marital deduction* and the estate-tax *charitable deduction*. They are unlimited in amount, as is also the case for transfers to a spouse or qualified charity during an individual's lifetime for gift-tax purposes. However, both types of property transfers need to be left in a qualifying form before the deduction is permitted. Specifically, property transfers to a spouse at death must be left without restriction, and property transfers to a qualified charity must generally be left in the form of a charitable trust.

Assume that you leave all your property outright (with no restrictions) to your spouse at your date of death under your will or by beneficiary designation. This is acceptable and qualifies the full amount of transferred assets for the unlimited estate-tax marital deduction. However, if you left your property to your spouse only for their lifetime use or for a term of years (in other words, with restrictions), the transfer typically does *not* qualify for the unlimited marital deduction. Next, assume that you leave property in remainder interest to a qualified charity but reserve the right to the income from the property during your lifetime through a **charitable remainder trust (CRT)**. The remainder interest left to charity at the time of your death qualifies for the unlimited estate-tax charitable deduction. But if you tried to accomplish this same transfer during your lifetime without establishing a trust, the unlimited charitable deduction would likely *not* be allowed.

Several credits also are available in estate-tax planning, the most useful of which is the *unified credit*. The unified credit is equal to a certain amount of property that may be transferred estate-tax free at death. However, as with income tax, this credit is applied only *after* computing the total tax liability. For example, in 2018, the amount of estate tax on $11.2 million of taxable estate property is $4,425,800. To that amount, you must apply the allowable unified credit (assuming you made no previous lifetime taxable gifts) of $4,425,800, so your net estate-tax liability is zero. When you hear that you may transfer up to $11.2 million in property free of estate tax (actually more, if your only beneficiary is your spouse or a qualified charity), you know it to be true, because you have an allowable unified credit of $4,425,800 to offset the tax due on that amount.

But you need to be aware of one circumstance that *reduces* the $4,425,800 unified credit at death. Because the gift- and estate-tax systems are linked (which is where the term *unified* comes from), any taxable gifts that you make during your lifetime in excess of the gift-tax annual exclusion impact the amount of unified credit that is available to your estate at your death. As such, if you make any taxable gifts during your lifetime, the credit amount that you use to offset that gift-tax liability *reduces* your allowable unified credit at death. For example, assume that you die with a taxable estate of $11.2 million in 2018 and you leave it all equally to your two children. During your lifetime, however, you made taxable gifts of $75,000 to each of those children. In operational effect, this means you have a tentative tax base of $11.35 million, leaving you with an estate tax due of $60,000 ($150,000 excess over the $11.2 million exempted amount times the applicable marginal estate-tax rate of 40 percent). Looked at another way, you have *reduced* your allowable unified credit by $60,000 and thus have available at your death only an allowable unified credit of $4,365,800 ($4,425,800 less $60,000).

Tax Rates and the Possible Repeal of the Death Tax

In recent years, one of the transfer taxes—the estate tax—has become somewhat of a political football. Specifically, some legislators have urged the repeal of what they believe to be an unnecessary and even punitive tax, while others are worried about the revenue effects of eliminating this tax. However, the ongoing debate over the estate tax was likely settled—at least for now—with the doubling of the estate-tax (and gift-tax) exemption from $5 million to $10 million, as indexed for inflation, in the 2017 TCJA. This provision is effective for estates of decedents dying after December 31, 2017, but the exemption amount will revert back to the $5 million indexed amount after 2025 unless amended by a subsequent Congress.

Moreover, the American Taxpayer Relief Act of 2012 included a permanent extension of the *portability* of exclusion amounts between married couples. Specifically, portability allows the estate of a decedent who is survived by a spouse to make an election to permit the surviving spouse to apply the decedent's unused exclusion to the surviving spouse's *own* transfers during life and at death. In effect, to the extent that the decedent's spouse's $11.2 million exclusion is not used at all during their lifetime or at death, the married couple enjoys a joint $22.4 million ($11.2 million times 2) exclusion amount before any transfer tax is payable in 2018. However, note that to take advantage of portability of the unused exclusion, an estate-tax return needs to be filed for the first spouse *regardless* of whether any estate tax is due for that spouse.

Do I Really Want to Leave It All to My Spouse or Charity?

As we have discussed, the deduction available for transfers made at death to a spouse or charity is *unlimited in amount*. But as a planning technique, do you really want to take full advantage of either deduction?

Although the tax law allows you and your spouse to leave each other all property free from estate tax, you may end up increasing or overfunding your spouse's estate if you leave everything to them. This is particularly the case if your net worth is already at or near the estate-tax exemption equivalent of tax-free property ($11.2 million in 2018). If your spouse is much younger than you (and thus there is considerable time for your bequeathed assets to grow in value), it may *not* be the best idea to leave it all to them.

This possibility is one of the major problems with titling all your property in **joint tenancy with right of survivorship** (JTWROS) with your spouse: from a planning perspective, JTWROS titling limits your flexibility, because all property passes directly to your spouse. It may result in too-great-an-amount

Plan Your Financial Future

of property taxable in the surviving spouse's gross estate, a problem commonly referred to as *overfunding the estate*.

Insofar as federal transfer-tax law is concerned, there is, since the 2015 US Supreme Court decision of Obergefell v. Hodges, no debate about who constitutes a spouse for the purposes of taking advantage of the unlimited marital deduction allowance; the spouse may be a member of either the opposite or the same sex. As a result, gay and lesbian individuals who enter into marriage must be recognized as a lawful union by all States. This entitles such individuals to several important estate-tax benefits, chief among them the use of the unlimited marital deduction for the making of lifetime gifts and transfers at death. The titling of property among gay and lesbian individuals in joint tenancy with right of survivorship also remains as a planning alternative.

If your estate or the combined estate of you and your spouse is currently equal to or expected to be more than the allowable exemption equivalent, you may wish to consider seeking the counsel of an estate-planning attorney relatively soon.

You may also wish to do so if you have questions about the possible application of the portability exclusion election. When and if you do seek assistance, ask the attorney about including in your estate plan a **disclaimer trust**, which will allow your spouse or estate executor to do some after-death planning and legally refuse the amount of your property that may **overfund** their estate. It will save your ultimate estate beneficiaries a great deal of money in the long run.

In contrast to property left to your spouse, you do not need to be concerned about possibly overfunding a charity. If the charity is tax-qualified, it is a tax-exempt entity and does not pay any income or transfer taxes on bequeathed property. You do, however, need to take into account how best to take care of family members who have otherwise been disinherited because their portion of your estate went to a charity. In most states, your surviving spouse may elect against your will to take the portion of your estate that they normally would have been entitled to—usually half of all your property at death—but your children, siblings, and close friends are not permitted this election.

There are several ways to benefit, or "re-inherit," your children or other disadvantaged heirs. The most popular is to buy a life insurance policy and name your children as its beneficiaries. If you buy a policy in the name of an ILIT, the death proceeds from the policy are removed from your gross estate for transfer-tax purposes. However, because the proceeds are paid from a life insurance policy, they are *not* taxable to your children or other beneficiary for income-tax purposes. In estate-planning terminology, setting up an ILIT in this manner, and for the reason of making up an inheritance otherwise lost to charity, is known as a **wealth replacement trust**.

For example, assume that, as an unmarried individual with two adult children, you wish to benefit the American Cancer Society (ACS) with the majority of your $11.2 million estate in 2018. As a result, you make a bequest in your will of $10 million to the ACS. Meanwhile, at the time you write your will, you also establish an ILIT and name your two adult children as the trust beneficiaries. You then have the ILIT purchase a $10 million life insurance policy on your life. Accordingly, you get the benefit of both claiming the estate-tax charitable deduction and accomplishing your philanthropic goals. Plus, you meet these objectives without disadvantaging your children, who would otherwise expect to be the beneficiaries of your estate.

The Unintended Danger of Generation-Skipping Transfers

Many high-net-worth individuals are unaware that there is a *third* transfer tax on gifts and estates that skip a generation, such as those made by a grandparent to a grandchild. The additional tax that is assessed on this transfer is known as the *generation-skipping transfer tax (GSTT)*.

The rules with respect to skip transfers are complex, but here is what you need to know to avoid the GSTT:

- The tax is designed to impose the equivalent of the gift or estate tax that the intervening generation (or the parent's generation) would have paid for the transfer.

- The tax is imposed *in addition to* either the estate or gift tax; thus, the tax can only add to an otherwise sizable transfer-tax burden.

- The tax is assessed at the *maximum* estate-tax rate in a flat rate at the time of a generation-skipping transfer

- There is no progressivity leading up to this maximum rate as there is with other lifetime or testamentary transfers (for example, in 2018, a flat 40 percent rate applies to any generation-skipping transfer).

- The tax potentially applies to a gift made either directly from grandparent to grandchild during the grandparent's lifetime (known as a *direct skip*) or at the time of the grandparent's death via a trust, wherein the grandchild is benefited to the exclusion of the parent (otherwise referred to as a *taxable termination* or *indirect skip*).

- The tax potentially applies to a gift made from one unrelated individual (transferor) to another (transferee), where the transferee is at least 37.5 years younger than the transferor.
- The liability for paying the tax falls on different individuals depending on the type of generation-skipping transfer made.

Fortunately, most individuals can escape the payment of the GSTT—even if they do make a generation-skipping transfer—rather easily. This is because the transferor has an $11.2 million exemption (in 2018) that they can allocate to the transfer to avoid the imposition of the tax. This allowable exemption, to be used on an elective basis by the transferor or their estate, tracks the estate-tax exemption equivalent or exclusion that was previously discussed. Direct gifts to grandchildren that qualify for the gift-tax annual exclusion ($15,000 in 2018) during the grandparent's lifetime also are not subject to the tax.

Let's say, for example, that in 2018, a wealthy grandfather makes a direct gift of $11,215,000 in appreciated stock to his adult granddaughter. If he *elects* to allocate his full $11.2 million generation-skipping exemption to the transfer (the $15,000 gift-tax annual exclusion is automatic and does *not* need to be elected), no GSTT is imposed. However, be aware that the generation-skipping tax exemption amount is now fully allocated and may not be used to offset any additional generation-skipping transfers at the time of the grandfather's death. Also, not only may the GSTT apply to the direct gift, but so potentially does the federal gift tax on any transfers made from a donor to a donee in excess of $15,000 annually in 2018.

In summary, the GSTT may be easily avoided with a little planning. If your will or trust was drafted before 1987, when this tax came into effect, you should ask your estate-planning attorney or financial planner to review it to see whether the tax applies. If the tax does potentially apply, amend your will so as to *defend* your hard-earned wealth. If you are fortunate enough to avoid the imposition of the tax in your estate planning, be aware that the GSTT constitutes an unintended danger to the *accumulation* and *distribution* of wealth from one generation to the next.

Now, to conclude this section of the book, let's look at common events that may threaten the accumulation of lifetime wealth. Among these are the divorce of married couples and the unexpected loss of employment in today's economy. Life events that endanger wealth are the title and focus of the next chapter.

CHAPTER 14

Life Events that Endanger Wealth

As you go through life, you sometimes experience events that endanger or threaten the amount of wealth that you have accumulated. We have already discussed the importance of obtaining an individual disability income policy in the event of physical disability, and we will discuss how to plan for your own possible mental incapacity later in this chapter. Specifically, however, we identify important planning considerations with respect to six potentially financially devastating life events, including divorce, the loss of a job for an extended period of time, the death of a spouse or life partner, a parent incurring a debilitating condition, caring for a developmentally disabled child, and physical or mental incapacity.

Divorce

Statistics indicate that one of out of every two marriages ends in divorce (the legal ending of a marriage) or separation (the establishment of a separate and independent lifestyle from that of your spouse). How do you financially make the best of (and hopefully recover from) divorce or separation?

Likely the first financial task that you, your attorney, or your financial planner should undertake—either before the divorce is finalized or immediately after property settlement—is to separate your and your spouse's assets and liabilities. You need to prepare new statements of personal financial position. Unlike before, when assets and liabilities could be listed as joint or individually owned on one statement, you now potentially need to prepare *three* personal financial statements: his, hers, and ours. If you live in a community property state, such as California or Texas, the division of assets and liabilities is easier, because all marital property must be divided equally between spouses. This may not be the case in non-community-property states, also referred to as *common law states*. Nevertheless, the preparation of separate financial statements is still prudent divorce planning in all states.

Once you have identified and reduced to writing your and your spouse's total assets and liabilities, each of you needs to prepare separate income or cash-flow statements. Doing so will assist you in determining whether temporary alimony or child support is possible before the divorce is finalized, and it also will help you establish any future amounts that may need to be paid. As a general rule, many divorcing spouses do not fully understand how their living expenses will change after divorce. As a result, ex-spouses typically *underestimate* how much money they will need to sustain their pre-divorce standard of living. The notable exception to this rule is a celebrity divorce, wherein divorcing spouses typically *overestimate* their future income needs.

Three basic provisions of most divorce or separation agreements should be carefully considered by separating spouses:

- The amount and necessity of alimony payments from one spouse to the other
- The amount of child support payments, if there are minor children from the marriage
- The division of property accumulated during the marriage (otherwise known as the *property settlement agreement*)

If the spouses own a home at the time of the divorce, attention should also be given to how best to divide equity in that important asset.

Alimony

Alimony, if it is to be paid, is often the most contentious aspect of any divorce proceeding. This is complicated by the fact that the payer of the alimony receives an income-tax deduction for payments made, thereby encouraging them to allocate *as much* of the total payments from the divorce to alimony as possible. To prevent this abuse, some years ago Congress added a provision to the Internal Revenue Code known as *excess front-loading alimony rules*, commonly referred to as *alimony recapture*. If violated, these rules make the payer go back and include in their income statement some portion of the alimony paid and deducted.

For example, assume that a husband made an alimony payment of $50,000 in the first year subsequent to a divorce and nothing thereafter. Under the alimony recapture rules, at the end of the third year after the divorce, the husband is required to file an amended income-tax return and include a portion of the $50,000 first-year payment in his income. This excess payment is referred to as *disguised alimony* because, inevitably, the real intent of the payment was as part of a property settlement agreement between the husband and wife. This payment could also have been intended as child support in the event that the couple had minor children at the time of the divorce.

The payee, for their part, must include in their income any alimony paid by the payer. Although not technically income in the sense of salary or wages, alimony constitutes earned income as characterized by a traditional IRA contribution. This means a stay-at-home ex-wife receiving alimony from her husband may contribute and deduct up to the specified annual amount for IRA savings and her own eventual retirement.

To qualify as tax-deductible alimony, payments stipulated in the divorce or separation agreement cannot be designated as something other than alimony (such as child support, for example). In addition, the payments cannot be scheduled to continue after the death of the payee spouse and must be made in cash or its equivalent. As such, transferring appreciated securities to an ex-spouse does not constitute alimony. However, payments made to a third party on behalf of the payee—such as life insurance premiums payable on the life of the payer—*do* constitute alimony.

For example, assume that a wife receives a sizable alimony award as a result of her divorce from her physically ailing husband. She is very concerned about how these alimony payments will be made if her husband predeceases her. Accordingly, as a part of the divorce decree, she mandates that the husband continue his premium payments on his life insurance policy and retain her as the irrevocable beneficiary. These premium payments constitute qualifying, deductible alimony for income-tax purposes.

In this example, what happens if the husband *fails* to make the premium payments on his life insurance policy, leaving the wife without income protection? The husband may be held in contempt of court and punished with jail time. This complicates the wife's situation even further, though, because if the husband is in jail, it is extremely unlikely that he will resume making life insurance premium payments. There is a better way.

As a planning technique in the context of this example, consider having the wife own the life insurance policy and make the premium payments. This prevents changes from being made to the policy without her knowledge. In addition, if the wife can afford it, have her buy life insurance that can build cash value on the life of the husband (for example, a whole life, universal life, variable life, or variable/universal life policy). The cash account in this policy is now hers to do with as she pleases, and she may even borrow against the policy for her own retirement if she so chooses. If any *new* life insurance is needed as a result of her changed financial circumstances after the divorce, the wife should apply for the insurance *before* the divorce is final. Then, if the husband cannot qualify for the life insurance (for example, because of poor health), the wife may still modify the final divorce decree to make up for the loss of the insurance proceeds. The treatment of alimony for tax purposes changes in the year 2019. Specifically, under the 2017 TCJA, alimony paid by one spouse to the other is *not* deductible, and the spouse receiving the alimony no longer pays taxes on the alimony amount. This creates a unique set of planning circumstances in the year 2018. The alimony-seeking spouse has an incentive to delay the divorce until 2019, whereas the alimony-paying spouse has an incentive to accelerate the making of the payment to the year 2018. It will be interesting to observe how divorce attorneys consider these competing goals.

Child Support

Each state has applicable guidelines with respect to the amount of child support that may be appropriate in any divorce agreement. If you are working with a divorce attorney or financial planner, they will be familiar with these guidelines. However, as with any cash-flow issue, be sure you, as the payer, can afford the minimum recommended child-support payment. For most divorcing individuals, the question is not whether child support should be paid, but rather how much should be paid. As such, be sure you are comfortable with the amount specified by the court—and pay it! Although it is against the law for an employer to fire you because you are not current with child-support payments, there is no prohibition against garnishing your wages to pay back-due amounts. If this happens, the employer may use other reasons to terminate your employment, notwithstanding that the real reason was your failure to assume the parental responsibility of supporting your children.

Child-support payments are neither deductible by the payer spouse nor taxable as income to the payee spouse. However, sometimes there is a question as to whether a payment is, indeed, child support or disguised alimony. Here is the standard rule you can use to tell the difference: if any portion of the agreed-on payment may be reduced because of circumstances related *to the child*, it is child support for income-tax purposes. For example, if the payment is reduced after the child goes to college, it is treated as nondeductible and nontaxable child support. This differentiation is likely important to high-income divorcing couples, where the higher-wage earner wants as much of the payment as possible treated as deductible alimony. This is in marked contrast to the lower-income earner, who probably is not nearly as concerned with the tax treatment of the payment.

Child Tax Credit

One other consideration in divorce also becomes important in light of 2017 TCJA changes: qualifying for the increased **child tax credit** of $2,000, up to which $1,400 is potentially **refundable**.

The definition of a *qualifying child* for taking advantage of the child tax credit is the same as that for claiming a dependency tax exemption except that the child must not have attained the age of 17 by the end of the year. As such, whether the child may be claimed as a dependent by either one of the divorced spouses is critical to clarify in the making of the divorce settlement. Typically, the dependency exemption for a child who is qualifying child for purposes of also claiming the child tax credit will accrue to the parent who has primary custody of the child for the current taxable year. However, the custodial parent can waive the exemption, thereby permitting the noncustodial parent to claim the qualifying child for purposes of the credit. As a result, the determination of the custodial parent for purposes of the child tax credit (and the increased amount) should now be considered more carefully in light of the 2017 TCJA changes.

Property Settlements

The overriding issue in finalizing a property settlement agreement is to be fair to both spouses. In **community property** states, where both spouses own half of all property acquired during the marriage, an equal division is relatively easy. However, a notable exception occurs when one spouse brings an already-thriving small business to the marriage, but the business is worth considerably more at the time of the couple's divorce or legal separation. The question then arises: how is the appreciation of the business during the couple's marriage best handled? The answer varies depending on state community-property law, but generally, the founder-of-the-business spouse is awarded the value of the business at the time they brought it to the marriage in addition to half of the appreciation in the business thereafter. The nonfounder spouse receives the other half of the appreciation.

Assume that you live in California and recently started a computer software business. It is worth $1 million when you marry your spouse. Eight years later, you get divorced, and at the time of your divorce, the business is worth $10 million. It is likely that the court will award you a settlement of $5.5 million with respect to the business—your original $1 million for your interest in the business prior to your marriage and another $4.5 million for the appreciation of your business during your marriage. You now have to come up with another $4.5 million to buy out your spouse's interest or sell the business entirely to make the required payment. (Can you see why divorce can be financially devastating to your accumulated wealth?)

There are currently eight community property states in the United States, and a ninth—Wisconsin—has a similar form of property law known as *marital property*. The two largest community property states—California and Texas—are relatively well known to most Americans. The other six states with community property law systems are as follows:

- Arizona
- Idaho
- Louisiana
- Nevada
- New Mexico
- Washington

In addition, Alaska allows for the establishment of community property among married couples on an elective basis.

All the remaining states (41, after accounting for Wisconsin's variation of the community property form) are referred to in property law as **common law property** or *individual property* states. In these states, either the husband or wife (even with property acquired *during* the marriage) can title property in their *individual* name. However, for those who think this may be an advantage when it comes to making an inordinate or unequal division of property at the time of divorce, think again! Most—if not all—common-law property states follow a concept in property settlements known as *equitable distribution*. Under this model, each spouse has a legal right during marriage to the other spouse's earnings and to the assets acquired with those earnings. As a result, common-law states end up in essentially the same place as community property states with respect to property acquired during the marriage: it is typically split in half between each of the spouses at the time of divorce or separation.

Often, the most contentious part of property-settlement negotiations is how to fairly divide one spouse's present or future retirement benefits. If this issue pertains to you, you should obtain a valuation of your (or your spouse's) current 401(k) or other retirement plan balance at the time of divorce. Once you have this valuation, make sure, if you are the payee spouse, that you obtain what is known as a *qualified domestic relations order* (QDRO) from the court. This order awards you the same rights that the plan participant would have had under the 401(k) or other retirement plan, including the right to choose your own investments.

As a divorcing spouse, you can also receive current or future Social Security benefits based on your former spouse's employment record if the following conditions are met:

- You were married to your former spouse for at least ten years.
- You are not remarried.
- You are at least 62 years old.
- Your former spouse is at least 62 years old and entitled to retirement or disability benefits.

Note that if you remarry *after* you have attained the age of 62, your eligibility for Social Security benefits based on your former spouse's employment record is not affected.

Principal Residence

Typically, the major asset that most couples own at the time of divorce is their house or primary residence. Because most couples are jointly obligated on the home mortgage, half of each mortgage payment may qualify as deductible alimony by the departing spouse. The other half of the mortgage payment is deductible by the remaining spouse under normal mortgage interest deduction rules; in other words, the remaining spouse should itemize their deductions on a separately filed income-tax return. Proceed carefully, however. Remember, under the alimony tax rules, any payment that constitutes deductible alimony may not be specified as anything other than alimony. Therefore, if you are the departing spouse and will be responsible for half the mortgage, add a sufficient amount to your required alimony payments to cover your portion of the monthly mortgage interest liability.

For example, assume that you and your wife are getting a divorce. You have agreed to pay her alimony of $3,000 per month. Your mortgage payment each month is $1,000, and $600 of that amount is interest. You remain obligated for your half of the mortgage payment. As such, add or recharacterize half—or $300—of the mortgage interest payment as deductible alimony, resulting in a total alimony payment of $3,300 per month (the $3,000 original amount plus the additional $300 recharacterized amount).

It gets even more complicated if you, as the departing spouse, are solely responsible for the mortgage payment. Although you are considered to have paid all the monthly interest on the mortgage, you are not necessarily entitled to the full itemized interest deduction. Rather, once you have moved out of the house, the house is no longer your primary residence (which, as you know from Chapter 11, can have serious tax implications if your ex-spouse sells the house immediately or if you did not live in it for at least two years before it is sold). You may be able to claim the house as a secondary residence and deduct the mortgage interest in that manner. The catch in this strategy, however, is that you must let your ex-spouse remain in the primary residence rent-free. Some spouses do not want to do this, particularly if it is a bitter divorce proceeding.

The key takeaway from this discussion is this: if you are involved in a divorce, do not try to represent yourself. The potential damaging consequences to your accumulated wealth are much too significant to forego seeking the assistance of competent legal and financial counsel.

Loss of Employment

Beyond the major psychological trauma of losing your job, particularly if you were terminated "for cause," are the financial consequences that should be considered in the aftermath of such an event. Chief among these is how to immediately reduce your ongoing living expenses. If you have not done so already, consider refinancing your current mortgage to obtain a lower interest rate. Although refinancing extends the life of the mortgage obligation, your monthly payment is reduced. What's more, refinancing usually frees up cash that can be used for any reason, including the payment of living expenses until you can find new employment. Note that this is not the case with a home-equity loan or line of credit under the 2017 TCJA: beginning in 2018, those proceeds may be used only for purposes of home improvements.

Another key issue involved in managing job loss is the reevaluation of your and your family's health insurance needs. As discussed in Chapter 5, remember that you can exercise your COBRA rights after losing your job. Yes, you will likely have to pay your previous employer's share of the group medical insurance, but this option is probably much less expensive than purchasing an individual health insurance policy. Alternatively, cost savings may result from funding a health savings account (HSA) and purchasing a high-deductible individual health insurance policy. In addition, current tax rules stipulate that, as a former employee, you may take distributions from your IRA to pay health insurance premiums while unemployed *without* being subject to a 10 percent early distribution penalty. However, unless you own a Roth IRA—and have done so for a specified period of time—you must pay ordinary income tax on the distribution.

Should you file for unemployment benefits after you have lost your job? There are several considerations to keep in mind. The first is psychological: do you feel embarrassed, or are you reluctant to file? Some workers, particularly those who have been terminated from a management position, simply cannot bear to file for unemployment benefits. Nevertheless, you should be aware that, in most cases, unemployment is available *regardless* of the position you left and your job status at your former employer. Your former employer has paid a tax under the Federal Unemployment Tax Act (FUTA) for just this reason.

The second consideration with respect to unemployment benefits is a more practical one: are you eligible to receive benefits? The answer depends on why you left your former employer. Assuming that you earned enough money to qualify for unemployment benefits during the previous 12-month period, you must, then, have left your job for one or more of the following reasons:

- You were terminated (laid off) through no fault of your own.
- You voluntarily quit your job for good reason.
- You were involuntarily terminated, but not because of embezzlement, violating the company's drug policy, or anything else unrelated to poor job performance.

The biggest uncertainty in any of these reasons is what constitutes "good reason" for you to voluntarily leave your job. Unfortunately, you do not get to make this determination; your local unemployment agency caseworker does (sometimes along with your former supervisor). As a result, if you left your job voluntarily and file for unemployment benefits, carefully document in writing why you left before speaking with your caseworker, and justify that it was for reasons unrelated to personal preference or desires for another career.

Death of a Spouse or Life Partner

As with job loss, psychological and financial issues are associated with the premature death of a spouse or life partner. Unlike with job loss, however, assuming that the life of the spouse or partner is adequately insured, the psychological aspects of overcoming the loss are probably paramount.

Normally, countless financial questions confront the survivor of the spouse or partner, including these:

- Do I pay off or pay down the mortgage now while remaining in the house?
- Do I sell the house and move?
- If I am not retired, do I retire now (or as soon as financially possible)?
- Do I continue to work?
- Am I entitled to retirement or life insurance benefits?
- How do I distribute any retirement or life insurance benefits to which I am entitled?
- Can I afford to live in the same lifestyle to which I am accustomed?
- Should I seek the assistance of a financial advisor?

None of these questions is easy to answer, particularly during the grieving process. Nevertheless, they need to be addressed—and sooner, rather than later—to avoid damaging the lifetime wealth you accumulated together.

Not only is the surviving spouse or life partner the beneficiary of all or most of a decedent's estate, but they are also often the named executor or administrator of that estate. Legally, the difference between an executor and an administrator depends on whether the decedent dies with or without a will. If the decedent dies after having written a will (or dies *testate*), the individual named to handle the decedent's financial affairs is referred to as the *executor*. If the decedent dies without a will (or dies *intestate*), the individual appointed by the court to handle the decedent's financial affairs is said to be the *administrator* of the estate. In either case, if the spouse or partner survives, he or she is normally the named executor or appointed administrator of the estate.

This raises the question of whether the surviving spouse, as the named executor or administrator, should take a fee for the rendering of services. Under the probate code of most states, the surviving spouse is entitled to such a fee, but they should consider the usual circumstances of most estates. In most circumstances, the surviving spouse or executor is also the primary (if not sole) beneficiary of the deceased spouse's property. Furthermore, under federal transfer tax, property that is inherited by the spouse or any other beneficiary is *not* income taxable. However, if the surviving spouse or executor collects a fee for administration services associated with the estate, that fee *is* income taxable. As a result, by accepting a fee, the surviving spouse converts nontaxable income into taxable income. The better option, clearly, is for the executor to receive all (or their share) of the decedent's property at death in the form of an inheritance and *not* reduce this amount by an after-tax payment of executor fees.

As is discussed further in Part 5 of this book, whether a court becomes involved in administering your estate depends on whether your estate goes through *probate*, which is a legal proceeding administered by the local court to verify title to a decedent's assets and distribute them to your heirs at death. Generally speaking, many individuals do not like the potential costs and delays inherent in the probate process and search for ways to plan around it. There are three primary means of doing this, and we will examine each in turn:

- Title all your assets jointly (in joint tenancy with right of survivorship) with someone else, such as your spouse or life partner.
- Use beneficiary designations on as many assets as permitted by law.
- Establish a revocable living trust and transfer as many assets as you can into it during your lifetime.

Titling Assets Jointly

Titling all your assets in joint tenancy with right of survivorship (JTWROS) with someone else is sometimes referred to as "the poor man's way of avoiding probate," because it does not involve the drafting of a trust or acquiring any other assets for which a beneficiary designation is possible, such as a life insurance policy. Typically, only spouses title assets jointly, although such titling was heavily used by same-sex domestic partners in states where the marital relationship was not legally recognized.

Joint tenancy titling may be both a blessing and a curse, because it provides an easy way to dispose of property at death while avoiding probate, but it can be relatively inflexible from a transfer-tax standpoint. Specifically, if a surviving spouse already has significant property of their own, leaving even more property to them by operation of law only adds to an existing taxable estate. Fortunately, under current tax law, it is possible for a surviving spouse (or other surviving joint tenant) to refuse, or *disclaim*, the receipt of this additional property. However, the survivor must do so within nine months of the decedent's death and in a certain manner, referred to as a *qualified disclaimer*. Otherwise, the survivor is considered to have made a subsequent gift to whoever receives the property in their stead.

For example, assume that you are a joint tenant at your death with your already-ultra-wealthy spouse (particularly, given the increased estate-tax exemption from 2018–2025). To avoid potential additional estate taxes at their death, your spouse should refuse the property within nine months of your death by making a qualified disclaimer. They must do this before accepting any benefits from the disclaimed property and without separately directing to whom the property should now pass. If you have children, they normally receive any disclaimed property under state law. If you do not have children, your closest blood relative (or relatives) receive the property.

Using Beneficiary Designations

Beneficiary designations are typically contractual agreements used to leave property to others upon the death of the owner. Common examples of assets for which beneficiary designations are used are life insurance policies, employer-sponsored retirement plans (such as 401(k) plans), and IRAs. It is also possible to use a beneficiary designation to avoid probate on brokerage or advisory accounts.

Given that you should access taxable brokerage or advisory accounts before accessing any tax-deferred accounts during your lifetime, you may have few or no assets to pass in this manner. Nevertheless, you can avoid the probate process on these types of accounts by asking your broker or financial advisor for a transfer-on-death (TOD) form. Fill out that form for each of your brokerage or advisory accounts, and ask that it be sent back to the broker-dealer with whom you established the account. If you are investing online, ask whatever company or mutual fund family you are investing with to send you the comparable form. By proceeding in this manner, you should be able to avoid the probate process on those particular assets in the state of residence where your estate is potentially subject to court administration. Note that the same result may be accomplished with individual bank accounts, but the form used in this instance is referred to as a payable-on-death (POD) form.

Establishing and Funding a Revocable Living Trust

As discussed, *revocable living trusts* are frequently promoted for several reasons, but the most prevalent of these is their ability to avoid probate. Be careful, though: many grantors or creators of revocable living trusts believe all that is necessary to avoid probate is to purchase the trust document from the promoter. *This is not correct!* Rather, to avoid probate, your assets must be transferred into the name of the trust before your death and while you are still legally competent to know the ramifications of that action. If the assets (or any assets you may have acquired after establishing the trust) are not in the name of the trustee of the trust at your death, they do *not* avoid probate.

If you are electing to establish a revocable living trust and pass on all your assets via the trust outside probate, *you must fund the trust during your lifetime*. Alternatively, if you are not concerned about the delay or cost of probate, you can use the trust only to distribute your assets in a transfer-tax-efficient manner subsequent to your death. As a third option, you may elect to pass on all your property by using joint-tenancy titling or beneficiary designations and use the trust only as a standby document in the event that you become mentally incompetent during your lifetime.

For example, assume that you and your spouse own most of your property jointly, including your house, checking and savings accounts, and investment accounts. In addition, let's say your retirement plans and life insurance policies name your spouse as the primary beneficiary, and you are not concerned about having your estate or that of your spouse subject to transfer tax at death. Under such circumstances, you may wish to establish a revocable living trust to be used to manage your assets only in the event of your own mental incapacity. If this event occurs, you can name your spouse as the successor trustee or, if they are not able to serve in such a capacity, someone else (such as, perhaps, your favorite brother). Because you will be legally incompetent at the onset of your mental incapacity, you must also give your spouse a durable power of attorney to transfer property to the trust and avoid probate. (Durable powers of attorney are discussed later in this chapter.)

Now let's proceed to a common issue confronting many members of the baby-boom generation: how to pay for the long-term care expenses of a dependent parent.

Dependent Parents

Certainly, more issues are involved in caring for dependent parents other than paying for their long-term care expenses. (As a reminder, *long-term care* is defined in this context as daily care provided in a nursing home for a chronic medical condition.) Nevertheless, the payment of the ongoing expenses of a parent who cannot live alone independently or whom you, as a concerned child, cannot care for properly is a significant threat to your accumulated wealth. This is not to mention the additional emotional burden that taking care of a formerly able-bodied and responsible parent entails.

As you know from the discussion of Medicare and Medicaid in Chapter 5, Medicare provides only a limited benefit for skilled nursing facility care; and although Medicaid does cover long-term care, qualifying is extremely difficult. Remember also that some states have filial statutes that may require you to take care of your parents' long-term care expenses. In the absence of such a statute in your state, you are faced with the following options:

1. The best option is that your parent or parents are financially educated enough to recognize the need for long-term care insurance and have previously purchased a long-term care policy. Unfortunately, many seniors do not recognize this need before they can no longer qualify for the coverage or the protection is so prohibitively expensive that they cannot afford it.

2. The next best option, if your parents are likely to need long-term care but are unable to pay for the cost of the insurance themselves, is for you to buy the policy for them. The risk of this approach is that your parents may never need long-term care, and the expended premium dollars are lost forever.

3. A close alternative to the second option is that you set aside money to pay for your parents' long-term care needs. This option gives you more flexibility, because you do not lose the money if your parents do not need long-term care, but it means an added monthly or other periodic expense for which you have to budget.

4. The least-best option is that you do nothing and then the need arises for long-term care for your parents. In this instance, you are likely to see the wealth your parents accumulated (and your potential inheritance) slowly depleted over the years, at the end of which Medicaid is the only option.

As noted, the preferable option is that your parent does not place the burden of funding their long-term care on you. If they do, you should purchase a long-term-care insurance policy for your parent while they can still qualify for the coverage. You also need to consider how long an insurance benefit period you should purchase. Remember, the *longer* the benefit period, the *greater* the premium costs associated with the policy.

You may wish to purchase a lifetime benefit period for your parent to be absolutely sure that proper long-term care will be there for them when they need it. You may also wish to purchase a higher-than-normal daily benefit as part of the policy (currently, the average cost of nursing-home care for a semiprivate room is approximately $270 per day). If you do purchase a high daily benefit (beyond the average $270 per day), it is possible that you can *make* money from the policy. This is because you can pocket the higher daily benefit paid under the policy in excess of the actual daily cost charged by the facility. However, before you purchase such a high benefit, check with the insurance company or issuer of the policy, because such a motivation may be frowned on in your particular state.

You also need to consider what Medicare will and will not cover when your parent reaches age 65. For example, although Part D of Medicare has been fully implemented and now covers the cost of most prescription drugs for your elderly parent, a privately owned policy may provide better coverage. In addition, many deductibles and co-insurance payments are associated with Medicare Part A (hospital insurance) and Medicare Part B (physician's care) that you need to provide for.

The preferable way to cover these costs is to purchase a supplementary health insurance policy, commonly referred to as a *Medigap* policy. All Medigap policies are standardized according to federal law, with Medigap Policy A constituting the least expensive and least comprehensive form of coverage, and Medigap Policy F constituting the most expensive and most comprehensive coverage. As such, the purchase of a Medigap policy means you or your parent are protected by federal regulations with respect to supplementary medical care, a fact that may be of some comfort to you. It is also important to note that you may purchase only *one* Medigap policy for your parent at any given time under current law. In addition, your parent may not be turned down for supplemental coverage, regardless of any preexisting, potentially disqualifying medical conditions, as long as they apply for such coverage within six months of reaching age 65.

Claiming Your Parent as a Dependent for Income-Tax Purposes

Under the provisions of the 2017 TCJA, a *new* credit of $500 is permitted, beginning in 2018, when caring for a dependent parent. The dependency rules are the same as that for the child tax credit just discussed. However, unlike the child tax credit, which is partially refundable, the dependent parent or *nonchild dependent care credit* is nonrefundable.

A Developmentally Disabled Child

A developmentally disabled child presents special challenges in wealth accumulation and management. Specifically, what is the optimal way to pay for the tremendous expenses associated with raising a developmentally disabled child to independence?

The numerous planning techniques that may be used cannot be fully explained here, but certainly a prevalent strategy is to establish a **special needs trust** for the benefit of the child. To properly establish and maintain such a trust, the child must first meet the Social Security definition of *disability*, even though, typically, public assistance benefits are paid at the state or local level rather than from the federal government.

The purpose of the special needs trust is to allow the child to maintain eligibility for certain public assistance benefits, such as Supplemental Security Income (SSI) or Medicaid, while at the same time providing for needed services that are not available from the government. The trust document must state that the trust income and principal are to be used *only* to provide for extra services required to care for, maintain, and educate the child beyond those government-provided benefits. If the document does not state this or include similar language, the state may attach the assets transferred to the trust to pay for its cost of providing required care.

An alternative to the substantial cost incurred with a special needs trust for a disabled child is an **A.B.L.E. account** (created by the Achieving a Better Life Experience Act of 2014). An A.B.L.E. account is a tax-advantaged savings account for a disabled individual modeled after the Section 529 private savings plans when planning for a child's higher education needs. (See Chapter 15 for more on Section 529 accounts.) Whereas contributions to the A.B.L.E. account of not more than $15,000 annually in 2018 are *not* federally income-tax deductible, some States do afford the contributor a State income-tax deduction. The beneficiary of the account is the account owner, and income earned by the account is not taxed.

Why establish an A.B.L.E. account? Like a special needs trust, but at much less cost, an A.B.L.E. account preserves the disabled individual's eligibility for public assistance benefits. Eligibility for these benefits requires that a disabled individual retain no more than $2,000 in cash savings, including retirement funds. A.B.L.E. savings accounts do not affect eligibility for these public benefits (they are not counted) and permit funding for the wide range of other expenses incurred by the disabled individual.

At a minimum, if you are the parent of a developmentally disabled child, you should consider the implementation of an A.B.L.E. account. Beyond that, you also need to consider who will care for the child in the event of your or your spouse's death or incompetency. Under law, parents are the natural guardians of their child only until the child reaches age 18 or the otherwise-specified state age of legal majority. Hence, if your disabled child needs care after the age of 18, you may wish to seek court appointment as your child's legal guardian. Further, in the event of your death or incompetency, you may wish to have your spouse succeed you in this capacity. In your will, you should provide for the naming of a guardian, likely first your spouse and, in the event of a joint death, a willing and competent family member or members. If you fail to do so, the court will normally appoint a guardian for your child, but you will have no say with respect to whom this person is or where your child will live subsequent to your death.

The need for the implementation of a **contingent family trust** is important in all cases in which a minor child may be left without their natural parents, but it is even more important when one or more children are developmentally disabled. The guardian named for your child and the trustee of the contingent family trust will probably be the same individual, but you should give careful consideration to the different skill sets required for each duty. A *guardian* needs to possess considerable empathy and compassion for your disabled child's ongoing needs, whereas a *trustee* needs financial acumen. Just because a family member has one set of these skills does not mean they have the other. Moreover, although your first thought may be that your parent (the child's grandparent) is the perfect choice, do you think it is fair to ask your parent to take on a second family, particularly one involving a disabled child, late in their life? Only you can gauge the correct way to deal with this situation, but do not overlook considering it.

Your Own Physical or Mental Incapacity

Disability and *incapacity* are frequently used interchangeably, but the terms differ. *Disability* refers to a *contractual* status, whereas *incapacity* is a *legal* status. You are typically disabled if a contractual definition, such as that included in a disability income insurance policy, says you are. However, you are incapacitated or incompetent to act only if the *law* says you are.

An example of a legally incapacitated person is a minor or child who has not yet reached the age of legal majority. Such an individual cannot take legal title to property and can execute only what is known as a *voidable contract*, meaning that when they turn 18 (or reach the state's legal age of majority), the child can revoke the terms of any contract that was previously signed. For this reason, financial and other institutions often require a parent's co-signature on any contract entered into with a minor.

An individual who suffers from Alzheimer's disease would also be considered legally incapacitated. Such an individual may be physically fine, at least for some period of time after the initial diagnosis is made, but mentally they may not have the legal capacity to act. Someone must act on their behalf. Typically, this surrogate is a close family member (usually the spouse) who was granted power of attorney by the Alzheimer's patient while they were still competent. This leads to an important point in planning for your own or your parent's possible legal incapacity: *the power of attorney must be executed while the author (or principal) is still legally competent.* How do you determine legal competence? Usually, it is done by asking the author's primary physician to render an oral or written opinion that the author is legally competent at the time of granting the power. Absent a positive affirmation from a physician, or if a power of attorney is never completed, the family must ask the local court to appoint someone as the legal guardian of their incapacitated loved one.

Is one type of power of attorney preferable to another? Yes. Under the property laws of every state, the principal's authority to grant someone else the right to act on their behalf *terminates* at the date the principal becomes legally incapacitated (for example, they become so severely demented that they do not readily understand the consequences of their actions). What's more, when the principal most needs their power of attorney (or agent) to act, the individual with power of attorney is legally prohibited from doing so. To avoid these consequences, you should always seek to execute a **durable power-of-attorney** form, which specifically includes in its language that the power of the agent to act continues *even after* the principal is declared legally incompetent. Again, if this language is not included in the power-of-attorney form, family members will be forced to request court intervention.

If you execute a durable power-of-attorney form for yourself or your parent, you have a choice with respect to the date that you request your agent to act on your behalf. You can grant the agent the right to act immediately (a *nonspringing* durable power of attorney) or postpone this right until you, the principal, are declared legally incompetent (a *springing* durable power of attorney). Although many authors or principals are concerned about giving someone else the ability to act immediately with respect to their financial affairs, as a practical matter, the agent named is almost always a close family member. Typically, if you are married at the time of executing the power, your spouse is named as the agent. Many authors therefore draft a nonspringing durable power and continue conducting their own affairs as if the power was never granted. This avoids the inherent problem presented in the drafting of any springing durable power, where someone (usually, the concurring opinion of two physicians) must determine *when* you have become legally incompetent.

You may want to execute a durable power of attorney to plan for your own possible legal incapacity, but there is often a practical problem with third-party acceptance of the document. This is particularly the case with financial institutions that either want you to execute their own durable power-of-attorney form or refuse to recognize an outdated form. To avoid this issue, you should adopt the following two measures:

- Have an attorney draft the broadest possible durable power-of-attorney form in the hopes that all conceivable actions that the financial institution may require of your agent are covered by the power.

- Periodically (every three years or so) reexecute the durable power-of-attorney signature page; this ensures that the form is executed while you are still legally competent to grant the power.

Most states provide for the execution of *two* durable power-of-attorney forms: a general durable power-of-attorney form for *property* or financial management, and a *medical* or health care durable power-of-attorney form. This second form is intended for you to grant authority to an agent (again, usually a close family member) to give informed consent to any needed medical procedure on your behalf if you are unable to do so. Some states allow the inclusion of living-will provisions in the medical durable power-of-attorney form, whereas others require two separate documents. However, of the two documents (living will and medical durable power-of-attorney), the medical durable power is likely the *more important*, because it is much broader and covers additional health-care situations in which terminal illness is not the diagnosis. A sample general durable power-of-attorney form is included in Appendix C. You may wish to adopt it or discuss adopting it with your attorney.

We now move on to planning for the distribution of wealth to others, including yours via the retirement-planning process. The next chapter considers wealth distribution via a similarly important financial goal for many parents: planning for your child's higher or post-secondary education.

PART V

Distributing Wealth During Your Lifetime

CHAPTER 15

Planning for Your Child's Higher Education

We now move to the last step in the PADD process of wealth accumulation and management: *distributing* your wealth. Toward that end, this section of the book focuses on the distribution of wealth during your lifetime and considers the common financial goals of saving and planning for your child's higher education and your own retirement. It also discusses how to save and plan for other lifetime financial goals you may have, such as starting your own business. Then, the last section of the book takes up the process of distributing your wealth at *death*.

If you are married and have children, one of your first goals when evaluating how to distribute wealth during your lifetime is probably to afford your family members the best opportunity to pursue a profitable career—and that requires, at a minimum these days, a college degree. There are many colleges and universities, public and private, and your children's costs of attendance will vary dramatically based on their eventual choice. The common thread to whatever choice they make is that college is *expensive*—and getting more expensive by the year. According to the **College Board**, over the ten-year period of 2017–2018, tuition at public four-year institutions increased by an average of 5.1 percent per year nationally (tuition increases at private four-year

© Keith R. Fevurly 2018
K. R. Fevurly, *Plan Your Financial Future*, https://doi.org/10.1007/978-1-4842-3637-6_15

Chapter 15 | Planning for Your Child's Higher Education

institutions averaged 4.6 percent per year nationally over the same period). This compared to an average annual inflation rate of only 1.9 percent over the same period. For the 2017–2018 school year, the total annual cost of attending a four-year public college or university for an in-state student was approximately $20,000 ($36,000 for an out-of-state student) and close to $47,000 at a private institution. It is closer to $66,000 annually at an Ivy League institution.

Fortunately, the availability of financial aid increased during this same ten-year period, although most of this aid is based on financial need, with the amount necessary to qualify decided by the school and other factors beyond the control of the average middle-class parent. The key thing to keep in mind, then, is that it is important to plan for your child's higher education as early as possible.

How Much Will I Need?

As with any financial-planning goal that may be quantified, the first question to answer with respect to planning for your child's higher education is how much money you will need. The answer depends on several factors, including how many children you have and whether you wish for them to attend public or private colleges or universities. In 2018, private-college Ivy League institutions (elite institutions), such as Harvard and Yale, are among the most expensive to attend, with tuition, fees, and room and board costs averaging at least $66,000 per year. Meanwhile, private liberal arts schools throughout the country are not far behind in cost. Finally, the cost of attendance at public schools varies greatly, but for planning purposes, using the average of the current cost of attending a public university for an in-state and out-of-state student—or $28,000 annually—is not unreasonable.

The first step in computing the cost of your child's education is to inflate, or calculate in today's dollars, what the current cost of attendance—say, $28,000 annually—will be when your child is ready to attend college. To do this, you need to assume an annual increase in costs of a certain amount—say, 6 percent annually—to account for additional future increases. You can input these numbers into a web-based calculator (for example, at www.tvmcalcs.com), or you can enter them on a financial function calculator. Here is an example using the Hewlett-Packard 10BII financial function calculator illustrated at the cited web site:

1. Enter $28,000 as the present value (PV). Note: With this calculator, you need to enter this amount as a negative number so the calculator can distinguish between the PV amount you are entering and the future value amount (FV) for which you are solving.

2. Enter 6 as the projected annual percentage increase (I/YR).
3. Enter the number of years (N) until your child enters college; for instance, if your child is 3 years of age, enter 15, because 18 is the typical age for beginning college.
4. Solve for the FV of the cost of one year of attendance: in this case, the cost would be $67,104 per year.

Once you have completed this calculation, you need to determine the present value of the total sum that will be required to fund your child's college education for their estimated four years of attendance. The steps are as follows:

1. Shift your calculator into BEGIN mode (you will need the money at the beginning of the period when your child enters college at age 18).
2. Enter $67,104 as a payment (PMT). Note: You may need to enter this amount as a negative number because it is a cash outflow to you, depending on what calculator you are using.
3. Enter 4 as the number of years (N) of college attendance.
4. Enter an inflation-adjusted annual rate of return (I/YR) on the monies set aside to fund the education; for example, if you believe you can make a 10 percent annual before-tax rate of return on your investments, the number you will enter is 3.7736 (1.10 divided by 1.06 less 1 times 100).
5. Solve for the PV or lump-sum amount needed to pay for the cost of a four-year college education in today's dollars. Using the assumed numbers, the amount is $254,127.

The third and final step (after you've picked yourself up off the floor!) is to determine the amount of annual savings required to accumulate a lump sum of $254,127. The steps are as follows, assuming that you intend to save monthly in order to accumulate this sum:

1. Enter $254,127 as a FV amount, because you are solving for the amount of monthly payment needed today, while the child is 3 years old.
2. Multiply 15 years by 12 months (180) for the payments you need to make over the period you are saving. Enter this as N.
3. Divide the 10 percent annual assumed before-tax rate of return by 12 to convert to a monthly rate, and enter this as I/YR (here, 0.8333).

4. Solve for the monthly payment or savings amount needed: $608.09 per month ($613.16 if you do not save this amount until the end of each month). Annually, this is a savings of $7,271.22 or $7,998.34, respectively.

A word of caution as you consider the challenge before you: many people do not have the financial resources to accumulate this amount of money quickly. The important point is *not* to focus on the *end* of the process, but rather the *beginning*. In other words, begin to save *some amount*, even if it is not the amount that you *should* be saving. Probably the worst planning alternative is to *do nothing*, because you will quickly find other ways to spend the required savings. As part of the "pay yourself first" savings strategy, at least do what you can to provide for your child's college education.

The next concern relates to whose name you should use to save for this education: your child's or your own?

In Whose Name Do I Save?

Before you begin to save for higher education, you need to consider whether your child is likely to qualify for federal financial aid. As you ponder this issue, ask yourself the following questions:

- What do you expect your income to be at the time that the child enters college—or, more precisely, when you complete the Free Application for Student Aid (FAFSA) form in the second semester of your child's junior year of high school? Most federal financial aid is need-based; and if the child's parent makes too much money, the child is unlikely to qualify for the aid.

- Do you believe it is your responsibility or financial obligation to provide the child with a college education? Do you expect the child to assist financially or cover the complete cost of attendance?

- Do you anticipate that your child will receive an academic or athletic scholarship to cover the cost of college attendance? Be realistic: although we all believe our children are uniquely talented, more realistically, this is probably not the case.

- Do you have relatives or family members such as grandparents who have offered—or expect to offer—financial assistance when the child goes to college?

Fundamentally, you may be somewhat ambivalent about whether your child attends college or pursues higher education, but remember this: studies have shown that over the course of a lifetime, a college graduate will earn in excess of a *million dollars* more than an individual who receives only a high-school diploma.

Let's return to the question of in whose name you should save for college, which is a critical concern if you anticipate that your child will need financial assistance to cover the cost of college attendance. As you complete the mandatory FAFSA form, you are asked to list your assets and income as well as those of the child. This is necessary so the federal government can determine an amount of **expected family contribution (EFC)** toward the cost of college attendance. If your child needs financial aid, you want to achieve an EFC determination that is *as low as possible*. Accordingly, you should know the formula the federal government uses to compute the amount that the family is expected to contribute.

The most critical component of this formula is the fair market value of the assets held in the name of the child vs. those that are held in the name of the parent. In other words, what percentage of these assets is expected to be contributed to the cost of a college education and should therefore be counted *against* the family in the formula? The answer is 35 percent for the child and less than 6 percent (5.64 percent, to be exact) for the parent. Just from this entry into the formula alone, it is generally much more advantageous to save for college *in the name of the parent* rather than in the name of the child. If you decide to save for your child's college education in your own name, you should probably embark on a **Section 529 private savings plan**. Meanwhile, if you have decided to save for your child's college education under their name, you may want to open a **custodial account**, such as a Uniform Gifts to Minors or Uniform Transfers to Minors account.

Other savings strategies may also reap dividends when you are saving for college. They are as follows:

- Spend down the student's assets first. This may easily be understood when recognizing the disparity in countable children's assets (35 percent) vs. parental assets (approximately 6 percent).
- Maximize contributions to your retirement fund. Whereas annual contributions to your 401(k) (or other) retirement plan are included in the computation of countable parental income, the vested account balance in a retirement plan is not counted among available parental assets that may be used to help pay for college costs.

- Consider the use of a Roth IRA as a college savings vehicle. Your child will need earned income to contribute to this type of savings vehicle, but the work experience gained may be valuable in teaching the child discipline.

- Pay off as much as possible of your credit card and other unsecured debt before filing the FAFSA. This will reduce the amount of cash or other assets that you must list and that are counted against you when applying for federal financial aid on behalf of your child.

- Try to pay down your original mortgage as much as possible before applying. This yields two benefits: it can free up cash flow that you may need to fund your child's college education, and the amount of equity in your home is not included among parental assets when computing the expected family contribution.

To determine the amount of assistance required, most publicly funded college financial aid offices use a formula determined by the federal government known as the *federal methodology*. This formula does *not* consider the value of a family's home in arriving at the EFC. Meanwhile, some private colleges and universities use a formula known as the *institutional methodology* when computing the EFC. In this formula, the amount of equity in your home is *added back* (and is thus counted against you). You know that a school is using the institutional methodology if it asks you to file the more detailed CSS/Financial Aid Profile along with the FAFSA form. Unlike the information requested on the FAFSA, the CSS Profile requires the parent's expected income during the child's college years and not just your current or past year's income.

As a parent, be aware of a bait-and-switch tactic used by some colleges or universities in enticing your child to attend their institution. Although this practice is not as prevalent as it once was, some schools may offer an extremely lucrative financial aid package to a student whom they want to attend the institution, only to reduce the amount of financial aid given to that student after their first year of attendance. If the student is not comfortable at the school, they are then forced to consider transferring to another school (often with the disadvantage of not being able to transfer credit hours) or continuing studies at the same school and trying to resolve acclimation problems. As a result, once your child has obtained a financial aid package from a school, be sure to ask the financial aid officer how long the current aid package will be offered or, absent that, whether your child can easily transfer credit hours to another school if they become uncomfortable at the institution.

Types of Financial Aid

The two most common federal need-based loans are the Perkins and Stafford loans. Unlike grants or scholarships that do not need to be repaid, both Perkins and Stafford loans require repayment by the student after graduation.

The federal Perkins loan is a campus-based loan, meaning the school disburses the loan proceeds to the student through its financial aid office. The loan may be taken out by both undergraduate and graduate students, although the annual limit is slightly higher for graduate students than it is for undergraduates. Financial need must be demonstrated to qualify for a Perkins loan, but repayment is not required to begin until nine months after the student graduates from graduate or undergraduate school. Interest on the loan does not accrue on the loan principal until repayment is required.

The federal Stafford loan (also known as a *direct loan*) may be subsidized or unsubsidized. A *subsidized* Stafford loan means the US Department of Education pays the interest on the loan while the student is in undergraduate or graduate school, as well as during grace and deferment periods. An *unsubsidized* Stafford loan, on the other hand, means the student is responsible for the repayment of interest during the life of the loan and should repay the loan interest while they are still in school. If the student does not repay the interest as it is due, it is simply added to the principal of the loan for repayment at a later date. For both subsidized and unsubsidized Stafford loans, financial need by the student must be demonstrated.

A third type of federal loan is made available to the parent of a student in the parent's name: the Parent Loan for Undergraduate Students (PLUS). This is the only type of loan available on behalf of a student for whom financial need is not determined under the FAFSA formula. As a parent who makes too much money or has a significant net worth such that the child cannot qualify for federal financial aid, a PLUS loan is the only recourse offered by the federal government to assist with the child's college education. Good financial planning dictates that you have already planned for the cost of your child's college attendance; but if you have not, the PLUS loan will be offered to you. Interest begins to accrue immediately on the loan, and repayment begins 60 days after you receive the money.

Need-based government grants, which do not need to be repaid, also may help you pay for your child's college education. The most prevalent grant is the federal Pell Grant, for which the student is eligible if the family's EFC does not exceed a specified amount as determined annually. Scholarship awards do not affect student eligibility for the Pell Grant, although there is a limit on the amount of grant money that any student may receive annually (the maximum is $5,920 for school year 2017–2018). The student must be eligible for the Pell Grant on the basis of need before they can also qualify to receive federal Perkins or Stafford loans. Furthermore, the Pell Grant is available to undergraduate students only.

: Chapter 15 | Planning for Your Child's Higher Education

How Do I Save?

Now, let's proceed to the important question of in whose name do you save—the student or parent—for private school or higher-education expenses.

Custodial Accounts

Prior to the advent of **education savings accounts (ESAs)** and Section 529 private savings plans, custodial accounts were the primary methods of saving for a child's college education. Using this method to save still has advantages, although they are likely outweighed by the fundamental disadvantage that the opener of the account (usually the parent or grandparent) loses control of the money when the child attains the state's legal age of majority. It is also possible that the custodian of the account, such as a parent or grandparent, can roll over a custodial account to a Section 529 plan, but the custodian first must sell all of the assets in the account and pay taxes on any gains.

Two types of custodial accounts have been established by all states: the Uniform Gifts to Minors Act (UGMA) and the Uniform Transfers to Minors Act (UTMA). In most states, UTMA accounts are the norm, because that legislation superseded the earlier UGMA law. Operationally, however, the two types of accounts are the same, except that the UTMA allows for a broader range of investments to be made on behalf of the child, including a direct or indirect investment in real estate. Ownership of both accounts is vested in the child, with the custodian (usually the child's parent or grandparent) managing the account investments on behalf of the child.

As discussed in Chapter 13, anyone can give a child up to $15,000 ($30,000 for married couples who use the gift-splitting planning technique) each year free of federal gift tax. As a result, this amount is usually how much is initially transferred to custodial accounts on an annual basis. Appreciated securities or expected-to-appreciate securities are a common funding mechanism for custodial accounts; but as the child approaches college age, the custodian should gravitate toward more conservative and less volatile investments, such as bonds or CDs, to preserve the principal of the account. Keep in mind, however, that disadvantageous taxable implications are associated with too much annual unearned income (such as dividends or interest) generated from the account on behalf of a child under the age of 18 (or under age 24 if a full time-student). Specifically, a separate tax is imposed on such unearned income. Colloquially referred to as *the Kiddie Tax*, this tax was introduced by Congress to deal with the perceived income tax abuse of using your child as a tax shelter by shifting income to them, presumably to be taxed at a lower marginal income-tax rate.

Custodial accounts offer two advantages as compared to ESAs or Section 529 plans:

- The funds held in the UTMA or UGMA account may be used for anything that benefits the child, not just education. But if the funds are used to pay for expenses that otherwise constitute an obligation of support of the parent, depending on state law, all or part of the earnings on the account may be taxed back to the parent.

- The parent realizes a nominal income-tax benefit if saving in a custodial account. Specifically, for children under the age of 19 or a full-time student under the age of 24 benefiting from the account, the first $1,050 of income (in 2018) or other specified annual amount is permitted as a standard deduction. The next $1,050 or similar specified amount is then taxed at the child's marginal tax rate—typically, the lowest tax rate of 10 percent. As such, income splitting between the parent and child is possible, but only to a limited extent.

As mentioned, as attractive as these two advantages of custodial accounts may be, they are likely outweighed by the accounts' disadvantages. One has already been mentioned: at the legal age of majority, the child can do with the money in the account as they wish, including *not* go to college if the child chooses to pursue another path. In addition, several other disadvantages are associated with establishing custodial accounts on behalf of your children:

- The unearned income tax on minors applies after a specified annual amount of interest or dividends on the account is generated. Accordingly, when this amount is reached (for example, $2,100 in 2018), any further income is taxed to the child at the heavily compressed trust and estate income-tax rates. This is the taxable result even if the child's grandparent or other relative funds the account.

    For example, assume that your parent (your child's grandparent) has transferred $150,000 over the years to a UTMA established on behalf of your child. Further assume that this $150,000 generates a 10 percent return in the account ($15,000 of unearned income to the child). Thus, the child incurs a tax of $3,159.50 (+$105 as explained later in this paragraph) on the net taxable income of $12,900, or 37 percent of the amount in excess of $12,500 plus a base amount of $3,011.50 using the 2018 trust and estate income-tax rates. Note that you, the parent or grandparent, received a nominal income-tax benefit in avoiding tax on the first $1,050 of income from the account, with the child subsequently paying only $105 tax on the next $1,050 of income ($1,050 times 0.10)

- As compared to a Section 529 private savings plan, which allows a one-time contribution of up to $75,000 to be made in 2018 (or $150,000 for married couples who split the gift), the amount that may be contributed annually to the custodial account free of any federal gift tax is extremely limited. For example, currently no more than $15,000 may be contributed to a custodial account in any one year on behalf of any one child without having to report the gift as taxable for federal gift-tax purposes.

- As a general rule, custodial assets are treated as assets of the child when determining qualification for federal financial aid. As a result, these assets are usually counted against the child in the amount of 35 percent when computing the EFC.

There is one major exception to the federal financial aid disadvantage incurred in saving for college using custodial accounts. Given the recent introduction of the much more favorable Section 529 private savings plans, many parents are transferring (or should be transferring) UGMA or UTMA monies into Section 529 plans. The resulting account is known in the financial world as an UGMA/Section 529 plan or UTMA/Section 529 plan, depending on which type of custodial account is possible under state law. Although current financial aid law states that either an initially established Section 529 plan or a converted UGMA/Section 529 or UTMA/Section 529 plan is treated as an asset of the *parent* if the student is dependent, the parent is *not* permitted to change the beneficiary of a converted *custodial account* (as would be possible with the initially established Section 529 plan).

Education Savings Accounts

Named after Senator Paul Coverdell of Georgia, who sponsored the initial legislation that championed this education savings alternative, a *Coverdell education savings account (ESA)* is an investment account opened with a bank or other financial institution and funded with cash. Contributions to an ESA are not income-tax deductible, but the earnings generated from the contributions grow tax-free in the account. This is the case only so long as distributions made from the account are used to pay a child's educational expenses. If they are not, the earnings are taxed to the account owner—usually the parent—along with a 10 percent penalty.

Contributions to the ESA are permanently limited to no more than $2,000 annually for the benefit of a child under the age of 18. The ability to make account contributions is phased out for single taxpayers with an adjusted gross income (AGI) of between $95,000 and $110,000 and for married taxpayers filing jointly with an AGI between $190,000 and $220,000. This phaseout does not adjust annually for inflation, unlike other similar tax provisions. Thus, Congress elected to "schedule" the limit and deny the ability of higher-income individuals to take advantage of the ESA planning opportunity.

A major advantage of funding an ESA, which is the successor to the well-known (although not well understood) Education IRA, is that distributions or withdrawals from the account may be used not only in payment of college education expenses, but also to cover costs associated with attending public or private elementary or secondary schools. If you anticipate sending your child to a college-preparatory elementary or high school, you may wish to seriously consider saving via an ESA. Preparatory school costs may include the expense of school uniforms, computers, and even tutoring services, all of which may be paid with ESA money.

When the beneficiary of an ESA attains age 30 (unless the beneficiary is developmentally disabled, otherwise has special needs, or dies prior to that age), the account proceeds must be distributed to them within 30 days. But at such time or before the child attains the age of 30, the account proceeds may be rolled over, income-tax free and penalty-tax free, into an ESA for the benefit of another, younger family member. Moreover, beginning in 2018, the provisions of the 2017 TCJA permit a rollover to be made from the ESA to a Section 529 plan at any time.

Finally, what about the financial aid implications of saving using an ESA? The answer to this question depends on who is the owner of the account: the child, the parent, or the grandparent. If the child is both the owner and the designated beneficiary of the ESA, and they are still considered a dependent at the time of filing the FAFSA form, none of the ESA assets are counted against financial aid. On the other hand, if the child is both the owner and designated beneficiary of the ESA, and they are considered independent of their parents, 20 percent of assets are counted against financial aid. If the owner of the ESA is a parent, 5.64 percent of the assets are counted against financial aid. Finally, if the ESA owner is a grandparent, none of the assets should count against financial aid, because there is no place to report ESA assets owned by people other than a parent or the child on the FAFSA form.

Section 529 Savings Plans

Two types of savings plans are described in Internal Revenue Code Section 529 (from which the savings plans get their popular name). The first is a *qualified prepaid tuition plan* (QTP) that may have been established by your state to assist your child financially while they attend college. A QTP allows the contributor (typically the parent) to prepay tuition at a particular school using today's tuition price. As such, the parent is protected from future increases in the annual cost of the child attending college. In addition, the earnings made on the prepaid tuition grow income-tax deferred. If the parent withdraws the accumulated contributions and earnings in a QTP (or a private-savings type of Section 529 plan, which we discuss shortly) only for payment of higher-education expenses, the entire distribution is free of income tax.

The problem with a QTP, however, is that the child is restricted in choosing where they will attend college. For example, the state of Florida may dictate that the prepaid tuition feature is valid only if your child attends a publicly funded institution in that state. If your child attends a private school in Florida or another state, or a public college or university outside Florida, you may not be able to use the money accumulated in the QTP. This is also the result if your child is unfortunate enough to be denied entrance to the qualifying public school under the provisions of the state plan. Another problem associated with a QTP is that most plans cover only tuition, fees, and books at the qualifying institution and *not* room and board.

As a result of the disadvantages associated with the QTP, in 2001 Congress adopted a second type of Section 529 plan: the *private savings plan*. This plan is similar to a private investment account, but unlike the QTP, a private savings plan does not lock in future college tuition payment at today's prices. Rather, the private savings plan affords the contributor the opportunity to earn a rate of return on funds invested that hopefully exceeds the annual increase in college tuition (currently, averaging 5 to 6 percent annually). Earnings in the account grow income-tax free as long as distributions are used to pay college education expenses, including room and board. In addition, although contributions to a private savings plan are not federal-income-tax deductible, some states permit a state income-tax deduction for contributions offered by their state for state residents. Generally, however, Section 529 private savings plans are open to investors from any state.

In addition to possible state income-tax deductibility for contributions, another major advantage of a Section 529 private savings plan is the significant amount that may be contributed to the plan on a one-time basis every five years. In 2018, this one-time amount is $75,000 for a single donor (or five times the annual gift-tax exclusion of $15,000) and $150,000 if the contribution is made jointly by a married couple. There is also a maximum amount that may be accumulated in each of these plans, usually $300,000, on behalf of each plan beneficiary. A relatively unknown but significant estate-planning technique is that the donor may establish a Section 529 private savings plan on behalf of each family member beneficiary and exclude as much as $300,000 per family member from their gross estate. This can be achieved even though the donor controls the distribution of these funds until the date of their death.

Another significant advantage of a Section 529 private savings plan is that it is funded with your own money. Thus, for federal financial-aid purposes, it is counted among parental assets at a much *lower* percentage when computing the EFC than if a custodial account was established on behalf of the child. Most private savings plans permit you to change the beneficiary of a Section 529 private savings plan at any time, as long as the account proceeds are transferred to a member of the beneficiary's family (a sibling, a cousin, a grandparent, or even back to the parent). Therefore, you can take money back from a 529 plan, although you must then use it only for your own higher education or you will pay taxes plus a 10 percent penalty on the distribution. There are no age limits associated with the distribution of money from a Section 529 private savings plan, unlike with custodial accounts or the Coverdell ESA. Finally, the 2017 TCJA allows for tax-free plan distributions, up to a maximum of $10,000 annually, in payment of K-12 private school tuition. Previously, before 2018, 529 plan distribution could be used only in payment of higher or post-secondary education expenses.

If this all sounds too good to be true, it isn't—but Section 529 private savings plans have one minor disadvantage. In any Section 529 private savings plan, you cannot directly manage the invested money yourself. Instead, you must choose an investment manager who then decides where the money is to be invested, just as would happen if you were making a contribution to a mutual fund. To minimize the effects of this disadvantage, many plans have increased the number of investment choices (typically, mutual funds) in which you can invest. Furthermore, states have been careful in selecting whom they choose to manage investors' monies. Usually, only major brokerage houses or mutual fund companies are chosen.

So, what should you look for when selecting among the many choices offered in Section 529 private savings plans? Here are among the most important factors:

- Look for a plan that offers a variety of good investment choices—typically, mutual funds. Ask the same questions you would ask before investing in any mutual fund, such as what its investment objective is, how much investment risk you will assume, and what the fund's longer-term, risk-adjusted investment performance has been.

- Try to choose a plan with relatively low expenses. Some of this total amount depends on the mutual-fund manager in charge of the assets, but the higher the fund expenses, the more the manager must beat the market. And remember, the market in this instance is the ever-increasing annual cost of attending college.

- Consider the possible availability of a state income-tax deduction for contributions made to the plan. A top-performing fund of another state plan may offset the loss of the deduction from not investing in your own state's plan, but you should at least consider the advantage of the possible state income-tax deduction.

- Approach an investment in a private savings plan as you would an investment in any mutual fund. If you like the manager and the funds in the fund family, you may wish to invest in the plan of the state where the fund company is responsible for managing the plan investments. If not, consider another state's plan.

Other Methods of Saving for College

Several other methods are available for saving for your child's higher education, including establishing a trust on their behalf. (See Chapter 13 for further discussion of trusts.) All trusts that may be used for this purpose are irrevocable, meaning you cannot get the money back, and ultimately the trust principal must be distributed to the minor. Perhaps the most popular trust used in planning for the college education of a child is the Section 2503(c) trust, also known as a *minor's trust*. This trust must be drafted by an attorney, with the trust principal (and any unexpended income) made available to the child when they reach age 21. The age of distribution may be extended at your discretion by adopting an alternative trust, referred to as a Section 2503(b) trust, but the income from the Section 2503(b) trust must be distributed annually to the child, thus resulting in additional Kiddie Tax concerns.

You can also purchase Series EE and inflation-adjusted Series I US Savings Bonds and dedicate them to the purpose of paying for your child's college education. With both of these alternatives, the bond must be purchased in your name or in the name of an adult who is at least 24. Furthermore, adjusted gross income (AGI) limits apply at the time of redeeming the bonds. For example, if you purchase the bond in your name with the intent to use it to pay for the college expenses of your child, and your AGI is too *high* (a specified amount under law) when the child attends college, you will have to pay income tax on the bond interest at the time that you redeem the bond. However, if your AGI is *below* the prescribed amount, you will not be taxed on the interest as long as the bond is used in payment of qualified higher-education expenses.

Tax Deductions and Credits Available for Paying for College

This section addresses the benefits provided by the income-tax law to help you or your child pay for costs incurred while in college or pursuing some other type of higher education. The deductions available are a deduction for interest paid on student loans and a qualified higher-education tuition deduction. Important credits include the American Opportunity Tax Credit and the Lifetime Learning Credit. But since 2001, these deductions and credits cannot be taken *together* in payment of the same expense. As such, the use of each must be planned for carefully so as to take maximum advantage of every benefit available to you.

Deduction for Student Loan Interest

Under current law, the interest paid (never the principal paid) by any individual who is obligated to make repayment on a student loan is deductible regardless of whether the taxpayer itemizes their deductions. However, the deductible amount is limited to a maximum of $2,500 per year, and an income phaseout range applies based on the taxpayer's AGI level. Although these phaseout ranges are high, particularly for a student borrower, they can operate to deny the deduction for high-income taxpayer borrowers, such as parents who opt to take out a PLUS loan to pay for their child's education.

For this deduction to be taken, any debt incurred by the borrower must be used solely to pay for qualified higher-education expenses, including tuition, fees, books, and room and board. There is no restriction with respect to whether this debt is incurred for study toward an undergraduate or a graduate degree, but as part of the definition of a qualified higher-education expense, the debt must be taken out for study at a **qualified educational institution**.

Qualified Higher-Education Tuition and Fees Deduction

This deduction expired at the end of 2016 and was not extended by the TCJA of 2017. Therefore, the deduction is no longer available except if the tuition and fees also qualify as an allowable business expense (a Schedule C deduction). The maximum deduction available under prior law was $4,000 per student per year.

As we discuss shortly, a parent may also potentially claim a tax credit, such as the American Opportunity Tax Credit (AOTC) or Lifetime Learning Credit (LLC), for higher-education tuition and fees expenses. But if they do so, payment of tuition and fees expenses, for example, using a Section 529 plan distribution, is not permitted for the same expense for the same student. This presents an interesting dilemma if you are a parent with two children in college at the same time. You should give some thought as to how to best maximize any tax credit that is allowable for one child and any payment of tuition and fees expense for the other. In essence, although a two-student parent may mix and match tax credits and payment of tuition and fees expense, you cannot double-dip when trying to take advantage of both tax breaks for the same student.

Higher-Education Tax Credits

As discussed in Chapter 12, a tax credit (or a dollar-for-dollar reduction in tax due) is a valuable tax-avoidance technique. In most cases, if a taxpayer can qualify to take advantage of any tax credit, they should structure their financial affairs to do so. When a tax benefit is sought in paying for the considerable cost of pursuing higher education, two credits are permitted: the American Opportunity Tax Credit (AOTC) and the Lifetime Learning Credit (LLC). Prior to 2009, a third credit—the Hope Scholarship Credit—was permitted. It was replaced by the AOTC effective for the payment of certain higher-education expenses after December 31, 2008.

American Opportunity Tax Credit

The *American Opportunity Tax Credit (AOTC)* is a modification of the Hope Scholarship Credit for tax years beginning after December 31, 2008; it was preserved through the year 2025 by the TCJA of 2017. The AOTC amount is the sum of 100 percent of the first $2,000 of qualified tuition and related expenses plus 25 percent of the next $2,000 of qualified tuition and related expenses for a maximum credit of $2,500 per eligible student. Thus, a maximum of $4,000 in qualifying annual expenses may be taken into account in computing the credit. The student may take the AOTC themselves, if he or she is not claimed as a dependent; otherwise, the parent, or someone else, is paying the student's tuition and takes the credit, if claiming the student as a dependent.

What is a *qualifying expense* for the purposes of the credit? Unlike the Lifetime Learning Credit, for which *only* tuition and fees may be considered, the American Opportunity Tax Credit also includes such expenses as books, school supplies (including computers), software, and other class materials.

The credit is available for the first *four years* of a student's undergraduate education, but phaseout rules apply. In 2018, the credit amount phases out for single taxpayers with annual AGIs between $80,000 and $90,000. For married taxpayers filing jointly, it phases out between $160,000 and $180,000.

Lifetime Learning Credit

In contrast to the Hope Scholarship or the AOTC, the *Lifetime Learning Credit (LLC)* is much broader in application and may therefore be used by more parents. This credit is available for tuition and fees incurred for expenses associated with an undergraduate, a graduate, or a professional degree program. Furthermore, there are no credit-hour enrollment requirements, as is the case with the AOTC, where the student must be enrolled at least half-time. All that is necessary to claim the Lifetime Learning Credit is that the student incur the expense and that you, the taxpayer claiming the credit, are below an applicable income-phaseout range.

The maximum amount of Lifetime Learning Credit that may be taken in any year is $2,000 per family. Therefore, depending on the number of children you have attending college at any given time and what year of school they are in, the per family limitation may or may not be an advantage. If you have two children in their undergraduate years of college and you are under the income-phaseout range, the AOTC may afford you a maximum annual credit of $5,000 ($2,500 times 2), whereas the Lifetime Learning Credit yields a credit of only $2,000. With this limited exception, however, if you have to choose between the two credits (remember, you cannot take both credits for the same expense), you are better off claiming the Lifetime Learning Credit.

Unlike the AOTC, the LLC may be claimed for an *unlimited* number of years. You may even take advantage of it as an employee looking to improve your job skills by taking a single or several courses not leading to an eventual degree.

Finally, there are also phaseout rules associated with the availability of the Lifetime Learning Credit. For example, in 2018, for single filers, the LLC begins to phase out at $55,000 of AGI and disappears completely at $65,000 of AGI. For married couples filing jointly, these thresholds are $110,000 and $130,000, respectively.

The Tax-Coordination Rules: Why Can't I Do That?

Paradoxically, Congress does not want you to take too much advantage of a good thing—the "thing" here being double-dipping by using allowable tax credits and deductions in payment of the same expense. But what about withdrawals that you may anticipate making from your college savings accounts—notably, the Section 529 private savings plan? Remember that one of the major advantages of the Section 529 private plan is that, if you use those withdrawals to pay college tuition and fees, the earnings on them are income-tax free.

The answer to that question is that Congress has permanently shut down the opportunity to pay college tuition expenses and fees with tax-free Section 529 private savings plan withdrawals and then subsequently claim the AOTC or Lifetime Learning Credit for the *same* expenses. Technically, this prohibition is included in the tax law under the tax-coordination rules.

However, if you have been reading this chapter closely, you know that a Section 529 private savings plan withdrawal may be used to pay for room and board expenses, books and school supplies, and tuition and fees. This is in contrast to any of the permitted credits, which may be used only in payment of tuition and fees (or related expenses). Therefore, you have your answer with respect to how best to maximize *both* tax benefits: save for college with a Section 529 private savings plan, and subsequently make withdrawals from that plan to pay for college education expenses *other than* tuition and fees. In the same taxable year, then, depending on your AGI at the time your child attends college, you can also claim either the LLC or AOTC when you pay for your child's college tuition and fees.

Using a Roth IRA in College Funding

Many individuals think of a Roth IRA only in conjunction with planning for their own retirement (the subject of the next two chapters). But this vehicle may also be effectively used as a college savings technique. Although most retirement savings plans and accounts may be titled only in the name of the participant or owner, it is possible to title a Roth IRA in the name of a minor child—therefore avoiding the need to also name a custodian for the account. Keep in mind, though, that Roth IRAs require that the child accumulate some earned income (as defined in the Tax Code) before contributions are possible. The same rule applies before contributions may be made to either your or a child's deductible traditional IRA.

In planning for your child's college expenses, consider *hiring* your child to perform household duties, and pay them at least the maximum amount of annual contributions permitted to a Roth IRA (in 2018, $5,500 per year for taxpayers less than age 50). Do this at least five years before your child is planning to attend college, and the child can withdraw the after-tax contributions and earnings *income-tax free* for college use. Alternatively, if the child does *not* go to college or if you have otherwise saved to pay for those expenses, the child now has a wealth-accumulation vehicle that is powerful. For example, if you contribute the maximum amount of $5,500 per year to a child's Roth IRA between the years the child turns age 10 and 13 and make no further contributions, and assuming you can earn an 8 percent annual before-tax return on that money, the child will have over $1.4 million in the account ($1,464,278.30, to be exact) when they reach age 65.

Now let's proceed to most individuals' number-one financial planning goal, the topic you probably have been waiting for or planning for most: retirement. We discuss this broad area in two ways over the next two chapters: planning for the *financial aspects* of retirement, and planning for the *lifestyle needs* of your retirement years.

CHAPTER 16

Planning for the Financial Aspects of Retirement

There are many opinions as to when it is best to start planning for your retirement, but the best strategy is to do so as soon as possible. As part of the PADD process, recognize that accumulating sufficient funds to retire comfortably should be your *number-one* financial goal. If you are married with children at the time of your planned retirement, having sufficient retirement funds will help you avoid becoming a burden to your family, and, as a result, will make your retirement years that much more enjoyable. Adequate retirement monies will also prevent you from becoming overly dependent on the Social Security system, which is heading for financial difficulty absent Congressional action.

© Keith R. Fevurly 2018
K. R. Fevurly, *Plan Your Financial Future*, https://doi.org/10.1007/978-1-4842-3637-6_16

How Much Will I Need?

Similar to the lifetime distribution of your wealth in planning for your child's higher education, the first question in planning for the financial aspects of retirement is how much you will need. Generally, we can say you will need a lot of money, but a specific computation using a financial function calculator can give you a more approximate amount. Let's use the following example to describe the steps: assume that you are 35 and make $100,000 a year. You should anticipate that you will need approximately 75 percent of your before-tax income in today's dollars to retire comfortably, or $75,000 annually. As part of your retirement-planning assumptions, you anticipate that inflation will average 3 percent annually prior to and during your retirement and that you can earn a 7 percent after-tax return on your investments. You plan to retire 30 years from now at age 65 and plan to be in retirement for 20 years.

■ **Note** All amounts are calculated using a Hewlett-Packard 10BII financial function calculator, such as that illustrated at www.tvmcalcs.com.

Follow these steps to figure out the amount you will need for retirement:

1. Compute your annual retirement income need in today's dollars until your planned date of retirement:
   - PV = $75,000 (Enter this as a negative number if using the HP 10BII calculator.)
   - I/YR = 3
   - N = 30
   - Solve for FV = $182,045
2. Compute the lump-sum capital needed to generate this annual income during the period of retirement:
   - PMT = $182,045 (You need to be in BEGIN mode if using the HP 10BII calculator, and the amount needs to be entered as a negative number.)
   - I/YR = 3.8835 (This is an inflation-adjusted rate of return, so enter 1.07 divided by 1.03, less 1, times 100 on your calculator.)
   - N = 20
   - Solve for PV = $2,596,849

3. Compute the annual amount of savings needed to accumulate this lump sum (assuming you have not already begun a retirement savings program and have not accumulated any invested assets for retirement):

- FV = $2,596,849 (Round to $2.6 million. If using the HP 10BII calculator, you now need to convert back to END mode.)
- I/YR = 7
- N = 30
- Solve for annual savings deposit required or payment = $27,524.65

Again, as in education funding, the important action to take here is to *begin to save some amount now*. The amount that needs to be set aside from your salary is intimidating—over 25 percent of your *gross* pay, and *not* your take-home pay (from which the percentage to be saved would be even greater). Nevertheless, do not fixate on the required annual savings or total lump-sum amount as much as on the financial goal of beginning to save for your retirement.

If you do not want to purchase a financial function calculator or would rather not compute a retirement needs analysis yourself, a number of financial calculators and worksheets are available online (for example, at www.tvmcalcs.com) that can assist you. In addition, helpful charts are available in financial magazines that, given certain assumptions, tell you how much money you will need to accumulate at a certain age in order to retire comfortably.

There are three basic methods to saving for retirement:

- Contributing to employer-sponsored retirement plans, such as Section 401(k) plans
- Contributing to personal tax-deferred savings plans, such as traditional deductible IRAs or after-tax Roth IRAs
- Contributing in the form of payroll taxes to the Social Security system

Even after maximizing all these retirement savings methods, you will likely also have to set aside money in a *taxable* account to accumulate the necessary amount for retirement. When you do so, follow the investment strategy of dollar-cost averaging discussed in Chapter 3 and, if investing solely or primarily in mutual funds, try to choose funds with low expenses and tax-efficient investments.

Other Questions to Ask When Planning for Retirement

You have not only financial questions to answer when planning for retirement, but also questions that are softer in nature. In other words, you must also determine where you will live and what you will do when you stop working. Questions such as these are the focus of the next chapter, but you need to consider two more financially related issues when planning for retirement:

- Is my mortgage paid off (or at least paid down to a manageable amount)?
- How will I cover major expenses during retirement, particularly the rising cost of health care expenses?

Mortgage Expenses

The possibility of using a reverse mortgage to generate additional income during your retirement period is discussed in detail in the next chapter. Regardless, studies have shown that individuals who have been able to free up cash by paying off as much of their mortgage balance as possible prior to retirement tend to be much happier. Certainly, if you can remove your monthly mortgage payment from your list of fixed expenses, you will have that much more cash to live on and enjoy during retirement.

It is true that there is a debate about whether you should pay off your mortgage early, given the corresponding loss of the mortgage interest deduction when itemizing deductions for income-tax purposes. However, you should keep in mind that, at most, you are receiving a 37 percent offset from your ability to deduct any mortgage interest. Further, depending on the type of mortgage you signed, you may be accumulating little—if any—equity in your home. For example, if you signed an interest-only mortgage, you probably are not reducing your mortgage principal (and thus are relying only on the possibility of your home appreciating over time). As a result, paying off as much of your mortgage as possible before you retire will likely prove to be wise financial planning.

There is also the issue of refinancing your mortgage prior to retiring, to lower your monthly fixed expenses. Although refinancing may prove to be a good decision, the disadvantage of doing so is that you have probably extended your mortgage payment term to a greater number of years. For example, assume you have a 15-year mortgage and are planning to retire in 3 years. The remaining term on this mortgage is 10 years. In an effort to free up needed cash and reduce your monthly payment, you refinance your mortgage at a lower interest rate and take out another 15-year mortgage. Thus, you have an additional 12 years of mortgage payments to make during your retirement period instead of only an additional 2 years after you retire. Similarly, if you signed a new 30-year mortgage instead of another 15-year one, you would have an additional 27 years of mortgage payments to deal with.

One way to avoid this consequence of refinancing is to sign a mortgage with a shorter repayment term, such as ten years. The trade-off for doing this is that your monthly mortgage payment goes up and not down. Accordingly, unless you have budgeted for such a situation, the increased mortgage amount may result in cash-flow pressures throughout the remaining seven years of the mortgage term after you retire.

Health Care Expenses

As almost everyone is aware, there is a health care crisis in the United States. This crisis is particularly acute for retirees, many of whom are relying on a fixed income to pay for their retirement years. According to Fidelity Investments, a 65-year-old couple who retired in 2017 will need approximately $250,000 to cover medical costs after they stop working—and this amount is *in excess* of Medicare coverage, which typically covers catastrophic expenses of an individual age 65 or older. To make matters worse, for individuals retiring after 2017, the amount needed to cover medical costs in excess of Medicare coverage is even greater, because health care costs have continued to rise.

What is the best strategy to cover the rising costs of health care during retirement? Short of being fortunate enough to be provided with retiree health insurance from your prior employer, the best plan is to save even more while you are working. For example, the 35-year-old wage earner noted earlier in this chapter should plan to save more than the $2.6 million lump-sum capital needed for retirement; at the very least, they need approximately $250,000 (actually more, because the noted amount has not been inflated for 30 more years of growth) for their future health care costs. Another option is to apply for Medigap coverage within the first six months of qualifying for Medicare, to assist with the payment of these expenses. Finally, a third option, at least for self-employed individuals, is to establish and save for current and future medical costs via a health savings account (HSA).

Note that this estimated $250,000 cost of medical care does not include possible long-term care expenses. Contrary to common knowledge, Medicare does *not* cover the cost of custodial care. As such, it is critical that you consider the purchase of a qualified long-term-care insurance policy while you still qualify for coverage and can afford it. It is probably too early for a 35-year-old individual to consider purchasing such a policy (unless it is for their parent), but once they reach the age of 50 or so, investigating the purchase of an individual long-term-care policy (or participating in an employer's group policy, if available) should be a top financial-planning goal.

The Financial Risks of Retirement

Similar to the general investment risks discussed in Chapter 9, retirees face several special financial risks. Specifically, these are as follows:

- *Inflation or purchasing-power risk:* A daily risk of any retiree living on a fixed income. Succinctly, it may be asserted that the purchasing power of fixed dollars is less in the future than it is today.

- *Longevity or the risk of superannuation:* The risk that a retiree will run out of money before they die. It is this type of risk that most frightens the average retiree and is the primary reason that annuities are important retirement-planning vehicles.

- *Market risk:* The general risk of investing in the stock or bond market. It is sometimes referred to as *volatility risk* because the values of those investments fluctuate daily.

- *Investor behavior risk:* The risk that investors are irrational and subject to herd mentality. For example, they tend to purchase today's hot stock at the top of the market and then sell that same stock at the bottom of the market. Thus, many investors are not positioned for optimal, or even average, returns. A whole new field of finance has arisen, known as **behavioral finance**, to study just this type of risk.

- *Point-in-time or sequential risk:* The risk that a retiree begins retirement during a market downturn and then withdraws too much money initially, thus accentuating the risk of superannuation.

The most important of these risks is likely longevity risk—the risk of outliving your money. There is only one surefire way to avoid this risk, and that is to purchase an immediate fixed or variable annuity. But many retirees are dubious about purchasing annuities, for two reasons: they do not like the idea of spending down the money invested in the annuity; and they fear making such a large investment, dying shortly thereafter, and losing their money to the insurance company. There certainly are ways to resolve or at least minimize these concerns, but another way of managing longevity risk is to establish the withdrawal of a fixed percentage of retirement savings and then adhere to that percentage, adjusted for annual inflation, until your death.

What fixed annual percentage should a retiree withdraw? Many studies have been conducted in an attempt to answer this question, but the consensus of most academics and financial-planning practitioners is to annually withdraw 4 to 5 percent of your initial account balance, and then step up this percentage each year after accounting for inflation. In other words, the actual dollars you spend in any year should be 4 to 5 percent of the total amount you have saved at the time of retirement, adjusted for the effect of inflation in the subsequent years. It is important to keep in mind, however, that this percentage is dependent on the market remaining relatively stable (not significantly decreasing in value) throughout your retirement period.

Assume that you are 65, have been a diligent saver throughout your working years, and have accumulated retirement savings of $1.5 million. In your first year of retirement, you would withdraw $67,500 (or 4.5 percent of your initial account balance). Assuming that inflation for that year is 3 percent, in the next year you would withdraw $69,525 ($67,500 times 1.03), and so on throughout your retirement period. In such a manner, it is estimated that you have approximately a 90 percent chance of *not* outliving your money over a 30-year retirement period.

Two big challenges are associated with this strategy:

- As you enjoy your retirement years, you need to average an after-tax return of more than 4.5 percent annually, or you will invade the principal of your retirement savings.

- If you have begun this strategy in a down market, your withdrawal of more than 4.5 percent annually will deplete your account balance much more quickly than it otherwise would. In other words, you are not living off the interest and will not have as much—if any—money to leave to your heirs at the end of your retirement period. You can make up this deficiency in later years by earning more annual investment returns than you have otherwise assumed. But what happens if you do not achieve your expected rate of return or even lose money? For example, if you lose 2 percent from your portfolio from a previous return of 4 percent, that is a mathematical loss of 50 percent. To recover that loss or get back to even, you now need to earn back that lost 2 percent or achieve a mathematical gain of 100 percent.

It is critical that you associate point-in-time risk with longevity risk. Practically, this means the investment climate at the point in time when you retire is important. You want the first few years of your retirement to be enjoyed in an *up* market—or at least in a market environment that is relatively stable. You also do not want to be overly invested in fixed-income securities, such as bonds and cash equivalents, or you probably will *not* achieve an after-tax return that is equal to or more than the inflation rate. Accordingly, that is why financial planners and investment advisors recommend approximately a 60 percent equity / 40 percent bond and cash mix throughout retirement.

The "Three-Legged Stool" of Retirement Savings

Historically, financial planners have tended to view saving for retirement as consisting of three legs of a retirement "stool":

- Pension income from an employer-sponsored retirement plan, such as the traditional defined-benefit plan
- Personal savings income from either a tax-deferred personal savings plan, such as an IRA, or a taxable mutual fund account
- Social Security income

Recently, however, given the rapid increase in defined-contribution plans, wherein investment risk is transferred to the employee or participant, a fourth leg of retirement-period earnings has also been included among retirement savings. As such, the stool is really more like a table—one that needs to be "set" more and more by your own retirement-plan contributions.

Employer-Sponsored Retirement Plans

Most medium- to large-size employers now offer their employees the opportunity to participate in an employer-sponsored retirement plan. Generally speaking, most employer-sponsored retirement plans today fall under the classification of **defined-contribution retirement plans** (sometimes lumped together under the heading of *profit-sharing plans*). The plan of choice in this category is often a Section 401(k) plan, which is a type of profit-sharing plan wherein the employer may choose at its discretion whether to make a separate, matching contribution in any given year.

Unfortunately, though, according to a recent survey by the American Benefits Council, almost 21 percent of eligible employees do not participate in their employer-sponsored 401(k) plans. Even though this percentage should decline in the future, with the popularity of automatic contribution plans through which employer contributions are made in the absence of an employee "opt out," as a society, we still have a long way to go in retirement education planning. Particularly when the employer matches all or a portion of the employee's before-tax contribution, the employee is essentially leaving found money on the retirement-savings table. Moreover, even if the employer does not match a portion of employee contributions to the plan, the employee is still contributing to a 401(k) plan with before-tax dollars. As a result, not only does contributing to a 401(k) plan represent an opportunity for the employee to save for retirement, but it also allows them to reduce their current income taxes at the same time.

As a substitute for defined-contribution plans, employers may elect to offer their employees a second category of retirement plans known as a **defined-benefit retirement plan** (or traditional pension plan). But as has generally been well-documented, defined-benefit plans are a dying breed of employer-sponsored retirement plans because of their complexity and cost. According to a Bureau of Labor Statistics report in 2013, only about 16 percent of private sector workers participate in a traditional pension plan—and for workers now in their 20s, the outlook is even worse. It is likely that 10 percent or fewer of those workers will receive a monthly pension check. For employers, this is a positive trend; but for employees, it is not so favorable, because those employees assume sole responsibility for funding their retirement. Hence, in addition to the lack of a promised retirement benefit, the now-predominant defined-contribution plan requires considerable investment expertise on the part of the employee—a trait that many do not possess.

The retirement outlook for younger workers, the vast majority of whom will not be offered a defined-benefit plan during their working years, is not all bad, however. Certain defined-contribution plans dictate that employer contributions are *not* discretionary. For example, a governmental Section 401(a) plan requires mandatory employer contributions equal to a percentage of employee salary, plus investment of those contributions on behalf of the employee at their direction. Furthermore, because of the 2001 law that equated the percentage deduction of a mandatory-contribution employer plan, such as a money-purchase plan, to that of a discretionary-contribution plan, such as a Section 401(k) plan, profit-sharing plans have become much more popular. You should respond in one of two ways:

- Participate in and contribute to a defined-contribution plan in whatever amount you can afford. Remember, the lump-sum amount you need to accumulate for a comfortable retirement is substantial.

- Educate yourself as much as possible about the concepts of investment risk and return. Know the minimum amount of risk you are willing to assume for the maximum possible amount of return you wish to achieve.

Contribute to your employer-sponsored retirement plans *first* and *before* you attempt to separately contribute to any personal tax-deferred savings (such as an IRA) or taxable investments. In this manner, you can best take advantage of any matching contributions your employer may choose to make to encourage you to save for your retirement.

Personal Savings Plans

If you wish to supplement the retirement savings you are accumulating in an employer-sponsored retirement plan, you may want to consider allocating additional money into either a tax-deferred or a taxable personal savings plan. Tax-deferred personal savings plans include the traditional deductible IRA, the traditional nondeductible IRA, and the Roth IRA (although qualifying Roth IRA distributions are actually tax-free). There are also rollover IRAs, which are used as receptacles for lump-sum distributions from employer-sponsored (defined-benefit and defined-contribution) retirement plans. All these types of IRAs may be established without the assistance of your employer, although other types of IRAs—notably the Simplified Employee Pension (SEP) IRA and the Savings Incentive Match Plan for Employees (SIMPLE) IRA—must be established and contributed to by the employer on behalf of the participating employee.

The traditional deductible IRA is the oldest and best-known type of IRA. The annual amount that may be contributed to this type of IRA is established by law, but whether this same contribution amount may be *deducted* on the owner's income-tax return depends on various factors:

- If neither spouse is an active participant in an employer-sponsored plan, such as a Section 401(k), or if a single taxpayer is not an active participant, then contributions to the traditional IRA are deductible without regard to the participant's adjusted gross income (AGI) in the year of contribution.

- If one spouse is an active participant in an employer-sponsored plan but the other spouse is not—for example, one spouse stays at home—then the nonparticipant spouse may deduct contributions to their traditional IRA as long as the couple's AGI is less than a specified annual amount in the year of contribution.

- If both spouses are active participants, or if a single taxpayer is an active participant in an employer-sponsored plan, then the deduction is phased out if their income exceeds a separate, specified annual AGI ranges in the year of contribution.

The important point to take away from these complex rules is that if you are a relatively high-wage earner and participate in a retirement plan offered by your employer, you are likely prohibited from deducting your contribution to a traditional deductible IRA. As such, you have only two other options to personally save: either take advantage of a traditional nondeductible IRA or elect to open a Roth IRA.

Traditional deductible IRA contributions may be invested in any type of asset, with three specific exceptions:

- You cannot invest IRA contributions in collectibles such as stamps, coins, and antiques.

- You cannot invest IRA contributions in life insurance policies (although annuities are permitted).

- You cannot write yourself a promissory note and invest in that manner; that is a form of borrowing, and borrowing of any type is strictly prohibited from an IRA.

An individual or a married couple may also make traditional nondeductible IRA contributions up to the same specified annual amount as those of a traditional deductible IRA. But there are no complex rules or AGI limitations associated with nondeductible traditional IRA contributions. If you are a high-income wage earner and cannot otherwise contribute to a Roth IRA, you should consider contributing to a nondeductible IRA. Note, however, that you should do this only *after* fully maximizing whatever contributions you can make to an employer-sponsored plan, because those contributions are fully deductible from your taxable income without regard to how much you earn.

For example, assume that you are making $200,000 annually and that your employer offers a Section 401(k) plan. Because you make too much money, you are prohibited from deducting your contributions to a traditional IRA. Therefore, you should first contribute as much of your salary as you can afford and is permitted under law on a pretax basis to your employer's Section 401(k) plan. You should then make a contribution to a traditional IRA—in this case, a traditional *nondeductible* IRA—even though you cannot deduct the contribution in the current year.

A second option to consider in the event that you cannot make a deductible contribution to a traditional IRA is to make this same contribution to a Roth IRA. The Roth IRA was introduced in 1997 and for the most part is still an extremely underutilized personal-savings retirement plan. It does have its own annual AGI contribution limits, meaning that very high-income wage earners (like the taxpayer in the previous example) cannot contribute. For most of us, however, a Roth IRA is an effective personal retirement tool if you do not distribute the funds you put into it until at least five years after its establishment and are at least 59.5 years old. Why? Because if you meet these requirements (a qualified distribution), the withdrawal made from the Roth IRA is completely *income-tax free*. In addition, unlike with either form of traditional IRA, you can make contributions to a Roth IRA *after* you have reached the age of 70 and 6 months, meaning that throughout your retirement, assuming you are within the AGI limits, you may continue to accumulate wealth.

The major disadvantage of the Roth IRA is that your annual contributions are *never* income-tax deductible, meaning you cannot deduct those contributions on your income-tax return. But in exchange for this disadvantageous tax treatment going in, distributions from a Roth IRA that has been owned for more than five years are taxed extremely favorably going out. Specifically, not only are the earnings generated from Roth IRA investments income-tax free at the time of distribution, but so are the contributions. This is not the case with the traditional deductible IRA, in which only the earnings, not the contributions, are income-tax free.

Social Security

If you want to get into a political discussion quickly with a business colleague or friend, just ask them their opinion of the Social Security system. Many people, particularly younger individuals, do not believe that Social Security benefits will be available for them when they retire. They believe this even though they have paid into the system for most—if not all—of their working years. To view Social Security in this way is probably a mistake: your ability to receive a benefit under the system is a contract between you and the federal government. Thus, despite all the political hand-wringing over the Social Security system, Congress is likely to do whatever it takes to shore up the system and make good on its part of the contract.

Who is eligible to receive Social Security retirement payments? Anyone who is *fully insured* under the system. A fully insured individual is any worker who has earned 40 quarterly credits (worked for ten years) before their full retirement age under the system. A nominal amount of income must be earned each quarter for a credit to be awarded, but most of us easily exceed this amount and have no problem qualifying for retirement benefits. Once you are fully insured, you—and, usually, your surviving spouse—are entitled to Social Security retirement benefits at a certain age. Many people think the age at which they will receive retirement benefits under the system is 65, but your full retirement age (FRA) depends on your date of birth. For instance, if you were born in 1962 or after, your FRA is age 67, not age 65. Table 16-1, which is also included in Social Security publications, will help you determine your FRA and when you and your spouse are entitled to unreduced retirement benefits under Social Security.

Plan Your Financial Future

Table 16-1. Social Security Full Retirement Ages

FRA for Retired Worker	Year of Birth	FRA for Surviving Spouse
65	Before 1938	65
65 and 2 months	1938	65
65 and 4 months	1939	65
65 and 6 months	1940	65 and 2 months
65 and 8 months	1941	65 and 4 months
65 and 10 months	1942	65 and 6 months
66	1943	65 and 8 months
66	1944	65 and 10 months
66	1945–54	66
66 and 2 months	1955	66
66 and 4 months	1956	66
66 and 6 months	1957	66 and 2 months
66 and 8 months	1958	66 and 4 months
66 and 10 months	1959	66 and 6 months
67	1960	66 and 8 months
67	1961	66 and 10 months
67	1962 and after	67

The third column of the table shows the FRA for the surviving spouse when they are entitled to retirement benefits from *your* employment record. It is also possible for the spouse to be entitled to retirement benefits as a result of their *own* employment and earned credits under the system. In that case, the spouse is entitled to the *greater of* the retirement benefits computed under your employment record or those determined using their own employment history.

Unlike Medicare, it is also possible for a retired worker under the Social Security system to receive retirement benefits before age 65 or the otherwise applicable FRA. If you are fully insured, you may elect to receive permanently reduced benefits as early as the first full month after your 62nd birthday, regardless of your date of birth. Whether you should elect to do so is the subject of the next section of this chapter.

When Should I Elect to Begin Receiving Social Security Retirement Benefits?

According to Social Security Administration figures, approximately 70 percent of all beneficiaries are collecting reduced benefits because of early retirement. Is this the correct decision?

The choice to receive Social Security retirement benefits early is a complex one and should take into account several factors. Certainly, if you are in poor health at age 62 or have an unfavorable family history with regard to your expected future health, it is prudent to elect to receive Social Security benefits early. Given a number of reasonable assumptions, the break-even point between making an early election and delaying the receipt of benefits until you reach your FRA under the system is approximately age 81 or later. As a result, if you believe you will live beyond age 81, you are generally better off delaying the receipt of Social Security retirement benefits until your FRA.

Individuals who are fortunate enough to decide between the early receipt of Social Security benefits vs. delaying the receipt of those benefits may be categorized into two groups: those who can or want to continue working after age 62, and those who do not need to work after age 62 because they can fund their retirement years through personal retirement savings and/or an employer-sponsored retirement plan. If you plan to continue working after age 62, you need to be aware that your Social Security benefits will be reduced by $1 for every $2 received in excess of a specified amount (for example, $17,040 annually in 2018). As a result, if you anticipate making *more* than this amount at whatever post-retirement job you decide to take, it will prove beneficial for you to delay the collection of your benefits until your FRA, when no benefit penalty exists.

The actual percentage reduction suffered by a 62-year-old recipient depends on their date of birth and how far they are from the FRA. Benefits are reduced on a sliding scale, ranging from a total of 20 percent for individuals born before 1938 who retired at age 62 to 30 percent for individuals born in 1960 or later who elect to take early benefits. For more information, you may wish to consult the reference table found on the US Social Security Administration web site (www.ssa.gov), which lists the percentage reduction you will suffer for early receipt of benefits, depending on your date of birth.

Your other option is to postpone collecting benefits until you turn 70. If you do so and reach your FRA on or after 2018, the increase in retirement benefits for each month of delay is two-thirds of 1 percent of your otherwise-payable normal retirement benefit. This works out to an increase in benefits of 6 to 8 percent for each year you delay—a relatively reasonable rate of annual return, particularly in a volatile stock market.

How should you decide what to do? Should you take benefits early at age 62, delay until your FRA under the system, or postpone your receipt of benefits until you are 70? Perhaps the simplest way to make this decision is to ignore alternative uses of the money and plot the percentage reductions and increases based on your monthly retirement benefit payable at FRA. You can determine the amount of your otherwise-payable monthly benefit by contacting the SSA or referencing the projected payment estimates found on the statement at the SSA website, www.ssa.gov/. Then run the numbers on a spreadsheet and determine which decision gives you the maximum gross benefit over your anticipated life expectancy. When you apply actuarial life-expectancy tables, if you live exactly as long as the tables predict, you should have the *same* amount of gross benefit, regardless of which option you choose.

You need to consider one other factor with respect to receiving Social Security retirement benefits. Benefits are income-tax free for the majority of Social Security beneficiaries; but for taxpayers with relatively modest annual incomes, up to 85 percent of all benefits received must be included as income for federal income-tax purposes. Special step-rate thresholds apply. The first of these thresholds requires inclusion of 50 percent of all benefits, and the second threshold mandates an 85 percent inclusion. Currently, these two thresholds of modified AGI are as follows, depending on taxpayer filing status:

- *Single taxpayer:* $25,000 and $34,000
- *Married couple filing jointly:* $32,000 and $44,000
- *Married couple filing separately:* $0

When computing modified AGI for the purposes of Social Security benefit taxation, it is important to keep in mind that you must add back to your regular AGI any tax-exempt interest income you may have. Thus, a retiree whose investment portfolio consists primarily of municipal bonds or municipal bond mutual funds will likely pay more when filing their return than a retiree whose portfolio is heavily weighted with stocks. This is all the more reason a retiree should continue to diversify their portfolio among equities, corporate bonds, and cash or cash-equivalent asset classes.

Understanding Distribution Options from an Employer-Sponsored Retirement Plan

Depending on plan provisions, four basic options are available to a participant in an employer-sponsored retirement plan when you terminate employment or retire:

- Take a lump-sum distribution from the plan.
- Receive an annuity or other periodic distribution from the plan.
- Roll over the distribution to an IRA or to your new employer's retirement plan.
- Leave the accumulated funds in the employer's plan.

This last option is infrequently offered, because most sponsoring, past employers do not want the responsibility of continuing to manage and invest your retirement monies. Of the three remaining options, most participants choose a lump-sum distribution if it is available. Presumably, this is because most participants believe they can invest the retirement monies at least as well as the plan trustee. In reality, though, many people choose the lump-sum option because they think they need the money. This is unfortunate, because, given the power of tax-deferred compounding, the *younger* the participant, the *more advantageous* it is to roll the distribution into an IRA and continue the tax deferral. Alternatively, if you elect to receive the distribution in a lump sum, you must first pay income taxes on the total and then may use only the net amount for your personal needs.

The decision to receive an annuity or other periodic distribution option is the most common and prudent course of action for a retiring or soon-to-be retired participant. The primary advantage of selecting the annuity option from an employer-sponsored plan is that *you cannot outlive their money* from the plan. But this does not mean the employer is underwriting the annuity for you. Rather, many employers transfer the risk of future investment performance and liability to an insurance company at the time that you retire. Thus, they buy a commercial annuity on behalf of the participant to fund their retirement payment obligation.

The fact that many employers purchase a **tax-qualified annuity** with the employee's retirement monies raises the issue of whether you are better off taking a lump-sum distribution and purchasing the annuity yourself. This is not a simple question and is the subject of a separate discussion with respect to the use of annuities in retirement, but here are some general guidelines to assist you in making this decision:

- If you are married at the time of taking an annuity payout from most employer-sponsored plans, under law, the plan must provide for at least a 50 percent joint and survivor annuity for your spouse *unless* your spouse waives the survivor annuity in writing. This protection for your spouse in turn *reduces* your monthly annuity payment, although alternatives can provide for your spouse while also ensuring that your monthly payment amount is higher.

- If you purchase the annuity yourself, investigate a payment term with at least a *guarantee* of payment to your survivor: for example, a life annuity with a period certain. This ensures that if you die before the end of the period (for example, 20 years), your survivor will receive payments for the remainder of the term.

- Consider the purchase of an **immediate fixed annuity** if you need to begin annuity payments as soon as possible. Conversely, if you do not need the money immediately, consider a low-cost **variable annuity (VA)** with a lifetime guarantee withdrawal benefit (GWB) rider or guaranteed minimum income benefit (GMIB) rider.
- Try not to annuitize the annuity (use up the principal of the annuity) during your lifetime, but live off the earnings from the annuity's underlying investments. This will ensure that the greater of the annuity's account value or death benefit will pass on to your heirs.
- Annuities can be expensive, so look for as low-cost an annuity as possible.
- If the annuity you are considering does not provide as high an annual return as the annuity your employer will otherwise purchase for you, you are better off letting the employer provide the benefit. Before you make this decision, ask your employer's human resource office what the internal rate of return on their annuity will be. In other words, what assumed discount rate is used to determine the present value of your monthly annuity payment?

Because more and more defined-contribution retirement plans are being offered by employers, a lump-sum payment option may be your only choice of distribution. If, on the other hand, you are fortunate enough to be entitled to a pension from your employer's plan, an annuity payout or other periodic distribution will likely be among your distribution options. Assuming an annuity payout is available, you should carefully consider the advantages of that payout if you are concerned about the longevity risk associated with retirement.

Required Minimum Distributions

By April 1 of the year following the year in which you reach the age of 70 and 6 months, you must generally begin to take taxable distributions from either an employer-sponsored retirement plan or a traditional IRA. Note that an exception to this rule exists for some workers who have not yet retired as of age 70 and 6 months. In that instance, a required minimum distribution does not have to be made until April 1 of the year following the year in which the worker retires. For each subsequent year after your required beginning date, you must withdraw a required minimum distribution by December 31 of that year.

Because the amount of distribution you must take in a given year is established by tax law, these distributions are often referred to as *required minimum distributions (RMDs)*. The RMD for any given year is computed by dividing your account balance in the employer plan or traditional IRA as of December 31 of the preceding year by an applicable divisor or distribution period. This divisor or distribution period is determined by referencing your age as of December 31 of the distribution year in an IRS table known as the Uniform Lifetime Table. Table 16-2 shows a portion of that table for participants age 70 through age 80.

Table 16-2. Uniform Lifetime Table

Participant's Age	Applicable Divisor or Distribution Period
70	27.4
71	26.5
72	25.6
73	24.7
74	23.8
75	22.9
76	22.0
77	21.2
78	20.3
79	19.5
80	18.7

Once you begin distributions, each subsequent divisor goes down by a factor of approximately one. This is because you are getting older and your life expectancy is, accordingly, reduced. For example, assume you were born in June 1948 and are age 70.5 as of year-end 2018. Further, assume that the account balance in your traditional IRA was $500,000 as of year-end 2017. (Remember, you have to use the previous year's account balance in computing the necessary RMD.) Your RMD for 2018 is $18,248 ($500,000 divided by 27.4). You may delay this distribution until April 15, 2019, but doing so requires you to take *two* distributions for that year (one for 2018 and one for 2019). Next, in 2019, you divide your year-end 2018 traditional IRA account balance by 26.5 (because, by year-end 2019, you will have reached age 71). All things considered, you are probably better off from a tax standpoint if you take the first distribution in 2018 and the second in 2019. If you do not take any

Plan Your Financial Future

distribution or fail to take the correct amount of RMD, the IRS will penalize you in the amount of 50 percent of the difference (that is, what you should have taken as an RMD and the amount of distribution you actually made).

The Uniform Lifetime Table is used for all situations and individuals with one exception: if you are married and your spouse or beneficiary is more than ten years younger than you, a different table is used. This second table, known as the Joint and Last Survivor Table, is based on the actual joint life expectancies of the respective spouses. Although the Joint and Last Survivor Table also reflects a divisor that begins when you turn age 70 and 6 months (or age 70 as shown on the table), the applicable divisor is a greater number, thus allowing for a smaller taxable RMD.

There are also post-death RMDs that must be made when a plan participant or IRA account owner (including a Roth IRA owner) dies before the entire account balance has been distributed. The application of these rules is based on, among other factors, the individual named as the designated beneficiary of the plan or IRA. If the spouse is named as the beneficiary, they are a favored subsequent owner and may therefore roll over the remaining account balance to their *own* IRA, free of income tax. It is important to note, however, that as of 2007, a *nonspousal* beneficiary of an employer-sponsored plan may also take advantage of the rollover provisions to an IRA. Accordingly, as a plan participant, if you name a child as the beneficiary of your Section 401(k) plan, they may now transfer the money accumulated in that account directly into a properly titled inherited IRA and stretch the distributions over their own lifetime. To title this IRA properly, it must read as follows: "John Doe IRA (deceased 00-00-07 or later) for the benefit of Mary Doe, adult daughter."

Be careful. According to recently issued IRS notices, an employer-sponsored retirement plan does *not* have to allow a nonspouse beneficiary to make a direct transfer to an inherited IRA. Further, a nonspouse beneficiary who inherited funds from an employer-sponsored plan before 2006 cannot take advantage of the direct-rollover opportunity. If you inherit a retirement plan account balance from someone other than your spouse, the first step is to check with the plan administrator to see if the plan has accorded you the opportunity of a direct rollover.

No Loopholes

You may wonder if there is a planning technique you can adopt to avoid making a taxable RMD from your employer-sponsored retirement plan or traditional IRA. In other words, as a higher-income retiree, you may not need the money and not want to pay taxes on the distribution. Unfortunately, there is no longer a planning technique that precludes the necessity of an RMD. One of the most popular alternative planning techniques to avoid making an RMD used to be as follows: in years when you did not wish to take an RMD, you transferred the previous year-end account balance from a traditional IRA to a Roth IRA before December 31 of the required distribution year. Then, after January 1 of the next year, you transferred (or recharacterized) the money back to the traditional IRA. Thus, the previous year's traditional IRA account balance was zero, and no RMD was necessary for the distribution year.

Under current federal tax rules, however, this technique does not work. Rather, as the owner of a traditional IRA, you must make an adjustment to the previous year-end balance of the account to reflect the return of any recharacterized Roth IRA transfers. You must look back and add the money that you subsequently transferred to the Roth IRA to the traditional IRA account balance of zero. If you refuse to do so, the IRS will penalize you in the amount of 50 percent on any difference or shortfall. Bottom line: do not do this, or you will unnecessarily deplete your hard-earned accumulation of wealth.

It is interesting to note that, beginning in 2018, *all* recharacterizations, whether attempting to implement the just-discussed technique or otherwise, are prohibited by the TCJA of 2017.

IRA Rollovers and Conversions

A *rollover* is a direct or indirect *income-tax-free* transfer of all or part of the participant's account balance from one employer-sponsored retirement plan, such as a Section 401(k), to another employer-sponsored plan or IRA. Thus, continued tax deferral of the plan assets and earnings is achieved, at least until the participant reaches age 70.5 and is required to start taking an RMD. An additional advantage of this planning technique is that, if you roll over the account balance to your IRA, you are still in control of the money and can direct your investment decisions yourself.

The mechanics of an IRA rollover are relatively simple: you take the money or distribution from your employer's retirement plan and transfer it to a previously established or newly established IRA on your behalf. But these mechanics can be deceiving and troublesome if you do not properly transfer the money. For example, after you receive the distribution from the employer plan, you have only 60 days in which to roll over or deposit the funds into your IRA. If you exceed this time frame, you must pay income taxes on the amount that you failed to roll over. Further, if you have the distribution check made out in your name, under law, the employer must withhold 20 percent from the amount you are due. As such, you net and roll over only 80 percent of the total account balance to which you are entitled. You can get this 20 percent withholding tax back when you file your income-tax return the next year, but why wait? There is a better way.

To get around the 20 percent withholding tax, ask that your employer *directly* roll over the distribution to your new employer's retirement plan (if the plan will accept the money) or your individual IRA. The easiest way to do this is to have your employer's human resources department make the distribution check payable to the trustee of your new employer's plan or the custodian of your IRA. Have your employer cut the check *on your behalf*, otherwise known as an FBO check (*FBO* stands for *for the benefit of*). In this way, you avoid the application of the 20 percent withholding tax.

For example, assume that you are 45 and have recently changed jobs. You have an account balance of $200,000 in your previous employer's Section 401(k) plan and are entitled to a lump-sum distribution from the plan, because you have separated from service. To avoid the 20 percent withholding tax, you have two planning options:

- If your new employer has a Section 401(k) plan that will accept the $200,000 account balance, ask your previous employer to make the distribution check out to the new employer's plan trustee on your behalf.
- Roll over the distribution into your previously established or newly established traditional IRA with a check made payable to the IRA custodian on your behalf.

In this example, assuming that you have both choices—a new 401(k) or a new IRA—which is preferable? This is a common question confronting many Section 401(k) participants who either do not need the money from the 401(k) plan or wish to continue the tax deferral. Consider this: if you directly roll over the distribution to the new Section 401(k) and then subsequently leave your new employer when you reach age 55, you may take the total 401(k) balance without the imposition of the 10 percent premature-disposition penalty that otherwise applies to employer-sponsored retirement plans. Alternatively, this is *not possible* if you roll over the distribution to your own traditional IRA; in that case, you must generally wait until the year in which you reach age 59 and 6 months to take the money without penalty. Furthermore, if you choose the new 401(k) plan option and like the investment choices offered to you under that plan, you may self-direct those investments and perhaps achieve a greater return than the IRA.

Whatever choice you make, the *younger* you are at the time you receive the distribution, the *more advantageous* it is for you to roll over the money and continue the tax deferral.

IRA Conversions

Prior to 2010, it was the law that you could not convert your traditional IRA to a Roth IRA if your AGI exceeded $100,000 in the year of conversion. However, now there is no income limit, providing a potential planning opportunity for those who are willing to pay the income tax due on the proceeds at the time of conversion. There are two reasons for converting your IRA to a Roth IRA:

- You believe you will be in a higher income-tax bracket at retirement than you are currently and will pay no subsequent tax when you distribute the account balance from the Roth IRA.

- You plan to keep the converted assets in the Roth IRA for a considerable period of time (generally, more than ten years) and will make up the dollars expended in payment of taxes due at the time of the conversion. To ensure that this will be the result, you should pay the up-front tax from assets other than those in the traditional IRA. Doing so will permit you to invest an even greater amount in the Roth IRA.

Converting your traditional IRA to a Roth IRA raises the possibility of an intriguing—and potentially profitable—income-tax strategy:

1. If you have not done so already, establish a nondeductible traditional IRA.

2. Make the maximum allowable annual contributions to this nondeductible IRA for as many years as possible before conversion.

3. Just prior to your planned retirement, convert the entire account to a Roth IRA.

What is the result? Well, remember that you have already paid taxes on the money that you have contributed to the nondeductible traditional IRA—in other words, you made those contributions with *after-tax dollars*. Therefore, the only tax you owe on the nondeductible account when you make the conversion to the Roth IRA is on the earnings generated from the nondeductible account. In return for this relatively small amount of income tax due, your new Roth IRA will grow income-tax free *forever*. Although it does not get any better than this when it comes to accumulating and growing your personal wealth, there is one catch: you should have only *one* traditional IRA (deductible or nondeductible) at the time of conversion. If you have more than one IRA, the IRS will assume that the conversion is coming pro rata from each IRA, and thus you will owe *more* tax.

For example, assume that at the time you convert your nondeductible IRA to a Roth IRA in 2018, you also own a traditional deductible IRA. The nondeductible IRA has an account balance of $50,000, and the deductible IRA has an account balance of $250,000. Further, assume that you have made after-tax contributions of $40,000 to the nondeductible IRA and must pay tax on $10,000 of earnings ($50,000 less $40,000). Because the converted amounts will be distributed pro rata from both the deductible and nondeductible IRAs, you must treat a total of $300,000 ($250,000 plus $50,000) as potentially subject to tax. As a result, you owe taxes on $42,000, not just $10,000, in 2018.

Note The $42,000 is determined by multiplying the fraction of ($50,000 divided by $250,000) times $250,000—or $50,000—and subtracting the product of (0.20 times $10,000)—or $2,000—from the $10,000 of earnings—or $8,000.

If you want to contribute to a nondeductible IRA, you are probably ineligible to take advantage of a deductible IRA in the first place because of AGI limitations and active-participation requirements. However, if you *do* have a traditional deductible IRA and participate in a Section 401(k) or other employer-sponsored plan, ask your employer if you can do what is called a *reverse rollover*. That is, roll over your deductible IRA account balance to the Section 401(k) plan, leaving you with only the one nondeductible IRA—and *without* the worry of the pro rata rule.

The Use of Annuities in Retirement Planning

According to the McKinsey Consumer Retirement Surveys, the proportion of US working-age adults who consider the lack of a guaranteed retirement income to be an extremely important risk increased from 28 percent in 2004 to 61 percent in 2009. This percentage has likely only increased from 2009. Indeed, outliving one's money is the number one retirement planning concern expressed by a majority of retirees. As such, immediate fixed or variable annuities with a lifetime GWB rider at the time of retirement have increased in importance. This reflects the primary advantage of using an annuity in retirement planning: annuities allow you to own a safe investment with a *guaranteed lifetime income stream*. In other words, as the annuitant, or person receiving the annuity payments, you cannot outlive your money.

Annuities offer other advantages in planning for the financial aspects of retirement:

- If you purchase a deferred variable annuity, you have the opportunity to grow your account balance through investment in mutual funds as part of the annuity's subaccounts. It is also possible to purchase a GMIB rider with this form of annuity, ensuring a minimum amount of guaranteed investment return on your money.

- You can plan the timing of income receipt to take advantage of years when you are in a lower tax bracket.
- If you have purchased a **nonqualified annuity**, such as a nondeductible IRA, you have to pay tax only on the earnings accumulated in the annuity at the time of distribution.
- You never have to make required minimum distributions from a nonqualified annuity and therefore can leave the entire account balance to your heirs at your death.

When should you consider purchasing an annuity as part of the lifetime wealth-accumulation and distribution process? When you want the following:

- A guarantee that you cannot outlive your money during the retirement period (in other words, you avoid longevity risk)
- An opportunity to grow any invested funds on a tax-deferred basis
- An alternative or supplement to a traditional or Roth IRA that permits unlimited annual contributions
- An alternative beyond maximizing contributions to an employer-sponsored retirement plan or a traditional deductible IRA

But as a general rule, you should *not* consider the purchase of a nonqualified annuity or any after-tax retirement-planning savings vehicle until *after* you have annually contributed all that you can on a pretax basis to your employer-sponsored plan or deductible IRA.

How Much Should I Withdraw Annually During Retirement?

To steal the name of a popular game show from many years back, the $64,000 question is, "How much should I withdraw annually during retirement?" Before you can answer, you need to ask three corollary questions:

1. Over what time frame should my retirement money be expected to last?
2. In what assets should I invest to have the least probability of outliving my retirement money?
3. Once I begin making withdrawals, what retirement monies should I access first to most effectively minimize income tax due?

Plan Your Financial Future

With respect to the first question, several academic studies have determined that a 4.5 percent annual withdrawal rate, adjusted for inflation each year, provides the greatest chance that a retiree will not outlive their money. Therefore, you should assume a retirement distribution period of approximately 30 years with a 4.5 percent after-inflation withdrawal rate. Specifically, studies have shown that you have only about a 10 percent chance of outliving your money over that period using the optimal 4.5 percent withdrawal rate.

The second question begs the issue of what you should invest in during your pre-retirement period to optimize your chances of not outliving your money. Empirically, it has been shown that a constant asset allocation of approximately 60 percent equities and 40 percent bonds and cash or cash equivalents in your retirement savings portfolio affords you the greatest chance of not outliving your money. Specifically, I suggest that your retirement portfolio should consist of a 40 percent allocation to large capitalization, blended stocks, or mutual funds (*blended* means a combination of value and growth stocks), a 20 percent allocation to international stocks, a 30 percent allocation to intermediate-term investment-grade bonds, and a 10 percent allocation to cash or cash equivalents.

Once you begin making annual retirement withdrawals, a basic rule of thumb can minimize income tax on those withdrawals:

- Withdraw money first from taxable accounts, thus reducing your future tax bills as much as possible.
- Next, withdraw funds from tax-deferred retirement accounts, such as a traditional deductible IRA, where RMD requirements apply beginning at age 70 and 6 months.
- Last, tap Roth IRA monies, because no taxes are paid on qualified distributions made from those accounts.

To summarize the process of planning for your financial needs in retirement: *keep a constant allocation of 60 percent equities and 40 percent bonds and cash or cash equivalents in your portfolio, and withdraw only a real rate of 4.5 percent annually from a portfolio of taxable, tax-deferred, and Roth IRA accounts, in that order.* If you follow this rule, you will have a high probability (approximately 90 percent) of *not* outliving the money you have saved for retirement.

Now let's move on to other, nonfinancial aspects of planning for retirement, such as where you will live and what you will do to experience a prosperous retirement.

CHAPTER 17

Planning for the Lifestyle Needs of Retirement

Now that you have decided how you will finance your retirement, you need to consider where you will live and what you will do during your retirement. For many retirees, the choice of where to live is fairly simple: they continue living in the home they purchased prior to retirement. But you have many choices to make regarding where you will live, including the type of facility you will live in, as discussed shortly. What you will do in your retirement, however, is more complicated.

Many newly retired individuals, who worked for 35 to 40 years, need to find a new identity after they retire. This is not easy. While you are working and thinking about retiring, the first thing most casual acquaintances ask is what you will do when you stop working. Part of this chapter is dedicated to helping you answer that question when you are retired.

© Keith R. Fevurly 2018
K. R. Fevurly, *Plan Your Financial Future*, https://doi.org/10.1007/978-1-4842-3637-6_17

Housing Options for Retirees

Newly retired individuals have at least 11 housing options:

- Single-family dwellings
- Town homes
- Condominiums
- Apartments
- Living with one or more of your children
- Independent-living communities
- Assisted-living communities
- Memory care units
- Continuing-care retirement communities (CCRCs)
- Skilled nursing-care facilities
- Traditional nursing homes

Recently, several more types of housing have been added to this list of options, including row homes and lofts, but these are likely to be of more interest to your children or younger generations.

Single-Family Dwellings

Many members of the baby boomer generation grew up with plentiful single-family dwelling choices, many of which could be found in planned communities. As boomers have advanced in their careers, they have typically purchased larger and more expensive houses.

Upon retirement, at least some boomers—particularly those with children who are now independent—wish to downsize their homes, meaning they seek smaller and less expensive ones. Builders are well aware of this trend and are attempting to meet the lifestyle needs of retirees looking to downsize. This strategy may permit boomers and other newly retired individuals to access the equity in their homes, which are typically the single largest financial asset they own. If they are lucky enough to receive sufficient funds for this equity, boomers may even be able to pay off their mortgages, one of the financial keys to a prosperous retirement.

As a retiree, if you choose to remain in a single-family dwelling during retirement, you should determine where you want to live. In addition to the choice of the subdivision or community where you will buy, you must also decide in which region of the country and state you would like to live. These decisions are often relatively easy to make, because retirees generally choose to live close to one or more of their children and grandchildren. You should also consider the income-tax status of the state you choose. Some states, notably Florida, Texas, and Arizona, do not have state income taxes, which contributes to their allure as retirement havens. Others, including California and New York, are known for relatively high state income taxes. Still others, such as Colorado, provide partial exclusions for income derived from pensions. If the tax implications of where you live are important to you (remember, inflation and taxes are the two biggest threats to your accumulated wealth), you should consider carefully the state in which you will live during retirement.

If you wish to live in a single-family dwelling, even one you have downsized to, you should be aware that you will need to continue maintaining and improving that dwelling. As you advance in age, depending on your health, this may become a burden. If you are unable to maintain your home, you will have to call on your children for help (if they live close by) or pay someone to do certain necessary daily and weekly chores. The next two options—town homes and condominiums—may provide a resolution to this problem.

Town Homes

According to Webster's dictionary, a *town home* is "usually a single-family dwelling of two or three stories that is connected to a similar house by a common sidewall, thus forming a continuous group." The town-home owner also owns the land on which the town home sits. In essence, this means a purchaser of a town home owns their own individual unit but may be surrounded on both sides or above and below by other owners.

Residing in a town home may not be how you envision retirement living, but if it is, be aware that, unlike with an apartment, you *own* rather than *rent*. If you have a mortgage on your town home, you are entitled to deduct the interest on that mortgage for tax purposes, just as a single-family dwelling owner can. Town-home owners also typically pay a monthly maintenance fee to a homeowner's association. The amount of this fee varies greatly, depending on the location and quality of the property, but it usually covers maintenance of the common areas of the development. A town home is appropriate for a retiree who does not want the burden of property maintenance and does not mind living closely with multiple neighbors.

Condominiums

Condominiums are much like town homes, with two significant differences: the owner owns not only their individual unit, but also an additional percentage of the surrounding property; and the condo unit may be on any floor, not just from the ground up. The condo owner does not own the ground on which the condo is located. Furthermore, because they own an additional percentage of the surrounding property of their condo, condo owners typically face more homeowner restrictions than do town-home owners.

As with town homes, condo owners have to pay a monthly maintenance fee, although this fee may cover more property-maintenance and upkeep features. For example, balcony and patio repair may be covered by fee payments made by condo owners, whereas town-home owners may have to pay for these repairs themselves. As such, condos are best for retirees who want others to maintain the exterior of their property and reside and interact with other owners.

Apartments

Apartments may be thought of in several ways for retirees (for instance, retirees may reside in apartments in independent-living, assisted-living, or continuing-care facilities), but the important feature to understand is that the apartment dweller usually rents rather than owns. As such, you are not entitled to favorable income-tax treatment, such as being able to deduct any portion of your rent as an itemized deduction. Most renters take advantage of the standard deduction and do not itemize their deductions when they file their tax returns.

Living with One or More of Your Children

For many retirees, living with one or more of their children is the *least* favorable of all the housing options. However, whether because of poor health or lack of funds, they often have no other choice. If you live with one or more of your children, try not to be a burden to them. Help out around the house and offer to pay your fair share of the rent or mortgage. If you are in poor health, make sure your child can adequately attend to your daily needs. If your son or daughter works, they may not be able to care for you, so you might want to consider investigating the option of adult day care.

Another frequently overlooked consequence of living with your child is that, if the child is married, their spouse must also approve of your residing in the house or apartment. Many marriages of adult children can be strained (some to the point of divorce) if the child and their spouse do not agree on how to take care of the parent.

Independent-Living Communities

Independent-living communities are designed for retirees who are fully capable of attending to their daily living needs without assistance. Usually, an independent-living community is age-restricted and may even be gated or feature restricted entry. Sometimes, considerable amenities, such as the use of golf courses and tennis courts, may be offered in exchange for the payment of homeowner's fees by community residents. Homeowner's fees also generally cover lawn service. Accommodations include single-family dwellings, town homes, and apartments.

Assisted-Living Communities

Assisted-living communities generally combine the attributes of independent-living communities with limited nursing-home benefits. Assistance is provided for bathing, dressing, and other activities of daily living (ADLs). Assistance in administering medications to retirees or seniors is also typical. Lodging in such a community varies from small cottages or apartments to larger-scale housing.

Confusion often arises about the attributes of assisted-living and those of a nursing home (discussed next). An easy point of differentiation is that an assisted-living community is more "home-like," whereas nursing home care is more "hospital-like." Each is also commonly regulated differently among states. The monthly cost to the elderly recipient for both facilities, however, may be approximately the same (although generally nursing-home costs tend to be more because of 24/7 care).

An important point to understand if you or your parent moves into an assisted-living community is that you are likely eligible to receive benefits under a long-term care insurance policy. Long-term care eligibility usually requires the inability to satisfy at least two of six ADLs. For example, not being able to dress or bathe independently is typically enough to qualify for benefits, as is needing assistance with eating, transferring from a bed to a chair, and using the toilet. Medicaid assistance from the state may also be available if you qualify.

Memory Care Units

Memory care can be a unit located within a traditional nursing home or an assisted-living facility. Typically, the unit is "locked down" (restricted entry) and is available to individuals with profound dementia or Alzheimer's disease. These units also usually have a common sitting area and/or dining facilities.

Medicare may cover memory care, but only for 100 days following a hospital stay. Medicare will also pay for home health care for up to 35 hours a week, but the individual must be certified as "homebound." Alzheimer's patients may or may not qualify for home care benefits, because home health care is not supposed to be for a long-term need. Finally, because Medicare covers only mental conditions from which the patient is expected to improve, a diagnosis of severe dementia or Alzheimer's disease does not qualify for long-term coverage. Alternatively, Medicaid does cover some patients in facilities providing long-term memory-care services, but some facilities do not accept Medicaid patients.

Continuing-Care Retirement Communities

Continuing-care retirement communities (CCRCs) combine the independent-living, assisted-living nursing-home, and memory-care approaches to retirement living in that they segregate retirees according to the level of care they require. Generally, a fairly hefty fee is required for entry into a CCRC. In addition, residents are expected to pay ongoing monthly maintenance fees, which vary in amount based on the level of care needed. Some CCRCs charge a fixed amount for maintenance rather than a varying fee, although you may be disadvantaged by this method if you require only independent living. The type of CCRC may be distinguished by whether any portion of the entry fee is refundable, as well as whether the monthly maintenance fee is fixed or flexible.

CCRCs are becoming more popular, in part because the retiree does not have to move residences as their health deteriorates and they require more care. However, CCRCs are not available in all states and, if they are permitted, are usually lightly regulated. As with assisted-living coverage, individuals who need nursing-home care or memory care can access the benefits of a long-term care insurance policy, provided they meet the eligibility requirements of the policy (for example, the inability to perform two or more ADLs). Medicare coverage may also assist with the first 100 days of care.

Skilled Nursing-Care Facilities

Skilled nursing-care facilities and nursing homes are sometimes thought of synonymously, but Medicare makes a differentiation between the two. Basically, a skilled nursing-care facility provides acute (short-term) care, whereas nursing homes are designed to meet chronic (longer-term) care needs. Both skilled nursing-care facilities and nursing homes provide 24-hour assistance by a registered nurse or other medical professional. Keep in mind, though, that nursing-home care is more long-term in nature, and nursing-home residents typically do not require as much daily attention as those in need of skilled nursing care. Medicare pays a limited benefit for skilled nursing-care attention, but it does not cover nursing-home or custodial care.

The requirements that must be met in order for Medicare Part A to cover skilled nursing-care facility expenses are as follows:

- You must have been hospitalized for at least a three-day period.

- You must enter the facility within 30 days of hospitalization at a physician's direction. You do not need to go directly from the hospital to the facility to be covered by Medicare, but you do need to enter the facility within the 30-day period.

- You must be making improvement as certified by your doctor or other medical specialist; in other words, if you are not making either mental or physical improvement during the period of Medicare coverage, payment of expenses will not be afforded (for example, payment of expenses for Alzheimer's disease is *not* a qualifying condition, because mental deterioration is inevitable).

If you meet these three requirements, Medicare will pay for 100 percent of your expenses during your first 20 days of residence at a skilled nursing-care facility. After that, you are subject to a government-specified daily patient co-payment through day 100 of your stay. After you have received 100 days of skilled nursing-care benefits, Medicare Part A will no longer provide coverage in a given benefit period.

Nursing-Home Care

Traditional nursing-home care is continual or chronic in nature, which is one of the reasons it is referred to as *custodial* care, and you pay a sizable monthly fee for coverage. For example, as of 2018, the average monthly expense for nursing-home care in a private room is approximately $8,000 per month, or $96,000 per year. Depending on the state in which the nursing home is located, the monthly expense may be much higher.

There is no precise way to determine when you or your parent should enter a nursing home, but usually a logical progression occurs, wherein seniors move from independent living to assisted living to a nursing home. Adult children who have to make the decision to move their parent or parents into a nursing home typically experience a great deal of angst before and after the decision is made. Sometimes, if more than one child is involved in the discussion, disagreement arises over the best time to take such a step. Furthermore, if the senior is mentally competent, there may be troubling discussions with them before they enter the nursing home. The living-with-a-child option is frequently tried in the interim.

There are three ways to pay for nursing-home care, although impoverishing yourself to achieve Medicaid coverage (the third way) is not much of an option. The other two ways are from your own savings—private pay—or via receipt of long-term care insurance benefits. You should be aware that, at $96,000 annually, it may not take you or your parent long to deplete all private savings and then have to turn to other alternatives, such as the children paying for the parent's care out of their own pockets. If you do not want this to happen and you can qualify, buy a tax-qualified long-term care insurance policy or life insurance policy with a long-term care benefit rider.

Using Your Home to Fund Retirement: Reverse Mortgages

You are likely familiar with the terms *mortgage* and *mortgage note*, because you probably had to execute such a note to help finance the purchase of your house. You might also have mortgage insurance, which lenders generally require if you cannot make a down payment of at least 20 percent of the purchase price of your home. Seniors may now have another option involving a mortgage note: a *reverse mortgage*, with the term *reverse* coming from the fact that instead of you paying the lender, the lender pays you.

A reverse mortgage is a means of accessing the equity in your home, and seniors are the most likely candidates for such mortgages, because they usually have considerable equity built up in their homes. With a reverse mortgage, the homeowner is able to remain in the home and usually receives a monthly payment from the lender based on a percentage of the principal due on the home. In some cases, this payment may take the form of a lump sum instead of a periodic monthly payment; but if the senior is looking for an income stream during retirement, a monthly payment is the preferred alternative. Under law, the minimum age to qualify for a reverse mortgage is 62, and the senior cannot take a mortgage for more than the home is worth at the time of the loan. If the homes has an existing mortgage, it must first be paid off with the proceeds of the reverse mortgage.

Here is an example of how a reverse mortgage is structured and how you may be able to use it. Assume that you are at least age 62 and otherwise qualify for a $150,000 reverse mortgage (there are no income or health-status requirements with a reverse mortgage). You have an existing mortgage of $100,000 on your house. You will have enough money from the reverse mortgage to both pay off your existing mortgage and benefit from $50,000 in cash to use in whatever manner you wish. A reverse mortgage is even more advantageous if you have no original mortgage, because then you have the full $150,000 available for your use.

If you do qualify, does this sound too good to be true? There are some facts to consider before entering into a reverse-mortgage arrangement:

- No monthly payments are due on the mortgage while it is outstanding. However, when you die or sell the house, the loan must be repaid. If you are married at the time of your death, the loan typically does not have to be repaid until the death of your surviving spouse, but it then must come out of the spouse's estate, thereby *reducing* the amount that subsequently passes to your children or other heirs.

- Like a home-equity loan, you may receive the proceeds from a reverse mortgage over a set term, in lifetime payout, or via a line of credit. If you take the proceeds in a line of credit, a growth feature is built into most reverse mortgages that benefits you if your home appreciates in value over the years (in other words, your payments from the reverse mortgage may *increase*).

- In general, the amount of money you receive from a reverse mortgage depends on your age. The older you are, the more money you will receive.

- A reverse mortgage does *not* affect your receipt of Social Security or Medicare benefits, and the payments are not taxable or treated as taxable income (for example, the 50 percent or 85 percent special step-rate thresholds in Social Security taxation do *not* apply).

- Because of the closing costs associated with a reverse mortgage, you should *not* enter into the arrangement if you intend to sell your home within two to three years after you begin to receive the proceeds. You will not financially be able to recover the closing costs in such a short period of time.

This last point speaks to an important consideration you should be aware of before executing a reverse mortgage: such mortgages are relatively expensive. There may be other, less expensive ways to access the equity in your home, such as a home-equity loan or line of credit. These should be investigated before committing yourself to the drawbacks of a reverse mortgage.

Do I Need Life Insurance During Retirement?

When you retire and your children become independent, you may wonder why you need life insurance. This is particularly the case if you are divorced or separated from your spouse. If you are thinking about ditching your life insurance policy, though, you may need to think again, particularly if you have a high net worth (say, $10 million or more) and are involved in estate-planning and estate tax–reduction techniques. After all, life insurance remains an effective way to pay both any estate taxes you may owe at death and the final expenses associated with settling your estate, because it is purchased with considerably discounted dollars from what your estate will receive in death benefits.

For example, assume that you purchase a $250,000 annual renewable-term life insurance policy and die during the term of the policy's coverage. Depending on numerous factors (including your age and health at the time of purchase), the premiums you paid for coverage may be extremely low. If you assume a total premium payment at your time of death of $25,000, your estate receives a discounted dollar benefit of $225,000 ($250,000 less $25,000). In addition, your heirs receive a total dollar, *income-tax-free* benefit of $250,000 upon receipt of the life insurance proceeds.

Be careful here. If you do not properly title or arrange for the purchase of the $250,000 term life insurance policy, the death proceeds from the policy will be included in your gross estate for estate-tax purposes, thus *adding* to your estate-tax problems. The simple way around this, of course, is to title the policy in your spouse's or adult child's name. But if you do this, you add to the spouse's or child's gross estate. Further, what if the new owner does not make the premium payments on the policy? The policy will then lapse, and your intended beneficiaries will lose the insurance protection on your life. The better way to arrange for the titling of life insurance is to establish an **irrevocable life insurance trust (ILIT)**.

If you are married at the time you enter into retirement and are entitled to a pension, you have a different problem, commonly referred to as *the pension dilemma*. Specifically, under current law, if you are to receive a pension (*not* a lump-sum distribution from a Section 401(k) plan), you must provide for a survivorship payment on the pension to your spouse. When you do this, your own annuity or pension payment is *reduced*, which may potentially impact your future cash flow.

For example, assume you are 65, married, and entitled to a pension payment from your company's pension (defined-benefit) plan of $5,000 per month, or $60,000 per year. This amount is payable to you in a single life annuity form, meaning when you die, the pension terminates, which also means your spouse must replace $60,000 of lost income. To avoid this possibility, you *must* elect under law—unless your spouse elects to waive it—a joint and survivor payout so that your spouse is protected upon your death. However, because your pension payment must now be spread over two lives instead of one, it is reduced, sometimes by as much as 30 percent. Using the numbers in this example, this means your pension payment is now $42,000 ($60,000 times 0.70). Taken over a 25-year life expectancy, you sacrifice approximately $450,000 of lifetime benefits that may otherwise have been payable to you ($18,000 per year difference in payments times 25). Of course, the sacrificed benefit becomes even larger, the greater the pension payment is.

One option that allows you to retain those benefits is to have your spouse consent in writing (signed in front of a notary) to waiving the joint and survivor benefit. But if you proceed with this option, you are right back to where you started: leaving your spouse without loss-of-income protection at your death. Therein lies the pension dilemma. A preferable option is to elect the single life annuity from the pension and then purchase a life insurance policy for the amount of the sacrificed benefit if paid in the joint-and-survivor form (in the example, $450,000) and name your spouse as the policy beneficiary. Doing so has the advantage of partially converting potentially taxable pension benefits to your spouse to nontaxable insurance proceeds. In the financial world, this is known as the *pension-maximization planning technique*, founded on the idea that you use some of the additional pension payment you receive ($18,000 per year, in the example) to pay the premiums on the life insurance policy in order to keep the policy in force until the time of your death. Indeed, you can likely purchase much more coverage than $450,000 with an $18,000 annual premium. This technique works particularly well when the plan participant's spouse is in poor health. In such instances, the cost for the amount of insurance needed to provide income for the poor-health spouse for their remaining life (assuming the plan participant predeceases the spouse) may often be *less than* the cost of providing the survivor benefit from the retirement plan.

Why doesn't everyone entitled to a pension payment from an employer-sponsored plan take advantage of the pension-maximization technique? A primary reason is that the 65-year-old, soon-to-be-retired individual may not be able to qualify for life insurance coverage because of poor health. Another is that life insurance is simply too expensive at that age. Finally, there is always the risk that premiums will not be paid and the insurance will not be there when needed. You need to look closely at a number of factors—including health, age, cost, and whether the pension payment is adjusted for cost of living each year—and see whether the pension-maximization technique is right for you. Hopefully, you will do this with the assistance of a competent financial advisor or life insurance agent.

Retiree Health Insurance

Health insurance coverage for retired individuals is becoming less common. Among businesses with 200–999 employees in 2017, approximately only 23 percent of them provide retiree health insurance, according to a study by the Kaiser Family Foundation. The statistics are even worse among businesses with fewer than 200 employees. Studies have shown that no more than 5 percent of these small businesses can afford to offer retiree health insurance.

What should you do if you want to be insured against poor health during retirement? It depends on your age and whether you are working enough hours to be eligible for your employer's group health insurance policy. Once you reach age 65, you probably will not be concerned about private health insurance coverage, because you will be eligible for Medicare. However, if you are newly retired, but not yet 65, you do not have a great many options.

Your first option is to exercise your COBRA rights. Under the Consolidated Omnibus Reconciliation Act (COBRA) law of 1985, after you leave your job—as long as you were not terminated for gross misconduct—you may remain on your previous employer's group health insurance coverage for a period of up to 18 months. To do so, as noted in Chapter 5, you must pay your former employer's share of the group premium as well as your own previous share. But you should not overlook the opportunity to take advantage of these rights if you retire before age 65. Alternatively, once you reach age 65 and qualify for Medicare, your younger spouse or dependent children may continue group coverage under the COBRA law for a period of up to 36 months.

A second option is to begin to fund a health savings account (HSA), which is established much like the traditional or Roth IRA forms of saving for retirement but includes a high-deductible individual health insurance plan. You may make a tax-deductible annual cash contribution to your HSA and then use this contribution, plus its earnings, to reimburse yourself for medical expenses income-tax free. Moreover, once you become eligible for Medicare, you may draw on your HSA funds tax-free to pay your share of monthly premiums for Medicare Part B and any other co-insurance you share with the government under the Medicare system.

A third option is to purchase an individual health insurance policy. Although such policies are relatively expensive, you can save money by being a prudent shopper of policies, remaining healthy, and taking advantage of certain techniques. For example, if you are between ages 55 and 64, consider separating your coverage from that of your family at the time of application. Typically, individual health insurance is underwritten by companies according to the age of the *oldest* participant in the plan. Thus, if you have a younger spouse, you may be able to classify them for separate coverage under the plan and then combine their age with yours for a more favorable overall rating. You may also wish to consider titling the health insurance policy in the name of the younger spouse to ensure that they continue to have coverage after you become eligible for Medicare.

Another idea that is similar to paying premiums on individual health insurance coverage is to pay a monthly fee for service to a health maintenance organization (HMO). In return for the payment of this fee, you can receive the services of medical professionals for any medical condition that may present as you age. There will be some months (hopefully many months) when you do not need health care–related services, but it is nice to know that treatment will be provided at little or no additional cost when you do need it. The same idea applies for direct-payment medical services now being offered by a number of private physicians (so-called *medical concierge practices*).

If you find individual health insurance premiums or monthly service fees to be so high that they are prohibitive, investigate state-guaranteed policies. Typically, these types of policies are efforts by state governments to cover the uninsured or those who are so unhealthy that no insurance company will provide coverage. To become eligible for state risk pools, you must be rated as a high-risk, unhealthy individual, and you must have been rejected by private insurers. If you can withstand the blow to your ego with respect to being classified in such a manner, you may be able to obtain relatively inexpensive coverage.

Medicare and Medicare Supplemental Insurance (Medigap)

Both Medicare and Medicare supplemental policies (Medigap) were discussed in Chapter 5 as part of the first step in the PADD approach to wealth accumulation and management—*protecting* yourself, your family, and your property. However, you might find it helpful to be reminded of the considerable gaps in Medicare Part A and Part B coverage. Once you become eligible for Medicare, you should purchase the standardized Medigap policy that is most relevant to your needs and health status at the time. I hope you have heeded the advice in this book with respect to your possible long-term health care needs and have been (or will be) paying the premiums on a long-term care insurance policy. Remember, neither Medicare nor private Medigap policies cover long-term care expenses, except in a limited manner, so it is up to you to provide for such coverage.

So, I am Retired! Now What?

You experience a significant life change when you retire, no matter your age. Among the issues you should consider when you retire is the need to establish a new *identity*, but there are also other lifestyle-related issues. Among these are the following:

- Will you continue to work, even if it is only part-time?
- Do you plan to pursue educational opportunities that you were too busy to consider while you were employed full-time?
- Do you plan to travel? What will you do for recreational activities?
- Perhaps most important, how do you accommodate the change from employment to retirement?

Let's consider these issues in more detail.

Future Work

In recent surveys, over 70 percent of baby boomers (individuals born between 1946 and 1964) said that they planned to continue working in some capacity during retirement. This statistic may be somewhat misleading, because in many instances boomers will *have to* continue working due to poor savings habits and lack of planning, but there is no doubt that the members of this generation will be more active in their retirement than previous generations were. Employment of some kind, even if part-time, may be useful, because it eases the transition from a working career to the more leisurely time of retirement.

If you will continue to work after you are retired, you need to consider the impact of your earnings on your eligibility to receive Social Security benefits. For example, if you elect to receive Social Security retirement benefits early (beginning at age 62), be aware that an earnings limit applies until you are 65 or until your otherwise specified full retirement age (FRA) under the Social Security system. If you are under your FRA throughout a given calendar year and earn more than a specified amount, then $1 of Social Security benefits is withheld for every $2 you earn in excess of this limitation. Further, this earnings limit is separate and apart from any income-tax requirements to which you may be subject. In other words, between the age of 62 and your FRA, not only will your Social Security retirement benefits be reduced, but you will have to pay income taxes on those benefits if your income exceeds either of the special step-rate thresholds.

You should also consider the possibility of self-employment during retirement. As part of their desire to stay active, many boomers have started their own businesses. According to a survey by *Bloomberg's Business Week* magazine, boomers are twice as likely to pursue self-employment than the generations that retired before them. This is particularly true for boomers with professional skills, such as medical doctors, lawyers, accountants, and financial planners. Moreover, it is generally advantageous from an income-tax perspective to become self-employed, because self-employed individuals usually are better able to benefit from certain tax deductions and credits than are salaried employees.

Keep in mind, however, that self-employment also carries many risks, chief among them the willingness to assume the financial risk associated with becoming self-employed. Most businesses do not generate a profit until at least three years after the business was started. In the meantime, these businesses must find a way to cover expenses during the years when a profit was not generated. Hence, many self-employed individuals seek financial assistance from banks and other sources of capital to run the business in its formative years. Typically, banks require a personal guarantee of repayment on any monies loaned. This often means that if you become self-employed and require the bank's financial assistance, you must pledge personal assets, such as your house, as collateral for the loan. Venture capitalists—private money lenders—are even more demanding: they may require not only a personal guarantee, but also a percentage of the profits after the business becomes profitable.

Unless you consider yourself a risk-taker—the primary attribute of any entrepreneur—you may wish to remain in the employ of a larger company. For instance, Walmart has become known for aggressively seeking senior workers, and other companies are quickly doing the same, given the wealth of experience that today's retirees bring to any business.

Education

What should you do if you are retired and want to pursue a degree or return to the college coursework you always meant to finish? Normally, if you withdraw money from a traditional or Roth IRA before you reach the age of 59.5, you pay a 10 percent early distribution penalty in addition to regular income tax (you would pay tax on the contributions and earnings from a traditional IRA, but probably only on the earnings from a Roth IRA). There is an *exception* to this penalty when you use the money in payment of qualified higher-educational expenses, however. If you are a retiree under the age of 59.5, you can withdraw money from your traditional or Roth IRA if the expenses incurred are for the education of you, your spouse, your children, or your grandchildren and include only tuition, fees, and books used in a degree program. Meanwhile, if you are over age 59.5, you pay neither a penalty nor income tax on a qualified Roth IRA distribution made for purposes of education.

A second suggestion is to do what increasing numbers of traditional college students are doing: request financial aid. There is no age maximum on financial-aid packages offered by schools or the government. As a result, if you can demonstrate a need for the money to attend school, just like your children or grandchildren, you may be awarded financial aid. In addition, if you are attempting to fund your post-retirement education from your traditional or Roth IRA, the assets accumulated within that account are sheltered from the financial-aid need analysis; in other words, they are not counted against you.

Finally, consider borrowing for your education from an employer-sponsored retirement plan, such as a Section 401(k). In practical effect, you are borrowing from yourself to fund your education, but you are doing so at an extremely favorable interest rate—usually only a percentage point or two above the prime rate. The funds you borrow from a retirement plan are still tax-deferred and are not subject to income tax when you borrow them. Then, when you pay the funds back, they return to your retirement account, and all you have sacrificed in the meantime are any earnings that could have been made on the account if you had not taken the loan.

Travel and Recreation

As mentioned in Chapter 16, the standard rule of thumb in saving for retirement is to attempt to replace approximately 75 percent of your pre-retirement gross income for use during your retirement years. This amount comes from the presumptions that you will be saving less, paying a lower amount of taxes, and not commuting (or commuting very little) during retirement. But what if one of your retirement goals is to travel extensively or spend considerably on recreational activities that you postponed while working? In this event, should you strive to replace more than 75 percent of your pre-retirement gross income?

Studies have shown that even with increased expenses for travel and recreation, the most you should budget for your retirement is probably 90 percent of your pre-retirement gross income. Still, if your pre-retirement gross income averaged $100,000 per year, this means you need to save for $90,000 per year in today's dollars (after accounting for the effects of inflation). This is not an insignificant sum. Keep in mind, however, that travel and recreation do not usually add substantially to the total amount of retirement dollars needed. The expense that most retirees typically underestimate is the cost of health care during their retirement years.

Under federal tax law, some of the travel costs you incur during retirement could be income-tax deductible. But these travel expenses must be primarily for and essential to medical care. Thus, a trip to an out-of-state specialty facility, such as the Mayo Clinic in Minnesota or Sloan-Kettering Medical Center in New York City, may be deductible within limits. To remain within these limits, you cannot deduct meals on the trip, and the deduction for lodging is restricted to an amount that is not lavish or extravagant. Even if you can pass these tests, though, you still may not be able to claim a deduction unless the aggregate total of your medical expenses exceeds 7.5 percent of your adjusted gross income (AGI) in 2018, after any health insurance reimbursements. As a result of these limitations, the chances are small that you will receive a travel expense deduction in the pursuit of most noncatastrophic medical care. Similarly, some taxpayers have tried to deduct from their taxes the cost of living in a warm locale during the winter after getting a note from their physician that it is advisable to do so for their good health. Nice try, but the US Supreme Court has ruled that such expenses are primarily personal and not medical, thus denying the claim for the average taxpayer.

Accommodating Change

For many retirees, the most difficult part of retirement is not what we have discussed so far, but rather the simple fact that their daily life has changed. For example, before retirement, when you got out of bed each morning, you had somewhere to go and something to do! This routine changes considerably when you retire.

Just as you need to prepare for the financial aspects of retirement, you also need to prepare for the lifestyle change that retirement brings. Many seminars and workshops are available to help you deal with retirement issues and life as a retiree, but the most important lifestyle challenge you will face at retirement is establishing a new purpose for your life. This may be as simple as being there for your children or grandchildren, or it may involve working part-time. Whatever you do, you should strive to maintain good physical health and keep mentally active. Keeping mentally active does not necessarily entail writing the next great American novel, but it does mean that exercising your mind is an integral part of a fulfilling retirement. Also, cultivate as many friendships as possible during your retirement years, because studies show that retirees are generally happier when surrounded by family and friends.

If you can accept change and, hopefully, thrive on it, you will probably find yourself among the 90 percent of Americans who say they are pleased with their retirement and are happy with the lifestyle decisions they have made while in it.

This chapter and the previous one have addressed what is likely everyone's number-one financial goal: personal retirement. But as with life, the personal financial process is not so simple, because different people may have different—or other—financial planning goals. Among these goals may be starting your own business, buying a second home, and eventually selling a substantially appreciated personal residence. These goals are the focus of the next chapter.

CHAPTER 18

Planning for Other Lifetime Financial Goals

Although most people's number-one financial goal is planning for a comfortable retirement, you may have other financial goals that you wish to include in your wealth-distribution process. Among these may be starting your own business (and perhaps subsequently selling that business), buying and selling a personal residence, purchasing a second or vacation home, or investing a windfall, such as lottery winnings or a substantial inheritance. This chapter considers all these goals in turn and, to the extent possible (you cannot really *plan* to win the lottery), discusses how to attain them.

Starting Your Own Business

The term *entrepreneur* is defined in Webster's Dictionary as "someone who organizes, manages, and assumes the risk of a business." Does that sound like something you would enjoy? If it does, you are not alone, because many individuals of all ages (particularly baby boomers who are just beginning retirement) harbor the dream of starting their own business. However, according to the

© Keith R. Fevurly 2018
K. R. Fevurly, *Plan Your Financial Future*, https://doi.org/10.1007/978-1-4842-3637-6_18

Small Business Administration, the sad fact is that approximately 56 percent of start-up businesses fail within five years. Another 33 percent fail within *two* years of beginning operation. Therefore, your business has an approximately 45 percent chance of being successful.

Numerous books have been written on the subject of how to avoid becoming a failed business owner. To summarize all these ideas, success in starting your own business comes down to the same initiative that applies throughout the financial-planning and wealth-management process: you have to *plan* to be successful.

The following are five commonly agreed-on steps you can use to help ensure your success when starting a business:

1. Begin a business in a trade, skill, or service that you know.
2. Write a business plan.
3. Consider your form of business operation. Do you wish to operate as a sole proprietor, partnership, corporation, or limited liability company?
4. Recruit individuals to the business who possess strengths that are different from your own.
5. Give some up-front thought to how you will pass on the business to others—usually family members—if that is important to you.

Begin a Business with What You Already Know

According to a study by the Kaufmann Foundation, a center for research and education for entrepreneurs, people ages 55 to 64 are more likely than those in any other age group to start their own business. In part, this is because these individuals are retiring or getting close to retiring from the workforce and are preparing for their retirement years. It is also because people of this age group have readily transferable skills that can help them start and grow their own business.

For example, if you have worked for all or the majority of your career in product development, who knows more than you about that particular product and how it may be adapted to the broader consumer market? Alternatively, if you have worked in sales for the duration of your career, who knows better than you how to sell this or some other product? Meanwhile, if you are younger than 55, starting your own business may be more difficult, because you probably have not accumulated sufficient financial resources and expertise to do so.

Regardless of your specific area of expertise, all successful entrepreneurs share several common characteristics. Among these are a take-charge attitude, organizational skills, and enormous self-confidence in their own abilities. In addition, for lack of a better description, entrepreneurs are skilled at thinking outside the box. They are able to think creatively about other potential uses for a given product or service. Bill Gates, for instance, was told many times that consumers would have no need for personal computers (PCs), yet he persisted in his vision that consumers would accept and subsequently demand access to this technology. In essence, what Bill Gates saw was not the physical box that was to become the PC, but rather what that box could do for people to make their lives easier. As such, he proved his ability to think outside the box and is among the richest men in the world because of it.

Write a Business Plan

A critical mistake that many young entrepreneurs make is failing to write a business plan before they open the doors of their new business. Just as it is troublesome to structure your personal finances without first having written a forward-looking budget, it is terribly difficult to operate a business profitably if you do not anticipate where that business is going—and what risks you have to assume to get it there.

Not only is a well-thought-out business plan key to operational success, but it is also an important document for raising business capital. It is unlikely that you will be able to fully finance your start-up and its first few years of business operation out of your own pocket, particularly if you are young. Instead, you will probably have to seek capital from friends or family or—more likely—a bank. And guess what? Most banks will *not* lend you the necessary money before they have seen and analyzed your business plan. Similarly, if you seek financing from a venture capitalist or a private equity group of investors, they are exceedingly likely to ask you to prove to them in writing how you intend to grow the business and what untapped niche your product or service will fill in the marketplace. A business plan forces you to think about the answers to these questions.

The components of a business plan are up to you, but among the more common parts are the following:

- A detailed description of your product or service
- A marketing plan and strategy
- The management team you plan to assemble
- Financial plans and projections
- Timelines for accomplishing certain metrics

- An analysis of the potential problems and risks you will encounter when bringing your product or service to market, including a competitive SWOT (strengths, weaknesses, opportunities, and threats) analysis

Estimates of start-up costs and profit-and-loss projections for the next three to five years should also be included, as should a break-even financial analysis. Many web sites and books are available to assist you in drafting and implementing a business plan, so refer to them often and *before* you begin business operations.

After you take the time to write a thorough and complete business plan, you may decide that you don't want to start the business after all. In that case, the business plan served its purpose: it convinced you that the time is not right to begin your business and that perhaps you should think again before pursuing your entrepreneurial dream.

Consider the Form of Business Operation

Often, business plans outline the form of operation that the business will take. This is particularly true if you plan to start the business with partners. Under law, if a business is to have two or more owners, it cannot take the form of a sole proprietorship (the most common form of business operation today). Instead, a multiple-owner business must be a partnership, a regular (also known as a C) corporation, an S corporation, or the increasingly popular limited liability company (LLC), which is now permitted in all 50 states. Note that all states also permit the formation of a one-member LLC in lieu of a sole proprietorship.

Commonly, any potential business owner should consider three primary formational issues before beginning business operations:

- The possibility of incurring personal liability for any business acts or operations
- The ease of the business entity's formation and its ability to assist the owner in raising capital
- The income-tax consequences of operating the business in a particular form

Briefly, the following three sections detail concepts to think about with respect to each of these issues.

Possibility of Personal Liability

In both the regular and S corporation forms of doing business, as well as in the LLC form, the business owner's liability is limited to the amount they have *invested* in the business. Conversely, in the sole-proprietorship and general-partnership forms of conducting business, the owner or partner retains unlimited *personal* liability for all acts of the business; in other words, no distinction is made between the business entity and the business owner or owners. As a result, the business's creditors (including the bank) may foreclose on the owner's personal assets to satisfy any outstanding obligations.

It is currently possible in all states to operate your business like a sole proprietorship but otherwise limit your personal liability. This may be done by structuring a one-owner business as a single-member LLC. The LLC entity may be formed relatively easily by filing standard documents with your Secretary of State or other prescribed office and declaring that you wish to operate as a single-member LLC. Alternatively, a business attorney can advise you of the consequences of conducting your business in this form.

Ease of Formation and Ability to Raise Capital

The sole-proprietorship approach to conducting business is the easiest to form. No formal documents are required by the state, and you may simply hang out a sign and open your doors to business (although in some cases you may need a state license to conduct the business). However, the relative ease with which you can form a sole proprietorship should be balanced against the assumption of personal liability that is inherent in operating your business in this manner.

There is also no written agreement necessary to conduct your business as a general partnership. Nonetheless, it is generally prudent to spell out the obligations and capital contributions of each partner before the partnership begins operation. At some point in the future, the partnership may dissolve and dispose of partnership assets and obligations, and this process generally proceeds much more smoothly if the possibility was considered at the time of commencing business operations.

The regular and S corporation forms of doing business both require the filing of articles of incorporation with the state. Note that an S corporation is simply a regular corporation that has elected to be taxed as a partnership for income-tax reasons. If you plan to do business as a corporation, you need to seek the services of an attorney. Although it is possible to form a corporation or LLC on your own without legal assistance, consulting with an attorney before you do so is generally advisable.

With respect to raising capital for the business, there is one clear winner among the various forms of business operation: the regular or C corporation. That is because this type of corporation may issue both common and preferred stock shares and solicit financing from the public through the sale of such shares (an initial public offering, or IPO). Nonetheless, given the complexity of forming a business as a regular or C corporation, not to mention the double taxation of corporate income, most start-up businesses shy away from corporate organization, at least initially. It is interesting to speculate, however, given the sizable reduction in C corporation tax rates in the 2017 TCJA (from a maximum rate of 35 percent to 21 percent) how many entrepreneurial businesses may choose to incorporate anyway beginning in 2018.

Income-Tax Consequences

Fortunately, all business entities, with the exception of the regular corporation, may be categorized as flow-through entities for income-tax purposes. This means all business income and losses are reported on the owner's individual tax return—not through the filing of a separate tax return. Because most start-up businesses experience losses in their first few years of operation, the impact of added business income on your individual tax return probably will not be significant. But the attribution of tax losses that you can take as a business owner on your tax return may assist greatly with your cash-flow needs. Remember, in many cases the cash flow of the business and of the business owner are one and the same. Unlike capital losses, which are restricted to no more than a $3,000 income-tax deduction in any one calendar year, ordinary businesses losses are fully deductible *without limitation*. As such, a loss may be incurred by the business in one year and offset against the business owner's other taxable income in that same year.

For example, assume that you have elected to conduct business as a sole proprietorship and experience a business loss of $10,000 in your first year of operations (after considering any income you received from the business). You report all of this loss on Schedule C of IRS Form 1040 and offset any other nonbusiness income by the $10,000 loss. You can do this *regardless* of whether you itemize your deductions for income-tax purposes.

The one exception to flow-through tax rules is the regular or C corporation form of doing business. If you conduct business this way, a separate tax return, with the application of a separate set of tax brackets, is required. As with individual tax rates and brackets, corporate tax rates are progressive in nature. As such, it is possible to have some corporate income taxed at a *lower* marginal tax rate than that of the corporation's shareholders. Keep in mind, however, that this advantage is usually offset by the fact that corporate income is double taxed: once at the corporate entity level and again when it is paid out in the form of a dividend to shareholders. In addition, business losses may be taken by only the separate corporate taxable entity and may *not* be applied against the owner's individual taxable income.

Recruit Individuals with Different Strengths

It is unlikely that you (or any other potential business owner, for that matter) possess the myriad skills necessary to conduct and grow your business in the way you anticipated when you first drafted your business plan. In reality, you probably need the services of others to ensure the success of your business. As such, you should try to recruit individuals to your business with strengths and skills that are different from your own, to fill any gaps that may arise as you develop and operate your business. For example, if you possess strengths in product development, you should hire someone with the marketing skills to sell that product. If you can sell, you need to ensure that the product you are selling is of the utmost quality, so seek out someone who is skilled at product development.

Plan for Business Succession

It is estimated that 70 percent of family businesses do not survive the transition from the original founder or founders to a second generation of family members. Why? Because most business founders fail to plan for the succession of their business. Although the failure to plan for succession may be due in part to the founder's temperament (for example, when the founder acts as if they are immortal and succession will never occur), perhaps the major reason founders fail to plan for the succession of their business is that they just do not wish to talk about the possibility of their eventual death or disability.

One way to preemptively address the eventual succession of your business is to include provisions for possible successor owners in your business plan before you begin operations. Doing so has the advantage of forcing you to think about how you will pass on the business to others without the attendant pressure of developing a formal estate plan. The most probable successor owner is a family member who either previously worked in the business or has indicated an interest in taking it over. But a trusted non-family-member employee with many years of experience in the business is also potentially a worthy successor.

Regardless, if you want the business to continue after your death or disability, you must develop a business-succession plan. This should be accomplished in as tax-efficient a manner as possible for the sake of the business seller (usually a senior family member) and the buyer (usually a junior or younger-generation family member). Accountants and tax attorneys may provide an invaluable service in this regard and should be consulted as early as possible in the business-succession process.

Buying a Personal Residence

The tax implications of buying and selling a personal residence were addressed in Chapter 11. The discussion here focuses on saving enough money to buy a home (particularly a first home) and the types of mortgages available to finance such a large purchase.

Saving for a Home

The cost of a home depends on local market conditions, but you should attempt to save at least 20 percent of the purchase price so as to avoid the additional cost of private mortgage insurance. Let's consider an example.

Assume that you are considering the purchase of a starter home for $150,000. In this case, you should attempt to save at least $30,000 as a 20 percent down payment on the home. How long will it take you to accumulate $30,000? The answer depends on how much money you can save each month, as well as the rate of return you can earn on those savings.

If you can put away $500 per month and earn a 6 percent before-tax rate of return on those savings, you will have $30,000 after approximately 53 months of saving. However, if you can earn a 12 percent before-tax rate of return (in other words, *double* your rate of earnings), you will achieve $30,000 in savings six months earlier, after approximately 47 months. Of course, if you can save more than $500 per month, you can achieve the needed down payment even sooner. Keep in mind that some mortgages allow you to put down *less* than 20 percent of the home's purchase price, but the conventional mortgage marketplace requires 20 percent as a minimum.

Just as with any other financial goal, to save the funds necessary to buy a home, you have to plan to do so. This goes back to the financial-planning fundamentals discussed in the first section of the book: *you must establish a savings strategy and then implement it.* If you need to prepare a budget to allow you to accumulate the necessary savings, then you should do so. You must have the discipline to save, or you will not accumulate wealth.

Understanding Types of Mortgages

Historically, four primary types of mortgages have been offered to homebuyers, although recently a fifth—the interest-only mortgage—has been added to the mix. Each is discussed in turn in the following list, along with some factors to consider before choosing which is most appropriate for you. Keep in mind that regardless of which type of mortgage you choose, all demonstrate a primary advantage of investing in real estate: the use of borrowed money to leverage an investment and thereby achieve a greater return on your money.

- *Conventional mortgage*: This is a fixed-rate mortgage for the term of the loan—usually 15 or 30 years—that gives the borrower a guarantee that the interest rate will not increase. These types of mortgages are for individuals who have a stable cash flow and anticipate this stability to continue in future years.

- *Adjustable rate mortgage (ARM)*: With this type of mortgage, the interest rate charged may change on a monthly or yearly basis according to a specified index or benchmark, such as the current yield on the ten-year US Treasury note. ARMs are for individuals who want lower monthly payments and do not anticipate remaining in the home for a considerable period of time.

- *Federal Housing Administration (FHA) mortgage*: The payment of this mortgage is guaranteed by the federal government and as such normally has a lower interest rate than a conventional mortgage. A low down payment is also a feature of the loan. FHA mortgages are usually available only to lower-income homeowners.

- *Veterans Administration (VA) mortgage*: This type of mortgage features the same federal guarantee of repayment as that for FHA mortgage but is for veterans of the armed services only. A feature of the loan is that no down payment is required.

- *Interest-only mortgage*: In this form of mortgage, the borrower pays only the interest on the loan for a specified number of years. Little reduction of loan principal is possible, thereby effectively preventing the borrower from building much, if any, equity in the home. When executing an interest-only mortgage, the borrower is anticipating that the fair market value of the home will appreciate from the purchase price, allowing a payoff of the mortgage balance from any sale proceeds. By their nature, interest-only mortgages should be executed only by relatively risk-aggressive individuals.

Purchasing and Using a Vacation Home

Purchasing a vacation home is a *direct* form of real-estate investment. Although sometimes a vacation or second home is rented out and generates rental income for the purchaser, more times than not such a home is purchased as a private getaway for the purchaser and their family. As a result, treating the home as an income-producing investment in lieu of an income stock or fixed-income bond portfolio probably is not foremost in the purchaser's mind. Moreover, if the purchaser does rent out the vacation home for more than 14 days per year, the IRS will tax it as a rental. This could push the purchaser into the next marginal income-tax bracket, resulting in higher overall income taxes.

Presuming that you, as the purchaser, are buying a vacation home for your own private use or that of your family, you can use several techniques to take maximum advantage of the tax laws. The first, known colloquially as a *like-kind exchange* or *Section 1031 exchange*, may allow you to defer taxes on the gains realized from the sale of the vacation home. The second, known as a **qualified personal residence trust (QPRT)**, is an estate- or transfer-tax planning technique that allows you, if certain conditions are met, to exclude the fair market value of the vacation home from taxation in your gross estate.

Like-Kind Exchanges

Let's first discuss like-kind exchanges. Under Section 1031 of the income tax code, it is possible to execute a nontaxable exchange of one investment property for another investment property, such as real estate or a vacation home. You should note that, under the provisions of the 2017 TCJA, exchanges of personal property held for investment no longer qualify as nontaxable after December 31, 2017. However, it is *not* possible to execute this same exchange if real property is held for personal use. As a result, if you plan to use your vacation home for more than 14 days during the year (which is likely, because you probably bought the home for personal use), you are definitely out of luck, because it will *not* qualify as a nontaxable or like-kind exchange.

Alternatively, assume that, for whatever reason, you plan to use your vacation home for only one week during the year. In this case, you could argue that the vacation home is strictly held as an investment property, and nontaxable exchange treatment should be possible. The key word here, though, is *possible*, because the law is unclear with respect to the taxable result of an exchange of vacation homes wherein each home is used by the owner for fewer than 14 days out of the year. This is certainly aggressive tax planning, but it may work if the facts are right.

Section 1031 nontaxable exchange treatment is much more clear-cut if you rent out your vacation home instead of owning it for personal use. In that case, assuming that you keep your personal use of the vacation home limited to 14 days or fewer during the year, it probably *will* qualify as a like-kind exchange, and any realized gain will be deferred. Remember, though, that the trade-off for the deferral of gain is the annual reporting of all income from the home as a rental property.

QPRT

Now let's move on to the second planning technique involving a vacation home: the Qualified Personal Residence Trust (QPRT). In a QPRT, the vacation home must definitely be used as a *second* personal residence. As such, you cannot rent out the vacation home for any period of time during the year. As a result, if you subsequently establish a QPRT and make the vacation home part of its corpus or principal, you may potentially exclude the fair market value of the home from your gross estate and avoid estate tax on that value.

The mechanics of the QPRT technique are as follows:

1. Establish a QPRT with the assistance of an estate-planning attorney.
2. Retitle the vacation home in the name of the trustee of the QPRT.
3. Provide for your right to use the home for a period of years. Be aware: if you die during the period of time when you have the right to use the home, the value of the home at your death will be included and taxed as part of your gross estate.
4. Transfer the title to the home at the end of this period of reserved use to a separately named trust beneficiary or beneficiaries (typically, your adult child or children).

It is also possible to stipulate that the trust beneficiary *lease* the vacation home back to you at the end of the reserved period. In this instance, although the value of the home will be excluded from your gross estate, the trust beneficiary will have to report taxable lease income. Nevertheless, you can further reduce your gross estate by the amount of the lease payments you are making. For example, assume that you are 65, are in a high marginal estate-tax bracket, and establish a QPRT, funding it with a vacation home as the corpus of the trust. You reserve the right to use the vacation home for a period of 15 years, or until you turn 80. If you die before age 80, the fair market value of the home is included in your gross estate. But if you survive the term of the trust, the value of the home is totally *excluded* from your gross estate. In addition, if you still wish to use the home, you can enter into an arm's-length rental arrangement with a family member as the trust beneficiary when you turn 80.

Carefully consider the practical consequences of establishing a QPRT. If you establish the trust and do not outlive the trust term, you are in no worse taxable shape than you would be if you had done nothing. Therefore, for only the cost of establishing the trust, you can possibly enjoy a sizable potential estate-tax savings. In addition, you have also defended your wealth from one of the often-cited primary threats to its distribution at your death: the imposition of taxes.

Investing a Windfall: So You Won the Lottery!

There are ways you could come into unexpected money or experience a windfall other than winning the lottery. Among these is the receipt of a substantial inheritance, the awarding of an unexpected bonus, or the settlement of a sizable lawsuit in your favor. Still, when most people hear the term *windfall*, they think of winning the lottery. What do you do after you learn that you hold the lucky winning numbers resulting from an investment of only a dollar or two?

The following are three commonsense tips to be used in managing unexpected wealth:

- *Do not tell anyone*—most of all, do not tell the media! This will allow you to make important financial decisions about how to invest the windfall without everyone telling you what you should do with the money. The obvious exception to this rule is that you do want to consult with financial and legal professionals about how best to invest the money.

- *Decide how best to receive the money*—that is, in a lump sum or over time. If you tend to be a spendthrift, structure the payment so it is received over time. Alternatively, if you consider yourself a pretty good investor and saver, you may wish to take the lump sum. Regardless, both forms of payment are immediately income-taxable, so you will receive a greatly reduced after-tax amount.

- *Invest the money*, at least for the time being, in a money market mutual fund or savings account that you can easily access without fear of losing any principal. This will enable you to meet with a financial expert with respect to how you should invest the money for both your short-term and long-term needs. Further, it should help you avoid making any immediate bad investment decisions when your judgment may be clouded by the excitement of coming into so much money.

Remember a basic rule of debt management: pay off high-interest debt immediately, such as credit card interest. With such a significant windfall of money, you should be able to get rid of your credit cards entirely and pay cash for all future expenses.

This chapter concludes the section of this book that discusses how to distribute your accumulated wealth during your lifetime. Of course, one inevitable event remains in anyone's lifetime: their death. This brings us to the next section of the book, which covers distributing your wealth at death, and the topic of estate planning.

PART VI

Distributing Wealth at Death

CHAPTER 19

Estate Planning

We have now reached the last stage in a person's financial life (and physical life, for that matter): death. In this chapter, we discuss how to distribute wealth to your spouse, family members, or other specified individuals or charities when you die. Estate planning and the distribution of an individual's assets at death may best be thought of as the second component in the last step of the PADD process: *distributing* your lifetime accumulation of wealth at death so as to benefit others.

Most people think of estate planning as a lifetime mission to avoid the possible imposition of sizable (some would say *punitive*) estate taxes, but estate planning is much more than that. More properly, the process can be described as the efficient distribution of an individual's property to the person's heirs or beneficiaries in the proper amount at the proper time. The *proper amount* in this context means generally whatever distribution among your heirs is the most preferable; however, the term takes on special meaning for high-net-worth individuals, who must distribute the assets of their estate in a transfer-tax-efficient manner. Meanwhile, the *proper time* is not only at the decedent's death, but also when they are still alive. Lifetime gifting is a prudent and effective way to distribute your wealth on a trial basis to see how your intended heirs manage and use the property you give them. If you do not like the way your intended beneficiaries are using the assets you have gifted them, in most cases you have the opportunity to amend your estate plan.

As a general rule, everyone should prepare certain estate-planning documents *regardless* of whether they believe they will owe any estate taxes at death. Among the estate-planning documents that almost all individuals should have are these:

- A last will and testament
- A financial durable power of attorney
- A medical or health care durable power of attorney (also known as a *health care proxy*)
- A declaration as to medical and surgical treatment (commonly referred to as a *living will*)
- A personal letter of instructions

We begin our discussion of these documents specifically and the estate-planning process generally with the last will and testament.

Do I Need a Will?

The short answer to the question of whether you need a will is yes! Regardless of your personal and financial circumstances, a last will and testament allows you to express how you wish your property to be distributed to your beneficiaries when you die. The writing of a will also permits you to name an individual of your choosing to administer your estate at your death.

If you do not do either of these things, your estate will probably be distributed not only *how* the state in which you reside when you die wants it to be, but also *by whom* this state chooses to administer your estate. This process, known as **intestate succession**, can be summarized as the execution of the will that the state has already written for you. If you do not like the state's will—to the extent that you even know what that is—the private writing of a will to carry out your personal wishes in the manner you deem fit is a prudent estate-planning technique.

The writing of a will is particularly critical for a young married couple with minor children, because a will is the primary document that allows them the opportunity to name a guardian for their children. It is not necessary to name a guardian if one of the natural parents is still living when the other dies. But what about the unfortunate circumstance in which both natural parents die in a common disaster or accident? In that event, the court (known here as the *probate court*) names a guardian if a will is not in place. If either set of grandparents of the minor children is alive, they may be a likely choice. But what if your parents (the children's grandparents) are in poor health or do not reside close to you at your death? If this is the case, the court will probably look to a sibling to assume the guardianship role. If neither a grandparent nor a sibling (or any other family member) is close by, or even exists, the court will look to a trusted friend or perhaps a foster family. Regardless, as a young married individual, if you do not wish for the court to decide the fate of your minor children, be proactive and write a will providing for a guardian.

Keep in mind, however, that parents must do more than just name a guardian for minor children in their will. Your parent or sibling may be able to assume the guardianship role for your minor children, but what if this individual is not good at handling the money you leave them for the children's care? If this is the case, you may wish to consider including a trust in your will for the purposes of receiving and investing the money on behalf of the children for later distribution. You need to name a trustee for this trust—but remember: the skills necessary to effectively perform the legal duty of a trustee are *not the same* as those of a guardian. In other words, the empathetic skills of a person suited to be a guardian and the financial skills most important for a trustee may not be present in the same person or family member. As such, you may wish to name a separate individual for each role. If you do, make sure these individuals can work together effectively. After all, you will not be there to serve as a go-between if your guardian and trustee do not get along, and your minor children may suffer the consequences!

If you do include a trust in your will for the benefit of your children (known in estate planning as a **contingent trust**, because it takes effect only on the contingency of the simultaneous death of both parents), you need to change all your beneficiary designations to include the name of the trustee. It is particularly important to name the trustee as the contingent or secondary beneficiary of a life insurance policy on your life; otherwise, the insurance company will need to obtain a probate court order allowing it to pay out the proceeds to the trustee. Moreover, under the laws of all states, a minor cannot take title to property in their own name. If you have left property to a minor child in your will and have not named a guardian, the court must appoint a guardian to receive the property on the child's behalf. All things considered, it is much easier to complete the necessary components of estate planning while you are alive so as to avoid these consequences.

Given its importance, why do many individuals never write a will? For two primary reasons:

- Writing a will reminds us of our own mortality, a topic that many people do not wish to consider.
- Many people believe the writing of a will is prohibitively expensive.

With respect to overcoming the first objection, consider the situation in which you may leave your survivors if you do *not* write a will. More than likely, your survivors will want your passing to be as easy as possible on them—and knowing that they have been provided for in your will give them great comfort. Further, if you have gone so far as to establish a trust in your will, you may direct the disposition of your property at a time when you believe it will be most appropriate for your survivors. This is colloquially known as "speaking from the grave," and the more direction you give in your estate-planning documents, the louder you speak!

The cost objection to writing a will is often resolved by investigating your alternatives. For example, most attorneys charge a flat fee for drafting a will, with this charge varying according to the amount of drafting that must be done. A simple will, or one that does not involve any estate-tax planning, may not cost more than several hundred dollars—or even less, if it is part of a package of estate-planning documents drafted by the attorney. In addition, many web sites now have standardized wills and other estate-planning documents that you may wish to consider using.

Leaving Property via Beneficiary Designations

It is possible to avoid the probate process and leave your property to others via *beneficiary designations*, such as those included with your life insurance policy, IRA, and retirement plan at work. Although many educated consumers are aware of this possibility, what about property for which a beneficiary designation is *not* possible, such as your checking and savings accounts, brokerage accounts, and articles of personal or real property? Unfortunately, each of these must be considered separately when it comes to distributing property to others.

Checking and savings accounts may generally be left to others only by a will (or your state's laws of intestate succession). If you are married, you may wish to consider titling these accounts in joint tenancy with right of survivorship to your spouse. If you title the accounts in such a manner, they will pass directly to the other named joint tenant, and not under a will, at your death. However, be aware that during your lifetime, each spouse owns 100 percent of the monies in the accounts and can do with them as they wish—without the consent of the other spouse. If you are not married but nevertheless want a second name on your checking and savings accounts, ask your bank to establish a joint account for convenience only (otherwise referred to as a *convenience account*). In most states, titling your accounts in this manner means the second party to the account may withdraw monies from the checking or savings account—but only for the benefit of the primary joint tenant. At death, a convenience account may or may not be left to the second party without having to write a will, depending on the law of the particular state.

Brokerage accounts are usually easier to pass directly to others without writing a will. As mentioned in Chapter 14, if you are working with a stockbroker, ask them to title the brokerage account by using a transfer-on-death (TOD) form. As with an IRA or retirement plan, you need only name a beneficiary for the account and fill out the requisite form for the broker or mutual fund family to honor the request. But be aware that if you have not completed a TOD form for your brokerage account during your lifetime, your will or state law will dictate its disposition at death. Note that a bank has a similar form, known as a **payable-on-death (POD) form**, to provide for the passing of bank accounts directly to a named beneficiary.

The disposition of personal property articles at death may not be of much concern to many decedents. This is because either they do not have significant articles of value or they simply wish to leave their personal property for others to sell or dispose of. However, if a particular piece of property is an antique or has been passed down through several generations of family members, you should attach to your will a *statement of personal property* memorandum to dictate the disposition of the item. All states provide for this statement. As long as the statement is incorporated by reference in your will, and as long as your will includes certain default provisions, you do not need to complete the statement at the time you execute your will. Rather, you may subsequently describe the articles you wish to leave to others and sign the statement at a later date. In other words, you have time to consider future circumstances in deciding how best to dispose of valuable items.

Finally, in most states, individually titled real property (such as your home) may be separately distributed via a beneficiary deed. Moreover, you do not have to be a resident of the state where the real property is located to use that state's beneficiary deed. The purpose of completing this deed is primarily to avoid the necessity of probating the real property or home at your death. As such, the proper completion of a beneficiary deed can be a substitute for the execution of a will in the disposition of such property. Keep in mind, however, that the state may or may not require the filing of the deed for it to be effective, so you should check your state laws after completing the deed.

Titling Property

We now move on to what is known as the *poor man's will* in estate planning—titling all or most of your property jointly so that it may pass to a beneficiary by operation of law in the state where you die. Proceeding in this manner means you may not have to write a will at all, although, as just discussed, you may wish to do so for other reasons. Keep in mind that although titling property jointly with another person is a simple and effective method of transferring your property at death, you may need to reconsider for estate-tax reasons. After all, leaving property via joint tenancy to a surviving tenant who already owns significant amounts of property in their own name may add to the survivor's potential estate-tax liability.

For example, assume that you own property with a fair market value of $10 million jointly with another person at your death. Depending on when the survivor dies and the estate-tax exemption amounts at that time, the survivor may end up owing a sizable amount of estate tax if they already own $10 million of property in their own name prior to receiving your property. Note that this may be a concern for both spouses *and* nonspouses who are the surviving joint tenants of another person's property.

If you do not believe you will have an estate-tax problem at your death, owning property jointly with another person may substitute for the beneficiary designation that is possible with other assets. In this case, even if you do write a will and leave your property to someone other than the surviving joint tenant, the will provision is generally ignored and the property passes by operation of law to the surviving tenant.

Should I Avoid the Probate Process at Death?

As discussed in Chapter 14, the probate process can best be described as the act or process of proving the legal validity of a will. But this entails numerous steps and court intervention, which may lead to both excessive cost and delay in distributing your property to heirs. For these reasons, among others, many decedents wish to avoid the process entirely. Individuals can avoid probate via three primary methods:

- You may use a beneficiary designation whenever possible to leave specific property to a named individual or individuals.

- You may title property with survivorship rights. In most states, this means titling property jointly with another person; but even in community-property states, such as California and Texas, it is possible to elect rights of survivorship with respect to property acquired during a marriage.

- You may establish and transfer assets to a revocable living trust.

Because of its popularity, the **revocable living trust (RLT)** deserves additional explanation. In order for the assets in an RLT to avoid probate, they must be transferred out of the individual names of the owners and retitled in the name of the trustee. It is possible, however, and common, for the original owner to also name himself or herself trustee of their RLT. To do so, the owner must simply prepare and file a quitclaim deed that transfers the title to the property from their individual name to their name as the trustee. For this to occur properly, a trust document must exist at the time the title is transferred. If no such document exists, the retitling from individual owner to trustee is not legally valid, and all relevant property must be probated.

Even if you write an RLT document, keep in mind that only the property that is *actually retitled* in the name of the trustee may avoid probate. Accordingly, many individuals couple the drafting of an RLT with a **pour-over will**, which is executed for the express purpose of transferring forgotten and after-acquired property into the RLT. In other words, the will "pours over" this property to the RLT at the decedent's death and distributes it according to the terms of the trust. Because certain pieces of property are still owned by the decedent in their name at the moment of death, the property passing via the will is subject to the probate process. Nonetheless, the fair market value of this property is typically so nominal that many state laws provide for an exemption.

We have now discussed the reasons for avoiding probate and the primary methods available to individuals who wish to do so. But this discussion begs the question: *should* you avoid the probate of assets at your death? After all, probate has several advantages. It provides a mechanism to clear title to the decedent's property, and it also implements the provisions of the decedent's will. Another frequently overlooked advantage of the probate process is that it protects the decedent from an untimely filing of claims by their lifetime creditors. For example, let's say you own a small business and have many creditors at the time of your death. If your interest in the small business undergoes probate, the business creditors must file their claims against the estate within nine months of your death—or another specified period under state law—or *they are forever barred*. As such, should you anticipate the filing of some unknown creditor's claim at your death, forcing these creditors into a time-specific period to make their intentions known is prudent estate planning.

Ultimately, the only person who can make a decision about whether you want your estate to avoid probate is you! You should recognize the advantages of having your property probated at death and keep in mind that probate's frequently cited disadvantages—cost, the potential for delay, and the public nature of the process—may not be so important that you should skip the process altogether.

Estate Taxes

Estate taxes may be assessed at both the federal and state levels (for example, New York has an estate tax), but typically only the *federal* tax rates are of concern to most decedents. Regardless, be aware that your state may have a *lower* exemption level than federal law for the taxation of gross estates, so you may end up owing estate tax at the state level even if you are not required to file a return or pay tax at the federal level. If federal or state estate taxes are likely to be due on either your or your spouse's estate, you may want to include some tax-planning measures in your will or trust. The inclusion of these measures initially makes the writing of a will or trust more costly, but the planning will pay for it many times over in estate taxes saved.

Estate taxes at the federal level are part of what is known as the *unified transfer tax system*. In practical effect, this means the tax rates and brackets are the *same* regardless of whether you make a lifetime gift of property to others or transfer this property to others at your death. Thus, operationally, any lifetime taxable gift you make *reduces* the amount of property you can leave to your heirs or beneficiaries at death.

Assume, for example, that in 2018 you make a taxable gift of $1 million to someone other than your spouse (if to your spouse, an unlimited deduction applies). Although you pay no federal gift taxes—an allowance of $11.2 million is permitted before any gift tax is due—you have reduced your current aggregate $11.2 million estate-tax exemption to only $10.2 million. If you die with a tentative tax base (after adding back in the lifetime gift) of $11,200,001 in 2018, that $1 of additional property is taxed at a marginal tax rate of 40 percent.

Note that the reduction of your exemption for estate-tax purposes does not mean you should avoid lifetime gifting. Rather, this means, first, that you should take advantage of the annual gift-tax exclusion ($15,000 per person in 2018), because this exclusion is applied *before* you begin to calculate tax liability on a taxable gift; and second, and perhaps even more important, you may be able to exclude the subsequent appreciation of gifted property from your estate. For instance, in the example, let's say you do not die until 2020, and the property gifted in 2018 appreciates 50 percent over the course of those two years. Because you previously gifted the property, you will *avoid* estate taxes on $500,000 (or the 50 percent of appreciation).

Once your taxable estate has been computed at your death, your executor may apply a specified amount of credit—known in estate-tax language as the *unified credit*—against your tentative estate tax due. As with income tax, a credit is a dollar-for-dollar reduction against taxes, so what you should really be concerned about is the amount of that credit in the year of your death. In turn, that credit equates to an amount of property that may be transferred estate-tax-free to others at your death (hence the term *exemption equivalent* or *applicable exclusion amount*). For example, in 2018, the amount of allowable unified credit is $4,425,800, which is equivalent to an exempted property amount of $11.2 million.

Let's look at another example. Assume that you die with a taxable estate of $11.2 million in 2018 and have made no previous lifetime taxable gifts that operate to reduce this amount. The applicable unified transfer tax table indicates that the estate-tax liability on this $11.2 million of property is $4,425,800. Because you have an allowable credit equal to that same amount, you may reduce your tax liability by the allowable credit, resulting in an actual

Plan Your Financial Future

tax due of zero ($4,425,800 tentative tax liability less the $4,425,800 unified credit amount). When you hear estate planners say that you will not pay any estate taxes unless you die with property in excess of $11.2 million in 2018 (or the otherwise applicable exemption equivalent for the year of your death), what they are really telling you is that you qualify for a unified credit that is equal to the estate tax due on $11.2 million.

The preceding discussion of the complexities of the estate-tax system should make clear that you need to understand how the federal estate-tax system works and what measures you may adopt to reduce the amount of your taxable estate at death. This is in part why you should contact a financial planner or estate-planning attorney if you are currently or expect to be a high-net-worth individual. Nevertheless, the more you can educate yourself with respect to the estate- and gift-tax laws, the better you will understand the planning techniques you may undertake to minimize those taxes.

Toward that end, examine the following two important tables, which relate to estate-tax transfers and estate-tax planning. Table 19-1 reflects the tax brackets and marginal tax rates that apply to taxable transfers through 2014–2018 and forward (or at least through 2025, when the TCJA of 2017 "sunsets"). Table 19-2 specifies the amount of applicable unified credit and exemption equivalent amounts for those same years.

Table 19-1. Unified Federal and Gift Tax Brackets and Marginal Tax Rates If the amount is:

Over (Column 1)	But Not Over (Column 2)	Tax on Column 1	Excess Tax on Column 2 (Marginal Tax Rate)
-0-	$10,000	-0-	18%
$10,000	$20,000	$1,800	20%
$20,000	$40,000	$3,800	22%
$40,000	$60,000	$8,200	24%
$60,000	$80,000	$13,000	26%
$80,000	$100,000	$18,200	28%
$100,000	$150,000	$23,800	30%
$150,000	$250,000	$38,800	32%
$250,000	$500,000	$70,800	34%
$500,000	$750,000	$155,800	37%
$750,000	$1,000,000	$248,300	39%
Over $1,000,000		$345,800	40%

Chapter 19 | Estate Planning

Table 19-2. Unified Credit and Applicable Exemption Equivalent Amounts for Estates

Year of Death	Unified Credit	Applicable Exemption Equivalent
2014	$2,081,800	$5,340,000
2015	$2,117,800	$5,430,000
2016	$2,125,800	$5,450,000
2017	$2,141,800	$5,490,000
2018	$4,425,800	$11,200,000*

*Applicable Exemption Equivalent of Exclusion Amount increased to $10 million indexed amount by TCJA of 2017; note that annual exemption equivalent or exclusion amount indexed for inflation for years 2018–2025.

The Importance of Durable Powers of Attorney

Although many people use the terms *disability* and *incapacity* interchangeably, they are not the same thing. In the context of understanding and applying powers of attorney, it is important to recognize that their use is triggered only in the event of *legal incapacity* (or *incompetency*). In other words, the individual granting the power of attorney may be physically disabled and still be legally competent to conduct their financial and health-related affairs.

Let's review some of what we discussed in Chapter 14 in considering how to plan for your own physical or mental incapacity. First, there are two parties to a power of attorney: the *principal*, or the individual granting the power; and the *agent* (also known as the *attorney-in-fact*), or the individual responsible for carrying out the duties of the power. It is essential for the principal to be legally competent when granting power of attorney to the agent; if they are not, the power cannot be effective. Moreover, unless the power of attorney is specifically written to continue in the event of the principal's incompetency (a *durable* power of attorney), the power of the agent to act on behalf of the principal will *terminate* on the date of the principal's incompetency. In other words, a nondurable power of attorney is *not* effective just when it is needed most—on the date of the principal's inability to act!

There are two types of powers of attorney. The first is used for the management of the principal's *property*, including their financial accounts, subsequent to the principal's incompetency. This is frequently referred to as a *financial* or *general durable power of attorney* (DPOA), because it covers a multitude of financial situations in which the agent may act on behalf of the principal. It is also possible to limit the power of the agent to act through the writing of a special or limited DPOA.

A DPOA becomes effective in one of two instances: either *immediately* (at the time that the principal grants powers to the agent) or *in the future* (when the principal becomes legally incompetent). If the power becomes effective immediately, it is referred to as a *regular* or *nonspringing* DPOA. If the power does *not* become effective until the principal becomes incompetent, it is referred to as a *springing* DPOA. If the power is springing, there must be some method of determining *when* the principal has become legally incompetent. Normally, legal incompetence is determined by the mutual agreement of at least two physicians that the principal cannot act on his or her own behalf and needs the assistance of the agent. Because a principal may derive comfort from knowing that they have not relinquished immediate control over their property, many times they execute a springing DPOA. However, this concern is exaggerated in the majority of cases: typically, the designated agent is a trusted family member and is exceedingly unlikely to act until it is clear that the principal cannot do so.

The second type of durable power of attorney provides for a surrogate or substitute to make decisions with respect to the principal's health. This type of power commonly goes by the name of a *medical durable* or *durable power of attorney for health care* (DPOAHC), although it may have a different name in your state (for example, a *medical proxy*). In contrast to the general DPOA, the DPOAHC is *always* springing in effect. In other words, as long as the principal is able to give informed consent with respect to their own health care, the medical community will look to the principal to do so. It is only in the event that the principal is *not* able to give consent that the advice of the agent is sought.

The selection of an agent to make medical decisions on a principal's behalf should be considered even more carefully than the selection of an agent of a DPOA. Although some individuals may not be overly concerned about their financial affairs or who takes over these responsibilities in the event of their incompetency, the same probably cannot be said when it comes to their health. It is essential that the principal give considerable thought to the individual whom they choose to make medical decisions on their behalf. Note, too, that the individual named as the power of attorney for a principal's health need not be the same individual named to manage the principal's money or property.

How should you proceed with planning for your own possible incompetency? Do you need one or both of these powers of attorney? Yes, and you preferably should draft *both* documents—even if you do not see the need for a separate last will and testament. Statistics show that your chances of becoming incompetent at any given time in your life are much *greater* than your chances of dying, so the importance of writing durable powers of attorney cannot be stressed enough. To assist you in the writing and implementation of these documents, samples of the general DPOA and DPOAHC are included in Appendixes C and D. Alternatively, you may wish to seek out an estate-planning or elder-care law attorney to aid you in the drafting of these documents.

Durable powers of attorney are a simple and, by and large, effective way to plan for incompetency, but their use presents several potential problems. First, if the powers are dated (say, more than five years old), the third party to whom the power is presented may not recognize its validity. Moreover, this third party (typically a financial institution) may ask the principal to execute their own durable power of attorney form in order to protect itself from possible liability when honoring the power. This is particularly a concern if, between the time the original DPOA was written and the time the power is needed, the principal becomes incompetent. As a general rule, you should ask the third party how long it is likely to recognize the validity of a general DPOA before executing one.

The other problem with a DPOA, whether related to a principal's finances or to his or her health care, is that, under law, the power terminates on the death of the principal. As a result, in cases where minor children depend on the principal to act on their behalf, a DPOA could present a problem if the principal dies. Fortunately, one of the advantages of writing a revocable living trust (RLT) as part of your estate-planning process is that doing so may serve as an effective method of planning for your own incompetency. Specifically, in contrast to a DPOA or DPOAHC, the power of a successor trustee to act on behalf of the grantor of an RLT does *not* terminate on the death of the grantor. Instead, a successor trustee may continue to act without impunity. In some states, because of this feature, many financial institutions prefer to recognize the legal validity of an RLT rather than that of a DPOA.

For example, assume that you granted a general DPOA on behalf of your oldest son ten years ago. Given the datedness of the general DPOA, some financial institutions may refuse to recognize its validity while you are still alive. Next, let's say you become incompetent while the general DPOA is in effect. In this case, your son may not be able to act on your behalf as power of attorney. Finally, let's say you die tomorrow. Upon your death, the power of your son to act on your behalf will be effectively terminated. All of these problems may be avoided if instead of, or in conjunction with, the DPOA, you execute a revocable living trust naming your son as the successor trustee.

Living Wills

Unlike a DPOAHC, which can take effect in a variety of medical situations, a living will takes effect only in the event of a *terminal illness*. In other words, you must be in a terminal condition and not expected to recover for a living will to go into effect. Due to recent medical advances, hospitals and other types of health care facilities can keep terminally ill patients alive for days, weeks, or months by allowing a respirator to breathe for them or feeding them intravenously—or both. As a result, in most states, you are permitted to execute a living will that directs health care facilities to act in one of three ways in the event that you become terminally ill:

- The health care facility must maintain an artificial means of life for you for an indeterminate amount of time.

- The health care facility must immediately discontinue the artificial means of life after you are pronounced terminal by two or more physicians.

- The health care facility must maintain the artificial means of life for a period of days—usually seven to ten—at your discretion.

Many individuals select the third option, but there is no proof that, after spending a certain number of days or weeks on life support, you will partially or fully recover. Usually the result is the opposite: if you have not recovered after a specified period of time, you are probably *not* going to recover. Unfortunately, this makes the execution of a living will that much more difficult, because most people do not wish to consider that they may find themselves in a terminal condition.

Unlike a DPOAHC, which names a substitute decision-maker with respect to health care matters, a living will is a personal directive from you to your physician specifying how you wish to be treated if you are terminally ill. As a matter of procedure, after executing a living will, you should give a copy to your family doctor and other physicians. Fortunately, the process of writing a living will is made easier by the publication in most states of a preprinted form that you can fill out prior to entering the hospital. Early completion of this form permits you to discuss with your physician the ramifications and possible unintended consequences of your decision.

Should you execute a living will? If you have not written a DPOAHC or medical proxy, you should. If you have already written a DPOAHC, you should check to see whether any living-will provisions are already included in that document. Some states permit an individual to dictate in a DPOAHC both living-will directions and to whom the durable power of attorney for health care should be given. As a result, you need complete only one document, instead of two, to address any conceivable medical decision that may need to be made in the case of your incompetence. Keep in mind, though, that this course of action may make it more difficult for your physician to determine what type of medical treatment you would prefer to receive. Consequently, it is all the more important (whether you have both a living will and a DPOAHC or one all-inclusive document) that you also communicate *orally* to your spouse or other close family member what should happen in the event you suffer a life-threatening condition.

A sample copy of a living will—sometimes referred to by its proper name of *Declaration as to Medical or Surgical Treatment*—and a DPOAHC are included in Appendix D.

Personal Letter of Instructions

A final, often-overlooked document that you can use to aid in the distribution of your wealth upon your death is a *personal letter of instructions*. This letter is an informal writing from you to the executor of your will, reminding them to contact certain individuals and perform certain tasks in the event of your death. Such a letter often also includes directions as to where the executor may find the original copies of your last will and testament, information on any trusts you have executed, forms specifying powers of attorney, and living wills. The letter should also specify how you wish to have your body handled subsequent to your death, as well as any other special wishes, such as organ donation.

It is important to understand that you do not have to draft a personal letter of instructions in any particular form, nor do you need to consult an attorney to draw one up for you. Rather, the form of and the inclusions in the letter are limited only by your current and anticipated circumstances (and perhaps by your creative skills). A sample personal letter of instructions as used by an attorney in his financial- and estate-planning practice is included in Appendix E.

When Should I Change My Estate Plan?

You should periodically review your estate-planning documents to consider whether your objectives have changed. To conclude this chapter, the following are some important events that may cause you to consider changing your estate plan, amending your current will or trusts, or rewriting those documents entirely:

- You have moved from one state to another. In this case, it is good practice to have your will or any other estate-planning document reviewed by an attorney who is licensed in your new state of residence.
- You have had a significant change in family circumstances, such as the birth of a new child or the death of a named or intended beneficiary to your estate.
- The executor or guardian you have selected for your estate can no longer serve.

Plan Your Financial Future

- You are a high-net-worth individual, and there has been a substantial change in the estate- or gift-tax laws subsequent to the implementation of your estate plan.
- You have come into a substantial inheritance (or another significant change in the amount of property that may be taxed) after the writing of your estate-planning documents.
- Any other important distribution or estate-planning objective has changed since you first implemented your plan.

In amending your plan or documents, it is prudent to seek the assistance of a financial planner or estate-planning attorney or both.

Now let's move on to techniques for engaging in philanthropy, which is a common estate-planning objective of many individuals, particularly those of high net worth. The topic of charities and charitable planning is so vast that it warrants a separate chapter. We look at the topic first from the standpoint of how to choose a charity to benefit from your largesse. Then we discuss how to best structure the gift or testamentary bequest to benefit that charity.

CHAPTER 20

Philanthropy

We conclude our look at wealth accumulation and management by considering a common financial-planning goal of many individuals, particularly married couples without children or those who are unmarried: benefitting, either at death or during their lifetime, the charity of their choice.

Before we begin this important discussion, allow me a note of caution: most taxpayers are aware that the government offers taxpayers an income-tax deduction for charitable gifts made during their lifetime. Although taking advantage of this deduction is a valuable tax-avoidance technique, you should not let your desire to reduce your taxes outweigh practical cash-flow management. In other words, just because the charitable income-tax deduction is permitted does *not* mean you should make a transfer to charity *if* this transfer will jeopardize your ability to maintain your standard of living. Your analysis should be quite the contrary: *if you cannot afford to make a gift to charity during any given year, do not make such a gift*. Furthermore, although you might consider it unfair tax policy, it is the law that you must be able to *itemize* your income-tax deductions before deducting any contributions to charity. This is still the case even after passage of the 2017 TCJA. If you are unable to itemize your deductions, you must take only internal satisfaction in giving to the charity of your choice.

Choosing a Charity to Benefit

For income-tax purposes, there are two types of qualifying charitable organizations: a *public* (also known as a 50 percent) charity and a *private* (also known as a 30 percent) charity. Each of these charities gets its percentage name from the respective maximum limitation that you, as the donor, may deduct as a percentage of your adjusted gross income (AGI) in the year when you

© Keith R. Fevurly 2018
K. R. Fevurly, *Plan Your Financial Future*, https://doi.org/10.1007/978-1-4842-3637-6_20

make a charitable contribution. For example, assume that you have decided that during the current tax year, you wish to make a sizable gift of $50,000 to the American Red Cross to benefit the victims of recent hurricanes. However, your AGI for this year as reported on your IRS Form 1040 is only $80,000. Thus, you are limited to an allowable itemized deduction of only $40,000 for this gift ($80,000 times 0.50) during this tax year. The remaining $10,000 must be carried over and deducted in a subsequent year, for up to a period of five years, when your AGI for that year is at least $20,000 ($20,000 times 0.50).

For *transfer-tax* purposes, on the other hand, there is *no* taxable difference with respect to which type of charity you benefit. Regardless of whether the charity is public or private, you receive an *unlimited* deduction equal to the amount of property that passes from you to the named charity at your death or during your lifetime. Keep in mind, though, that if you care to also benefit a noncharitable beneficiary, such as yourself, before transferring the property to charity, you must do so through the use of a specific form under tax law. This type of transfer is known as a *split-interest gift*. If you do not make this type of transfer in an approved form, the transfer-tax charitable deduction will *not* be permitted.

For example, assume that you are interested in benefiting your alma mater with a charitable gift of income-producing property at your death. But during your lifetime, you need the income from this property to maintain your current standard of living. Under current tax law, you must structure this split-interest transfer in one of only a few allowable ways, including a private transfer in trust (commonly known as a *charitable remainder trust*) or via a fund that has been previously established by your alma mater (commonly known as a *pooled income fund*).

Public Charities

A *public charity* is one that receives broad public support and is not established by a private individual. Examples of public charities are the American Red Cross, the United Way, the Salvation Army, and the American Heart Association. Public charities can also include local churches, as well as hospitals operated by a religious order or municipality that are not-for-profit for income-tax purposes. In addition, educational institutions are public charities—and they need not serve a particular demographic to be considered as such. Given the amount of tuition and fees that many pay for higher education, you may not immediately think of your alma mater as a qualifying charitable institution, but that is indeed the case! It makes no difference whether the college or university is publicly supported or privately operated; the educational institution to which contributions are made is considered a public charity.

All public charities afford the donor an income-tax deduction of up to 50 percent of your AGI in any one tax year (60 percent in the event of *cash* contributions) in 2018-2025. Contributions exceeding the 50 or 60 percent limit are generally allowed to be carried forward and deducted for up to five years so long as not exceeding the later year's "ceiling." However, depending on the type of property given to the charity, this percentage amount may be further limited. For instance, if you make a gift of appreciated stock to a public charity, you *may* be limited to a deduction of no more than 30 percent of your AGI in the year of contribution. The word *may* here is emphasized, because the actual deduction you can take depends on whether you ultimately choose to deduct the full fair market value of the stock or only your cost basis in the stock. There is a trade-off: if you choose to deduct the full fair market value of the stock from your taxable income, you are limited to a deduction of 30 percent of your AGI in the year of contribution. Alternatively, if you choose to deduct only your cost basis in the stock, you may deduct up to 50 percent of your AGI (depending on whether this basis equals 50 percent of your AGI for that year).

For example, assume that you previously paid $40,000 for 500 shares of XYZ stock. The value of these shares has appreciated to $50,000, giving you a potential capital gain of $10,000. You wish to give the shares to the Salvation Army in a year in which your AGI is $90,000. You have two choices:

- You can subsequently deduct the appreciated fair market value of the shares ($50,000) and deduct $27,000 ($90,000 times 0.30) in the year of contribution. You can then carry over the remaining $23,000 of allowable charitable deduction ($50,000 less $27,000) to a period not exceeding five years from the date of the contribution.

- You can deduct your cost basis of $40,000 in the shares in the year of contribution. This amount is less than 50 percent of your AGI ($90,000), so the full $40,000 deduction is permitted. But if you make this choice, you are *not* permitted to deduct *any* additional appreciation with respect to the shares or the remaining $10,000 ($50,000 less $40,000).

In most instances, it is to your benefit to elect the *first option*, because you avoid the capital gains tax that would be imposed on you if you sold the appreciated stock rather than gifting it to charity. An exception to this basic rule, however, occurs when the gifted stock has not experienced much appreciation from the time you bought it until the time you donate it to charity. In such cases, the basis election is preferable for income-tax purposes.

There are also restrictions on the income-tax deduction you may take for any tangible personal property, such as a painting, after it is given to charity. These restrictions, known as *use-related* and *use-unrelated* income-tax rules, are based not only on the *type* of property given, but also on the *use* the charity makes of the property after it is received. According to these rules, if the charity's use of the property matches that for which it was intended, the property can be considered use-related, and you may take a deduction for its full fair market value. Nevertheless, the 30 percent AGI limit applies in the year of contribution unless the taxpayer elects to deduct only their basis in the donated property. On the other hand, if the charity does not use the property in the way it was likely intended, the property is considered use-unrelated, and the donor is limited to a total charitable deduction of no more than the amount paid for the property. As a further limitation, if you are an artist and created a painting yourself before gifting it to charity, you are not permitted to take any income-tax deduction whatsoever, save for the cost of the materials you expended to create the painting.

For example, assume that you, as a collector of fine art, gift to a local university a painting you purchased. Although the university has an art museum, it intends to show the donated painting in its administration building. As a result, the university is making use of the painting in a "use-unrelated manner." Accordingly, as the donor, you are limited to a charitable deduction of no more than what you paid for the painting. Alternatively, if the university featured the painting in its art museum, you would be entitled to a charitable deduction for the current fair market value of the painting, because the university featured the painting in a use-related manner. Note that if you were the original painter of the painting, you would be entitled to a charitable deduction only for the cost of the materials you used to create the painting. This is the tax result *regardless* of the use the university made of the painting.

As the previous discussion makes clear, the tax rules with respect to charitable income-tax deductions are extremely complex. As a result, you should make gifts to charity only after consulting with a tax advisor or financial planner.

Private Charities

A *private charity* is best described as any charity that is not considered to qualify as a public charity. In practice, a private charity or private foundation is any charity other than a church, an educational organization, a hospital, or a governmental unit. Examples of well-known private charities include the Bill and Melinda Gates Foundation, the Ford Foundation, and the Rockefeller Foundation.

The tax rules permitting an income-tax deduction for contributions to private charities are similar to those for contributions to public charities, except that the percentage of AGI limitations are even further restricted. The percentage amount permitted also depends on whether the private charity is an *operating* or *nonoperating* foundation. For example, a gift of appreciated stock to a private nonoperating foundation is subject to a deduction of only 20 percent of a donor's AGI in the year of contribution, as opposed to the 30 percent deduction that donors to private operating foundations are eligible to receive. This is also the case when a gift of use-related tangible personal property is made and the donor does not elect to claim only their basis in the property as the allowable total deduction. Meanwhile, a gift of cash to a private charity is generally restricted to a contribution-year deduction of only 30 percent of AGI, as opposed to the 60 percent deduction that applies to a public charity donee.

Table 20-1 documents the most important deduction limits with respect to gifts made to charity during the lifetime of a donor.

Table 20-1. Charitable Contribution Deduction Limitations

Type of Property	Allowable Total Deduction Amount	Percentage AGI Limitation if Public Charity (and private operating foundation)	Percentage AGI Limitation if Private Charity (private nonoperating foundation)
Cash	Fair market value (FMV)	60% of AGI	30% of AGI
Appreciated stocks and bonds (securities)	FMV election	30% of AGI	20% of AGI
	Basis election	50% of AGI	20% of AGI
Tangible use-related personal property	FMV election	30% of AGI	20% of AGI
	Basis election	50% of AGI	20% of AGI
Tangible use-unrelated personal property	Basis in property only	50% of AGI	20% of AGI

Substantiation Requirements

As a taxpayer, after you have determined what type of property to give to which form of charity and in what amount, you need to be concerned about proving what you gave or *substantiating* the amount to the IRS. The law used to be that the donor had to obtain a written receipt from the charity only if their cash gift exceeded $250 in the year of contribution. For gifts of tangible property, the donor did not need a qualified appraisal establishing the fair market value of the gift unless it was reasonably estimated that the property exceeded $5,000 in value.

These rules changed, however, beginning with charitable contributions made in 2007. Now, regardless of whether they constitute cash or property, all contributions of any amount that are made to a public or private charity must be substantiated. In practical terms, this means unless you can produce either a bank record (such as a cancelled check) or a written communication from the charity (a "contemporaneous acknowledgement") indicating the amount of the contribution, the date of the contribution, and the name of the charity, your charitable income-tax deduction may be disallowed. If a donated item is valued at more than $5,000, and the item is neither cash nor a publicly traded security, the donor must obtain an appraisal (and attach it to his or her tax return).

Gifts to Charity Using Trusts and Annuities

Gifts made to charity in qualifying split-income form for income-tax deduction purposes must generally be made either in the form of a trust or in exchange for an annuity from the charitable institution. The following discussion provides the specifics for each form.

Charitable Trusts

There are two prevalent types of charitable trusts: the **charitable lead trust (CLT)** and the **charitable remainder trust (CRT)**. A CLT makes payments of income interest to a charity during its term. Then, at the end of the trust's term, the remainder of its assets are passed to a noncharitable beneficiary in an attempt to zero out any estate taxes that may be due from the donor's estate.

For example, assume that you have established a CLT as part of the provisions of your last will and testament. At death, you direct that $1 million be placed in this trust to benefit first the American Humane Society and subsequently your two adult children equally. From this bequest of $1 million, the Humane Society is to receive a payment of $80,000 for the next 20 years. Using a table to determine the present value of your total future bequest to the Humane Society, the executor of your estate determines that the estate is entitled to a charitable deduction of approximately $997,000. As a result, you have effectively zeroed out the value of the subsequent transfer of the trust property to your two children, as well as any potential estate tax that may be assessed on this same transfer. In other words, your two children receive the trust property estate-tax-free.

The second (and more popular) type of charitable trust is a CRT, which pays the donor (or another beneficiary) income during the donor's lifetime and then, at the time of the donor's death, transfers all remaining assets to the donor's charity of choice. This type of trust comes in two basic forms: a CRT that provides a *fixed annuity payment* to you throughout your lifetime (otherwise known as a *charitable remainder annuity trust*, or CRAT); and a CRT that provides a *fixed percentage of the trust assets*, as revalued annually, to you during your lifetime (otherwise known as a charitable remainder unitrust, or CRUT).

There are additional requirements for both CRATs and CRUTs to qualify for income-, gift-, and estate-tax deductions. But it is important to recognize that if you, as the donor, establish either trust during your lifetime, you are afforded *two deductions*:

- An *income-tax* charitable deduction during your lifetime for the present value of your future bequest to charity
- An unlimited *estate-tax* charitable deduction at your death for when the gifted property eventually passes to charity

As such, if you intend to benefit a qualified charity at your death, you should likely establish a remainder trust *now* and take advantage of the double tax benefit for income- and estate-tax purposes.

Both CRATs and CRUTs are irrevocable trusts, but have two basic differences. First, whereas a CRAT's fixed annuity payments may eventually cause your purchasing power to decline as inflation rises, a CRUT is capable of keeping pace with or exceeding the annual inflation rate. Because the CRUT guidelines include an annual income payment based on a fixed percentage of trust assets, as revalued annually, you may be able to keep ahead of inflation and preserve the future purchasing power of your trust payments. Second, unlike a CRAT, for which no additional contributions of property may be made after the trust has been established, a CRUT permits subsequent gifts of property.

Because both CRATs and CRUTs are customized, privately drafted documents, it is necessary to seek the assistance of a competent estate-planning attorney in drafting them. If you are worried about the out-of-pocket costs involved in the implementation of either document, you should ask the attorney to estimate the amount of money you will save in income and estate taxes by forming a CRT. Then compare this figure on a present value basis to the attorney's fee. In most instances, the present value of the tax savings will more than exceed the cost of establishing and maintaining the trust throughout your lifetime.

Charitable Gift Annuities

If you want to obtain the same benefits offered by a CRT without having to hire an attorney, you may want to establish a charitable gift annuity (CGA), which allows you to donate cash or property to a charity in exchange for the charity providing you with a lifetime stream of annual income. Like CRAT payments, CGA payments are often distributed in a predetermined, fixed amount and thus may cause your purchasing power to diminish as inflation rises. However, it is possible for the charity to purchase a cost-of-living rider on the annuity so that your payments keep pace with inflation.

Be aware that, as with other charitable transfers, the transfer of assets in exchange for a CGA is *irrevocable*, meaning after you begin to receive benefits, there is no turning back. In addition, keep in mind that if you decide to implement a CGA, you need to ensure that the present value of your annuity payments is less than the present value of the future property that will pass on to the qualified charity. If these amounts are equal, or if the present value of your annuity payments exceeds the present value of the future property that will pass on to charity, you are not entitled to a charitable income-tax deduction. For example, assume that the American Diabetes Association has purchased a CGA on your behalf, and you have determined that the present value of the annuity payments you receive from this CGA is $500,000. The present value of the future property you pass on to the American Diabetes Association must exceed $500,000. Otherwise, you are not entitled to a charitable income-tax deduction—even if you itemize your deductions.

Hail, Hail to Your Dear Old Alma Mater

If neither CRTs nor CGAs interest you as vehicles to advance your philanthropic endeavors, you may want to consider contributing endowment funds to your alma mater through a **pooled-income fund (PIF)**. Such a fund is created and maintained by a sponsoring educational institution, which then commingles your contribution with those of other donors and invests the sum total on its own behalf. The investments made by the institution and fund manager cannot include tax-exempt securities, such as municipal bonds, but aside from this special provision, the pooled-income fund operates much like a standard mutual fund.

The mechanics of participating in a pooled-income fund are relatively simple. First, you are contacted by your alma mater's planned-giving office, which explains to you the terms and restrictions of the fund. Next, you transfer property (usually cash) to the fund, which gives you an income interest in the fund for life, with the remainder interest in the cash or property passing to the educational institution. Your actual payment to the fund is determined by your pro rata share of the annual earnings generated by the fund manager. You are then entitled to a charitable income-tax deduction based on the annual return of the fund for your particular age and actuarial life expectancy.

For example, assume that you are 55 and transfer $100,000 in cash to your alma mater's pooled-income fund. The fund, as managed by the university, generates an annual return of 6 percent. When consulting the applicable table, you find that approximately 33 percent of your original $100,000 transfer will pass to your alma mater upon your death. As such, you are entitled to a charitable income-tax deduction of $33,000 ($100,000 times 0.33). As long as your AGI in the year of contribution does not exceed $55,000 ($33,000 divided by 0.60), you are entitled to deduct your entire contribution. If your AGI in the year of contribution is more than $55,000, you are entitled to carry over the difference and deduct it in the future, up to a maximum period of five years.

Private Foundations

A *private foundation* is usually established by an individual or family as either a not-for-profit organization (known as an *operating* foundation) or a charitable trust (known as a *nonoperating* foundation). An operating foundation uses the bulk of its income to actively run its own charitable functions, as in the maintenance of a museum, library, or historical property. In contrast, a nonoperating foundation does not engage in or actively run any charitable activity directly, but rather only disburses funds to other charities for their own use.

Perhaps the best-known private foundation in existence today is the Bill and Melinda Gates Foundation, a **family foundation** whose objective is to "bring innovations in health and learning to the global community." More specifically, the foundation is dedicated to caring for individuals in Africa who have been afflicted with HIV or AIDS. Categorized as an operating foundation, because Bill and Melinda Gates personally engage in and use their own money to further its charitable activities, the Bill and Melinda Gates Foundation has also attracted a pledge of $30 billion from mega-investor Warren Buffett to assist in its day-to-day operation and stated mission.

Typically, a private foundation is established by the pooling together of a principal fund of money—commonly referred to as an *endowment*—that is subsequently invested. Only the investment income generated from the fund—and not the principal—is spent, either as disbursements to other charities or to service the charitable works of the foundation, leaving the principal to grow. The foundation must not pay dividends to its shareholders, although it may pay reasonable compensation for services rendered by its directors, officers, and employees. Under current law, after a certain period of time, the foundation must make qualifying annual distributions totaling at least 5 percent of its net investment assets.

A major advantage of contributing to a private foundation is that the donor is entitled to an income-tax deduction in the year when the contribution is made. However, as with the charitable deduction income-tax limitations previously discussed, the donor's tax deduction is generally limited to no more than 30 percent of their AGI in the year of contribution if it is a private nonoperating foundation. Additionally, the deduction for contributions of appreciated stock or any other type of long-term capital gain property is limited to the donor's cost basis in the stock, which cannot exceed 20 percent of their AGI.

Wealthy donors are primarily interested in establishing private foundations because of the considerable flexibility that is afforded to them with respect to the management of the foundation's investment funds. In other words, the donor of a private foundation may control the investment and distribution of the foundation's assets, as well as train other family members to eventually manage the wealth that is accumulated in the foundation. The donor may also customize the investments of the foundation to meet any specific charitable objectives they believe are not being adequately addressed by other public or private charities.

Is the establishment of a private foundation right for you or your family? Unless you have substantial funds at your disposal to create and operate the foundation, it probably is not. But that does not mean you are precluded from making a contribution to such a foundation if you agree with its objectives. If you do decide to make a contribution to a private foundation that has been approved by the IRS as a qualified charity, you are entitled to a charitable income-tax deduction in the year of contribution—although, if a private nonoperating foundation, in a somewhat reduced amount than that afforded by a contribution to a public charity.

Donor-Advised Funds

Another possible option to further the philanthropic goals of an individual or family is to establish a *donor-advised fund* (DAF), which is an arrangement whereby a donor makes a gift to a giving account that is managed by a

Plan Your Financial Future

commercially available mutual fund. A DAF is sometimes called a *charitable IRA*. After contributing to a DAF, the donor can then make recommendations as to the fund's future disbursements to any qualified public charity. However, because the donor can only make recommendations, the sponsoring mutual fund is under no legal obligation to carry out or implement the donor's requests. Nevertheless, most DAFs do try to implement their donor's wishes.

DAFs have several benefits. First, they offer donors the opportunity to create a low-cost, flexible vehicle for charitable giving that is structured as an alternative to direct gifting or the creation of a private foundation. There are no setup costs to establish a DAF, and annual fees currently run at approximately 0.60 percent for the DAF and an additional 1 percent or so for expenses associated with the management of the mutual fund or funds. Additionally, unlike the minimum 5 percent disbursement requirement that is applied to private foundations, DAFs are not subject to mandatory distribution rules. Finally, DAFs make it easy to involve generations of families in philanthropy. As a result, you can imbue in your children the philanthropic mindset of "giving back."

What about the tax benefits of establishing a DAF? First, because a DAF is technically an extension of a public charity, donors are eligible for the same maximum income-tax deduction they would receive were they to contribute directly to a 50 percent organization. A donor receives this deduction at the time of contributing to the fund, no matter when the fund designates those contributions in the future. Next, current tax law affords those who donate appreciated securities to a DAF an income-tax deduction for the full fair market value of the donation. In addition, by donating appreciated securities to a DAF and then advising the fund to make donations to several charities, donors may obtain tax advantages without the necessity of transferring these securities in kind to the recipient charities. Moreover, donating to a DAF offers a way to avoid capital gains taxes that would otherwise be due on the appreciated securities if they were converted to cash before being gifted to a charity.

For example, assume that you are the owner of 1,000 shares of ABC stock, which has appreciated over the years from $20 per share to $100 per share. Further, assume that you are in the highest marginal income-tax bracket of 37 percent, which means your capital gains tax rate is 23.8 percent in 2018 (including the 3.8 percent Obamacare surtax). You want to donate your 1,000 shares of ABC stock to your public charity of choice, and because you are aware that the charity is likely to cash in those shares upon their receipt, you make the tax mistake of selling the securities yourself first and subsequently gifting the cash to the charity. Your net cost in making this charitable gift is $82,040, which is computed as follows:

$100,000	Cost of donation
+ $19,040	Capital gains tax due (($100,000 less $20,000) times 0.238)
$119,040	Total cost
− $37,000	Income tax saved ($100,000 times 0.37)
$82,040	Net cost of gift

Now, suppose that instead of making your charitable gift in this manner, you donate your 1,000 shares of ABC stock to a DAF. You then advise the DAF's managing mutual fund to transfer the cash proceeds of the stock to your public charity of choice. Accordingly, your net cost in making this charitable gift, using the DAF as a tax-exempt intermediary, is only $60,400, which is computed as follows:

$100,000	Cost of donation/total cost (no capital gains tax due)
− $37,000	Income tax saved ($100,000 times 0.37)
$63,000	Net cost of gift

In other words, by avoiding the administrative and tax costs that you incur when making the gift of appreciated securities directly to your public charity of choice, you effectively save $19,040.

You must keep one final tax-planning principle in mind if you are planning to gift property to a qualified charity. If the property appreciates in value from the time you purchase it until the time you plan to gift it to charity, let *the charity* subsequently sell the property. If you proceed in this manner, *no* taxes of any kind will be due, because the charity is a tax-exempt entity. Alternatively, if the property depreciates in value from the time you purchase it until the time you plan to gift it to charity, *you* should sell the property before gifting it to charity. Doing so permits you to take advantage of the loss in property value on your income-tax return. If you do not claim the loss before gifting, the allowable loss is lost forever, because the tax-exempt charitable entity cannot take it either.

If you are interested in establishing a DAF, shop the idea around first. Different mutual funds charge different annual fees to operate, which reduces the amount of monies that can go to the charities you wish to benefit.

Plan Your Financial Future

In summary, the following are the planning techniques you may wish to consider in accomplishing your philanthropic objectives. In all cases, at least one tax deduction, and in some cases two or three (income-, gift-, and estate-tax) deductions, may be permitted:

- An outright or direct gift to charity
- A charitable remainder annuity trust (CRAT)
- A charitable remainder unitrust (CRUT)
- A charitable gift annuity (CGA)
- A pooled-income fund
- A private operating foundation
- A private nonoperating foundation
- A donor-advised fund (DAF)

With this chapter, we have concluded our journey of planning for your financial future and, specifically, slowly and consistently becoming wealthy in that future. It is now time to summarize the PADD process and reap the rewards! That is the focus of the final chapter of this book.

PART

VII

Summarizing the Personal Financial-Planning Process

CHAPTER 21

Reaping the Rewards

This book has introduced you to a new method of ordering your financial life and planning for your financial future. It has also developed a novel definition of the term *wealth*—a definition that goes beyond the traditional meaning of accumulating enough financial riches to ensure that your current or desired standard of living is maintained throughout your working years and subsequent retirement.

How do you go about ensuring that you are wealthy in the fullest sense of the word? This book suggests that this sought-after status may be best achieved by following the PADD strategy for wealth accumulation and management:

- Protecting yourself, your family, and your property
- Accumulating wealth
- Defending your wealth
- Distributing your wealth during your lifetime and at death

Chapter 21 | Reaping the Rewards

Broadly, this process may be thought of as following these financial-planning steps:

1. Insuring yourself, your family, and your property against the possibility of significant loss
2. Taking advantage of benefits that are offered by your employer, most notably any employer-sponsored retirement plan
3. Investing in financial or real assets—or both
4. Minimizing the effects of inflation on your portfolio as much as possible
5. Practicing effective tax-planning and tax-management techniques
6. Preparing for your children's higher education
7. Planning for your retirement years
8. Distributing your estate at death to your intended heirs or beneficiaries in as transfer-tax-efficient a manner as possible

Maximizing the implementation of these steps is not easy. If it was, this book, and many others on the topic of effective personal financial planning, would not be necessary. However, it should be comforting to know that you are not alone in meeting this challenge! A number of professional advisors, among them Certified Financial Planners (CFPs), Certified Public Accountants (CPAs), securities and insurance professionals, and estate-planning attorneys, stand ready to assist you in meeting your financial-planning and wealth-accumulation goals. Alternatively, if you believe you are skilled and disciplined enough to take on this challenge yourself, you should by all means do so.

Attending to your financial life and affairs is analogous to Scarlett O'Hara's famous line in *Gone with the Wind*: "Oh, fiddle-dee. I'll think about it tomorrow!" In other words, the *longer* you put off thinking about the financial-planning process, the *longer* it will be before you become wealthy—and the *sooner* a financially challenging tomorrow will arrive! If this book has accomplished nothing else, I hope it has provided you with some basic principles and knowledge with which you can begin to take control of your financial life. If you adopt the process described in its pages, you will reap the greatest reward of all: a financially worry-free and independent life that you can enjoy to the fullest with family and friends.

I wish you good planning.

APPENDIX A

Sample Data-Gathering Form

Personal Information		
	Client	**Spouse**
Full Name		
Gender		
Maiden Name (if applicable)		
Current Marital Status		
Prior Marriages (if yes, date of dissolution)		
US Citizen (yes/no)		
Current Address		
Phone Number		
Cell Phone Number		
Prior State of Residence		
Birthdate		
Age		

© Keith R. Fevurly 2018
K. R. Fevurly, *Plan Your Financial Future*, https://doi.org/10.1007/978-1-4842-3637-6

Appendix A | Sample Data-Gathering Form

Birthplace		
Social Security Number		
Occupation		
Employer		
Length of Current Employment (years)		
Business Phone Number		
Family Members Who Depend on Your Support		

List any family members or individuals you wish to provide/plan for			
Parent/Child/Grandchild	**Birthdate**	**Birthplace**	**Social Security Number**
Other Individuals/Dependents	**Birthdate**	**Birthplace**	**Social Security Number**

Are there any major health problems in your family? If yes, please explain.		
Family Member	**Age**	**Health Issues(s)**

Plan Your Financial Future

Family Advisors and Representatives		
	Name	**Phone Number**
Attorney		
Banker		
Doctor		
Executor(s)		
Financial Planner		
Guardian(s)		
Insurance Agent		
Investment Advisor		
Minister/Rabbi		
Tax Preparer		
Other:		
Other:		
Other:		

Family Planning Goals

List all your financial planning goals (e.g., retirement, travel, large purchases) and a time frame for their achievement

Family Goals	Time Horizon (immediate, within 3–12 months, or 1 year or more)
Client's Individual Goals	

Appendix A | Sample Data-Gathering Form

Spouse's Individual Goals	

Family Objectives		
Indicate which of the following objectives are important for your family.		
Objective	Important to Client (yes/no)	Important to Spouse (yes/no)
Saving for education (yourself, children, grandchildren, etc.)		
Saving for retirement		
Being able to retire early (age 55 or earlier)		
Minimizing income taxes		
Minimizing estate taxes		
Providing support for an aging parent or relative		
Improving investment returns		
Improving insurance coverage		
Supporting a favorite charity		
Planning for your estate		
Improving your standard of living		
Changing or improving your employment situation		
Other:		
Other:		

Taxable Assets

List the current value for each of the following, and provide the latest account statement available.

Account/Investment	Client	Spouse	Joint
Cash on Hand			
Checking Account			
Savings Account			
Certificates of Deposit			
Money Market			
Life Insurance Cash Surrender Value			
Stocks			
Bonds			
Mutual Funds			
Closely Held Business Interest			
Limited Partnership Interest			
Other:			
Other:			

Appendix A | Sample Data-Gathering Form

Retirement Accounts

List the current value for each of the following, and provide the latest account statement available. If the account statements do not list designated beneficiaries, please supply.

Account	Client	Spouse
IRAs		
401(k)/403(b) Plan		
Pension Plan		
Profit-Sharing Plan		
Stock Options		
Deferred Compensation		
Other:		
Other:		

Real Estate

List the current dollar value for each of the following.

Type	Ownership (client, spouse, or joint)	Cost	Market Value	Loan Balance	Monthly Payment
Primary Residence					
Vacation Home					
Rental Property					
Other:					
Other:					

Personal Property

List the current dollar value for each of the following.

Type	Ownership (client, spouse, or joint)	Market Value	Loan Balance	Monthly Payment
Aircraft				
Art and Antiques				
Automobiles				
Boat				
Collectibles				
Fur(s)				
Household Goods				
Jewelry				
Other:				
Other:				

Insurance Coverage

List the following types of coverage you currently have.

Type	Amount	Owner	Insured	Beneficiary
Life				
Group Term				
Term				
Universal Life				
Whole Life				
Disability				
Short-Term				
Long-Term				

Appendix A | Sample Data-Gathering Form

Medical				
Health Care				
Long-Term Care				
Liability				
Umbrella				
Professional				
Property				
Auto				
Homeowner's				

Are you or your spouse engaged in any professional activities, paid or unpaid, outside your main employment (e.g., moonlighting, board memberships, volunteer work, professional association memberships)? If so, please explain.	
Client or Spouse	**Professional Activity**

Liabilities		
List the current balance for each of the following.		
Type	Ownership (client, spouse, or joint)	Balance Due
Alimony/Child Support		
Bank Loans		
Charitable Pledge		
Credit Cards		

Home-Equity Loan or Line of Credit		
Installment Loan		
Insurance Policy Loan		
Investment Debt (Margin)		
Personal Loan		
Retirement Plan Loan		
Student Loans		
Other:		
Other:		

Income

List the following sources of income in annual amounts.

Type	Client	Spouse	Joint
Employment Income			
Salary			
Bonus			
Commissions			
Self-Employment			
Other:			
Investment Income			
Dividends			
Interest—Taxable			
Interest—Tax-Free			
Rental Income (net)			
Annuities			
Other:			

Appendix A | Sample Data-Gathering Form

Miscellaneous Income			
Alimony			
Trusts			
Child Support			
Estates			
Gifts			
Retirement Accounts			
Sale of Property/Investments			
Social Security Payments			
Other:			
Other:			
Do you expect a significant change in income over the next two to three years? If so, estimate amounts.			

Expenses	
List the following current estimated expenditures in annual amounts.	
Type	**Amount**
Charitable Contributions	
Clothing	
Education	
Employment-Related	
Food	
Gifts	
Home Improvements/Repair/Maintenance	
Income and Other Payroll Taxes	

Plan Your Financial Future

Insurance	
Auto	
Homeowner's	
Disability Income	
Life	
Medical	
Long-Term Care	
Personal Liability	
Other:	
Medical Expenses (unreimbursed)	
Mortgage/Rent	
Personal Expenses	
Recreation	
Dining Out	
Vacations	
Other:	
Savings	
Taxes	
FICA	
Income	
Property	
Telephone	
Transportation	
Auto Fuel/Repairs/Maintenance	
Auto Payments	
Utilities	
Other:	
Other:	
When did you last prepare a family budget?	

APPENDIX B

Sample Budget

CASH BUDGET: ESTIMATED INCOME

Name(s): _____
For the period ending: _____

Sources of Income		Jan	Feb	Mar	Apr	May	Jun	Jul	Aug	Sept	Oct	Nov	Dec	Yearly Total
Take-home pay	Name													
	Name													
	Name													
Bonuses and commissions														
Pensions and annuities														
Investment income	Interest													
	Dividends													
	Rents													
	Sale of securities													
	Other													
Other Income														
	TOTAL INCOME													

© Keith R. Fevurly 2018
K. R. Fevurly, *Plan Your Financial Future*, https://doi.org/10.1007/978-1-4842-3637-6

CASH BUDGET: ESTIMATED EXPENSES

Name(s) _____

For the period ending _____

Expense Categories		Jan	Feb	Mar	Apr	May	Jun	Jul	Aug	Sept	Oct	Nov	Dec	Yearly Total
Housing	Rent/mortgage payment (include insurance and taxes, if applicable)													
	Repairs, maintenance, improvements													
Utilities	Gas, electric, water													
	Phone													
	Cable TV and other													
Food	Groceries													
	Dining out													
Autos	Loan payments													
	License plates, fees, etc.													
	Gas, oil, repairs, tires, maintenance													
Medical	Health, major medical, disability insurance (not provided by employer)													
	Doctor, dentist, hospital, medicines													
Clothing	Clothes, shoes, accessories													
Insurance	Homeowner's (if not covered by mortgage payment)													
	Life (not provided by employer)													
	Auto													
Taxes	Income and Social Security													
	Property (if not included in mortgage)													
Appliances, furniture, and other	Loan payments													
	Purchases and repairs													
Personal care	Laundry, cosmetics, hair care													
Recreation and entertainment	Vacations													
	Other recreation and entertainment													
Savings and Investments	Savings, stocks, bonds, etc.													
Other expenditures	Charitable contributions													
	Gifts													
	Education loan payment													
	Subscriptions, magazines, books													
	Other:													
	Other:													
Fun Money														
	TOTAL EXPENSES													

APPENDIX C

Power of Attorney

Durable General and Financial Power of Attorney

I, _____(Name)_____, currently of __(City and State)___, do hereby execute this durable general (and financial) power of attorney with the intention that the attorney-in-fact hereinafter named shall be able to act in my place in all matters.

Section 1: Designation of Attorney-in-Fact

1.01: I constitute and appoint _____(Name)_____, currently of _____(City and State)_____, to be my attorney-in-fact to act for me, in my name and for my benefit.

1.02: In the event that _____(Name)_____ for any reason shall fail to act or continue as my attorney-in-fact, I constitute and appoint _____(Name)_____, currently of _____(City and State)_____, to act as my attorney-in-fact.

© Keith R. Fevurly 2018
K. R. Fevurly, *Plan Your Financial Future*, https://doi.org/10.1007/978-1-4842-3637-6

Section 2: Effective Date of Power of Attorney

2.01: This General Power of Attorney shall be effective immediately, and shall not be affected by my disability or lack of mental competence, except as may be provided otherwise by an applicable state statute.

2.02: This General Power of Attorney shall *not* be affected by my incapacity or disability, it being my specific intention that my attorney-in-fact shall continue to act as such, even though I may not be competent to ratify the actions of my attorney-in-fact.

2.03: Third parties may rely on the representations of my attorney-in-fact as to all matters relating to any power granted to my attorney-in-fact, and no person who may act in reliance upon the representation of my attorney-in-fact shall incur any liability to me or my estate as a result of permitting my attorney-in-fact to exercise any power. Further, I authorize my attorney-in-fact to indemnify and hold harmless any third party who accepts and acts under this document.

2.04: This power is revocable, provided that insofar as any governmental agency, bank, depository, trust company, insurance company, other corporation, transfer agent, investment banking company, or other person is concerned, who shall rely on this power, may justifiably rely on the power. This power may be revoked only by a notice in writing executed by me or my attorney-in-fact and delivered to such person or institution.

2.05: This power shall not be revoked or otherwise become ineffective in any way by the mere passage of time, but rather shall remain in full force and effect until revoked by me or my attorney-in-fact in writing, as provided in paragraph 2.04 hereof.

Section 3: Powers

3.01: My attorney-in-fact shall have all of the powers, discretions, elections, and authorities granted by statute, by common law, and under any rule of Court. In addition thereto, and not in limitation thereof, my attorney-in-fact shall also have the powers set forth below.

3.02: My attorney-in-fact may collect and receive, without the institution of a legal cause of action, all debts, monies, gifts, objects, interest, dividends, annuities, and demands that now are due or may hereinafter become due, owing or otherwise payable to or belonging to me. My attorney-in-fact may use and take all lawful actions in my name or otherwise to recover the same or to compromise the same.

3.03: My attorney-in-fact may sell, convey, lease, exchange, mortgage, pledge, release, or otherwise deal with, dispose of, exchange, or encumber any of my property, either real or personal. This shall include the power to borrow money or otherwise obtain credit, upon such terms, conditions, and covenants as my attorney-in-fact considers as appropriate.

3.04: My attorney-in-fact may appear on my behalf in any litigation in which I am or may become a party during the duration of this General Power of Attorney.

3.05: My attorney-in-fact may give discharges, releases, consent, and receipts on my behalf.

3.06: My attorney-in-fact shall have the power to deposit funds in my name in any banking or savings institution or in any money market account, whether or not insured.

3.07: My attorney-in-fact shall have the power to pay any and all bills, accounts, claims, and demands now due by me or becoming due by me subsequent to the execution of this General Power of Attorney.

3.08: My attorney-in-fact may endorse all checks drawn to my order for deposit in any account in which I have funds on deposit or in any new account opened in my name.

3.09: My attorney-in-fact shall have the right to make gifts of cash or property in kind to any person or institution in connection with any estate planning that needs to be completed or to carry out any beneficial intent of mine as he/she may understand it.

3.10: My attorney-in-fact shall have the power to transfer or surrender any securities that I may own. In connection therewith, my attorney-in-fact may execute in my name or on my behalf any stock power or other instrument in order to implement any such transfer or surrender.

3.11: My attorney-in-fact shall have the power to enter into or renew any agency or custodian agreement with any bank or trust company at my expense for the investment or safekeeping of any property.

3.12: My attorney-in-fact shall have unrestricted access to, and the right to enter into, any safety deposit box, vault, or other depository that I may own or may be registered in my name.

3.13: My attorney-in-fact shall have the power to prepare, make, execute, and file any and all Federal, State, local, or other tax returns, claims for refunds, or declarations of estimated tax. This power shall include the power to represent me (directly or indirectly through other agents) in any matter before the Internal Revenue Service or any other Federal, State, or local agency.

3.14: My attorney-in-fact shall have the power to execute, seal, acknowledge, and deliver any instruments, documents, or papers deemed necessary, advisable, or expedient with respect to any property.

3.15: My attorney-in-fact shall have the power to hold, invest, reinvest, and otherwise deal with and manage all property in which I may have any interest and wherever situated.

Section 4: Ratification; Use of Photocopy; Revocation of Prior Powers: Construction of Instrument

4.01: I hereby ratify, allow, acknowledge, and hold valid all acts taken by my attorney-in-fact pursuant to this power.

4.02: I hereby authorize the use of a photocopy of this General Power of Attorney, in lieu of the original copy executed by me, for the purpose of effectuating the terms and provisions hereof.

4.03: I hereby revoke, annul, and cancel any and all durable general and financial powers of attorney previously executed by me, and the same shall be of no further force and effect. However, the preceding sentence shall not have the effect of revoking any powers of attorney that are directly related to my health care that have been signed and executed by me.

4.04: This General Power of Attorney is executed and delivered in the State of _____(State of Domicile)_____, and the laws of the State of _____(State of Domicile)_____ shall govern all questions as to the validity of this power and to the construction of its provisions.

4.05: This instrument is to be construed and interpreted as a general power of attorney. The enumeration of specific powers herein is not intended to, nor does it, limit or restrict the general powers herein granted to my attorney-in-fact.

4.06: Pursuant to _____(Applicable State Statute)_____, any person or organization that "arbitrarily or without reasonable cause" fails to honor this Power of Attorney, or fails to comply with the directions of my attorney-in-fact, shall be subject to costs, expenses, and reasonable attorney's fees required to effectuate the terms and provisions of this instrument.

IN WITNESS WHEREOF, I have executed this General Power of Attorney this _____ day of _____, 20xx.

PRINCIPAL

WITNESS:

_____
Witness

_____
Witness

STATE OF _____
COUNTY OF _____

The foregoing instrument was acknowledged before me this _____ day of _____, 20xx by _____, Principal, and the above stated witnesses, for the purposes therein stated.

Witness my hand and official seal.

(SEAL)

_____
Notary Public

My commission expires: _____

SPECIMEN SIGNATURE OF ATTORNEY-IN-FACT:

_____

ATTORNEY-IN-FACT

SPECIMEN SIGNATURE OF SUCCESSOR ATTORNEY-IN-FACT:

_____

SUCCESSOR ATTORNEY-IN-FACT

APPENDIX D

Declaration as to Medical or Surgical Treatment and Medical Durable Power of Attorney

Declaration as to Medical or Surgical Treatment

I, _____(Declarant)_____, currently of _____(City and State)_____, being of sound mind and at least eighteen years of age, direct that my life shall not be artificially prolonged under the circumstances set forth below and hereby declare that:

Life-Sustaining Procedures

If at any time my attending physician and one other qualified physician certify in writing that:

I have an injury, a disease, or an illness which is not curable or reversible, and which, in their judgment is a terminal condition, and I have been unconscious, comatose, or otherwise incompetent so as to make or communicate responsible decisions concerning my person, then I direct that, in accordance with _____(State of Domicile)_____ law, life-sustaining procedures shall be withdrawn and withheld pursuant to the terms of this declaration. It is understood that life-sustaining procedures shall not include any medical procedure or intervention for nourishment considered necessary by the attending physician to provide comfort or alleviate pain.

Moreover, it is my request that the term "terminal condition" be interpreted to include a state of permanent unconsciousness (permanent vegetative state).

Artificial Nourishment

If the only procedure that I am being provided is artificial nourishment, I direct that artificial nourishment shall also be immediately discontinued when it is the only procedure being provided. Notwithstanding any direction with respect to the discontinuance of artificial nourishment, if my attending physician has determined that pain results from such discontinuance, such physician may order that artificial nourishment be provided to me, but only to the extent necessary to alleviate such pain.

Other Specific Requests:

Note to user Common requests may include use or non-use of CPR (cardiopulmonary resuscitation) and possible organ donation.

Medical Durable Power of Attorney

Designation of Health Care Agent

I, _____(Principal)_____, currently of _____(City and State)_____, do hereby appoint:

Agent Name: _____

Address: _____

Phone: _____

Relation, if any: _____

as my Agent to make health care and personal decisions for me if I become unable to make such decisions for myself, except to the extent I state otherwise in this document.

The term "health care" as used in this document includes all medical treatment, the provision, withholding, or withdrawal of any health care medical procedure, including surgery, cardiopulmonary resuscitation, or service to maintain, diagnose, treat, or provide for a patient's physical or mental health or personal care, unless such authority is otherwise limited by this document.

Creation of Medical Durable Power of Attorney

By this document I also intend to create a Medical Durable Power of Attorney. This Durable Power of Attorney shall take effect only upon my inability to give informed consent, disability, incapacity, or incompetency, and shall continue during such inability to give informed consent, disability, incapacity, or incompetency. I have prepared this document while still legally competent and of sound mind. If these instructions create a conflict with the desires of my relatives, with hospital policies, or with the principles of those providing care, I ask that my instructions prevail.

General Statement of Authority Granted

Subject to any limitations in this document, I grant to my Agent full power and authority to make health care decisions for me to the same extent that I could make such decisions for myself if I had the capacity to do so. This authority shall also include all acts related to my personal care and any residential placement and/or medical treatment. In making any decision, my Agent shall attempt to discuss the proposed decision with me to determine my desires if I am able to communicate in any way.

In exercising this authority, my Agent shall make health care decisions that are consistent with my desires as stated in this document or otherwise made known to my Agent. If my wishes regarding a particular health care decision are not known to my Agent, then my Agent shall make the decision for me based upon what my Agent believes to be in my best interests.

Access to Medical Records

My Agent shall have complete access to my protected health information, as the personal representative of my estate, for all purposes under the HIPPA Act of 1996 (45 C.F.R. Sec. 164.502 (g) (1) and (2), and pursuant to _____ (Applicable State Law)_____ state law (State Statute _____(Applicable State Statute)_____). There is no limitation on the information I authorize to be disclosed, and there is no limitation on the period of time for which information may be requested or disclosed.

Advance Medical Directive

My Agent shall be permitted to execute an advance medical directive with respect to the administration of cardiopulmonary resuscitation (CPR) in accordance with the provisions of _____(Applicable State Statute)_____ if determining, after conferring with my attending physician, that a CPR directive is appropriate.

Autopsy, Anatomical Gifts, Disposition of Remains

I authorize my Agent, to the extent permitted by law, to make anatomical gifts of part or all of my body for medical purposes, authorize an autopsy, and direct the disposition of my remains.

Designation of Alternate Agent

If the person designated as my Agent is not available or unable to act, I designate the following person to serve as my Alternate Agent to make health care decisions for me as authorized by this document.

Alternate Agent: _____

Address: _____

Phone: _____

Relation, if any: _____

Nomination of Guardian and Conservator

If a Guardian of my person is to be appointed for me, I nominate my Agent (and, then, Alternate Agent) to serve as my Guardian. If it becomes necessary for a court to appoint a Conservator for my estate, the same nomination and order as for Guardian is hereby made.

General Provisions

Hold Harmless and Third-Party Reliance

All persons, including attending physicians, or entities who in good faith endeavor to carry out the terms and provisions of this document shall not be liable to me, my estate, my heirs, or assigns for any damages or claims arising because of their action. However, if any person shall endeavor to challenge the authority of my agent in bad faith, or intentionally contradict any provision of this document, my estate shall not be liable and is not obligated to pay any fees or expenses arising out of the action or actions of my agent acting on my behalf.

Severability

If any provision of this document is held to be invalid, such invalidity shall not affect the other provisions, which can be given effect without the invalid provision, and to this end the directions in this document are severable.

Statement of Intentions

It is my intent that this document be legally binding and effective. If the law does not recognize this document as legally binding and effective, it is my intent that this document is taken as a formal statement of my desire concerning the method by which any health care decisions should be made on my behalf during any period in which I am unable to make such decisions. This power of attorney is intended to be valid in any jurisdiction in which it is presented.

Inconsistency in Provisions

In the event of an inconsistency in provisions between the Medical Durable Power of Attorney and My Declaration as to Medical or Surgical Treatment (Living Will), the Medical Durable Power of Attorney shall control.

Appendix D | Declaration as to Medical or Surgical Treatment and Medical Durable Power of Attorney

Revocation of Prior Powers

I hereby revoke any prior power of attorney for health care and restate my intentions as specified above.

Applicable Law

All questions pertaining to the validity, interpretation, and administration of this document shall be determined under the laws of the State of _____(State)_____.

I have read and understand the contents of this document and the effect of this grant of powers to my Agent. I am emotionally and mentally competent to make this declaration.

Signed on this _____day of_____, 20xx.

Signature: _____

PRINCIPAL

Name of Principal:_____

Address of Principal: _____

SSN of Principal: _____

Birth Date of Principal: _____

Statement of Witness

The foregoing instrument was signed and declared by _____(Principal's Name)_____, PRINCIPAL, to be his/her Declaration as to Medical or Surgical Treatment and Medical Durable Power of Attorney in the presence of us, who, in his/her presence, in the presence of each other, and at _____ (Principal's Name)_____'s request, have signed our names below as witnesses, and we declare, that at the time of the execution of this instrument, _____(Principal's Name)_____, according to our best knowledge and belief, was of sound mind and under no constraint, fraud, or undue influence. Neither of the witnesses is _____(Principal's Name)_____'s attending physician or any other physician, an employee of the attending physician or health care facility in which _____(Principal's Name)_____ is a patient, a person who has a claim against any portion of the estate of _____(Principal's Name)_____ at his/her death at the time the declaration is signed, or a person who knows or believes that he/she is entitled to any portion of the estate of _____(Principal's Name)_____ upon his/her death, either as a beneficiary of a will in existence at the time the declaration is signed, or as an heir at law. Neither witness is a person appointed as agent by this document. Neither witness is a provider of health or residential care or an employee of a provider thereof.

Witness

Signature: _____

Name: _____

Address: _____

_____

Date: _____

Witness

Signature: _____

Name: _____

Address: _____

_____

Date: _____

State of _____

County of _____

On this _____ day of _____, 20xx, _____, known to me (or satisfactorily proven) to be the person named in the foregoing instrument, personally appeared before me, a Notary Public, within and for the said State and County, and acknowledged that he/she freely and voluntarily executed the same for the purposes stated in the document.

My commission expires: _____

(SEAL)

_____

_____

Notary Public

APPENDIX E

Sample Personal Letter of Instruction

WRITTEN BY: _____

This is a personal letter of instruction, written by me, to be referenced by my personal representative (as named in my will) at my date of death. Although this letter does not have the binding effect of law, it does fairly represent my wishes at my date of death, and I ask that it be honored by my personal representative.

THIS LETTER IS TO BE READ BY MY PERSONAL REPRESENTATIVE IMMEDIATELY AFTER MY DEATH.

1. Full legal name: _____
2. Maiden name, if female: _____
3. My date of birth: _____
4. My place of birth: _____
5. Parents' legal names: _____

© Keith R. Fevurly 2018
K. R. Fevurly, *Plan Your Financial Future*, https://doi.org/10.1007/978-1-4842-3637-6

Appendix E | Sample Personal Letter of Instruction

6. My citizenship: _____
7. My Social Security Number: _____
8. Military service information, if applicable, including location of any discharge papers: _____
9. Marital status at date of death: _____
10. Name, address, and phone number of spouse or partner: _____
11. Names, addresses, and phone numbers of any children: _____
12. Names, addresses, and phone numbers of any brothers and sisters: _____
13. Names, addresses, and phone numbers of any friends or business associates to be contacted: _____
14. Existence and location of advance medical directives (medical durable power of attorney, medical proxy, living will): _____
15. Existence and location of financial power of attorney: _____
16. Organ tissue and/or bodily donation information: _____
17. Religious affiliation, if applicable: _____
18. Designated preference of funeral home and/or other burial information: _____
19. Type of disposition of bodily remains (burial or cremation): _____
20. Location of any burial plot or crypt: _____
21. Preferable memorial donations, if any: _____

Glossary

A

A.B.L.E. account: A tax-advantaged savings account for a disabled individual created by the Achieving a Better Life Experience Act of 2014.

accelerated death benefit rider: An additional provision to a life insurance contract that permits the owner/insured to receive all or a portion of the proceeds of the contract before death so as to cover, for example, the costs of a last illness.

accidental death benefit (ADB): Also known as a double indemnity benefit; a provision in some life insurance contracts that pays twice the face value of the policy in the event of the accidental death of the insured.

amortization schedule: A schedule of monthly payments made by a borrower to pay off debt—typically, a mortgage obligation on a personal residence. The schedule includes both interest and principal paid over the term of the mortgage.

annuity: An insurance product that features an equal stream of payments over the owner's/annuitant's lifetime. An important retirement-planning technique, because the product ensures against the risk of *superannuation*, or the risk of a retiree outliving their accumulated retirement monies.

asset allocation: A method of allocating, or dividing up, an individual's collection of assets or portfolio among several asset classes, usually cash or cash equivalents, stocks, and bonds. Such allocations also include agreed-on percentages of assets among specified asset classes and are a staple of a properly prepared investment policy statement used by many financial advisors.

B

basis (or cost basis): An income-tax term meaning, first and foremost, the amount of money contributed by a taxpayer in the purchase of any real or financial asset. Sometimes alternatively referred to as an individual's *cost basis* in property, it is used to determine the amount of taxable gain or loss in the sale of assets. There are, however, other types of basis referred to in income-tax and accounting rules.

behavioral finance: A branch of finance that studies the interrelationship of psychology and investor behavior; an alternative to the traditional theory of corporate finance that assumes efficient markets and rational investor behavior. An important precept of behavior finance is *prospect theory*, which essentially posits that investors fear losses more than they value gains.

beneficiary: The individual named in a legal document, such as a trust, who benefits in the event of the writer's or creator's death.

bonds: A type of financial instrument commonly issued by corporations or governments to raise capital for needed projects or functions. Sometimes just referred to as *debt* or *debt obligations*, because the issuer borrows money from the holder of the bond and must repay the bond holder at the time the debt obligation reaches maturity.

C

capital gain: An income-tax and financial term meaning the increase in value or appreciation of the asset from the date of purchase to the date of sale. If such assets are owned for a requisite period of time before they are sold (or *long-term*), currently more than one year from the date of purchase, a favorable tax rate is awarded by the taxing authorities.

capitalization rate: A percentage rate or number applied to the future income from property (typically, real property) to determine its current value. For example, if the net operating income from an apartment complex is $500,000 and a capitalization rate of 20 percent is applied or divided into that income, the current value of the complex is estimated at $2,500,000.

cash value insurance: A type of life insurance that builds on the owner's behalf a cash reserve that may be accessed by the owner during their lifetime. Common types of cash value insurance include whole life insurance, universal insurance, variable insurance, and variable universal life insurance.

charitable lead trust (CLT): An irrevocable trust used in estate planning that is designed to provide either a fixed or variable income stream annually to a qualified charity for a certain period of time, with the remainder of the property left to a noncharitable beneficiary, usually the donor's child or children.

charitable remainder trust (CRT): An irrevocable trust used in estate planning that is designed to provide either a fixed or variable income stream annually for a certain period of time to a noncharitable beneficiary (typically, the donor), with the remainder of the property left to a qualified charity.

child tax credit: An income tax credit or dollar-for-dollar reduction against a taxpayer's income-tax liability that results from having a child or children currently under the age of 17. The maximum amount of the credit is established by tax law: for example, $2,000 per eligible child.

College Board: A not-for-profit membership organization committed to excellence and equity in education, particularly higher education. This organization also provides students an avenue to college opportunities, including financial support and scholarships.

Commissioner's Individual Disability Table A: A 1985 table published by the government that provides data on the probability of an individual becoming disabled during their lifetime.

common law property system: One of two property law systems (the other being the community property system) that permits the titling of property individually, even in the event of marriage. Currently, this is the system of property law in 41 of the 50 states.

community property system: One of two property law systems (the other being the common law property system) that does not permit the titling of property individually while married; any property acquired by either spouse during marriage generally belongs to "the community" and not the individual separately. Currently, this is the system of property law in 9 of the 50 states, most notably California and Texas, although Alaska permits community property on an elective basis among spouses.

contingent trust (for minors): A trust created in each parent's will specifying a trustee and provisions for the parent's property in the event of the simultaneous death of the parents. It is important that the trustee work in concert with the parent's named guardian for the sake of the children who benefit from the trust property. Sometimes also used synonymously with the term *contingent family trust*.

correlation: A measure of the movement of two variables, such as financial assets, in relation to each other. For example, if one financial asset declines in value at the same time another increases in value, the assets are said to exhibit *negative correlation*. The use of correlation is a key factor in the proper diversification of a portfolio of assets.

cost basis: See *basis*.

coupon rate: The percentage rate of interest on a bond; for example, 6 percent. If multiplying the rate times the stated or *par value* of the bond (typically, $1,000), it is possible to determine the annual cash payment received by the bondholder or owner.

custodial account: A type of account, commonly used in planning for a child's higher education, in which monies are set aside on behalf of a minor child but are managed by the child's parent or *custodian*. Such accounts are permitted in all 50 states, either in the form of a Unified Gifts to Minors Act (UGMA) account or a Unified Transfers to Minors Act (UTMA) account.

D

defined-benefit retirement plan: A tax-qualified employer pension plan that guarantees a specified benefit amount or level at the date of the participant's retirement; commonly offered only by large corporations and government entities.

defined-contribution retirement plan: A tax-qualified employer profit-sharing (or other type of) plan that establishes an individual account for each plan participant. Plan benefits consist of the amount accumulated in each account at the participant's retirement or the termination of their employment. The most common and popular type of defined-contribution plan is a Section 401(k) retirement plan.

dependent care credit: An income tax credit or dollar-for-dollar reduction against a taxpayer's income-tax liability because the taxpayer has incurred child-care expenses for a child under the age of 13. The maximum amount of credit is determined by tax law on a sliding-credit basis, with the maximum capped under law, regardless of the number of children receiving dependent care.

disclaimer trust: A type of trust used in estate planning that allows individual(s) to benefit from property that is otherwise refused, or *disclaimed*, by the named beneficiary or heir.

durable power of attorney (DPOA): A type of power of attorney (granted by the principal to the agent) that continues even in the event of the principal's or author's legal incapacity or inability to act; currently permitted by all 50 states in some form.

E

education savings account (ESA): Properly known as the Coverdell education savings account and the successor to the education IRA. A trust or custodial account created exclusively for the purpose of paying qualified educational expenses of the designated beneficiary of the account. Currently, certain taxpayers, not subject to phaseout limits, may deposit cash of up to $2,000 per year into the account for a child under the age of 18.

expected family contribution (EFC): The amount of money that a family is expected to contribute to pay for a child's higher education as determined by completing the Free Application for Student Financial Aid (FAFSA) form provided by the federal government.

F

401(k) plan: A type of tax-qualified profit-sharing plan that provides for before-tax salary-reduction contributions (known as *elective deferrals*) to be made by the employee. Such plans must not only be generally nondiscriminatory (all eligible employees must be permitted to participate), but also must meet *special* nondiscrimination rules if the employer matches employee contributions with additional monies.

family foundation: A type of private charitable foundation that is funded primarily by one family. Such foundations may be either operating or nonoperating in nature. An operating family foundation uses the bulk of its income to actively run the daily operations of the fund, whereas a nonoperating family foundation only disburses monies to other charities for their own use.

flexible spending account (FSA): A type of *cafeteria plan*—a plan under which employees may choose between cash and nontaxable fringe benefits—that is funded through salary reductions elected by employees each year. Among other provisions of the Patient Protection and Affordable Care Act of 2010, employee salary reductions used to provide for health-care reimbursement from an FSA are capped at $2,500 annually beginning in 2013 and indexed for inflation thereafter.

floater: An insurance term used to describe personal property that travels with the insured and remains insured wherever the insured is currently traveling. Commonly used in conjunction with the term *personal articles* and indicates insurance on property, such as jewelry or personal keepsakes.

G

grantor: The individual who creates or establishes a revocable or irrevocable trust. This term is also used in tax terminology to mean the individual who could be taxed on income generated from trust property as determined under a series of rules collectively referred to as the *grantor trust rules.*

H

highly compensated employee (HCE): A specific definition of certain employees who are the focus of the nondiscrimination rules determining, in part, whether a retirement plan is "tax-qualified" or granted certain tax advantages. Specifically, to be qualified for tax purposes, the plan cannot discriminate in favor of HCEs. An HCE is either an individual who owns a certain nominal percentage of the business (such as more than 5 percent) or an employee who makes in excess of a specified amount of annual salary.

I

immediate fixed annuity: A popular form of retirement insurance product whereby the retiree turns over to the insurance company a lump sum of money in exchange for a fixed payment that begins immediately (or, typically, within 30 days of his or her retirement date).

intestate succession: A series of state laws that specifies who inherits property at a decedent's death when the decedent dies without having written a last will and testament.

irrevocable life insurance trust (ILIT): A trust whereby the owner of a life insurance policy irrevocably relinquishes those ownership rights to a designated third party, the trustee of the trust. The death proceeds from the life insurance policy are removed from the owner's gross estate, and a trustee is chosen who can provide needed liquidity to pay taxes and other expenses incurred in the administration of a decedent's estate.

J

joint tenancy with right of survivorship (JTWROS): Also referred to as owning property *jointly.* A type of property ownership (most commonly found in common law property states) that is distinguished by automatic survivorship rights upon the death of the first joint tenant. The primary advantage of JTWROS property is that title passes automatically to the survivor without the necessity of the probate process.

L

Lloyds of London: A specialist insurance market, located in London, England, where syndicated members join together to insure risks. Most commonly known for insuring hard-to-insure or unique risks, such as Betty Grable's legs or famous baseball pitchers' throwing arms.

M

managed care health insurance plans: A type of health insurance plan noted for its emphasis on preventative medicine and characterized by such features as a network of physicians and copayments by insureds. Examples of managed care plans are health maintenance organizations (HMOs) and preferred provider organizations (PPOs).

marginal income-tax bracket: The rate on a specified amount of the taxpayer's next dollar of income. Important for income-tax planning purposes, because it affects tax decision-making.

master limited partnership (MLP): A type of limited partnership investment that is *publicly* traded (as contrasted to a private limited partnership, which is *not* publicly traded and does not have an active market if the owner wishes to sell their interest in the partnership).

mutual fund: More properly known as an *open-ended investment company*. A type of company that pools money from shareholders and invests in a variety of securities, including stocks, bonds, and money-market securities. Mutual funds generally continuously offer new shares to investors and redeem old shares.

N

net unrealized appreciation (NUA): A r favorable income-tax advantage given to the distribution of employer shares in a qualified retirement plan. Specifically, tax is not imposed on the appreciation of employer shares from the date of contribution to the date of distribution until the date of sale of those shares. Then, upon that sale, tax is imposed only at favorable long-term capital gains rates.

nondiscrimination tests: In retirement law, a general test that a tax-qualified plan cannot discriminate in favor a separately defined *highly compensated employee*. There are also special nondiscrimination tests that certain types of tax-qualified plans, such as a traditional 401(k) plan, must satisfy to remain "qualified" for business income-tax purposes.

O

ordinary income: A term used in income-tax planning to distinguish the taxation of salary and wages from that of the sale of assets (or capital gains or losses). Currently, the highest marginal tax rate on salary and wages (ordinary income) is 37 percent, but historically it has been as high as 90 percent.

overfund: A generic term used in the context of estate planning to indicate that improper use of the transfer-tax marital deduction has occurred. For example, if the second deceased spouse's estate is overfunded, it means too much property has been transferred to them from the first deceased spouse's estate. As such, the couple cannot engage in efficient estate-tax planning as a unit.

P

passive portfolio management: A theory of portfolio management that attempts to replicate overall market performance (or a specified market index, such as the Standard & Poor's 500 index of stocks) and involves little trading of assets in the underlying portfolio. Contrasted to *active portfolio management*, sometimes known as *stock picking*.

Patient Protection and Affordable Care Act of 2010: Otherwise colloquially known as *Obamacare*, an act signed into law by US President Barack Obama on March 23, 2010. The law is designed to provide coverage to over 32 million uninsured or underinsured Americans. The law reforms Medicare, Medicaid, and other government programs; reforms insurance markets; and establishes new state-based exchanges. To finance the cost of health care, the law imposes varying levels of taxes on insurers, employers, and individuals. It also implements an individual mandate that all individuals must have health insurance beginning in 2014 or incur a penalty tax.

payable-on-death (POD) form: A form used with bank checking and savings accounts that specifies who is to receive the individually titled account at the death of the owner. The form's primary advantage in estate planning is that it permits the transferred monies to pass automatically to the named beneficiary without the necessity of the probate process.

personal automobile policy (PAP): The most common form of automobile policy issued by insurance companies, as based on Insurance Services Offices (ISO) forms. It includes parts such as liability, bodily injury, property damages, medical payments, and collision.

pooled income fund (PIF): A trust generally created and maintained by a public charity, such as a public or private university or not-for-profit hospital. Used in estate planning both to provide a lifetime charitable income-tax deduction and to benefit the public charity at the donor's death.

portfolio diversification: A fundamental investment technique used to reduce the risk associated with capital market investing. This technique is characterized by the purchase of securities both within and across asset classes, such as stocks and bonds or stock and bond mutual funds.

pour-over will: A will used in conjunction with a revocable living trust that distributes, or "pours over," to the trust any assets that have not been titled in the name of the trust during the grantor's lifetime or any assets that the grantor may have acquired after the trust retitling first occurred.

price-to-earnings (P/E) ratio: The number by which the expected earnings per share on a stock investment is multiplied to estimate the stock's proper value. Also sometimes referred to as the *earnings multiplier*.

Q

qualified charity: A charity that is *qualified* for income-tax purposes, meaning it has met certain requirements that allow contributors to take advantage of an income-tax deduction after a contribution is made to the charity. The charity can be either public or private.

qualified educational institution: A ubiquitous term used throughout federal tax law with respect to allowance of certain taxpayer deductions and credits. This term is also used in student financial aid programs administered by the US Department of Education. It applies to virtually all accredited public, nonprofit, and proprietary post-secondary institutions and, specifically, institutions eligible to disburse financial aid under Title IV of the Higher Education Act of 1965, as subsequently reauthorized.

qualified personal residence trust (QPRT): An irrevocable trust whereby the grantor of the trust transfers ownership of their personal residence (or vacation home) to another but retains the right to occupy the residence for a period of years, at which time title to the residence passes to the beneficiaries of the trust.

R

rabbi trust: A trust established to hold property used for financing a deferred-compensation plan, in which the funds set aside are subject to the employer's creditors in the event of employer bankruptcy. As a result, the trust achieves an income-tax deferral of funds set aside on behalf of the beneficiary/corporate executive.

real estate investment trust (REIT): An investment (usually in the form of a publicly traded trust) that holds portfolios of real estate investments.

recognized: An income tax term often used by accountants to describe taxable income resulting from an economic event (such as the sale of an asset).

refundable: Typically used to describe a type of tax credit whereby the taxpayer will receive a "refund" from the taxing authorities, even though that taxpayer has paid little, if any, taxes on taxable income. Contrasted to a *nonrefundable* credit, whereby no payment is received by the taxpayer taking advantage of the credit.

revocable living trust (RLT): An important estate-planning technique that permits the grantor to avoid the probate process at death but still control and enjoy the benefits from their lifetime property. Contrasted with an *irrevocable* trust, which may achieve transfer-tax savings but cause the grantor to lose control of their property during their lifetime.

Roth 401(k): A relatively recent type of employer-sponsored retirement plan, part of a series of so-called *designated Roth accounts*, that features the combined advantages of 401(k) contributions and Roth accounts at the time of distribution. The Roth contributions are included in the participant's gross income when they are made but generally are not included in the participant's gross income when they are distributed.

Roth IRA: A type of individual retirement account (IRA) under which contributions may be made up to a specified limit on an after-tax or nondeductible basis. Withdrawals from Roth IRAs are tax free, presuming certain requirements are satisfied. A Roth IRA is the second form of personal savings plan available to help fund retirement, with the other being a traditional deductible IRA.

Rule of 72: A simple rule that may be used to estimate how long it will take for a given sum or deposit of money to double in value by dividing the rate of return into the numerator of 72. For example, if an investor achieves a before-tax rate of return of 8 percent compounded annually, it will take approximately nine years for the given sum of money to double in value (72 divided by 8 = 9).

S

Section 529 private savings plan: A form of college savings plan, governed under Section 529 of the Internal Revenue Code, whereby the account owner contributes cash to the plan for a beneficiary, and the contribution is then invested according to the terms of the plan. When the beneficiary attends college, the funds in the account plus all the earnings may be used to pay for the beneficiary's tuition and other college expenses income-tax free.

special needs trust: A type of trust established by clients who have children who are mentally or physically disabled and are entitled to receive supplemental Social Security Income (SSI) benefits or other types of governmental assistance. If structured properly, such a trust may permit the parents to furnish benefits to the developmentally disabled child without disqualifying the child from receiving governmental assistance.

standard homeowner's (HO) policy: A type of homeowner's insurance policy that follows Insurance Services Office (ISO) format and is written on an *open perils* basis. It ensures that losses to the home are covered, regardless of the peril or cause of the loss, unless specifically excluded under the terms of the policy.

stock: An evidence of ownership of a corporation. A major attribute of stock ownership is the ability to vote for the Board of Directors of the corporation that issued the stock.

T

Tax Cuts and Jobs Act of 2017 (TCJA of 2017 or 2017 TCJA): A major piece of tax legislation signed into law by President Trump on December 22, 2017 with an official title, but popularly known as the TCJA of 2017 or 2017 TCJA. The Act includes major tax changes for individuals and corporations, including the lowering of marginal tax rates generally. Most provisions of the law are in effect from 2018 through the year 2025, when the Act is scheduled to "sunset," or expire.

tax-qualified annuity: A tax term referring to the purchase of an annuity by the sponsor of a qualified retirement plan on behalf of the plan participant. Such annuities are characterized by the lack of any tax basis in the plan, thus making the entire annuity payment income-taxable to the participant at the time of payment or distribution. Contrasted to a *nonqualified annuity* that includes after-tax premium dollars contributed to the annuity product, resulting in a tax basis.

term insurance: A type of life insurance that is characterized by its temporary nature. In other words, for the insured's beneficiary to receive the insurance proceeds or death benefit, the insured must die within the stated term of the policy.

time value of money: A finance theory that posits a "dollar is worth more today than in the future," given that this dollar can be invested to generate additional monies.

traditional deductible IRA: An individual retirement account or individual retirement annuity under which deductible contributions, up to certain limits, and investment earnings are tax deferred. Interest earned and gains received while inside the protection of the traditional IRA are free of federal income tax until withdrawn. IRAs can also be offered on a nondeductible basis for individuals who cannot qualify for a deductible contribution.

transfer-on-death (TOD) form: A form used by securities firms to specify who is to receive the individually titled account upon the owner's death. The form's primary advantage in estate planning is that it permits the transferred funds to pass automatically to the named beneficiary without the necessity of the probate process.

trust: A legal arrangement whereby property is transferred or set aside on behalf of a beneficiary, and the distribution of that property is postponed or delayed by the grantor until some point in the future. Used for a wide variety of purposes in estate and financial planning, but particularly to pass property to family members either during the grantor's lifetime (inter vivos) or at their death (testamentary).

trustee: The legal owner of the property transferred into trust by the grantor. The trustee has a legal duty, known as a *fiduciary duty*, to act in the best interests of the trust beneficiary(ies) at all times.

U

umbrella liability insurance: An alternative to increasing personal liability limits in either an automobile or homeowner's insurance policy. Generally, the umbrella policy has high individual liability limits and can also protect the insured from personal risks, such as the risk of libel or slander, that are not typically covered under the underlying policies. A necessary part of protection planning for high-net-worth individuals.

V

variable annuity (VA): A popular form of (typically) pre-retirement insurance product whereby the investor turns over to the insurance company a lump sum of money in exchange for a variable payment, usually beginning at the time of the investor's retirement. The product also usually features certain guarantees, such as a minimum income benefit or percentage amount of annual withdrawal.

volatility: A commonly used term to describe the daily movements of the financial markets. For example, if the market index averages are significantly different today than they were yesterday, the market is said to be extremely volatile.

W

wealth replacement trust: A type of irrevocable life insurance trust (ILIT) that is used to replace the value of property left to a qualified charity at the grantor's death but that would otherwise pass to an heir or family member of the grantor. In such trusts, a life insurance policy is purchased on the life of the grantor, with a family member named as the beneficiary.

Index

A

Accidental death benefit (ADB), 104
Activities of daily living (ADLs), 259
Adjustable rate mortgage (ARMs), 281
Adjusted gross income (AGI), 139, 219, 222–223, 270
Alternative investments, 36
American Humane Society, 308
American Opportunity Tax Credit (AOTC), 223–225
American Red Cross, 304
Assets investment
  automobiles, 155–156
  home
    average annual real rate of return, 147
    average cost of home ownership, 148–149
    buying vs. renting, 151
    mortgage payments, 150
    ownership, 149
    planning strategies, 150–151
    sale, 153
    Wall Street Journal suggestion, 148
  tangible personal property and collectibles, 156–157

B

Bear market, 37
Behavioral finance, 234
Blue chip stocks, 130

Bond ratings, 125
Budgeting
  benchmark, 14
  emergency/contingency fund, 14
  expenses forecasting, 14
  financial goals determination, 14
  future income estimation, 14
  sample, 14, 333–334
Buffett, Warren, 43
Business, 274
  operation
    ability to raise capital, 277–278
    entity's formation, 277
    income tax consequences, 278
    personal liability, 276
  plan, 275–276
  property insurance, 98–99
  recruit individuals, 279
  succession, 279
Business owner's policy (BOP), 98
Buy-vs.-rent analysis worksheet, 151

C

Capital appreciation, 35
Capitalization rate, 141
Capital market, 121
Capital preservation, 34
Cash flow and debt management
  bad debt, 15
  debt reduction techniques, 15–16
  good debt, 15
  investment trade-off, 14
  liquid assets, 14

Index

Cash value insurance
  vs. term insurance, 52
  types
    traditional whole life insurance, 54
    universal life insurance, 54
    variable life insurance, 54
    VUL policy, 54
Certificates of deposit (CDs), 120
Certified Financial Planners (CFPs), 20, 320
Certified Public Accountants (CPAs), 23, 320
Charitable Gift Annuities, 310
Charitable remainder trust (CRT), 183
Charitable trusts
  annual inflation rate, 309
  attorney's fee, 310
  charitable lead trust (CLT), 308
  charitable remainder annuity trust (CRAT), 309
  charitable remainder trust (CRT), 309
  fixed annuity payment, 309
  income-tax charitable deduction, 309
  unlimited estate-tax charitable deduction, 309
Charity benefits
  charitable remainder trust, 304
  deduction limitations, 307
  income-tax purposes, 303
  pooled income fund, 304
  private charity, 306–307
  public charity, 304
  requirements, 308
  transfer-tax purposes, 304
Chartered Financial Consultant (ChFC), 23
Child's higher education
  BEGIN mode, 211
  college funding, Roth IRA in, 226
  custodial accounts, 213, 216
  EFC, 213–214
  ESAs, 216, 218
  FAFSA, 212, 214
  financial aid types, 215
    federal Pell Grant, 215
    federal Perkins loan, 215
    federal Stafford loan, 215
    PLUS loan, 215
  financial function calculator, 210
  future value amount, 210–211
  higher-education tax credits
    AOTC, 224
    Hope Scholarship Credit, 224
    Lifetime Learning Credit, 224
  inflation-adjusted annual rate of return, 211
  minor's trust, 222
  number of years, 211
  payment, 211
  present value, 210–211
  savings strategies, 213
  Section 529 private savings plan, 213
  Section 529 savings plans, 219
  tax-coordination rules, 225–226
  tax deductions and credits
    qualified higher-education tuition and fees deduction, 223
    student loan interest, 223
  UGMA, 216, 218
  UTMA, 216–218
Collision coverage, 96
Commercial package policy (CPP), 98
Commission-only planner, 21
Consolidated Omnibus Budget and Reconciliation Act (COBRA) 1985, 61, 67
Consumer Price Index (CPI), 126
Contingent trust, 289
Continuing-care retirement communities (CCRCs), 260
Conventional mortgage, 280
Corporate bond fund, 133
Corporate bonds
  bond-rating organizations, 125
  bond ratings, 125
  callable bond, 124
  convertible bond, 124
  mortgage bond, 124
  treasury bonds, 124
Cost of living adjustment (COLA) rider, 84
Credit-default swaps, 146
Criminal Investigation Division (CID), 167
Currency or exchange-rate risk, 136
Current income, 35
Cyclical stocks, 130

Index

D

Defensive stocks, 130
Direct loan, 215
Disability income insurance policy
  American Family Life Assurance Company, 80
  continuation provisions, 84
  disability definitions, 81
  group policies, 80
  important provisions
    benefit amount, 83
    benefit period, 83
    elimination period, 82
    income-tax-free, 83
  policy benefits, 84
  policy exclusions, 85
  social security system, 80
Dividend reinvestment program (DRIP), 42
Dollar-cost averaging, 39
Donor-advised fund (DAF), 312
Durable power of attorney (DPOA), 296
Durable power of attorney for health care (DPOAHC), 297–299

E

Education savings account (ESA), 216
  advantage of, 219
  benefit of, 219
  financial aid implications, 219
Employee stock ownership plans (ESOPs), 112
Employee stock purchase plans (ESPPs), 112
Employer-sponsored retirement plans, 236
Endanger wealth
  dependent parents
    developmentally disabled child, 203
    income tax purposes, 203
    long-term care, 201
    Medigap policy, 202
    option, 201
    physical/mental incapacity, 204
    planning technique, 203
  divorce
    alimony, 192
    child support, 192
    common law states, 190
    principal residence, 195
    property settlements, 194
    spouse separation, 190
  employment loss, 196
  spouse/life partner
    beneficiary designations, 199
    dies intestate, 198
    dies testate, 198
    psychological aspects of, 197
    revocable living trust, 200
    titling assets jointly, 199
Entrepreneur, definition, 273
Estate planning
  changes in, 300
  DPOA, 296
  DPOAHC, 297–299
  estate taxes
    annual gift-tax exclusion, 294
    federal and state levels, 293
    tax brackets and marginal tax rates, 295
    unified credit and exemption amounts, 295
    unified transfer tax system, 294
  intestate succession, 288
  living wills, 298
  personal letter of instructions, 300
  poor man's will, 291
  pour-over will, 293
  probate process, 292
  property, beneficiary designation, 290
  RLT, 292
  titling property, 291
  will, 278
    contingent trust, 289
    cost objection to, 290
    intestate succession, 288
    mortality, 289
    prohibitively expensive, 289
Exchange traded funds (ETFs), 134
Expected family contribution (EFC), 213–214

F

Family foundation, 311
Federal Housing Administration (FHA) mortgage, 281

Index

Federal Insurance Contributions Act (FICA), 164
Federal Perkins loan, 215
Federal Stafford loan, 215
Fee-and-commission planner, 21
Fee-only planner, 22
Financial assets investment
    bonds
        corporate bonds (see Corporate bonds)
        debt obligations, 123
        government bonds, 125
        municipal bonds, 127
        portfolio, 128
        yield curve, 123
    cash investments
        bank deposits, 120
        money market deposits, 120–121
        savings accounts, 120
        short-term, 120
    international investment, 136
    mutual funds
        balanced fund, 132
        bond mutual funds, 133
        ETFs, 134
        fund types, 132
        global funds, 132
        index funds, 133
        international funds, 132
        NAV, 132
        portfolio, 134–135
        professionally managed asset, 132
    stocks
        capital appreciation, 129
        common stock, 129
        dividends, 129
        market capitalization, 130
        portfolio, 131
        price-to-earnings (P/E) ratio, 131
        publicly traded stocks, 130
Financial goals
    business, 274
        ability to raise capital, 277
        business operation, 276
        business plan, 275
        business succession, 279
        characteristics, 275
        entity's formation, 277
        income tax consequences, 278
        personal liability, 277
        recruit individuals, 279
        transferable skills, 274
    mortgages
        ARMs, 281
        conventional mortgage, 281
        FHA, 281
        interest-only mortgage, 281
        VA, 281
    personal residence, 280
    unexpected money/windfall of money, 284
    vacation home, 281
        like kind exchanges, 282
        QPRT, 283
Financial planner
    approach, 26
    certified professional, 22
    charges, 26
    clients net worth and annual income level, 27
    engagement agreement, 25
    experience, 25
    FPA suggestions, 25
    investment risk profile, 28–29
    minimize inflation on portfolio return, 21
    offered services, 25
    paid option, 26
    professional code, 20
    public discipline, 26
    qualifications, 25
    recommendations, 27
    time value of money principles, 20
    types, 21
Financial Planning Association (FPA), 25
Financial planning process, 320
    financial and personal records gathering, 5
    goal, 6, 210
    investor's time horizon determination, 7
    net worth, 7
    personal balance sheet, 8
    record keeping, 5
    record types, 5
    return forces, 6
    safe-deposit box disadvantages, 6
    steps, 4

Index

Financial planning professional
  accountant, 24
  bank trust officer, 24
  estate planning attorney, 24
  financial planner, 23
  life insurance/property and casualty agent, 23
Financial products, 32
Flexible spending account (FSA), 103
Free Application for Student Aid (FAFSA), 212, 214
Fringe benefits
  company stock purchase plans, 112
  dependent care assistance, 106
  employer educational assistance, 107
  group disability insurance, 104
  group life insurance, 103
  group long-term care insurance, 105
  group medical and dental insurance, 102
  retirement plans
    Roth IRA, 112
    section 401(k), 109
    section 403(b), 110
  stock options
    nonqualified deferred compensation, 116
    restricted stock, 115
Full retirement age (FRA), 240–241, 268
Future value amount (FV), 210

G

Generation-skipping transfer tax (GSTT), 186
Global mutual fund, 136
Growth-and-income fund, 132
Growth fund, 132
Growth investing, 44
Growth stocks, 130
Guaranteed insurability rider, 85
Guarantee withdrawal benefit (GWB), 245

H

Health care expenses, 233
Health insurance, 57
  coverage continuation, 67
  coverage portability, 68
  Medicare
    drug coverage, 68
    federal government health insurance plan, 68
    free coverage, 70
    hospital insurance, 68
    skilled nursing care benefit, 69
    supplementary medical insurance, 68
  Medigap
    American Association of Retired Persons (AARP), 70
    supplemental policies, 70
  Patient Protection and Affordable Care Act 2010, 63
  policy selection
    co-payment and deductible provisions, 61
    employer-based health insurance system, 60
    flexibility plan, 62
    group health plan, 61
    legal rights, 62
    preexisting condition, 60
    state's insurance department plans, 60
    top-ranked plans, 60
  policy types
    health savings accounts, 66
    indemnity (fee-for-service) policies, 65
    managed care policies, 65
Health Insurance Portability and Accountability Act 1996, 62
Health savings accounts (HSA), 66, 233, 266
Homeowner's insurance
  automobile coverage
    medical payments, 95
    personal liability, 94
    physical damage/loss coverage, 96
    uninsured motorist's coverage, 96
  business property insurance, 98
  home coverage
    contents/personal property, 89
    dwelling, 88
    insures outbuildings, 89

Index

Homeowner's insurance (cont.)
    loss of use, 90
    medical payments to others, 91
    personal liability, 90
  no-fault insurance, 97
  policy types
    flooding/earthquakes, 91
    HO policy types, 93
    nuclear hazard losses, 91
    power failure or interruption, 91
    property losses, 92
    replaced/destroyed dwelling, 91
    war losses, 91
  umbrella liability insurance, 97
Hope Scholarship Credit, 224
Human life value approach, 50
Hybrid bond, 127

I

Immediate fixed annuity, 245
Incentive stock options (ISOs), 113
Income fund, 132
Income stocks, 130
Income tax planning and management
  AMT, 165
  FICA, 164
  rate, withholding and estimated tax, 163
  smart investing, 170
  tax return, 171
  technique
    income conversion, 169
    tax avoidance (see Tax avoidance)
    tax deferral, 168
Indemnity (fee-for-service) policies, 65
Index funds, 133
Individual long-term care plan, 106
Inland marine policy, 99
Insurance company rating agencies, 56–57
Interest-only mortgage, 281
Interest rate risk, 42
Intestate succession, 288
Investment assets, 36
Investment policy statement
  investment constraints, 35
  investment resources allocation, 36
  investor's objectives, 34
  performance monitoring, 37
  personal financial statement, 34
  risk tolerance, 34
Investment risks, 141
Investment strategies
  averaging down, 41
  buy and hold, 43
  dividend reinvestment programs (DRIP), 42
  dollar-cost averaging
    mutual fund shares increase, 40
    401(k) plan, 39
    poor man's saving method, 39
  laddering, 42
  market timing, 43
  real estate investment, 45
  value versus growth investing, 44
Investor behavior risk, 234
Irrevocable life insurance trust (ILIT), 180, 264

J

Joint tenancy with right of survivorship (JTWROS), 184, 199

K

Kaufmann Foundation, 274

L

Level premium term insurance, 53
Life-cycle fund, 38
Life-cycle planning
  accumulation stage, 17
  consolidation stage, 17
  estate planning, 18
  self assessment, 16–17
  spending phase, 17
Life insurance
  cash value insurance (see Cash value insurance)
  guiding principles, 49
  human life value approach, 50
  insurance company rating, 56
  insured person needs, 51

Index

needs approach, 51
term insurance (see Term insurance)
types, 55
Lifetime Learning Credit, 223–225
Limited liability company (LLC), 276–277
Long-term care insurance
  alternatives
    chronically ill, 75
    filial support, 76
    living benefits rider, 75
    Medicaid coverage, 76
    policy purchase factors, 77
    reverse mortgage, 76
    terminally ill, 75
  coverage types
    adult day care, 73
    assisted living, 73
    custodial care, 72
    home health care, 73
    hospice care, 73
    intermediate nursing care, 72
    skilled nursing care, 72
  exclusions and limitations
    benefit period, 74
    daily benefit amount, 74
    policy exclusions, 74
    preexisting-condition limitation, 74
    waiting period, 74
  HIPAA legislation, 71
  own home nursing care, 71
  policy criteria
    chronically ill, 73
    substantial services, 73
  tax-qualified, 71

M

Managed care policies, 65
Market risk, 234
Market timing, 43–44
Master limited partnerships (MLPs), 144
McKinsey Consumer Retirement Surveys, 251
Medicare and Medicare supplemental policies (Medigap), 267
Modified guaranteed issue policy, 105

Money market deposit accounts (MMDAs), 121
Mortgages
  ARMs, 281
  conventional mortgage, 281
  expenses, 232–233
  FHA, 281
  interest-only mortgage, 281
  VA, 281
Municipal bond fund, 133
Mutual funds, 38, 122

N

National Flood Insurance Program (NFIP), 88
Net asset value (NAV), 132, 142
Net operating income (NOI) formula, 140
Net unrealized appreciation (NUA), 112
No-fault insurance, 97
Nonqualified stock options (NQSOs), 113

O

Obamacare (Affordable Care Act), 57
Open peril coverage, 92

P

PADD approach, 4, 146
Parent Loan for Undergraduate Students (PLUS), 215
Partial disability rider, 85
Passive portfolio management, 43
Patient Protection and Affordable Care Act 2010, 63
Payable-on-death (POD), 200, 291
Pension Protection Act (PPA), 110
Permanent life insurance, 52
Personal automobile policy (PAP), 94
Personal cash flow statement
  advantages, 11
  cash inflows and outflows, 11
  cash surplus/deficit, 11
  specimen statement, 12–13

Index

Personal computers (PCs), 275
Personal residence, 280
Personal savings plans, 238
Pooled-income fund, 310
Portfolio diversification, 37
Present value (PV), 210
Price to earnings ratio (P/E ratio), 44
Private foundations, 311
Private purpose bond, 127

Q

Qualified personal residence trust (QPRT), 283
Qualified prepaid tuition plan (QTP), 219–220

R

Real estate
   direct investments
      commercial properties, 140–141
      rental homes, 139
      unimproved land, 141
      vacation homes, 138
   financial asset correlation, 145
   vs. financial assets, 146
   indirect investments
      Real Estate Investment Trusts (REITs), 142
      Real Estate Limited Partnerships (RELPs), 143
   leverage, 144
Real estate investment trust (REIT), 142, 169–170
   advantages, 142–143
   types, 143
Real Estate Limited Partnerships (RELPs), 143
Renewable term insurance, 53
Required minimum distributions (RMD), 245
Residual disability rider, 85
Retiree health insurance, 265
Retirement planning, 229
   accommodating change, 270–271
   annual retirement withdrawals, 252
   defined-contribution plans, 237
   education, 269
   employer-sponsored retirement plan, 243
   financial risks, 234
      challenges, 235
      inflation/purchasing-power risk, 234
      investor behavior risk, 234
      longevity/superannuation, 234
      market risk, 234
      point-in-time/sequential risk, 234
   future work, 267
   health care expenses, 233
   housing options
      apartments, 258
      assisted-living communities, 259
      CCRCs, 260
      children, living with, 258
      condominiums, 257
      independent-living communities, 258
      nursing-home care, 261
      single-family dwellings, 256
      skilled nursing-care facilities, 260
      town homes, 257
   IRA rollovers and conversions, 248
   life insurance, 263
   Medicare and Medicare supplemental insurance, 267
   mortgage expenses, 232
   retiree health insurance, 265
   retirement savings, "three-legged stool"
      employer-sponsored retirement plans, 236
      personal savings plans, 238
      social security, 240
   reverse mortgages, 262
   RMD, 245
   saving methods, 231
   social security retirement benefits, 242
   travel and recreation, 269
   use of annuities, 251
Return of premium, 84
Revenue bonds, 127
Revocable living trust (RLT), 292

Index

S

Savings Incentive Match Plan for Employees (SIMPLE), 238
Sector fund, 38
Separate Trading of Registered Interest and Principal of Securities (STRIPs), 170
Share averaging, 39
Simplified Employee Pension (SEP), 238
Social security system, 240
Split-definition policy, 82
Standard bond, 124
Standard homeowner's (HO) policy, 91
Statement of personal financial position
    considerations, 8
    personal cash flow statement (see Personal cash flow statement)
    specimen statement, 9
Subsidized Stafford loan, 215

T

Tax avoidance
    advantage, 166
    definition, 165
    vs. evasion, 167
    itemized deductions, 166
    nonrefundable credit, 167
    refundable credit, 166
    tax credit, 166
    tax deduction, 165
Tax-qualified annuity, 244
Tax-sheltered annuity, 110
T-Bills, 122
Temporary life insurance, 52
Term insurance
    vs. cash value life insurance, 52
    types, 53
Transfer-on-death (TOD), 199, 290
Transfer tax planning and management
    components and valuation, 181
    deductions and credits, 182
    GSTT, 187
    lifetime gift, 177
    Relief Act, 184
    trust
        advantages, 179
        irrevocable trusts, 180
        revocable trust, 179
Treasury bonds, 124
Treasury Inflation Protected Securities (TIPS), 126, 170
Treasury note, 125
Treasury Separate Trading of Registered Interest and Principal of Securities (STRIPS), 126

U

Umbrella liability insurance, 97
Uniform Gifts to Minors Act (UGMA), 178, 216, 218
Uniform Lifetime Table, 246–247
Uniform Transfers to Minors Act (UTMA), 178, 217
Unsubsidized Stafford loan, 215
U.S. government bond fund, 133
U.S. Treasury bills (T-bills), 120

V

Value investing, 44
Value stocks, 130
Variable universal life (VUL), 54
Veterans Administration (VA) mortgage, 281
Volatility, 34

W, X, Y

Waiver of premium, 85
Wealth, 319
    definition, 4
    financial planning process, 4
    PADD approach, 4
Wealth-accumulation and-management strategy, 319
Wealth management
    diversified portfolio, 37
    financial life examination, 33

Wealth management (cont.)
    investment policy statement (see Investment policy statement)
    investment strategies (see Investment strategies)
    PADD approach, 33
    permanent safety build up, 33
    rebalancing, 38
    wealth builders, 32
    wealth managers services, 33

Z

Zero-coupon bond, 126

Made in the USA
Monee, IL
28 April 2026

49136503R00214